URBAN DESIGN
IN
WESTERN EUROPE

URBAN DESIGN
IN
WESTERN EUROPE

Regime and Architecture, 900–1900

Wolfgang Braunfels

Translated by
Kenneth J. Northcott

THE UNIVERSITY OF CHICAGO PRESS
Chicago and London

WOLFGANG BRAUNFELS (1911–1987) was professor of art history at the University of Munich. Among his previous works is *Monasteries of Western Europe: The Architecture of the Orders* (English translation 1972).

KENNETH J. NORTHCOTT is professor in the Department of Germanic Languages and Literatures, University of Chicago.

The University of Chicago Press, Chicago 60637
The University of Chicago Press, Ltd., London
© 1988 by The University of Chicago
All rights reserved. Published 1988
Printed in the United States of America

97 96 95 94 93 92 91 90 89 88   5 4 3 2 1

Originally published under the title *Abendländische Stadtbaukunst: Herrschaftsform und Baugestalt,* © 1976 Verlag M. DuMont Schauberg, Köln; © 1977 DuMont Buchverlag, Köln.

LIBRARY OF CONGRESS CATALOGING-IN-PUBLICATION DATA

Braunfels, Wolfgang.
  Urban design in Western Europe.

  Translation of: Abendländische Stadtbaukunst.
  Includes index.
   1. City planning—Europe—History.   2. Architecture—Europe—History.   I. Title.
NA9183.B7213   1988   711'.4'094   87-30060
ISBN 0-226-07178-2

CONTENTS

Translator's Note   ix
Preface   xi

Introduction   1

One   CATHEDRAL CITIES   12
Cologne   19
Trier   26
Ecclesiastical Cities of the 10th and 11th Centuries   27
Halberstadt   28
Hildesheim   30
Bamberg   33
Cathedral Cities of the High Middle Ages   35

Two   CITY-STATES   40
The Tuscan City-States   46
The Florentine Republic   49
Pisa, Pistoia, and Lucca   54
Siena   61
Florence as the Seat of a Princely Court   67
The Swiss Cantonal Capitals: Zürich and Bern   69

Three   SEA POWERS   78
Venice and Amsterdam Contrasted   80
Venice   83
Lübeck   95
Amsterdam   102
Manhattan   105

CONTENTS

Four   IMPERIAL CITIES   110
     Self-representation as Self-interpretation   114
     Cathedral Cities as Imperial Cities   117
     Regensburg   118
     Augsburg   123
     Nuremberg as a Model City   126
     Ulm and the Small Swabian Imperial Cities   131
     Esslingen   133
     Reutlingen   135
     Rothenburg   136
     Ulm   137
     Imperial Residence and Imperial City   140
     Aachen   141
     Goslar   141
     Frankfurt   144

Five   IDEAL CITIES   148
     Aigues-Mortes and Richelieu   151
     Terre Murate or Bastides   153
     Star-shaped Fortifications of the Baroque   157
     Calais and Valletta   161
     Urbanization of the Swedish Baltic Empire   166
     City Plan and the Order of Salvation   172

Six   SEATS OF A PRINCELY COURT   176
     Early Forms in the 15th and 16th Centuries   186
     Turin   193
     Munich   204
     Berlin as the Seat of a Princely Court   212
     Dresden and Nancy   220
     Episcopal Seats in the Holy Roman Empire   230
     Salzburg   236
     Würzburg   242
     Versailles   253
     Potsdam   260
     St. Petersburg   267

Seven   CAPITAL CITIES   276
     Prague   278
     Vienna: The Conflict   294
     Paris as a Model City   307
     London   327

CONTENTS

Eight THE SECOND AND THIRD ROME   340
       The Second Rome   343
       The Vatican as Seat of Government   347
       The Opening Up of the City and Its Hills   350
       The Papal Squares   357
       The Capitol as Political Utopia   360

       Epilogue: The Unplannable   367
       Notes   373
       Credits   392
       Index   393

Translator's Note

The original version of this work was published in 1976; the translation was completed in 1987. In those cases where to my knowledge some updating was called for, or where I have identified obvious minor oversights in the original, I have made the necessary changes. That minor errors may still remain is probably unavoidable, since my expertise is in the German language rather than in the history of architecture. Professor Braunfels read the translation shortly before his death, however, and expressed general satisfaction with it.

I wish to express my thanks to Reinhold Heller of the University of Chicago for his invaluable help with the translation of a large number of technical terms.

KJN

PREFACE

This book may be regarded as the counterpart to *Monasteries of Western Europe: The Architecture of the Orders* (Princeton University Press, 1972), which involved roughly the same geographic area. In that work, the organizing principle was the rules of monastic order, for the more exact observance of which the building plans of monasteries were developed. Here, however, I am concerned with showing the dependence of the architectural organization of a number of successful cities upon differing political conditions. Forms of government and, even more, the forms of communal cooperation as well as the desire of both to express ideals and ideology in monumental buildings found their most precise testimony in the plans for and the physical appearance of these cities. Studying them broadens the horizons both of art history and of political science.

The exact number of European cities cannot be stated precisely because we cannot settle upon one single definition of what constitutes a city. Cities arise, and die; yet from the 12th century onward, thousands have survived. Today most of these are several hundred years old—some even as much as two thousand—and each has consistently regenerated itself on the same site. The literature on urban studies presents us with a whole range of different systems for arranging the unlimited and illimitable material. Each of these systems puts a different point of view in the foreground. Distinctions have been made by country—and works have dealt with German, French, Italian, Dutch, Swiss, and Scandinavian towns. Even individual provinces within modern national units have been distinguished—Westphalia, Tuscany, southern Germany, and Bohemia, for example. Distinctions have been made by epoch—there are works about the cities of the early Middle Ages, the Gothic city, the baroque or romantic city, the city in the "age of promoterism," and the postwar city. A third basis has been found in geographic location—mountain towns; hill towns; towns on plains, rivers, lakes, oceans, islands, or peninsulas. Economic situation provides another principle of organization: market towns, harbor towns, towns on through roads or on fords, commercial or purely agricultural centers. It is at this point that we approach the organizing principles of the present work.

In all areas of urban studies, the questions asked determine the principle upon which material is selected. This book deals only with the architectural history of those cities in which a political goal and ideality of design have mutually conditioned and promoted one another. It deals only with those centers that were able to develop "from the inside out." Chapter 5, "Ideal Cities," explains why. The great achievements of urban design have taken place wherever a bishop, an aristocratic society, a free burgher community, even an absolutist prince, or the nation as a whole, either on their own initiative or as a result of unconscious historical pressures, managed to design their cities as reflections of forms of government and ideals of order. The greatest successes were those cities where, for centuries, new goals were constantly enriching and redesigning their overall structures.

The extent of my field of inquiry—in time from A.D. 900 to 1900, though sometimes extending to the present day, and bounded in space by the much disputed and disputable concept of "Western Europe"—challenges criticism, as does the small number of towns and cities with which I deal. I have chosen a broad panorama in order to be able to make comparisons, and I have taken into account the fact that my examples must be limited and that each must be described as tersely as possible. Research has produced material for every one of these cities, which cannot here be surveyed in toto. The wealth of information about events threatens to obscure the paths of history. Brevity as a scholarly method and comprehensiveness of view are not characteristics of modern historiography. They were forced upon me by the goals of my research.

Nowhere else do I find such a broad base of observation for a comparative study of cities in terms of their architectural forms vis-à-vis the political structures by which they are conditioned, even though most of the facts are known to those with expert knowledge of each individual city. What were the economic, sociological, political, and religious prerequisites that permitted cities to develop into the abundant forms we see today? The principle of selection determined the terms of inquiry. A whole series of achievements in urban design are not—or are, at best, barely—taken into account. The humanistic cities, those areas of happily unburdened existence, were beyond the limits of this study. Pompeii has thus not been treated, nor Bath. The name Aix-en-Provence does not appear in the index any more than Palladio's Vicenza or James Craig and Robert Adams's Edinburgh, the palace street in Genoa, the idylls of Spain, modern vacation resorts, or garden cities. My limitation is not criticism of the research which has been done into the urban design of these centers, nor of the centers themselves. I merely wanted to treat structures with a more active life and a greater power of self-renovation.

The current style of research precludes our trying to take insights from the "manual of history," which has significance for the past and the future. The dangers are obvious. History was; cities continue to be. Concern with them links the old and the new. I cannot deny that, while I was writing the book, my thoughts were constantly being diverted toward the present.

INTRODUCTION

This book grew out of a sense of uneasiness. The uneasiness, in turn, arose out of the state of cities in the 20th century. Why, when every ancient urban nucleus, even in its reproductions in late medieval, Renaissance, and baroque engravings, right up to the early 19th century, captures the imagination with its order, do the Saturn rings of late 19th and 20th century urban expansion burden it with their disorder? The more the new forms penetrate the old, the more frightening the overall picture becomes. Where in earlier days a small number of laws and ordinances were enough to achieve that order, today the most comprehensive and precise codes no longer suffice to maintain it. What are the causes of such antitheses?

It cannot merely be the fault of architects, their limited ability, their lack of training, their thirst for novelty, their refusal to accept the teachings of the past, their disturbed sense of proportion. But in part it is their fault.

Nor can the blame be ascribed solely to theories of urban design, simplistic concepts of the planning process, lack of scientific investigation into *all* functions of a city, if such investigation has been undertaken at all. Yet the hasty, incomplete programming of new planning projects is in part to blame.

The reasons must be sought in changes in the general political function of cities. Cities no longer form unities but serve both the interests of the individual and those of the state with its manifold business, the new "one world." They represent only to the most limited extent an independent body corporate, for their areas of existence are interwoven in different ways, with the states to which they are subordinated and with the rural areas that surround them.[1] The Industrial Revolution, the unprecedented population growth as a result of medical advances, changed sociological conditions, new forms of traffic, the separation of work, living, and leisure areas first stretched the old organizational structures and finally broke them up. Despite numerous critical analyses of changed conditions and equally numerous attempts to outline the theoretical prerequisites for change, no one has yet been able successfully to predict or program the way to change. We are surrounded by failures. Historians are powerless to give advice. They can only indicate the reasons for old forms of order, reasons that may still be valid for modern forms.

These reasons lie in overlapping political areas. It has always been known that every important city represented a political fact. Political science arose out of the proposals for a perfect *polis*. The laws of order which gave form to cities also determine those of the states that have been governed by cities. Constitutions, which regulated the coexistence of men and gods, rulers and ruled, free citizens and tied wage-earners, created for themselves the architectural image appropriate to the occasion. Each city lets us know who governs it and how it is governed. We can read in a skyline or in any ground plan the standing of the controlling powers, whether rivals or mutually supportive: a dynasty, the church and its organizations, the patriciate, the nobility, the merchant class, the craftsmen and their guilds, the associations which served to defend or to oppress the city. New governmental programs always demanded new architectural programs. Every description of the architectural condition is at the same time a description of the economic bases and sociological composition of the population.

Individual institutions have always tried to express the ideals that quickened them. Monumental buildings propagandize for forms of government. They also propagandize for forms of coexistence and for the comprehension of the world and the ultramundane by means of everything that is called art. At the same time, they define, by their appearance, political ideologies, which they elevate to the realm of the ideal—thanks to their status as works of art. The architectural form of churches, city palaces or town halls, cloth merchants' halls and guildhalls, even the fountain in the market place and its sculpture, bears witness to the meaning of those ideologies. Castle, city walls and their gates, interpret and justify existing orders— or even orders which are sought after. They define ideal notions in an imperishable language and in this way give them a higher reality. The Doric temple, the Gothic cathedral, the Renaissance palazzo, the baroque residence, 19th century museums and the buildings of world expositions, even transportation buildings of the 20th century, airports or broad-spanned bridges, attempt, each in their own way, to interpret existence.

These words should not be taken to mean that I am emphasizing the contrast between the art of the rulers and the misery of the ruled, though that contrast has occurred all too often. St. Jerome himself complains that the most magnificent works of art were torn from the sweat and poverty of the poorest members of society.[2] The architectural form of many cities serves as illustration: the citadel and the city of Milan (fig. 96), the episcopal Marienburg in Würzburg and the little burgher town around the market with the Marienkirche in its shadow (fig. 134). The populace, convicts, prisoners-of-war, and slaves were condemned to build tyrants' castles for their own oppression. Yet, more frequently, we find examples that show how these contradictions were balanced out. The merchant settlements of the early days of European towns—designed to serve a castle which, in its turn, offered them protection—could be mentioned here.[3] We have reports to the effect that participating in the statute labor associated with the building of Gothic cathedrals fulfilled the lives of the population of whole areas of the country.[4] Many later depictions of towns illustrate the fact that political tasks evolved from conditions of tension which could also be mastered architectonically. We shall see this in Venice, in Florence, and in Prague, as in earlier episcopal centers or, later, in modern capital cities. The merchant city and the Louvre in Paris, the City of London, and the City of Westminster are among the most successful solutions to arise from the conflict between king and people. Likewise, architectural masterpieces grew out of the cooperation between all classes of the population: the city churches of the free imperial cities, the colonial cities of the Hanseatic League, and Amsterdam in the Golden Age. Prince Eugene was to erect the Belvedere both as a symbol of the new "peace style," after his victories over the Turks, and as a way of creating jobs for the veterans of his wars (see chap. 7). At all events, we must closely examine the attitudes and convictions of the various periods if we are to evaluate the task set for each building in the society that built it or saw it built.

Every architectural work can be regarded as a sign of the power, wealth, idealism, even the misery of its builders and their contemporaries. A good farmhouse not only serves its purpose; it reflects, thanks to its architectural and decorative forms, the worldview in which the farmer's family feels secure. Only by this means does it become a form of architecture in its own artistic genre. A good town house can be perceived as a textbook of bourgeois virtues. It is the area in which bourgeois diligence, sense of order, cleanliness, and careful accounting are all cultivated.[5] The rows of houses in a city show the efforts of families to regulate and distinguish themselves. If a good monastery confirmed by its appearance the ordering of life for which the monks had left the world, then in other forms, every palace, every princely castle, every city hall, every cloth hall, cathedral, or city church tries to do the same thing.

It will be shown again and again that these works serve an institution, whether it be a state or a family, and illustrate, by their architectural form, that institution's essence, its goals, and its ambitions. The Palazzo Strozzi advertises the financial might of the Strozzi bankers and bears witness to their self-confidence. The Palazzo Farnese needed a Michelangelo to give it that form which, in their eyes, was suited to the House of Farnese. A family's house stands for that family and thus becomes a self-representation of the rank and pretensions of that family within the social order in which it lives. Every architectural patron identifies himself, and the institution into which he is coordinated and to which he is subordinated, with the building he is having built. A city, as an all-encompassing institution, is composed of a multitude of different institutions. A prerequisite for its success as an architectural and political unit is for every building to take the form that is suited to it and yet at the same time stand on the exact spot in the overall architectural fabric that corresponds to its function and significance. For the topological harmony of a city is among the essential characteristics for its perfection. It was achieved in London and Berlin in the 18th century just as it was in such successful structures as the Piazza San Pietro, the Piazza San Marco, the Maximilianstraße in Augsburg, the market district in Lübeck, or the Ringstraße in Vienna. We read the plans of Munich, Zürich, or Prague with a more precise understanding if we bear in mind the dependence of the topographical situation upon the political tasks assigned to the monumental buildings. When the iconological plan of individual buildings and groups of buildings can be deciphered, every form of architecture gains in clarity.[6] The cathedral of St. Vitus in Prague can only be fully understood by someone who grasps the political meaning of its relation to the imperial palace of Charles IV.[7] The architectural form of the cathedral of St. Stephen in Vienna only reveals itself to someone who can extract from it the struggle for influence between the citizenry, the ecclesiastical authorities, and the ducal house.[8] The contrast between the palaces of Versailles and Sanssouci can only be described properly if we are conscious of the dependence of the building plans and forms—down to the last decorative detail—upon the different views of the state entertained by the kings who built them.

The dependence of every architectural form upon an ideology and a set of ideals which is above and beyond it comes from the fact that all monumental buildings owe their existence to unavoidable historical pressures. Victories sparked euphoria and led to projects that could not be realized even over the course of centuries. The first plan of the new cathedral in Pisa, after the victory over the Arabs before Palermo in 1063, is an early example (fig. 4). We do not know how many of the later buildings on the cathedral square were projected at the same time. Political or economic successes found their expression in monumental buildings that far surpassed any need. The Gothic cathedral, just as much as the baroque castle, derived from such historical pressures. Only that set of ideals to which all the leading spirits of every community felt themselves attached was able to create great architecture. And if the rationalism of the Enlightenment had not already been transcended in the Napoleonic period, more mundane forms of architecture would have been able to prevail everywhere.[9]

Pressure forced the bishops of Laon, Chartres, and Amiens to build cathedrals of a size and luxury completely beyond the scale of all earlier, or even later, buildings in these cities. And it was an all-subordinating force that made the citizens of Florence or Siena, Ulm or Nördlingen disposed to erect their enormous city churches: these were ventures whose cost could not be calculated financially or statistically in advance. Such pressures became apparent wherever a prince built himself a castle on an overwhelming scale in order to govern a city or where citizens exhausted the means earmarked for the defense of their freedom by building extensive systems of fortification. Rome, in the 17th century, could do nothing but build monument after monument to that successful Counterreformation it had striven for, while Amsterdam, at the same time, felt the necessity of documenting, in new building programs, the victory of its Calvinistic citizens over the aristocratic world of Catholic absolutism. For similar reasons, many monarchs managed to forget the misery of their people so that they could build their massive palaces and gardens—Versailles and Heidelberg, the court buildings of Kassel and Nancy. Max Emmanuel of Bavaria, after the War of the Spanish Succession, in which he personally sustained many losses and his country was ruined by the Austrian occupation, felt bound to give expression to his return to power in new and expanded castle complexes. Nymphenburg, Schleißheim, Fürstenried, and Dachau were all completed at the same time. Was it really "fictional history," as Dehio maintains, or ruthless libertinage, as the romantic bourgeois averred, or merely the documentation of political conditions themselves, in a manner appropriate to the time? Buildings were to testify to the success of a form of state, and, where they have been preserved, they have performed this task to the present day. Cologne has remained the city of its cathedral, Paris the city of its royal buildings, Lübeck the city of the burgher cathedral. The sum of the history of all successful cities is condensed in their outward form. Regimes which went into debt in order to erect buildings that illustrated the ideals of their age have always been justified by posterity. To possess an urban history means, for a community, always matching the architectural tasks of the day to changed political, economic, and sociological conditions. Centers that are famous as masterpieces of urban design have been able to do this for centuries.

This principle compels me to treat only successful cities in this book. In the examples offered, political success will always correspond to aesthetic success. Cities of this sort were the result of fruitful developments. Every given situation became the starting point for continuing creative activities.

I use the term "development" in the way technology uses it, not in the way biology does. Developments in urban design are completed neither of their own accord nor merely as a result of external pressures. They are the result of creative concerns that repeat themselves. The same process is at work as that by which motors, rockets, new chemical compounds, whole computer systems are built. The condition for all successful cities was the creativity of generations of researchers. New experiments could be based on the results of earlier ones. People believed in the power of time and in the continuing development of greater capabilities. Often it was impossible to calculate in advance how many years would be needed to reach the goals that had been set. "Rome was not built in a day" is an apt proverb. Successful groupings of buildings, too, were the results of such developments. It is true that, in contrast to progress in the engineering sciences, the final goal itself could not be sketched out in advance. But cities, like engineering achievements, are the result of a self-renewing power of design. The development of a city like Hildesheim (fig. 13), of the municipality of Siena (fig. 30), or of St. Petersburg (fig. 146) as the seat of a court, offer the same illustrative material as those great ensembles I have already mentioned—the Piazza San Pietro in Rome, the Piazza San Marco in Venice, the royal axis in Paris, the political topography of London, or even a single monumental work that neither was planned nor could be built as one process. For these works were never built in the way they were projected at a given time, and they were never planned in the way they were built. Often decades, sometimes centuries, of work went into their embellishment, and a change in political or governmental thought always meant a change in the building program.

For the moving force in architectonic developments is history itself.

Changes in the political situation make demands upon design which can only be met with creative ideas.

The difference between planned or "laid out" cities and cities that have grown seems ineradicable.[10] These concepts, precisely because they are opposing ones, become imprecise. The architectural form of successful cities, as it appears to our eyes, is neither planned nor grown. In the face of achievements in urban design and in the face of urban personalities like Rome or Vienna, London or Amsterdam, Prague or Cologne, or even more modest centers like Mantua, Parma, Landshut, and Ulm, such distinctions serve no purpose, unless the aim is to contrast order to excrescence, which can be seen in almost all cities. It was precisely the "grown" towns of the Middle Ages that were perfectly ordered organisms. Many of the "planned," ideal cities of the Renaissance proved incapable of functioning (see chap. 5). In modern planning we experience the strange contrast of chaos and vacuum among the rows of houses along regular networks of streets. All forms of overplanning prevent order. For in successful urban centers, planning was such that the pressures of development were overcome creatively—pressures that changed from one decade to another. In those cases where the political forces responsible for design slackened and left the road clear for excrescences, the attempt was subsequently made to subordinate these to the laws of order. Urban design became slum clearance.

Even in the most successful cities there were developments in which the principle of inertia, which caused decay, was more powerful than the countercurrents of order. When we read descriptions of Paris or London in the Middle Ages or even the baroque period, of the traffic conditions in Milan or Naples from the 16th to 18th centuries, in Nuremberg too, even in Berlin and Vienna, any romantic transfiguration of the past seems out of place. The forces which promoted order proved over and over again too weak to prevent the streets from becoming clogged. Individual districts in many cities gradually became enclaves, completely closed off. They became districts in which laws of the state could not be enforced—zones of insecurity. In Palermo and many oriental cities we can still experience this process. Such areas are reappearing in New York and San Francisco. At other times, streets turned into workshops for craftsmen, as these were forced out of their dingy hovels. Medieval town statutes, especially in Italy, are filled with ordinances that try to regulate working life on the streets. The provisions for maintaining a sewage system were disproportionate to the amount of refuse deposited, and the architectural situation prevented any effective sanitary measures. Traffic accidents and the noise of traffic were even more of a threat than they are today. Neither the construction of houses nor of hospitals could diminish the social misery. Conditions in the overcrowded Parisian hospitals were just as terrible as in the equally overcrowded prisons of London, Naples, or Madrid. Countermeasures were hopelessly few and were only carried out when the economy was flourishing. The enormous optimism to which monumental buildings owe their construction was not, in many cases, confirmed by historical developments. Incomplete projects determined the appearance of many cities for centuries. For generations, people in Cologne, Siena, or Beauvais lived on the edge of the same building sites.

The Middle Ages, the Renaissance, and the baroque were all confronted with the same set of problems, which arose again and again from the fact that cities, like each of the monumental complexes within them, need an active life if they are not to decay. Cities demanded constant care, and if care were not to degenerate into mere conservatorship, it had to be borne on by necessities which would appear absolute in the eyes of contemporaries, especially of the leading personalities among them.

Trains of thought of this kind are open to misunderstanding and misinterpretation from two sides. On one hand I refer to those modern ideologies that judge a building or the general structure of a city according to the value of the political system, in the service of which—indeed for the security of which—both came into being. In this case the standards of judgment are generally derived from one's own political attitudes. We are experiencing the revival of faith in world history as world judgment. Monumental architectural structures, in the eyes of such critics, disguise social injustice that was caused, in part at least, by their very construction. Judgments of what was achieved in other ages are made according to what we see as the failures of those ages. Here we shall attempt to replace judgments with a more precise understanding.

On the other hand we find exactly the opposite point of view. This view isolates buildings, spaces, and compositions of streets into the timeless realm of aesthetic experience. The attempt is made to develop guidelines for future urban planning on the basis of formal results that were successful in the past. From Camillo Sitte (1889) to A. E. Brinckmann (1920) and P. Lavedan (1926), it was believed possible to determine the rules of form to which successful urban planning has always owed its success. As late as 1959, Paul Zucker managed to elevate similar questions to a higher level of consciousness.[11] But even the beguiling corrections that Sitte proposes for the design of the Ringstrasse in Vienna seem to obscure precisely those characteristics which, both originally and still today, tie that masterpiece of urban planning to its own time (see chap. 7).

The reading of a series of historical city plans was made easier for me by Edward N. Bacon's drawings in *Town Planning, Past and Future* (New York, 1967). Bacon illustrates highly successful towns from all ages. He compares his graphic depictions—and achieves detachment in the process—with the rhythmic figures and symbols of motion in Paul Klee's urban abstractions. Correspondences confirm for him the effective possibilities of immutable formal relationships, which he has tried to revive in his own area of activity—plans for greater metropolitan Philadelphia. We do not have to condemn, with Jane Jacobs, the two-dimensionality of research into modern urban planning as inappropriate to today's situation in order to reject such simplifications.[12] Cities can no more be understood by means of aesthetic norms alone than by means of standards borrowed from sociology and political science.

History tries to encompass overlapping processes. It has to take every aspect of life into consideration. Cities can be understood neither from their beginnings alone[13] nor from their final state. Nor is it possible to make a case in terms of the visual manifestations generated in successful cities by an auspicious process of development. Yet the mind cannot demand more of itself than simple understanding.

Art history looks more deeply than history in general, for the sources of art history are the thing itself; the buildings, the townscape that still exists, constitute the historical event. Old views of a town complete our knowledge by making past circumstances visible to us. What is handed down to us visually teaches us with greater precision about the genesis of buildings, their aesthetic, ideological, and semantic rank.

Among art-historical objects, cities and particular monumental groupings assume a special position insofar as stylistic stages and phases are surveyed in them. Only ideal cities were supposed to be built in a single style. Living cities have always renewed themselves. Every epoch of their history became architecture. They are enriched, torn down, extended, reinterpreted. There is constant rebuilding. Everything we can learn about this process from secondary sources has to be confirmed by visual examination, which is the more exact truth.

In the process, the whole and its parts mutually interpret themselves— the totality of the city, every building in it, as well as every ornament, every statue, every picture. Cities do not merely report their history. By the forms that served for their physical manifestation, cities provide the motives for the building of every house and every street. Written sources may contribute information; as far as art-historical research is concerned, they become tags which promise to take some of the work out of looking; but no other source can inform us as well as the building itself. No other historical process instructs us in the same totally undeceitful manner. We are present as eyewitnesses. Suppositions, obstacles, goals, and ideas are all visible to us. The architects prove to be interpreters of the building patrons' intentions. The changing forms by which existence is mastered stand side by side with the stylistic phases that follow one another to form a particular composition. We are received by the past whenever we set foot in an old city square, and at the same time we are taught about a past that never denies its ideals in the face of the present. In the squares of Rome, Florence, or Venice, in the great axes of St. Petersburg, Berlin, or Paris, in the medieval regularity of Siena, Bern, or Lübeck, among those baroque vistas—which seem larger than they are—in Salzburg, Turin, and Prague, the desire to understand knows no bounds and searches for communicating forms.

No one individual can satisfy this desire for understanding in every direction. For every question expands the scope. We can never pursue more than a few. Research finds it necessary to do art—in the fullness of its being—an injustice by paying attention only to those parts of the whole phenomenon that respond to the specific questions of the research in some particular case. In the following text these questions will lead us through several disciplines—history and art history, sociology and political science, town planning and semantics—but they will always pursue the one basic question that is addressed in the subtitle of this book. It is a question that opens our eyes to consummate form.

A. *Colonnes composites*
   rustiquées.
B. *Piliers Buttans.*
C. *Consoles en ailerons.*
D. *Fronton brisé avec*
   enroulemens.
E. *Couronnement.*
F. *Degrez rampans.*

Pl. 78.

Pag. 313.

PORTE DE LA VIGNE DU CARDINAL SERMONETE

Chapter 1

*T*HIS BOOK STARTS AT THE POINT where the ancient orders of life had completed their decline and the Middle Ages began. This starting point, however, confronts us with three difficulties.

First, the architectural revival was not generated by towns—or, at least, only by a few in provinces south of the Alps. It was the result of the consolidation of conditions in the new Germanic empires, those of the Langobards, the Goths, and the Franks, whose ruling class, the knightly aristocracy around the king, lived in rural areas. Among the Merovingians and the Carolingians the most important buildings were in the palatinates or the monasteries. St. Denis and Aachen are late examples. Numerous examples could be cited. We shall have more to say shortly about the cathedrals built in this epoch.

Second, there is no dividing line between antiquity and the Middle Ages. The process we are concerned with took a different course in different provinces and in each of their towns between the 4th and 11th centuries, and the continuity of ancient conditions has to be examined separately for almost every city. In a few, like Bordeaux, the Roman era lasted until the 8th century; in others, like Salzburg, all that the first missionaries found—at the beginning of the 8th century—were neglected ruins and grass-grown streets.[1]

CATHEDRAL CITIES

The revival of the cities was everywhere consciously linked to antiquity. It involved various renaissances. The bishops, especially, saw themselves as the successors of Roman administration. It was they that promoted continuity. Almost all the successful cities of the early Middle Ages had been Roman cathedral cities. Only a few centers of commerce—above all Venice—are an exception to this pattern. The continued existence of Roman culture can be measured according to whether the rolls of bishops are broken or unbroken. Every new beginning was understood as a *renovatio*.

Third, all the cities of the Roman Empire, insofar as they were not completely destroyed or dissolved into rural colonial areas, were subject to a process of attenuation. Between the 3d and the 6th centuries A.D., wherever we see a Roman population defending itself against the Germanic armies it was almost always behind city walls that had been shortened. The legions themselves had already reduced their defensive quarters to a half or a third of their original area, and the same was to be true of the Byzantine forces in their defensive battles against the Goths and the Huns. I shall depict the situation in Florence in chapter 2. The emperor Julian the Apostate was content, in 361, to remain embattled on Lutetia, his island in the Seine, which was joined to the banks of the river only by two wooden bridges, and it never occurred to him to dare to go to the old *palatium* of the Roman city on the left bank. In Gaul between the 5th and the 10th centuries it was common practice to renew the fortifications of the city core, which was most suitable for defense—more a citadel than a city.[2] Over fifty examples of this are known. Most of the Roman grave or votive steles that have been preserved are those that were reused in the walls of such emergency fortresses. In places like Trier, however, where the bishops as lords of the city had neglected to reduce the size of the Constantinian encircling wall, which had formerly embraced a population of 60,000 in an area of 285 hectares, they remained defenseless and were plundered by the Normans as late as 882. The emergency fortification of the cathedral area, carried out after that disaster, shows how little there was left to defend (fig. 9). In 955, St. Ulrich of Augsburg chose from the outset a small defensive ring of this

Figure 1. Augsburg at the end of the 11th century (after E. Herzog): 1, St. Ulrich and Afra; 2, cathedral; 3, St. John; 4, St. Gertrude; 5, St. Stephen; 6, St. George; 7, Perlach and St. Peter; 8, St. George. The beginnings of the burgher settlement around the market on the Perlach contrast with the fortified ecclesiastical settlements.

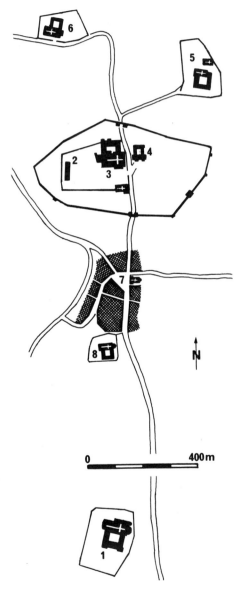

sort as the strongpoint in his defensive battle against the Huns (fig. 1). Long before this, not only in Trier and Augsburg, Cologne and Paris, but in nearly all the larger cities of the Roman area, a process of rustication accompanied the gradual attenuation that left ever larger parts of the original cities to agriculture or simply wilderness. How can we speak of city architecture as a continuous process when everything was subject to the constraints of reduction, restoration, and nest building in an inherited structure that was threatened with collapse?

There were reactions in three spheres. The first, of minor significance, was promoted by the fact that Germanic kings and princes built their residences and palaces in former Roman cities. Theodoric had already made a start in Ravenna. The Langobardic kings chose Pavia. The Langobardic dukes had rebuilt their city gates into fortresses. We shall encounter examples in Turin. And where there was no architectonic continuity, we still find a topographic continuity preserved. Thus, in Cologne the Merovingian princes established themselves within the walls of the Roman governor's praetorium, and the medieval as well as the modern city hall could arise out of those very ruins which now came to light.

The episcopal seats formed a second sphere. Almost all of them were cathedral-fortresses. In almost all the old cathedral cities after the 5th century the location of the cathedral remained unchanged. Pisa is one of a few exceptions. But apart from the Constantinian basilicas in Rome and the buildings of Ravenna, no cathedrals of late antiquity have been preserved to the present day essentially undamaged. Yet in many places portions of the Roman structure were incorporated into the new buildings. Trier and Aquileia are the finest examples but by no means the only ones. A similar complex developed everywhere alongside the cathedral: a baptistery, the bishop's palace, the hospital, bell tower installations, the cemetery, and—from the 9th century onwards, north of the Alps always, south of the Alps sometimes—cloisters, inhabited by the cathedral canons who according to the rule of Chrodegang of Metz, an uncle of Charlemagne, were bound to a communal life. There is a small group of newly founded cities in areas of ancient culture in which we find medieval buildings largely unchanged. Grado and Torcello, for example, reveal the plan of an episcopal complex with cathedral, campanile, baptistery, and palace. Torcello is one of the few sites not buried beneath later buildings (fig. 2). An entire series of architectural plans of the High Middle Ages has been preserved that renewed the old program in the town center at a time when the bishops had long since forfeited their political predominance. Parma, with cathe-

Figure 2. Torcello: cathedral and related buildings

Figure 3. Parma: cathedral square

dral, campanile, and baptistery, a large square in front of the cathedral and an ambitious episcopal palace standing opposite, is probably the most complete example from the 13th century (fig. 3). We shall come across numerous different expressions of this plan, especially in Italy. It represented a challenge of design for the whole Middle Ages. It was developed into the most original unit still preserved in Pisa between the 11th and the 14th centuries (fig. 4). We enter an architectonically organized space which has stood the test of time, not only as a perpetual stage for the playing out of human life, but also as a place in which every building stands on the spot exactly suited to its function.[3] This topographical harmony became an element of architectonic perfection.

In the third sphere, the process of attenuation in the cities of antiquity was a reaction to the constant increase in ecclesiastical institutions. Research on urban planning as a constant process of building must pay particular attention to this increase, as Aldo Rossi has rightly stressed.[4] The 5th century to the end of the 11th, most old urban centers saw a growing number of convents and monasteries both within and outside the city walls. We can

Figure 4. Pisa: cathedral and related buildings

17

measure the size of these cities simply by counting the number of ecclesiastical foundations, which has been done in statistical surveys.[5] Research is by no means complete. By counting 54 institutions inside and outside Rome in 855—the year of Lothar I's death—and 17 each in Paris and Ravenna, 15 in Le Mans, 13 in Vienne, and 10 in Lyon, we can gauge the relative importance of these towns. Cologne, Milan, and Tours have 8 each, Lucca, Metz, Orleans, Pavia, and Trier 7. Continuing with the statistics, we find 6 each in Auxerre, Venice, and Verona; 5 in Autun, Bourges, Chartres, Florence, Limoges, Reims, Sens, Soissons, and Spoleto. There are no statistics for this period for Spain, which was still almost entirely in Arab hands, or for England, and the new cities in the Eastern Carolingian empire all contained fewer than five ecclesiastical institutions, most of them only one. All of these institutions lived on the harvests of their agricultural possessions. For the most part, bishops were the major landowners. The monasteries were constantly trying to obtain endowments from princes and counts to enrich their landed possessions. As a result, large areas in most medieval cities, inside and outside the walls, ended up in mortmain. I shall

Figure 5. Reims in the early 17th century (from an engraving by C. Chastillon)

point out the importance of these empty spaces for later possibilities in the development of architectonic planning in Regensburg, Paris, and London. A large monastery like Saint Germain-des-Prés is said to have owned 12,000 hectares in the 12th century. This was nine times the area encompassed by the Aurelian walls in Rome and more than the whole area of Paris until the end of the 19th century.

The collapse of Roman administration and of all the transportation connections on secure paved roads, the rise of the great Merovingian, Carolingian, and Ottonian empires and—for Southern Italy and Southeast Europe—of the Byzantine Empire led to a situation in which bishops, when not lords over the city, became lords within the city.[6] They were the only ones on the spot. After the 10th century, the dukes and counts of Italy retired once more to their country properties. In most of the successful cities, until the end of the 11th century and often much longer, the bishops were the partners and leaders of the urban populace. It was only then that a conflict of interest developed between the merchant class, which was growing more powerful, and the ecclesiastical authorities—a conflict which was to determine the domestic policies of most cities of the High Middle Ages. The cooperative spirit contrasted with the autocratic.[7] In the early period, the bishops felt themselves responsible for the whole city and made its development their concern.

The integration of the monastic clusters of buildings—most of which lay outside the city walls of Roman times—into the urban complexes of the Middle Ages represented for centuries one of the greatest tasks confronting urban design. There are many examples; Augsburg and Regensburg are two that we shall discuss. The union of the first cathedral city of Reims with the monastery city around Saint-Rémy is among the most famous (fig. 5).

Cologne

Cologne hit upon one of the boldest solutions.[8] In 1075, the year the last of the great founding bishops (Anno) died, and one year after the merchants of this Rhenish city had attempted a first uprising, the city boasted thirteen such institutions, with a fourteenth, the monastery of St. Heribert, on the other side of the Rhine. They all developed into monumental complexes, each appearing to the visitor to be a town of its own within the city (see fig. 6).

In the course of the city's history, no further units were to be added to these fourteen, the mendicant, preaching, or Teutonic orders of the late

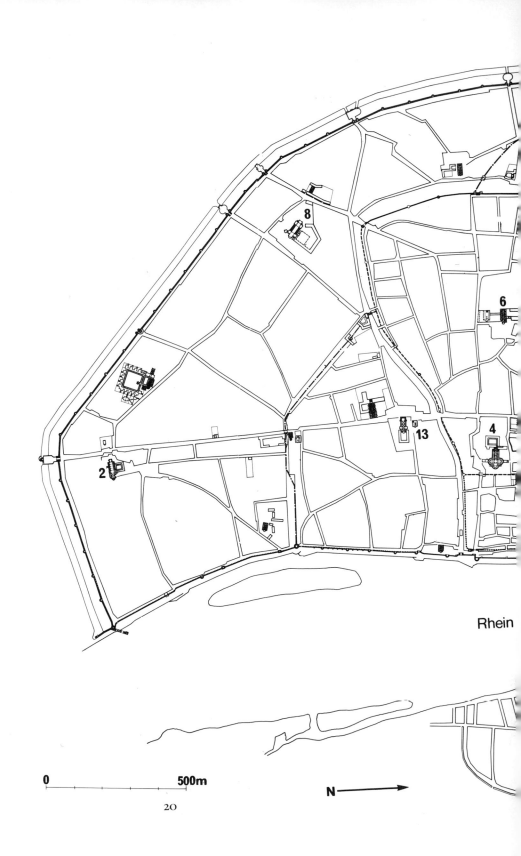

6

13

4

2

Rhein

0   500m

N

20

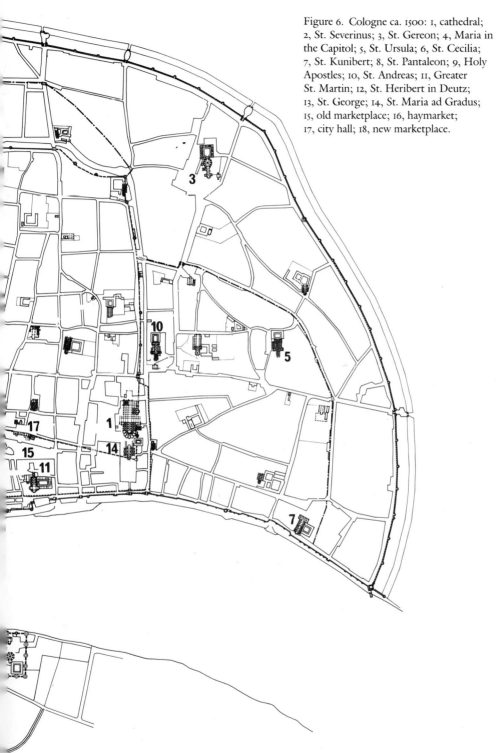

Figure 6. Cologne ca. 1500: 1, cathedral; 2, St. Severinus; 3, St. Gereon; 4, Maria in the Capitol; 5, St. Ursula; 6, St. Cecilia; 7, St. Kunibert; 8, St. Pantaleon; 9, Holy Apostles; 10, St. Andreas; 11, Greater St. Martin; 12, St. Heribert in Deutz; 13, St. George; 14, St. Maria ad Gradus; 15, old marketplace; 16, haymarket; 17, city hall; 18, new marketplace.

Middle Ages not being comparable to them. The design of the old institutions was supported by the conviction that they were established for all time, immortal in the constitution of their personnel—monks, clergy, nuns—as much as in their architectural form.[9] Some were already 500 years old in 1075 and, without exception, were to last another 750 years until, on June 2, 1802, they were all dissolved with a single stroke of the pen. The city's cultural climate was determined by them; the bulk of Cologne's art arose out of the competition among these institutions, which in the eyes of their contemporaries appeared immortal.

The rectangle formed by the Roman walls and the cemetery churches outside the walls constituted the points of departure. Within this rectangle, buildings arose at different times (see fig. 6): the cathedral (1), which has been renovated several times upon the same site; the two convents of Maria in the Capitol (4) and St. Cecilia (6); and finally the last collegiate church, St. Maria ad Gradus (14). Near Maria in the Capitol, its steward, Pippin of Herstal (d. 714), had built himself a residence in the Roman ruins. The cemetery churches outside the gates and on the roads leading from the city were St. Gereon (3), St. Ursula (5), and St. Severin (2). St. Gereon, built to an oval centralized plan dating from late antiquity and still preserved up to the third story in the present-day decagon, was called by Gregory of Tours, in 590, the church *ad sanctos aureos*. There, side by side with the martyrs of the Theban legion, bishops lie buried. The processional route from the cathedral to this church was one of the main streets in the Middle Ages, and its course is still preserved today.[10] An additional collegiate church, bearing the name of its founder, was added under Bishop Kunibert (626–63) in the northern part of the city (7). Still in the Carolingian period, the chapter church of the Holy Apostles was founded in the western part of the city (9) and also that of St. Andreas a little way from the north wall (10). Archbishop Bruno (953–65), a brother of Otto the Great, had renovated the cathedral, finished the construction of St. Pantaleon (8), and founded Greater St. Martin's (11) in the new merchant quarter. Under Archbishop Heribert (999–1021), St. Heribert's was added on the opposite bank of the Rhine with the express purpose of driving the demons out of the Roman ruins. The wish was to sacralize antiquity. St. Anno (1056–75) built both St. Maria ad Gradus (14) and the collegiate church of St. George (14) and renovated some existing buildings. The composition of the city now consisted of the cathedral chapter, seven canonical chapters, three convents, and three Benedictine monasteries. Most of the archbishops, from the 11th to the early 13th century, rebuilt, enlarged, or embellished individual colle-

Figure 7. Cologne: the choir facade of the church of the Holy Apostles from the new marketplace (before 1943)

giate or monastic churches. The hundred years from 1150 to 1250 have been called the "Golden Age" of church building in Cologne. It was then that most of the churches received the late Romanesque appearance they retain today, even if altered by restoration.[11]

With the exception of St. Maria ad Gradus, which, together with the cathedral, formed a monumental grouping, none of these installations related to any other in an urban design context. The choice of site was always determined by external historical factors. Each building therefore had to be integrated into the urban whole—a task individual architects have repeatedly confronted to the present day. The process was sustained by two contrary but interdependent movements. On the one hand, the burgher city overran the old ecclesiastical areas, which then became islands in the plan of the burgher settlement; on the other hand, the churches created decorative facades, which faced either the city or the bank of the Rhine. This is how the rich structures that have been called choir-facades were built—St. Gereon, the Church of the Holy Apostles, Kunibert, Greater St. Martin's, and St. Severin. They became monumental points of focus for streets and squares, in many cases the only ones, for none of the nineteen later parish churches strove for a form capable of dominating its surroundings (fig. 7).

The growth of the burgher city began with the merchant quarter on the Rhine. Whereas the Romans had built most of their cities some distance

IS ROMANORVM COLONIA

Figure 8. Cologne (Woensam's view, 1531, detail)

from rivers, because of the danger of flooding, medieval itinerant merchants accepted the risk so that they could build both their markets and houses near the river bank and the ships' moorings. The founding of Greater St. Martin's and the fact that it was granted permission to build its own wall are evidence that archbishops, as early as the 10th century, were promoting the strength of what was later to become the leading political and economic class. As we have seen, these merchants had already rebelled against the lords of the city in 1074, and we know both the causes and the details of that uprising.[12] At that time they were subdued. In an alliance with the aged emperor Henry IV against his son Henry V, a second uprising in 1106 was more successful, enabling the wall to be extended and reinforced. Five ecclesiastical institutions were now incorporated within the walls: St. Kunibert (2), St. Ursula (5), and St. Andreas (10) in the north; the wealthy church of the Apostles (9) in the west; and St. George (13) in the south. In the course of the 12th century, the burgher patricians of the city reached the point where it was possible for them, as a politically independent corporate body, to conclude contracts. No archbishop was in a position to oppose this new power. The new, third city wall, begun in 1180 and completed in 1210, is testimony to their surpassing success. Now, at last, all the chapter churches and monasteries were integrated. Inside the wall lay vast areas reserved for agriculture. Until 1882, for 700 years, the enclosed area was sufficient for the continuing growth of the population. It was only then that the wall was removed. If the wall extended far beyond the most distant monastery areas, St. Gereon (3), St. Pantaleon (8), and St. Severin (2), it was for strategic purposes. No medieval army was large enough to encircle the wall, especially as the frontage on the Rhine remained open, and none ever attempted to do so.

In popular consciousness, Cologne was the city of these church complexes. As late as 1530, Anton Woensam chose his points of focus so that all fourteen units were visible in his grand view of the city, and above them in the clouds he placed the patrons of the churches, under whose protection the people felt themselves safe (fig. 8). The single new, late medieval accent is the town hall tower, which stands as a symbol of the freedom of an imperial city.[13] This town hall represents a later conception of the city, in which the corporate principle has taken over from the governmental. It is also significant that it was only by destroying the ghetto that room was made for the new town hall and its square. We have documentary proof of the fact that the imaginative picture of all high medieval cities was stamped with the endeavor to claim higher legal rights as a "holy city." The social reality mirrored in the living conditions of the lower classes was not taken into account. For this reason it was only rarely, and late, that those conditions became an object of urban planning. The creative imagination occupied itself with an ideal picture in which art had become the higher ordering principle of all architectural efforts. What was best also had the greatest meaning for the city or the state.

We shall return, in the next section, to the medieval city north of the Alps as a composition of ecclesiastical buildings. Woensam's urban view also points to this chapter's third area of observation. The great century of Cologne's ecclesiastical architecture came to an end when the foundation stone of the new Gothic cathedral was laid in 1248. In the following centuries the bulk of all creative powers was concentrated upon this building. The reason it could not be completed in the Middle Ages lies less in the eviction of the archbishop in 1288 than in the city's political and economic failure since the 15th century. Nevertheless, Cologne has become the city of its cathedral. The new yardstick pushed the collegiate and monastery churches into second place.

Trier

In Cologne, as in many Roman cities in Italy—Florence, Pavia, Turin, and Verona—the line of the Roman walls and the Roman network of streets, at least the crossing of the two main streets, can still be seen today in the structure of the city. Trier (fig. 9) illustrates the very opposite solution.[14]

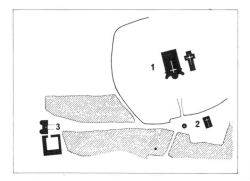

Figure 9. Trier, early formation of the city in the 11th century (after Noack): 1, cathedral precinct with the cathedral and the convent of Our Lady; 2, main market with St. Gangolf and the market cross; 3, Simeonsstraße with St. Simeon in the Porta Nigra.

Figure 10. (*below*) Trier: Porta Nigra and church of St. Simeon in the 18th century

The Roman streets were covered with debris. The course of the wall was retraced later and then only partially. On the other hand, a few large buildings could be put back to use. The present Cologne cathedral is the seventh or eighth new building to rise on the same site;[15] as for St. Severin, six earlier buildings can be traced at the same site. In Trier, on the other hand, a whole series of Roman monumental buildings were constantly being put back into service for the same or different purposes. Thus the nucleus of the present-day cathedral is an ancient building. The basilica was later incorporated into the castle of the episcopal city rulers, affording them the security of its brick walls (fig. 124). The Porta Nigra was closed off and developed as the church of St. Simeon in the 11th century (fig. 10).[16] The scattered cemetery or collegiate churches were not integrated into the city as a whole until the period of the city's modern growth. In the 11th century, Trier consisted of a cathedral precinct (fig. 9, 1) comprising the cathedral, the convent of Our Lady, the bishop's palace, and the cloister of the Dominicans; immediately outside the precinct gate, with the market- and parish church of St. Gangolf the main market (2); and, leading off from the market, all the streets on which the merchants and craftsmen lived. The axis leading from the church of St. Gangolf to St. Simeon's, which was built right into the Roman city gate (3), formed the first self-contained street area. The success of urban design in Trier—as in many Roman cities of southern France and Italy—lay in the ability to reuse monumental buildings and ruins, like the spoils of war, in a totally new plan.

Imperial Trier was too large ever to have been integrated either in the Middle Ages or in the baroque period. It was left to the monasteries and the convents to defend themselves. Many small settlements lay outside the medieval walls, and a few were outside the Roman fortifications. For even Roman Trier was not a garrison city and was not really set up for defense. Like Rome, Trier even in the Middle ages could not find its way from being an open city to being a closed one.

Ecclesiastical Cities of the 10th and 11th Centuries

The best work on early medieval architecture (Erich Herzog, *Die ottonische Stadt,* Berlin, 1964) illustrates that way for us. With the exception of Trier, Speyer, and Augsburg, Herzog examines only those cities that came into existence outside the Roman Empire under the Carolingians and the Ottonians. Of his seventeen examples, the thirteen most important were episcopal cities. Two more, Quedlinburg and Goslar, grew from imperial palaces. Only two, Halle and Lüneburg, began as purely market towns. Even in the comprehensive chapters that form the second part of Herzog's masterful work, the examples illustrating the main themes are all cathedral cities, the Roman cities of Strasbourg and Cologne and, of later founding, Liège, Utrecht, Hildesheim, and Osnabrück. Herzog is thus making an important statement: contrary to the overemphasis in historical research on the development of the medieval city from marketplace, or vicinage, under the protection of a castle, the successful cities show that political aims determined their beginnings. This was true of cathedral cities, founded in places where there was originally a castle or a market, as in Magdeburg, and of cities where there was neither, as in Osnabrück.[17] Although there was still a measure of uncertainty in the choice of sites in the case of new towns founded by St. Boniface and other missionaries, so that a whole number of cathedral cities were unable to sustain themselves, from Charlemagne's time onward every monarch who established an episcopal see managed to ensure the success of the new foundation by careful topographical planning. The last of these foundations was Bamberg, established in 1007 by the emperor Henry II. Later on, a few capitals or administrative centers were able to add a bishop to their urban prominence, for example, Vienna, Olmütz, Fulda, Munich, and—thanks to Napoleon—Freiburg-im-Breisgau in 1821. But in these cases the bishop came into a city that was complete, and did not start or restart one.

The development of these episcopal cities was sustained by two elements: first, the extension and multiplication of clerical centers, and, second, the growth of the merchant class, and shortly afterward of the craftsman class, around the market and outside the enclosed cathedral areas. Only the clerical element belongs, from the outset, in a history of urban design as a part of the general history of architecture. The merchant and craftsman element, over the centuries, made its mark in the history of settlement until it too could represent itself architecturally, having grown to political and economic power.

The city plans that Erich Herzog developed from the earliest land registry plans of the 19th century reveal the political evolution of various cities. I shall select two examples.

Halberstadt

Halberstadt (fig. 11) originally contained a fortified castle area in which two major ecclesiastical buildings, the cathedral and the collegiate church of Our

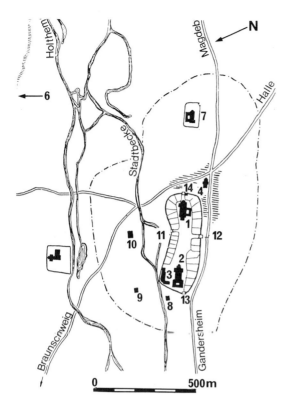

Figure 11. Halberstadt in the 11th century (after E. Herzog): 1, cathedral; 2, convent of Our Lady; 3, Petershof; 4, St. Martin; 5, Burchard convent; 6, St. Boniface convent (not shown); 7, St. Paul convent; 8, Alexius hospital; 9, Lundgeri hospital; 10, Pforten convent; 11, "watering gate"; 12, "dark gate"; 13, "dragon gate"; 14, steps to castle.

Lady, were erected opposite one another. At the crossroads below them, merchants and craftsmen had settled around the market church of St. Martin. Further monasteries and collegiate churches were widely dispersed in the lowlands; through their foundation the bishops hoped to enhance the political importance of their city. The plan illustrates how the market settlement depended upon the upper city.

The second plan (fig. 12) reveals that this relationship changed in the 12th and 13th centuries in favor of the citizenry. The cathedral and the collegiate Church of Our Lady had remained the high point of the town and had been built up. But their separate fortifications had had to be given up. The market area had expanded. The increase in population meant that the bishop's palace was now surrounded by the citizenry. There was, at least, a balance of power. Where the concept of the institution and external forces did not protect the bishop, he had to yield, as was the case in the numerous episcopal cities which became free imperial cities in the course of the 13th

Figure 12. Halberstadt, the city area of
the High Middle Ages with modern plan
showing the location of houses (after
E. Herzog): 1, cathedral; 2, Our Lady;
3, St. Martin; 4, St. Paul; 5, St. Andreas;
6, St. Moritz; 7, city hall; 8, hospital
of the Holy Ghost; 9, "broad gate";
10, Gröper gate; 11, Burchard gate.

and 14th centuries. The lofty concept of his office, however, led the bishop
to build ever larger ecclesiastical buildings, which, by their scale, were supposed to illustrate the meaning of "church." It was only later—just before
the end of the 13th century—that the huts of the lower city were expanded
into fancier, half-timbered houses, which, for their part, testify to the self-
consciousness of a citizenry gaining in power.

Hildesheim

As a second example, I chose Hildesheim (fig. 13). This cathedral city was
of Carolingian founding. A modest market settlement prompted the selection of the site. Hildesheim achieved particular prominence under the Ottonians, who for a time moved their court chapel—in which leading episcopal personalities received their training—to Hildesheim. As a politician
as well as an architectural patron, Bernward of Hildesheim (b. ca. 960,
bishop 993–1022) was one of the leading figures of his century.[18] He himself
had been educated in the cathedral school of Hildesheim and later became

a teacher of Otto III; until his death, he was also a friend of Henry II. We learn from his biography, by Thangmar, the head of the cathedral school, that he was considered in his day an active practicing artist. "He undertook with the greatest zeal to throw walls around our Holy Place—that is, the cathedral close—distributed the towers around the periphery, and did his work with such skill that there is nothing like it for beauty and strength in the whole of Saxony. Outside the walls he erected a splendid chapel in honor of the Holy Cross."[19] We have, therefore, to imagine the area around the cathedral (fig. 13, 1) as being strongly fortified. We shall describe later the construction of his chief work, St. Michael's (2), the oldest Benedictine church in Saxony. Again, in the lowlands, along the main road from Elze to Brunswick, there already existed a small and unprotected market settlement (A). The visual effect of St. Michael's as a basilica, well balanced in its dimensions, with two choirs, two transepts, and two towers at the intersection, can only be appreciated when one realizes that its broadside view could be seen from the cathedral, which was on the opposite hill.

Bernward's successor, Godehard, founded the church of St. Mauritius to the west (3) and St. Bartholomew's to the east (4), which also stood upon fortified eminences like the convent of the Holy Cross (5), which

Figure 13. Hildesheim in 13th century (before the circumvallation): 1, cathedral; 2, St. Michael; 3, St. Mauritius; 4, St. Bartholomew; 5, church of the Holy Cross; 6, St. Godehard; (A) first market settlement; (B) the 12th century old town; (C) the 13th century new town.

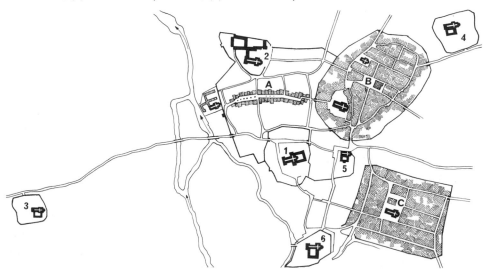

Bishop Hetzilo rebuilt in 1079. The last institution to be built was the monastery of Godehard (6) with its famous Romanesque church, begun in 1133.

In the meantime the little burgher community had moved from the unhealthy low ground on the ford (A) to higher terrain, where they built the first parish church loosely fortified by palisades (B). In the 13th century an orderly new settlement was added (C), by means of which the bishops tried to augment their income. But not until the end of the 13th and the beginning of the 14th centuries did the citizenry win the power and the rights to form a unified urban corpus, with enclosing walls, out of this open city of scattered settlements.[20]

It has often been stressed that the most important ecclesiastical institutions unite into the form of a cross whose beams meet at the cathedral. A series of cathedral cities—one example is Utrecht—confirm this observation. But the only surviving contemporary statement on this characteristic concerns Paderborn; we are told that Bishop Meinwerk, after completing his cathedral fortifications, wanted to found four institutions which would constitute the four ends of a cross. Only two were completed, the Benedictine church of Abdinghof to the west and the Busdorf church to the east.[21] But this one document teaches us to look at urban design of the 10th and 11th centuries with different eyes. The churches crowning the skylines of open cities of the earlier period were conceived as a unit. There was much discussion about what constituted a complete episcopal city. The goal was to have as many ecclesiastical institutions as possible, arranged in a significant order and dedicated to those saints to whom the city felt particularly indebted.

As late as the 17th century, Mattheus Merian's description of cities focuses on these churches, and the significance and beauty of cities was measured by the size and number of their churches.

The development of the "open" city of the 10th and 11th centuries into the "closed" city of the 12th and 13th came about in similar ways in many parts of Europe. Every language created its own concepts for the process: "dalle città a nuclei alla città compatta," from the scattered town to the compact town. If we look more closely, we see that the open city consisted everywhere of a number of clerical centers, whereas the closed city was a burgher city that had grown up around these centers. In open cities we see the ruling element in the foreground, whether a castle, an episcopal court, or an abbey; in closed cities, it is the associative element, the common works of the citizenry, that first meet the eye.[22]

Bamberg

Bamberg, the last episcopal see to serve for the founding of a city, furnishes the best example of what the 10th and 11th centuries understood by a functional city (fig. 14). The founder himself, Henry II, had determined the whole plan between 1007 and 1024, the year of his death.[23]

Figure 14. Bamberg: 1, cathedral; 2, old court; 3, new court; 4, cloisters; 5, St. Michael; 6, St. Stephen; 7, upper parish church; 8, St. Gangolf; 9, St. James; 10, town hall.

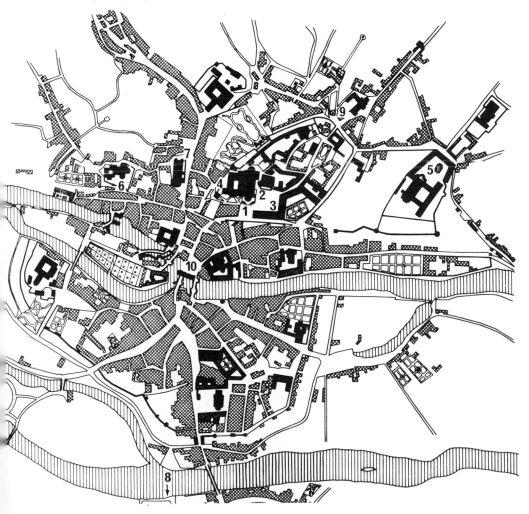

The point of departure was his own ancestral castle, which he offered to the new foundation. At its feet, on the Regnitz, was a fishermen's settlement which was also visited by merchants. The castle had previously belonged to the Babenbergs and retained their name. Its fortifications were preserved for the defense of the cathedral precinct. Two gates, in whose upper stories chapels were later built, led up to the Steigerwald and down to the ford.

Along with the cathedral and scattered lands, the emperor furnished his foundation with a Benedictine monastery, St. Michael's (5), the canonry of St. Stephen's (6), and probably the "upper parish church" as well (7). Later, St. Gangolf (8) and St. Jacob's (9) were added. From the beginning, the plan was to create a crown of churches up the long ascent, and in later centuries the plan was continually renewed but never altered. Down through the centuries, the castle hill preserved the essential parts of the architectural order it had had from the beginning. The contours of the "Old Palace" (2) followed the lines of the ducal castle. The original palace was not torn down until 1577. Most of the present-day buildings have Gothic and Renaissance origins. From the palace, one used the side entrance to the cathedral, the present-day "Royal Portal."

The first cathedral (1), the actual contours of which have only recently been excavated,[24] was almost the same size as the final one. The choice of the patron saints, St. Peter for the west choir and St. George—patron saint of the Teutonic order—for the east, embodied a political program. The new cathedral, the work of Bishop Ekbert von Andechs-Meran (1203–37) and his uncle Poppo, refined this plan. It could now take into account the fact that Bamberg was the only German church to contain the tombs of both an emperor (Henry II) and a pope (Clement II). With the apse facing the city, the portals and towers emphasize the importance of the choir of St. George.

On the other side of the "Old Palace" and lying sharply above the city, Lothar Franz von Schönborn erected the "New Residence" (1694–1705) designed by the architect Leonhard Dietzenhofer. He moved the imperial prelate's residence (3) to a point higher than the cathedral. Tradition was followed by having the cloister of the cathedral canons on the south side of the nave placed opposite the prince's side. Balthasar Neumann put his modest chapter house next to the choir of St. George's. The wealthy estates of the individual canons could extend over the whole of the hilly land that stretched out behind the city.

The fishermen's colony became a city. Rows of dwellings for merchants and craftsmen multiplied. The necessary parish and convent churches were incorporated. Because of the topographical situation, every later burgher uprising against the episcopal regime was condemned to failure from the very beginning (see chap. 6). The balance between the different sections of the town could only be achieved by putting the town hall in the middle, on the two bridges, and later between them (10). This was the one suitable place; and at the same time it afforded the baroque period the opportunity of developing it with enormous effect.

Cathedral Cities of the High Middle Ages

In another context we shall discuss the difficulties Maurice de Sully had to overcome in 1163 in order to get the empty space necessary for him to break ground for his new cathedral and its square on the overpopulated island on the Seine known as Paris (see chap. 7). Cologne's Gothic cathedral also took up more space than its Carolingian predecessor, but the problem here was to justify razing the venerable older building. Rumors that it was burned down by order of the architect have never been totally silenced. The new cathedral departed from the scale of its predecessor, a scale honored by all collegiate churches both before and after.

These Gothic cathedrals are of such a size as to dominate the whole urban landscape. With a few exceptions they are larger and always much higher than the buildings that preceded them. Even today the cathedral choir of Beauvais in front of the remains of the Romanesque church illustrates this relationship (fig. 15). In all cities in which the late 12th or 13th century had erected a cathedral, it was the largest building ever built there and would remain so until the present day. This is true of the cathedrals in Florence or Milan as late as the 15th and 16th centuries. We shall come across a similar phenomenon in the cathedrals of the imperial cities of Ulm, Nördlingen, and Dinkelsbühl, and also in a few other centers which, like Freiburg-im-Breisgau, merely aspired to such a status.

The relationship between city and cathedral appears all the more surprising, the less the population was permitted to increase prior to the industrialization of Europe. The cathedrals of Lyon, Chartres (fig. 16), Amiens, and Bourges were disproportionate in size to the city and the other parish or collegiate churches. Only Reims (fig. 5) had the power to erect—apart from a "Royal Cathedral" par excellence (begun in 1211)—a

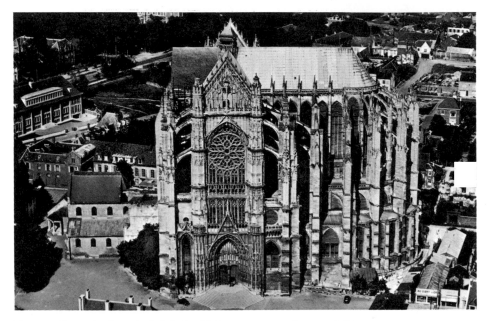

Figure 15. Beauvais: the cathedral choir with Romanesque predecessor (left)

Figure 16. Chartres

church of comparable proportions for the patron saint of the city, St. Nicaise (begun in 1229). All later churches of the mendicant orders in France and Germany are on a different scale. Where Gothic cathedrals stand, even the baroque never undertook massive church buildings. In the Holy Roman Empire, the only totally new cathedral that dates from this third great epoch of church building, after the Romanesque and Gothic, is that of Salzburg, which replaced what was allegedly a decaying 12th-century church. All the other great church buildings of the baroque are either monastic or shrine churches, and occasionally royal court churches. Only Spain and Italy, where in many cities the Romanesque cathedral was not followed by a Gothic one, offer some exceptions.

Hans Sedlmayr proposed the thesis that these Gothic cathedrals are monuments to the growing power of the French king.[25] As evidence he could adduce the fact that the chief buildings were constructed in the slowly expanding lands of the crown, the central power. The bishops and building patrons were relatives, retainers, and partisans of the king. A new royal peace created the economic prerequisites for such massive undertakings in these particular dioceses. For the time being a period of rest had begun. Otto von Simson pointed out that, in these same years, the cathedrals were to be understood as the expression of an image of the world that was formed by the scholastic thought and mystical ideals of the age.[26] The history of architecture has constantly reemphasized that, in every case, the creative thoughts realized in the previous building could be taken as a point of departure. Empirical knowledge was accumulated—up to the time of the catastrophic collapse of the choir in Beauvais because of its excessive height—that allowed interiors to be built which grew higher and higher and lighter and lighter.

Not a single one of these cathedrals, not even the last ones to be built in Regensburg, Prague, or Milan, represents the first large building on its site. The site was predetermined in the same way as the east-west orientation of the building with the transept running north-south. Whether we wish to regard achievements in design merely as the acquisition of an expanded building site depends on our definition of "urban design." In the case of Florence, we have exact information about the efforts the cathedral architects had to make in order to carve out an open area which would not only afford the necessary space for the building but would also make it possible, in the early Renaissance, to see the whole of the building.[27] Gothic cathedrals always dominated the appearance of their cities. The limits on height in modern building codes have proceeded from the principle that this dominance should be maintained, even though in many cases the codes have failed to prevent the construction of skyscrapers in the vicinity of a cathedral—for example, in Cologne or London. Such regulations indicate that people are conscious, even today, of the importance of a cathedral for the general image of the city.

This insight is of fundamental importance within our context. The "cathedrals and politics" theme was discredited by the fact that some authors tried to use it to promote the trends of their own times.[28] In the process, they generally corrected events according to the measure of their own goals.[29] It remains manifest that these enormous structures were to be understood as the expression of a world order in which the king, the bishop, the clergy, the nobility, and the common people all had appointed places they were to occupy within these buildings, and which their dwellings were to occupy around the buildings. The orders of magnitude illustrate the orders of value. The attitude of the bishops—who set out to burden generations of citizens as well as the countryfolk of their dioceses—was a combination of idealism, consciousness of the ruling class, and piety mixed with a desire to create a new order. It was a totality of relationships that could not be divided up. People built from historical necessity (see chap. 6). No other structures could define this totality more clearly than the cathedrals. Yet attempts to analyze the great syntheses have in every age led to the adoption of one-sided positions. In the meantime, art history has matured sufficiently to realize that every epoch and every author could emphasize only that which they considered appropriate for them.

In all medieval cities that have been kept more or less intact, there are productive, detailed solutions, which received a great deal of attention, for the site formation on rivers, on squares, in front of monastery or parish churches, in markets, in the area by the city walls and fortified gates. But these detailed solutions, especially in the smaller cities, are meaningless when compared with the effect of cathedrals from a distance, or their effect close up when viewed from every vantage point. Laon, Chartres, Bourges, and Salisbury (fig. 17) are outstanding examples. Almost every cathedral city spent fifty years or more building its cathedral. Its growth was the main event in the city's history for generations. And after its completion the power to repeat such an achievement seemed to have been lost for ever. Its presence denied any competing undertaking. Although older accents were everywhere retained and new accents added, the city as a whole preserved its monolithic character—its orientation toward one building. Even where, as in Amiens, the terrain itself granted no prominence to the large building,

Figure 17. Salisbury

the cathedral continued to dominate the city. Napoleon was not the first to
direct cross-country roads toward church spires. The majority of roads in
the Middle Ages were also built in such a way as to lead directly to the
spires of the cathedral or city church. Munich still serves as an example.

Cathedral cities represent one type of medieval urban design. The
growth of street networks does not belong in the history of urban architecture. It belongs rather to the history of settlement. An ideal notion of a city
is defined by a cathedral. The reference to a single building, of different and
larger proportions, unites this world and the life hereafter. It gives to everyday life the value that the Middle Ages thought proper to it, like the feast
day and the life to come. We may not relate the architectural form and the
size of cathedrals immediately to the actual power of a form of governance,
whether royal or episcopal. What we are dealing with is the representation
of principles of order which will become effective only in the context of a
belief in the life hereafter. The individual building sets limits on the whole
of the city. The demonstration of such a polarity was the true achievement
of urban design. It was preserved in its purest form where new political
aims did not cause new buildings to be built which disrupt our view of the
cathedral. That was the case in Chartres, Laon, and Bourges, but not in
Cologne, Milan, or Brussels, and it was true, with certain limitations, of
Paris, Regensburg, and Prague.

Chapter 2

*S*INCE THE END OF THE *11TH* century, the growth of the population and of its economic power allowed new forms of self-government to develop in many European cities. From the middle of the 12th century onward, hundreds of towns were founded under a variety of different conditions. They were granted municipal charters by their territorial rulers and these charters regulated the communal life of the burghers as well as their relation to their rulers and to other political units. Research in history, social history, economics, and, in particular, legal history[1] has paid scrupulous attention to forms of self-government and their development. Discussion of these forms falls outside the scope of this work, but, to the extent that they could directly influence city design, they are significant for our purposes.

The urban charters developed in the course of a struggle with older and superior ecclesiastical or state powers. Where the power of the princes diminished, self-government flourished; where it increased, self-government was limited. For this reason, cities in the Holy Roman Empire, especially in northern and central Italy, enjoyed greater independence than cities in France, where the central power was expanding, in Spain under the Reconquista, or in England under the Norman conquerors. My choice of examples here takes this

City-States

factor into account. Yet it must be emphasized that the diversity of legal conditions, even in medieval French and Spanish cities, determined their appearance so decisively that even later regimentation by the central power could not entirely destroy it. In many cases the historical life of the great centers, as they developed from communities that defended themselves to communities guarded by royal power and, finally, to those protected by the power of the state, could still be read from their ground plan and architectural profile. Bordeaux was first distinguished by the building of several carefully planned city walls, then by the crown's powerful citadel, and finally by the Place Royale, which, with the finest historical logic, adorned the space that had been made available on the site of the fortress (figs. 18 and 19). Within Germany, free imperial cities developed only where the territorial princes could not succeed in building a state composed of contiguous territories like Bavaria, Austria, Bohemia, and Brandenburg. However, the princes early recognized that prosperity and economic reward could only flourish where there was freedom, and therefore they gave their cities special rights from the outset. The Zähringer city of Bern (fig. 36) and Henry the Lion's seaport, Lübeck (figs. 44 and 45), outshine all of these new foundations in the very perfection of their design.

All free municipalities were ruled by town councils with one or several burgomasters. The composition of these town councils and their powers differed from one generation to another and from one group of cities to another. Aristocratic families, patrician merchants, upper and lower craft guilds struggled for power in the different centers for decades with varying degrees of success. The Italian municipalities had a number of councils, which kept an eye on each other. Mistrust promoted a constant differentiation of all the powers. The greatest successes in urban design were achieved wherever a patrician government could establish itself and, to an even greater degree, where its members were elected from an open burgher society rather than from a closed aristocratic one. The Welfs of the *popolo grosso* in Florence were members of such a burgher party, while the Ghibellines formed a predominantly aristocratic one. In Siena and, later, in Nuremberg and Lübeck we find similar conditions. The best cities were the work of the great burgher families, and even the princes were most successful where they allowed these "citizens" par excellence to develop freely.

The burgomasters, with the chief judges at their side, not only held different titles in various cities and languages—*Schultheiß, Schöffen, podestà, capitano del popolo, gonfalonieri della giustizia*—but had different powers and different terms of office. We see the doge, at one extreme, who not only enjoyed the title of duke but in the early period also had ducal rights, and, at the other extreme, the podestàs of the Lombard and Tuscan munici-

Figure 18. Bordeaux in the 17th century

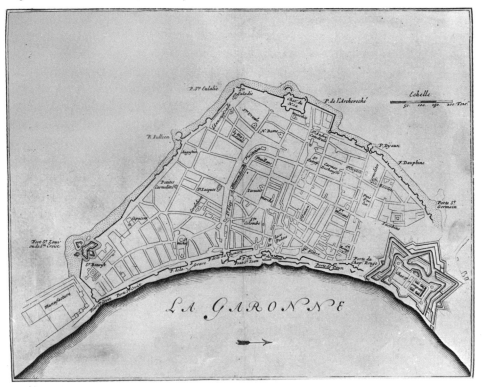

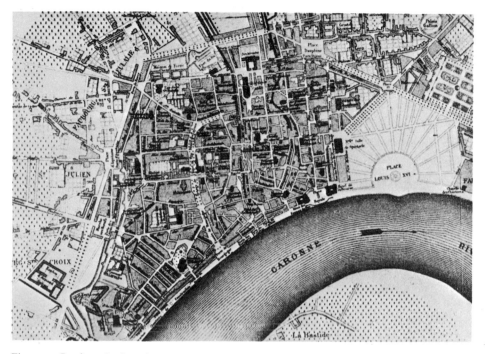

Figure 19. Bordeaux in the 18th century

palities, who were not citizens of those towns but were elected for a year and were under an obligation to carry out an immediately realizable program—a program preserved in municipal statutes, which were constantly being revised. Yet we must not overlook the fact that it was almost always to outstanding personalities, who far exceeded the powers accorded them, that we owe the greatest works of urban design. They were often architects, but more frequently they were rulers of the city. The various developments in the individual towns makes it impossible to group them merely from the point of view of a constitution, though it is from the constitutional point of view that I have derived the basic principles of their organizational schemes.

Comparable differences were created by orders of magnitude, which are often overlooked in research on the medieval city. Most of the towns in the ancient world were small; many were tiny. Many of the new foundations of the 13th and 14th centuries were dissolved again in the 15th. Around 1400, two hundred settlements in what was later to be Switzerland called themselves towns; in 1500 there were scarcely fifty.[2] In 13th-century Italy there were already twenty-three towns with more than 20,000 inhabitants. In England at that time, and this was true as late as the 17th century, London was the only town that large. In the German-speaking area, a town of 5,000 inhabitants was considered middle-sized. In the 13th century there were only two metropolises with populations of 40,000, Cologne and Vienna; and in 1300 a very few, among them Lübeck, exceeded 20,000. The Flemish towns of Bruges and Ghent were among these. From the point of view of urban design, cities like Florence, which around 1300 had a population of almost 100,000, or like Siena at the same period, with almost 40,000, can scarcely be compared with cities like Zürich and Bern, with populations between 5,000 and 10,000 around 1500. Even Nuremberg and Augsburg, the most powerful centers of commerce among the free imperial cities, scarcely exceeded 50,000 in their heydays in the 16th century.

With the division into city-states, maritime powers, and imperial cities, the cities we shall group together are not those with different constitutions, but rather those with a comparable architectural profile. This profile, it is true, tends to depend on the political achievements of the cities and on the development of their constitutions and economic and social structures.[3] The city-states of Tuscany and Switzerland were structures in which a capital city ruled over a larger area of land but was itself independent of all superior powers, unless, like the Swiss cities, it had entered into voluntary ties with other cities in the confederacies. The imperial cities, on the other hand, were municipalities which, in the first place, always recognized the imperial power as at least theoretically superior to all their decisions and, in the second place, had no rural area within their domain—or at most a small one. Nuremberg, with six small towns in its domain, and Ulm were the outstanding exceptions. Yet their territories, compared with those of Bern or Florence, were so small that they posed no administrative problems. The city ended with its walls. The walls themselves were the limits of jurisdiction, whereas in Italy—and this had been true since Roman times—at least the *borghi* on the arterial roads, and often a quite large area besides, belonged to the city and were subject to its ordinances. Roman law speaks of "1000 paces" around the fortifications. Third, the relationship between the ecclesiastical and the secular authorities was, at least in the Italian city-states, fundamentally different from that in the German imperial cities, and it was precisely this difference that gained architectural expression. The Swiss cantonal capitals, which were also—de facto until 1499 and de jure until 1648—imperial cities, assume a characteristic intermediate position.

The struggle with the ecclesiastical and secular authorities for influence, possessions, and rights ended in the north in many cases only with the Reformation; indeed, it compelled citizens to embrace the new doctrine rapidly and with political passion. The attacks of the iconoclasts were another expression of this passion.

The maritime powers differ externally from the city-states in that shipping was brought right up to the dwellings themselves. This fact determined the appearance of Venice and Amsterdam. For the same reason, Lübeck and even Manhattan have been included in our selection, but not ports like Genoa, Pisa, Naples, or Marseilles, which had no canals leading to the residential areas. Here I would rather have added Ragusa, or Bruges, Hamburg, Bremen, Danzig, or even Antwerp. The architectural profile and the cultural climate of these maritime cities, which have to be considered as belonging either, like Venice, to the city-states or, like Lübeck, to the imperial cities (whereas Amsterdam and Manhattan were incorporated into a superior federation of states), were also in part determined by the fact that they all had possessions and sovereign rights across the oceans. "Venice," it was said, "lay outside Venice as well." At times there were almost as many Venetians living in the Levant, Dalmatia, and Greece as in the capital itself. This was also true, for centuries, of Genoa and Pisa, and at least in Genoa it found suitable architectural expression. The Lübeck merchants had offices and political influence in all the cities of the Baltic. The East and West India Companies fulfilled this function for Amsterdam. The urban atmosphere and the architectural pattern were determined by the cosmopolitan nature of these cities, just as in Siena and Bern, though in a different way, they were determined by those cities' isolation.

Among the many cities that are not represented by an example of their type, the Flemish metropolises of the late 13th to the early 17th centuries represent the largest gap. Bruges, Ypres, Louvain, Ghent, and Antwerp were masterpieces of urban design, and Bruges is admirably preserved. In this way they form a type of city sui generis, for in their architectural structure the commercial center—the cloth hall or market hall—acquired a special significance, becoming in Ypres (fig. 20) and Bruges the city's dominant structure. In contrast to the Tuscan cities, the forces shaping the city did not turn in the first instance to the centers of political power but rather to those of commercial power. In size and cost these market halls remained unique. Even Venice and Lübeck have nothing to compare with them. I have not pursued the historical development of these Flemish cities because

Figure 20. Ypres: market and cloth hall

political conditions within them changed all too frequently. They could only achieve real freedom for short periods at a time. Their cloth halls must be understood as demonstrations of their pretensions, which, in the face of political adversaries such as the counts of Flanders, the dukes of Burgundy, the German emperors, France, and later Spain, could not be implemented. Their loss of freedom, however, was always accompanied by loss of creative capacity.

The Tuscan City-States

When not threatened by the imperial power, the free municipalities of Italy (unlike the German imperial cities) invariably began to fight among themselves to determine which was the leading power. These wars ended only when the stronger city had integrated the weaker into its territory. The large fishes swallowed up the small ones. Finally, after the subjugation of Siena in 1555—Siena having in its turn subjugated a whole series of rivals like Massa Maritima—only Florence remained, together with little Lucca, which was favored by special circumstances. By "finally" I mean not only until the Napoleonic conquest but up to the unification of Italy.

Cities maintained the creative power to monumentalize or reorder the urban organism only as long as they could also defend their charters. Dependence leads to unproductiveness. Even outstanding talents in painting or sculpture could develop no further in those conditions. The accents that central governments could later attach to or insert into the subjugated cities were of a different nature. Citadels were erected as strongholds, as done by Lorenzo il Magnifico in Volterra or, later, Cosimo I in Siena; or administrative palaces were built like those commissioned by the grand duke and provided for him by Vasari in Pisa or Arezzo. But these works lacked precisely that boldness of form which could only come from the desire to articulate oneself politically by means of large buildings. The cathedrals in Pisa and Florence possess this boldness in the highest degree. The Palazzo Publico in Siena and the Palazzo Vecchio in Florence were intended to be understood as demonstrations of political power, like the urban palaces in Perugia, Gubbio, Volterra, or the small town of San Gimignano.

The leading families in the Italian cities had for centuries been brought up to regard buildings as the conditions of political influence. Strategy based on fortified castles had now been transferred from the countryside to the town. Towers were built and tower associations formed. The rise of many cities was hindered by battles between different parties who were as enthusiastic about building their own towers as they were about destroying those of their enemies. In Florence, for example, the Ghibelline towers were destroyed before the Ghibellines set out for the battle of Montaperti in 1260, and after their victory they in their turn destroyed all the buildings of the Guelphs—103 palaces, 580 houses, 85 towers. Of these, 47 palaces, 196 houses, and 59 towers were inside the city walls, the rest of them in the countryside.[4] As we shall soon see, the 13th century shift of political thought from the great families to the town council and urban administration also conditioned a shift in the center of gravity of urban planning from the private sector to the public. Political rather than economic successes determined the citizenry's self-consciousness. Leading spirits were busy with questions as to what constituted a total political order. Dante, like Plato and Aristotle, developed political theories. The conceptual systems of economics and political science, insofar as they were not taken over from antiquity, originated in Florence.

A statistical record of numerous economic areas was first and most comprehensively developed in the Italian city-states, again primarily in Florence. One chronicler, Giovanni Villani (1280–1348), included the most

Figure 21. Florence and its 3(4) walls: 1, Mercato Vecchio; 2, baptistery; 3, cathedral; 4, San Lorenzo; 5, Santa Maria Novella; 6, Santa Croce; 7, Santa Maria del Carmine; 8, Santo Spirito; 9, SS. Annunziata; 10, San Marco; 11, Bargello; 12, Palazzo Vecchio; 13, Uffizi; 14, Palazzo Pitti; 15, Fortezza di Basso; 16, Fortezza di Alto; 17, Porta Romana; 18, Porta San Frediano; 19, Porta Prato; 20, Porta San Gallo; 21, Porta Santa Croce; 22, Porta San Nicolo, (A) Ponte Vecchio, (B) Ponte alla Carraia, (C) Ponte Santa Trinità; (D) Ponte alle Grazie.

precise calculations in his presentation of the city's history. No matter how highly the commercial spirit of the leading merchant families was developed, Italians always recognized that politics had pride of place, and they expressed this passion for politics in their buildings. A market like that in Nuremberg, or a string of street markets like those in Augsburg, never became the center of political life.

The Florentine Republic

Without such a fundamental attitude, this unique city would never have developed into the masterpiece of urban design that has been preserved for us. In the history of the six Florentine walls it was, it is true, only the last one that formed a part of this masterpiece, and this was because it was built as a demonstration of political power—which went far beyond the city's needs. Figure 21 shows the first walled enclosure, built by the Romans, that rectangle which was divided into quarters by Cardo and Decumanus, at the crossing point of which stood the forum—later the Mercato Vecchio and today the Piazza della Repubblica.[5] The figure does not show the second defensive ring, built by the Byzantines in 541–44, which made the city into little more than a citadel. What we understand by the third wall is the extension of the area to the south, and to the Arno, in the 10th century. To the north, the Byzantine fortifications, which left the cathedral and the bishop's palace outside the walls, were considered sufficient. It was only the fourth wall, Dante's *cerchia antica,* that enclosed the cathedral and palace and restored on three sides the course of the Roman wall, which embraced an area of 37 hectares. The fifth wall, which also appears in the figure, was built on the right bank of the Arno (the main bank) in the years 1172–75, but it was not until 1250 that it received its final form on the (secondary) left bank. In this way the city was enlarged to 97 hectares. This wall arose not as the result of large-scale planning but out of necessity—in response to the increasing population. If Florence had ceased to grow at this point, as did Pisa, Pistoia, and Lucca at the same time or perhaps a little later, its overall urban structure would have been comparable with these smaller centers rather than being the highly articulated structure it became in Dante's time.

The sixth and last wall grew out of a new political mode of thought. Built according to the plans of Arnolfo di Cambio, it took about fifty years to complete—from 1284 to 1333. It embraced 650 hectares, thus exceeding its predecessors more than sixfold. Contemporaries boasted of its length of 8,500 meters, its seventy-three towers, the strength of its fifteen fortified gates, and the regularity with which the ashlars were laid. The breadth of the entire installation was 70 bracchias or almost 41 meters, both to the north and in the plains to the south. Of these 41 meters, about 10 were taken up by the outer ring road, 20 by the moat, 2.1 by the wall itself, and just under 9 by the inner ring road. The city inside the new walls was not fully occupied until the final years of the 19th century. Extensive park areas were still left open. As a total undertaking in terms of size, cost, and clarity it can only be compared with the Cologne wall and the considerably smaller one built by Philip Augustus in Paris. In Florence, the new wall was not just the result of population growth, which rose sharply from the 11th century on. The 40,000 mark is supposed to have been passed shortly after the year 1200, and 100,000 around 1300. People simply wanted the wall to be that size. Villani himself, who was a member of the commission responsible for building the wall, emphasized the fact that the distance from south to north, from the Porta Romana to the Porta San Gallo, corresponded almost exactly to the distance from west to east, from the Porta Prato to the Porta Santa Croce.[6]

The growth of the city is illustrated by the increase in the number of bridges across the Arno and in the increase in the number of large churches. From Roman times until 1218, there was only one permanent crossing point, the Ponte Vecchio, which was only half as wide as it is today. The Ponte alla Carraia was built between 1218 and 1220, the Ponte Rubaconte (later delle Grazie) in 1237, and the Ponte alla Trinità in 1252. No further bridges were built until the construction of the iron bridge in 1836–37.

In the 12th century the city housed only one monastic institution, the Benedictine monastery, which for this reason could simply be called Badia (from Abbadia); in the 13th century, however, five large institutions were founded and constructed: these were devoted entirely to ministering to the populace. They were the settlement of the Dominicans in 1221, with its final church, Santa Maria Novella, built between 1246 and 1278; that of the Franciscans in 1226, with its church (Santa Croce) built between 1295 and ca. 1370; that of the Servites in 1248, whose church of the Santissima Annunziata was enlarged on a number of occasions; that of the Augustinians of Santo Spirito in 1250—they built themselves a large church as early as 1269; and finally the Carmelites, who erected their church, the Santa Maria del Carmina, in the 14th century. Four of these large buildings were situated outside the new walls when building started, and Santa Maria Novella was completed before the plans for the sixth wall were ready. In addition there were new buildings or remodelings undertaken by the Cistercians when they took over San Frediano, by the Umiliati for All Saints, the Vallombrosians for Santissima Trinità and Santa Maria Maggiore, and the Silvestrians for San Marco. All of these churches faced onto squares of a size hitherto unknown in Florence. These squares served as settings for the delivery of sermons, often as markets, and later on for popular festivals. Their monumental decoration, which became the rule after the 15th century, was to occupy many governments between the 13th and 17th centuries.

In the 11th century the city was divided into four *quartieri*, which were separated from one another by the north-south axis (Cardo) and the east-west axis (Decumanus). When the walls of 1172–75 were built, *sestieri* were created to which the twenty-four parishes or *popoli* were subject. In 1292 a return was made to the *quartieri*. All elections were held on the basis of these subdivisions. The army went on its campaigns according to *quartieri*, marching in parishes. What was significant was that even the palaces and, earlier, the towers of the *nobili*, of the magnates, and, later, of the *popolo grosso*—among which all the important names of future history were soon to be numbered—were divided fairly evenly among the various *quartieri* and parishes.[7] Even the upper-class cavalry went to war together with the foot soldiers from their own parishes. What is equally significant is that the division of the city into *quartieri* or *sestieri* was carried over into the rural area governed by the city when it was a question of drafting men for military campaigns. Not only the greater part of the arable land immediately outside the city walls but also that which was scattered far and wide in the *contado* was Florentine property. Everyone had invested a large part of his wealth in land. Even the leading artists from Giotto to Leonardo to Michelangelo bought land with the earnings from their works. The security represented by the possession of land encouraged people here, as everywhere else, to think in political categories that preferred the status quo to change.

The rise of the city was made possible by the gradual displacement of parties by guilds, both the great ones consisting of the upper class— merchants, bankers, doctors and apothecaries, judges and lawyers—and the lesser craft guilds. The guilds, which after 1284 were the bodies that made the political decisions, all belonged to the Guelphs in this later period. Nonetheless, increasingly sober assessments of the situation superseded the old factional feuds.

The growth of the city, which found its expression in the building of

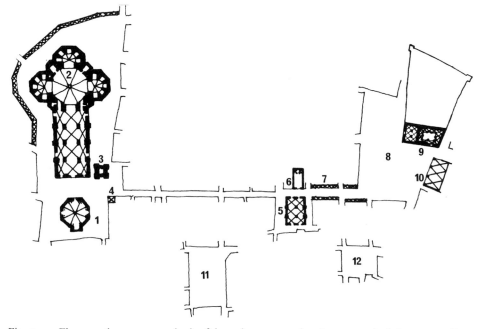

Figure 22. Florence, the monumental axis of the 14th century: 1, baptistery; 2, cathedral; 3, campanile; 4, Bargello; 5, Or San Michele; 6, San Carlo; 7, completion of the Via Calzaiouli; 8, Piazza della Signoria; 9, Palazzo Vecchio (dei Priori); 10, Loggia (dei Lanzi); 11, Mercato Vecchio; 12, Mercato Nuovo.

the city walls, was matched by a reorganization of the inner structures, manifested in public buildings. Throughout the 13th century we can see that governments that were close to the guilds or were sustained by the upper classes promoted public building, whereas in the Ghibelline periods it was neglected. In the period of the so-called *primo popolo* from 1250 onward, public squares and streets became much more distinct from private ones.[8]

Almost simultaneously with the minting of its own gold currency in 1252—the first to be introduced by a city in the Middle Ages—construction began on the first city palace, known today as the Bargello. The *secondo popolo* of 1282–83 then developed the magnificent master plan—though in piecemeal fashion and delayed by political setbacks—to which not only the new wall owed its existence but also the new cathedral (started in 1296); the Palazzo Vecchio (started in 1298); the vast Santa Croce (started in 1295), which like all the above-mentioned churches was financed in part by the city; the palace, which functioned as a grain silo above a loggia—the Or

San Michele (started in 1340); and, finally, the campanile (started in 1334) and the Loggia dei Lanzi (under construction since 1378). The present-day Piazza San Giovanni was built between the cathedral and the baptistery, and a little later the Piazza della Signoria was cleared from among a confusion of houses, a work which took years to complete. The intention was to build a processional route between the two, the present-day Via Calzaiuoli, with uniform buildings along it. This plan could only be partially executed. No other city possesses a street axis lined with such important and diverse buildings: the Palazzo Vecchio, the Loggia dei Lanzi, the Or San Michele, the campanile, and the cathedral, as well as the votive church of San Carlo across from the Or San Michele. The Bigallo foundation, which was devoted to charitable works and was situated opposite the baptistery, was also part of the plan (figs. 22 and 23). All these buildings were erected by the city administration itself represented by individual guilds. None of the great

Figure 23. Florence, the monumental center of the city with the cathedral, Or San Michele, and the Palazzo Vecchio: foreground, right, the front of the Uffizi; left, the covered way (Corridoio Vasariano), linking the Uffizi and the Palazzo Pitti.

merchant families had its residence on this street. None of the markets lay here, and the centers of popular piety had to be sought in the parish and monastic churches surrounding this inner axis. Throughout all the phases of its changing plans and in its execution, the building of the cathedral was understood to be just as much the task of the city administration as the building of the palace was. The contrast in style, mode, and material, ultimately a contrast between tower and cupola, fortress and church, was just as much a necessity as the interaction of podestà and bishop or, rather, of secular power and the Christian claim to salvation. People wished to see themselves secure in this world and the next. A good, strong, holy city needed prosperity, unassailable walls, and a city church dominating it all. On this axis and in the diversity of its buildings the city-state conceived of itself as a unit.

In spite of setbacks from plague, wars, social unrest, and political misjudgments, the 13th century was actually the heyday, in Florence, of urban planning seen as a means of political self-affirmation. The great epoch lasted from the revolution of the *secondo popolo* (1282–83) to the assumption of all businesses by Cosimo de' Medici (the Elder) and his friends. At that time, in 1434, the cupola had just been completed and Brunelleschi's lantern had yet to be started. No comparable municipal work came into being while the Medicis first flourished. A new surge of private palace building took place, by the Medicis, the Pitti, the Pazzi, the Rucellai, the Antinori, the Gondi, and the Strozzi. The most powerful building patrons, the Pitti, the Strozzi, and the Medici, used the ashlar facing style of the Palazzo Vecchio in *pietra forte,* thus testifying to their pretensions through the medium of materials and their use. Brunelleschi and Alberti developed a new ideal form for streets and piazzas in which an arrangement in perspective made it possible to see oneself surrounded on all sides by images of humanistic masters of existence. The perfectly beautiful was to become the backdrop to life. At the same time, Brunelleschi was still trying to create a new style of architecture for each commission he received. In his *urbanistica,* variety and unity occupied the two farthest poles. The municipality as a whole had ceased to be the object of plans that served only to represent themselves.

Pisa, Pistoia, and Lucca

Most of the remaining Tuscan city-states were overshadowed by Florence in the period of its greatness. In the 11th and 12th centuries Pisa, engaged in a constant struggle with its rivals, Genoa at sea and Lucca on land, had become the most powerful city in Tuscany.[9] It had conquered the Arabs of Palermo and integrated Sardinia into its territory. A monument to these successes was the cathedral square, which was outside the walls as they then existed—an ecclesiastical acropolis proclaiming its dependence upon the city government by the fact that the new bishop's palace, probably more modest than the early medieval building, was not integrated into the general composition. Construction of the cathedral was begun in 1064, of the baptistery in 1152, and of the campanile in 1173, but the Camposanto was not started until 1278, for the whole area in front of the Roman wall had been a cemetery in Late Antiquity. This was before it became the site of the first episcopal church, the original octagonal baptistery on the site of the present-day Camposanto with its great bishop's palace. The hospital on the city side was also part of the plan as was the fountain on the road to the city (figs. 4 and 24). The sites of the buildings corresponded to their functions. The bell tower rose diagonally across from the fountain. The portal in the transept through which the citizenry entered the cathedral was distinguished (after 1180) by Bonanno's bronze door. The city's pretensions to power were most clearly expressed in the number and size of the antique granite columns, spoils of war that had been brought back to the city by ship. With the exception of Rome and Constantinople, no other city possesses comparable ones; Pisa had first choice.

The new marble wall was not placed around the cathedral square until the end of the twelfth century (it was started in 1155); it takes a sharp turn behind the Camposanto, for presumably the city's Jewish community was also to be granted the right of participating in the sacred earth that had been brought back from Palestine, though it was not permitted to have its cemetery within the city walls.

The fact that no secular acropolis—which might serve as a counterpart to the ecclesiastical—could be built in the city center is linked to Pisa's devastating defeat in the sea battle against Genoa in 1285 and to the unfortunate history of this city-state, which was conquered by Florence for the first time in 1406. The Piazza dei Cavalieri (formerly degli Anziani or delle Sette Vie) contained nothing that could stand comparison with the monumental buildings of the Piazza della Signoria in Florence. It remained on the site of the Roman forum. Pisa did not aspire to any new city-state monumentality on a newly determined site. The relative increase in population reflected in census data from the 14th century could no longer be given expression in large buildings. The palace of the city government remained a modest one. There was no plan to build an axis to connect it with the cathedral quarter. One center could be reached from the other only by tortuous routes. The two never coalesced into a single optical image. Political decline was the reason the Romanesque structure of the city was never overlaid by a Gothic structure, as was the case in Florence and Siena.

Pistoia, too, remained a 12th and 13th century city and was able to exploit only in part the possibilities of the 14th.[10] Its square Roman bounds were extended somewhat in the 11th century. A circle of Romanesque churches, with the cathedral and its campanile in the middle, on the old Roman forum—which was both the new city square and the market—bear witness to the economic power of this community. In France, Pistoia's

Figure 24. Pisa, plan of the city: 1, cathedral; 2, Piazza di Cavalieri.

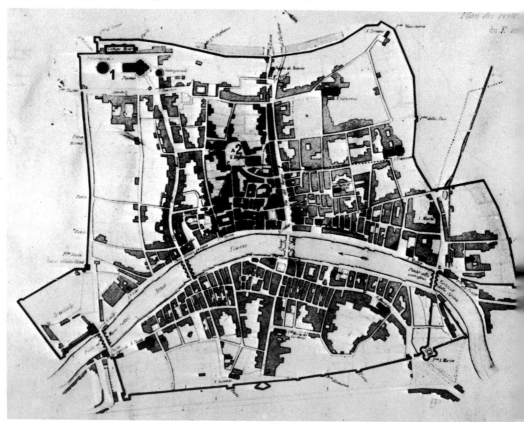

Figure 25. Pistoia: aerial view with cathedral, campanile, baptistery, Palazzo Communale, and Palazzo Pretorio

bankers and cloth merchants managed to compete with the Florentines. But, in 1254, a lost war robbed the city of its independence. Later, bitter factional struggles broke the power of the upper classes. Pistoia was frequently the cause of quarrels between Florence and Lucca and was besieged alternately by both. It had constantly to put up with either a Florentine podestà or a Luccan condottiere as governor. In a moment of confidence in 1305, work was begun on an encircling wall, which, however, enclosed an area far less likely to be filled than the previous wall, built by the Florentines; it has nevertheless survived. It encompassed 125 hectares, as opposed to only 10.6 and 40 by the two former walls. It was Florentine officials who began both the Palazzo del Comune on the city square in 1294 and opposite it, in 1367, the Palazzo del Podestà (fig. 25). Neither building had a tower. The inhabitants of Pistoia had to be content with the cathedral campanile as their city tower; the cathedral remained Romanesque.

The essential works undertaken to enhance the cathedral and other churches was undertaken by Florentine masters from the 14th century onward. The city of Pistoia ceased to be creative. Some churches of the men-

57

dicant orders, charitable buildings, and occasionally a palazzo were added. Reflections on future municipal planning were things of the past. The remains of the 12th century frescoes in the cathedral, which have now been rediscovered, reveal the high artistic level on which Pistoia once stood.[11]

More noteworthy is the history which can be gleaned from the architectural profile of Lucca.[12] This city with its surrounding rural area was, as mentioned, independent right up to the unification of Italy. In its periods of greatest prosperity it was governed by an oligarchy which knew how to be conservatively moderate and, in cases of doubt, was always content with the status quo. The expression of this independence is still the famous third wall with its bastions and casements, one of the first systems built to defy artillery. The wall had been started in 1504 and was converted in the 19th century into one of the most famous promenades to be preserved on a city wall (fig. 26).

Figure 26. Lucca, aerial view from the north: 1, cathedral precinct; 2, city square with San Michele; 3, Roman amphitheater and market; 4, San Frediano; 5, Palazzo Guinigi; 7, former citadel Agusta and Palazzo della Signoria.

Lucca also exemplifies the lack of individual development granted to Roman cities either in politics or in architecture. Not a single name or achievement from the flourishing Civitas Romana has come down to us in eight centuries. Under the Langobards, from the end of the 6th century Lucca was the main city of Tuscany, and Margravine Mathilde (d. 1119) still preferred it for her residence. After Pisa, this free municipality was the richest in Tuscany during the 12th and 13th centuries. Its superiority was expressed equally in architecture and in painting until the end of the 13th century. Particularly in the sphere of panel painting neither Florence nor Siena could compete with Lucca during the period 1150–1270.

Here, too, the history of the city walls reflects the history of the city. The first wall, the Roman, was built in the 2d century B.C.; the second was begun at the end of the 12th century and continued under construction until 1265, only to be extended again in the period after the city's heyday at the end of the 14th and the beginning of the 15th centuries. The third, and most famous, built between 1504 and 1645, embraced in a handsome oval what had already been achieved up to that point, greatly enlarging the eastern area in the process. We have to remember that the *borghi,* or suburbs, which were then incorporated into the city, belonged to the city itself in all Roman and medieval Italian cities. Thus the wall was neither a jurisdictional nor a city boundary, as was frequently the case in the north.

The cathedral area and the baptistery, along with the bishop's palace, occupy the southern edge of the Lucca (fig. 26, 1). In the northern section, the Roman amphitheater provided free space for a market (3). The political center and the meeting place of the leading merchant families was the forum (2), in which, during the Romanesque period, the city church of San Michele was built. It was not until the Renaissance that a splendid, though modest, city hall was built there by the one outstanding artist that Lucca could still lay claim to—Matteo Civitali.

A city church in the center of the city was to be found elsewhere in Tuscany—in Arezzo with its Pieve, for example, manifesting the tension that existed between the citizenry and the bishop, who in the 12th and 13th centuries had fortified his castle and his cathedral outside the city walls. Lucca's simple city hall was never meant to express the citizens' desire for political self-assertion. The city church (fig. 27) dedicated to the Archangel Michael, on the other hand, thanks to its choice of patron saint, can be regarded—both in its site and in its architectural profile—as a monument to the self-consciousness of the citizens, and as such it forms the counter-

Figure 27. Lucca: town square and parish church, San Michele

part to the cathedral. Work must have begun on the building shortly after the city achieved its new charter in 1120. The magnificent facade was not added until the beginning of the 13th century. We should recall that this was where the city council met: in the 12th century a church could still function as the city hall. In no other Italian city, however, has a building survived that served this function and that is either as large or as important as the one in Lucca.

The reason Lucca lacks a Gothic city hall is that the municipality had lost its freedom from 1314 to 1369. From 1314 to 1316 it was governed by the Ghibelline leader from Pisa, Ogoccione della Faggiola, and then from 1316 to 1328 by the most successful military commander in the history of Lucca, Castruccio Castracane, who squandered the city's wealth—which had been accumulated over the centuries—on the battlefield while gaining his famous victories over the Florentines. Lucca became so weak that Pisa was able to govern it from 1343 to 1369. It then recovered to a certain extent because of the silk industry and the silk trade, a recovery that at once proclaimed itself in the Gothic extension of the cathedral. Under Paolo Guinigi's rule (1400–30) the municipality experienced another period of prosperity, which found its expression in the size of Guinigi's palace (fig. 26, 5) and his "villa" (6) as well as in the quality of his artistic endowments. Yet this ruling merchant had no more desire to create a political center than did Cosimo il Vecchio or Lorenzo the Magnificent. In the early humanist period, art fulfilled different functions.

Castruccio had built himself a castle with the name of Agusta (7). Even his contemporaries criticized him for razing a heavily settled part of the city to create space for it. The castle, moreover, was built more for use against the city than to protect it. It was a citadel like those of Milan or Modena. In a swift and passionate uprising, the populace destroyed the building after the tyrant's death. The site seems to have remained unused until the late Renaissance, when the great administrative building was erected by Ammanati, who was brought from Florence for the purpose. For centuries, Lucca was without a political center of gravity.

Siena

Only Siena can be compared with Florence as far as building programs are concerned, but the two points of departure were as different as can be imagined. In the hills rising from the broad plain of the Arno where the Roman city lay, three citadels stood on three steep ridges. Since the 4th century A.D., these citadels had subordinated themselves to the bishop, the occupant of the highest one. In order to bind these heterogeneous elements into a unity, Siena developed the most precise building code that has been handed down from the Middle Ages, which was incorporated into the city's statutes. From the last third of the 13th century onward, the city council met regularly in May to issue numerous decrees for the building of walls, streets, fountains, churches, public buildings, and, last but not least, private dwellings. On 10 May 1297, twenty-six such decrees were on the program, among them the new code for the building of the city square and its palace, as well as for further building work on the cathedral, and one for the dismissal of the leading cathedral architect, Giovanni Pisano.[13]

Historical documents make it clear that, shortly before the middle of the 11th century, Siena had begun to pursue its own political course.[14] The rapid rise began with the temporary transfer of government in 1240 from

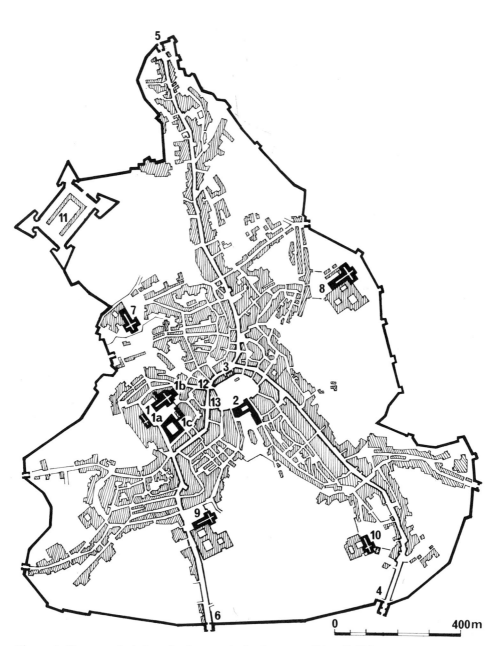

Figure 28. Siena: 1, cathedral; 1a, facade no. 1; 1b, facade no. 2; 2, Palazo Pubblico; 3, Croce di Travaglio; 4, Porta San Martino (Romana); 5, Porta Camollia; 6, Porta San Agostino (Tufi); 7, San Domenico; 8, San Francesco; 9, San Agostino; 10, Santa Maria del Servi; 11, Fortezza; 12, 1st ascent to cathedral; 13, 2d ascent to cathedral.

the aristocratic families to the leading merchant families. Constant wars against the barons of the diocese, conquests of small city-states, and a bitter struggle with Florence for supremacy could only delay the rise, not stop it. The same is true of the constant constitutional and factional struggles in the city itself. Scarcely any other city subjected itself to such complete regimentation. At times, over a thousand citizens, from a total of twenty to thirty thousand, were entrusted with particular public tasks. The real heyday of the city began with the government of the "Nine" in 1289. This system managed to sustain itself until 1355. The Nove Buoni Mercanti di Parte Guelfa had excluded the aristocracy as well as the craft guilds and the lower classes from exerting any influence upon the government. Thus it became apparent here, too, that a humane government consisting of merchants—as the true "citizens"—favored to a greater extent than any other form of government the development of urban design. It is true that the plague of 1348 broke Siena's power, even though there were some later flowerings which were much admired. Whereas Florence in 1355 decided to go ahead with an extension to the cathedral that had already been started, Siena in the same year decided to stop work on the enormous extension projects it had for its own cathedral.

Urban design in Siena was faced with the task of uniting and, at the same time, expanding the three sections of the city, the *terzi:* "di Città," which included the cathedral; "di Camollia," in the north, along with the fortified gate that faced Florence; and "di San Martino" in the southeast. In addition, the aim was to provide the whole city with a new center and to relate this suitably to the old one, which lay eccentrically on the cathedral hill. Siena is reckoned to have been enlarged eight times in the Middle Ages (fig. 28). The three main gates of the cathedral city—the Porta San Martino (4), the Porta Camollia (5), and the Porta San Agostino (6)—were moved outward on several occasions. The city's legislators paid great attention to the uniform development of the winding streets of this *città naturale.* The Via dei Banchi di Sopra, the Via dei Banchi di Sotto, and the Via di Città met at the Croce di Travaglio (fig. 28, 3) above the later Campo (fig. 29). The palaces of the leading families of all factions stood on these streets. Various municipal commissions—of which one was called the *ufficio dell'Ornato*—chaired by lawyers, watched incorruptibly over the preservation of the street lines, the use of homogeneous building materials, and the uniform shape of the ground floors of the structures. The political and geographical situation made it necessary to construct the city hall at the lowest

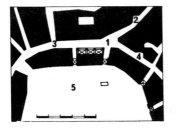

Figure 29. Siena, Croce di Travaglio: 1, Croce di Travaglio; 2, Via dei Banchi di Sopra; 3, Via di Città; 4, Via dei Banchi di Sotto; 5, Campo.

point between the three parts of the city so that no part should be placed at an advantage. Enormous substructures were necessary before building could begin on the Palazzo Pubblico in 1297. The city fathers were concerned not only that its tall, slender tower should dominate the towers of the residences of the nobility, but also that it should exist side by side in the overall view of the city with the cathedral tower and its cupola (fig. 30). We know the building ordinances to which all private owners were subject so as to ensure regularity in the development of the Campo; the smallest deviation from the basic scheme was a punishable offense. Not a single centimeter's deviation was permitted from the existing building line. The picturesque decoration of interiors by Simone Martini, Ambrogio Lorenzetti, and later painters illustrated the political ideology, which was also sustained by the urge to plan ahead.

In Siena, as in Florence, responsibility for building the cathedral was transferred from the bishop to the city. Around 1260, the small Romanesque cathedral with its cupola, campanile, circular baptistery and first hospital was completed. A suitable facade still had to be added, which was given its famous and final form by Giovanni Pisano after 1285. Yet this cathedral (fig. 28, 1) was soon too small for the growing city. This problem was one of constant concern to the city government and to many of its committees from around 1260 until 1377. In contrast to Florence, the old cathedral was not torn down, although architectural commissions had repeatedly urged that this should be done. Even in the Middle Ages, architects preferred to tear buildings down rather than remodel them, while municipal accountants often took the opposing view. The cathedral was extended first in the rear, then on the side of the facade, and was finally extended by the addition of the new cathedral. Three different facades were begun before the first was finished: the one on the west by Giovanni Pisano (1a) then, to the east there was the facade of a new baptistery (1b), which served as a sub-church for the extension of the new cathedral, and finally the new cathedral facade on the south (fig. 28, 1c, and fig. 31). It is significant that the oldest facade still did not relate to the new city center, the Campo, whereas the two later ones were expressly turned to face it. Attempts were made to drive a ceremonial road steeply down to the Campo from each of these facades (12 and 13), but this was only achieved piecemeal, for when it was decided not to complete the cathedral extension, there was no further point in building these roads.

Numerous building ordinances bear witness to the efforts of city government to unify city structure. The multiplicity of topographical formations, the enormous differences in elevation, the limited building sites which could only be acquired by the use of substructures, prevented any comprehensive building plan. The object was not only the church program, the erection and dispersal of fountains, the building of walls, and the uniform design of streets, but rather—indeed, primarily—the organic relation of the political center of the city, with the Campo and the Palazzo Pubblico (2), to the area around the cathedral, with the baptistery, the bishop's palace, the hospital, and the campanile (1).

Figure 30. Siena from the south, with cathedral precinct, fishmarket, and Palazzo Pubblico from the rear with the Torre di Mangia

Figure 31. Siena: cathedral complex with its three facades

The problems of building the cathedral on precipitous ground arose again in the case of the four large churches of the new monastic orders, which were built on the periphery of the city in the late 13th and 14th centuries, adding four new monumental accents to the city besides the Palazzo Publico and the cathedral. These four churches are San Domenico (7) and San Francesco (8) to the north, on either side of the great avenue that leads up to the Porta Camollia; San Agostino (9) on the edge of the cathedral quarter to the south; and, on the third range of hills not far from the Porta Romana, Santa Maria dei Servi (10).

The overall structure of the city of Siena can be looked at in two antithetical ways. The first is the picture created by those hundreds of ordinances, regulations, and directives to commissions and to architects which have been preserved in the Sienese archives of the 13th and 14th centuries.[15] They deal with all the details of the planning, design and financing of streets, squares, churches, fountains, gates, and much more. The control of building was recognized as a sober administrative task; the greater the difficulties presented by legal conditions and the topographical situation, the more resolute was the determination to exercise this control in all its details.

The second picture emerges when we realize the passion with which an ideal image was pursued—almost to utopian limits. The cathedral that could not be completed furnishes just one example. We must also take into account the strict determination of the street lines on the steep and winding main traffic axes. This fanatical desire for orderliness created a lyrical-aesthetic element which still has an effect today. It was this mentality that led to the inclusion of a clause in the architect Giovanni Pisano's contract that he was not only to look for, but to find, Diana, the legendary fountain that would at one stroke solve the city's water supply problems for ever. Dante pours forth his derision on this Sienese hope. Yet it was precisely hopes of this sort that stirred the optimism of the municipality in its building program. Generations of engineers had tried to pipe water to the Campo for a fountain. When they were finally successful, the fountain was called Fonte Gaia. Quercia later gave this installation the form that made him famous. It showed in the eyes of his contemporaries what an ample supply of water meant to the city's prosperity and security, and it also demonstrated that art of the very highest order was the only way to illustrate such an advantage.

Florence as Seat of a Princely Court

As the only city-state in Tuscany, Florence rose in the 16th century to become the capital city and the residence of a duke and, soon afterwards, of a grand-duke, who confirmed its proto-absolutist constitution in a new interpretation of the city as a whole. Two defensive installations were incorporated into the wall that had been built in 1284—the Fortezza di San Giovanni or di Basso to the northwest (fig. 21) and the Fortezza di San Giorgio or di Alto to the southeast. The first, the great citadel in the plain, was begun under the first Duke Alessandro in 1532. He had received a secure residential castle from Charles V as a condition for marrying the emperor's daughter Margaret (later Duchess of Parma). When Cosimo I's wife moved into the Pitti (which they acquired in 1549), the Fortezza above the park also seemed to be a necessity. It was not until 1590–1600 that Buontalenti finished it. Both the lower fortress, begun by Antonio di Sangallo, and the upper were pioneering works in fortification building. As late as 1720, under the rule of the last of the Medicis, their function was described by an English traveler: "The people of Florence are very highly taxed; there is an imposition laid upon everything they either wear or eat; and to keep the people in awe, and restrain them from entering into any seditious dis-

Figure 32. Florence: view of the city from the Boboli gardens of the Palazzo Pitti as the new residence

courses there were, when we were there, spies in all companies; by which his royal highness was acquainted with everything: and the cannon in the castle, which were planted towards the city, were always ready charg'd in case of any popular insurrection."[16]

The external security that the two citadels were supposed to guarantee corresponded to a new inner order in the city plan. Cosimo I had left the Palazzo Medici in 1540 to complete a new residence for himself in the Palazzo Vecchio. In the process, he severed the immediate relationship of his dwelling place with San Lorenzo (the church of the Medici), with the tombs of his ancestors, and with his family library, the Laurenziana. We know how Baccio Bandinelli and, later, Vasari added to and reorganized the inner structure in an effort to incorporate a royal residence into the medieval city palace.

At the same time, monuments were built on the Piazza della Signoria with the purpose of illustrating the power and importance of the prince. Among these monuments were Benvenuto Cellini's Perseus and Bandinelli's

Hercules. But it was only after he became a grand-duke that Cosimo I decided on a twofold extension of his palace. He had Ammanati enlarge the Palazzo Pitti by building an enormous palace square, and at the same time he changed the Boboli slopes into a palace garden. He ordered a densely populated area of the city to be razed, not only to create room in the Palazzo Uffizi for all the municipal authorities, which until then had been scattered about in various palaces, but also to create a new and personal forum in its extensive courtyard.[17]

It is significant that the buildings surrounding this courtyard were built from *pietra serena,* the same stone as the interior—the stone for the elegant courtly style, not the pietra forte, the use of which, in towers and fortified gates, for example, or in the Palazzo Vecchio and the Palazzo Pitti, was felt to be a demonstration of power.

A covered passageway, which also crossed the Arno at the Ponte Vecchio, joined the two great buildings, the Pitti and the Uffizi, which in their turn formed a transition to the impregnable city palace (figs. 23 and 32). The fact that the old palace bore no immediate and visual relationship, by way of the Uffizi, to the new residence in the Pitti presented a challenge to design skills so totally in keeping with late Florentine mannerism that second-rate architects, such as Vasari and Ammanati were, accomplished feats that are numbered among the greatest of the century.

Swiss Cantonal Capitals: Zürich and Bern

The capitals of the Swiss cantons had to all intents and purposes received their final form in the 14th and 15th centuries. Their development belongs to a later period than that of the Italian city-states. I have already pointed out that they cannot be compared to the Italian cities, being much smaller.[18] In 15th century Switzerland only two cities—Basel and Geneva—boasted around 10,000 inhabitants; three more—Zürich, Bern, and Freiburg in Üchtland—had between 5,000 and 10,000; while all the other cantonal capitals, among them Chur and Bellinzona, which did not even have 2,000, had fewer than 5,000. We must bear in mind that in the heyday of these cities or the period following it, that is, between the 14th and the 18th centuries, possibilities were more limited, though conditions were more peaceful than they are today.

I shall select only two, Zürich and Bern. None of these centers was ever a cathedral city, but Bern, like Lausanne, eventually managed to acquire a cathedral. Both Zürich and Bern had acquired their surrounding rural areas mainly by inheritance, by purchase, or by victories over noble families. They had not, in other words, won those areas from other cantonal capitals and had thus not forced the families of the territorial rulers to move into the city. For this reason there were virtually no palaces in either city.

In its origins, Zürich is the prime example of a palatinate locality which early became a clerical city. The abbess of the convent was its secular ruler until the 13th century. Bern is the prototype of a new city founded by the Zähringen family, who sought to use the city's favorable location to increase the fiscal productivity of their possessions and at the same time ensure their defense. The political prerequisites for the foundation and early development of both cities were just as different as their topographical situations.

In Zürich (fig. 33) there was a Roman customs fort at the crossing of the Limmat, in the ruins of which the Carolingians had erected a palace that stood until the 12th century. After the palace had been razed, around 1200, the site, known as the Lindenhof (1), was never again used for building. Upstream, the convent (2) was developed under the protection of the palace. The emperors donated all the land around the convent and also bestowed upon it administrative rights over the burgher settlement which was later to become the town. The only parish church, St. Peter (4), which is mentioned in 953, was also subject to the abbess. On the other bank of the Limmat, a canonry with twenty-four members developed almost simultaneously with the convent. Both centers created large ecclesiastical organisms. They appear as the guardians of the city in Merian's view of it in 1654 (fig. 34).

The development of the burgher community was directed against the ecclesiastical settlements. Its first town hall, as well as the one which is still standing (fig. 33, 6), had to be built on piles in the river since apparently the canons would not provide land for it. This town hall took over the role and functions of the imperial customs installation. The end of the Zähringer line, which had promoted the growth of Zürich, and the privileges granted to the town by Frederick II permitted the citizenry to establish ever greater gubernatorial rights. Here too, an increasing population was evidenced by the establishment of new monastic settlements. The Dominicans were here as early as 1231 (7); in 1252 the Franciscans arrived (8), and in 1274 the Augustine-Hermits (9). In 1336 a new fortified oval was completed which now included both of the monasteries, as we can see from figure 33.

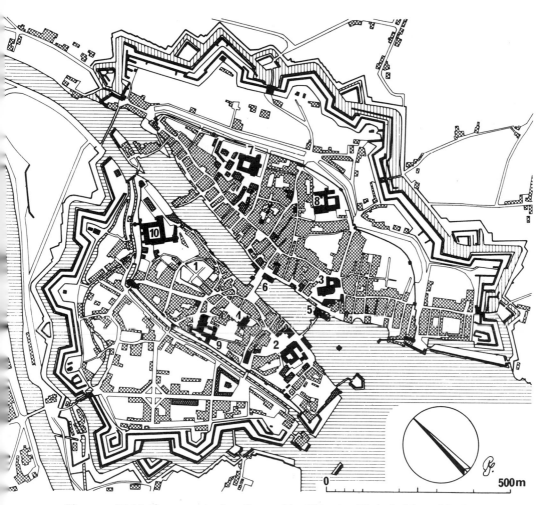

Figure 33. Zürich (from an engraving of 1705, with additions): 1, Lindenhof (imperial palace);
2, Frauenmünster; 3, Großmünster; 4, parish church of St. Peter; 5, Wasserkirche; 6, city hall;
7, Dominican monastery; 8, Franciscan monastery; 9, Augustine monastery; 10, convent of the
Dominicans, Oetenbach.

The baroque wall, begun in 1642 during the Thirty Years War, was intended to almost double the size of the city, but the whole area was not completely occupied until the 19th century. The wall was leveled in 1832—remarkably late. At that time the opportunity to use the land in a sensible manner was lost.[19]

The monasteries increasingly lost power when the wall of 1336 was built, even more so when the city was elevated to the status of a free imperial city and, later, united with the confederacy, thus increasing the power of the canton; but the monasteries still remained the largest landowners. There was a special monastic nobility, which allied itself with the noble families of the city and the countryside against the aspiring citizen guilds. In contrast to the state of affairs in Tuscany, where this role was assumed by the upper class citizenry, not by the magnates, the noble families in Zürich from the 13th to the 15th centuries sustained a culture that was expressed both in works of art and in buildings. Gottfried Keller, who was archivist in Zürich, has described the conditions that led to the production of the Manesse manuscript for a noble Zürich family. His treatment is sociologically correct even if his account is romanticized.

Zwingli's Reformation victory was a catastrophe for the development of art. The iconoclasts cleared out all the churches and sacristies in the canton—down to the smallest village church. Only bare walls were left.

Figure 34. Zürich (after Merian the Elder, 1642)

Figure 35. Zürich heraldic medallion, 1544

Since the search for works of art was carried out on the orders of, and under the protection of, the city council of the day, almost nothing escaped. Figural representations in the religious realm were forbidden for all time. Prodigious political energies had been generated by the antagonism between the burghers and the monastic nobility, but the enormous wealth of the monasteries in real property was used up within a few years. This elemental process of destruction was interpreted as a purification process.

The Reformation century produced no new churches in Zürich. Between 1694 and 1698 a city hall, large in the circumstances, was built above the Limmat on the site of the old one. The banqueting hall is an important example of extremely rich interior wooden detailing. Artistic efforts were concentrated less on private dwellings than on the guildhalls. Here, too, the emphasis lay on interior design. The whole city petrified into a parlor. Conditions remained cramped: in long years of peace, no one ever felt constrained to add so much as one new accent to the city.

If a city's neuroses were to be analyzed, Zürich would serve as an interesting example of the internalization of all cultural effort, a place where anything externalized was bound to be misinterpreted. Even the enormous growth that has taken place in its most recent history—first around the old city, then on the hills surrounding the city, and then around the lake—has affected this basic situation only in nonessentials. People were content, as citizens of a free city-state, to keep their own legal position and political significance before their eyes throughout the city by means of small plaques bearing coats of arms. Figure 35, dating from the year 1544, shows the im-

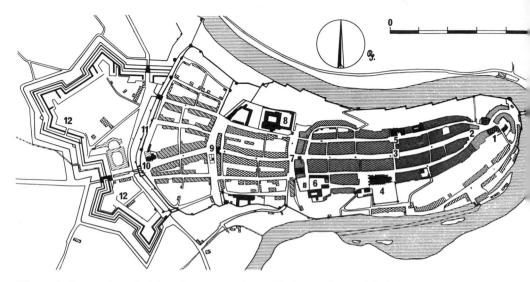

Figure 36. Bern at the end of the 18th century: 1, former Nydegg castle; 2, original city; 3, 1st defensive ring, after 1152; 4, city church; 5, 3d. city hall; 6, Franciscans; 7, 2d defensive ring, ca. 1191; 8, Dominicans; 9, 3d defensive ring, after 1265; 10, former Hospital of the Holy Ghost; 11, 4th defensive ring, after 1345; 12, 5th defensive ring, 1622–44.

perial city of Zürich with the imperial eagle and the imperial crown and the lion with the imperial orb and sword, garlanded by the coats of arms of all the subject cities and castles. This is how people perceived themselves and this is how the government of the city wished to be perceived.

In Bern the point of departure was different, the political success greater, but the political attitude nonetheless closely related in its essentials.[20] In Germany, Lübeck (see chap. 3) was the only place with a terrain comparable to the ridge of hills surrounded on three sides by the Aare that was chosen as the site for Bern (fig. 36). To the west, this ridge grew broader and needed to be fortified. It was the only place where later settlements could be built. The Zähringers owned the castle of Nydegg at the easternmost point (1). From there, Berthold V founded his city in 1190, after his grandfather had had plans drawn up for Freiburg-im-Breisgau and only a few years after his father had selected a rocky ridge in the horseshoe bend of the river Saane to build Freiburg-im-Üchtland. Such successes in design and the pleasure of planning *in vacuo* can hardly be imagined today. Below Burg Nydegg was a fortified river crossing (2). The main road was built across the brow of the ridge and was paralleled on either side by secondary roads. Thus, six sites for rows of houses were created. When the Zähringer family died out in 1218, Bern became a free imperial city. It was only then that new plans were embarked upon. Three times—in 1220, from 1225 to 1260, and from 1344 to 1346—the three roads were lengthened toward the west, first as far as the *Zeitglockenturm* (7), then to the *Käfigturm* (9), and finally, to the *Christophturm* (11) behind the Hospital of the Holy Ghost and its church (10). In the baroque period the city was extended a fourth time by bastions. In 1255 the Franciscans arrived (6), in 1259 the Dominicans (8). The townspeople had little difficulty in storming Burg Nydegg—which had remained an imperial castle—in 1266 and again in 1273. Immediately after this second attack the castle was destroyed. It was not until 1344 that the Nydegg church (1) was erected on the site of the castle chapel. It was much more difficult to evict the Teutonic Order from the collegiate church, which also functioned as the city church (4). The order had received gubernatorial rights from Frederick II. The townspeople were here faced with the same problem that Zürich had solved in its struggle with its two convents. The collegiate church had originally stood outside the walls of the newly founded city, while the old town hall, like the third one (5), still standing today, had been built within the walls at the extreme edge of the city. These two centers of political order had of necessity to face each other, both being equidistant from the main street and the market street.

By choosing a dominant site outside the walls, the founder of the city had placed the main parish church in a favored position. The accent this building gave to the row of houses was masterly. After buying part of the Teutonic Order's rights in the 15th century, the city could start thinking about the construction of a building which might—in the eyes of the world—compete with the cathedral in Lausanne, now subject to Bern. The city council entrusted Matthias Enzinger with the commission. Enzinger, the leading Gothic architect of the period, came from Ulm and worked in Bern from 1421 to 1452. Work was to continue on this, the most important late Gothic church in Switzerland, for 150 years until Daniel Heintz was able to place the arch over the nave between 1571 and 1575.

Precise building codes took care of the city's appearance.[21] Arcades in front of all the houses along the main streets were permitted, indeed prescribed. Although these remained the property of the municipality, they enlarged the living space of the citizens who dwelled above them. The building codes, between the 13th and the 19th centuries, made it possible for the facades to be renewed in accordance with the popular taste of the day, but the proportions always remained the same. The center of the city was always supplied with running water, feeding the numerous fountains of the city. After the Reformation the main street was named "the Street of Justice" *(Gerechtigkeitsstraße)*, and in 1543 the Fountain of Justice was added to it. On this fountain the figure of Justice was surrounded by four other figures—the pope, the emperor, the sultan, and the mayor of Bern, the three powers who had no say in the city and the one who had it all. The Madonna, too, that graced the portal column of the city church, underneath the Last Judgment, was replaced at this time by the figure of Justice.

The ecclesiastical and the municipal authorities formed a unit from the time of the Reformation onward. Even though the power of the municipality was increasing all the while—its oligarchical constitution remained unchanged from 1224 to 1798—there was scarcely any new building. For the followers of Zwingli the carefully tended appearance of the city, with its many running fountains and the clock which kept exact time on the gate tower, was decoration enough. True, in the 18th century a few buildings of classical dignity were put up, some even with a touch of the rococo. The city council gave the upper community, that is, the one farthest out, permission to build a new church in place of the Church of the Holy Spirit (10). The city architect of Bern built the pleasing gallery that was renowned as the most beautiful Zwinglian sacred building of the Swiss baroque period. Toward the end of the epoch it was even possible to build a sort of *Danzlhaus* (ballroom), something every imperial city possessed. I am speaking here of the Hôtel de Musique, built between 1765 and 1775 by Nikolaus Sprüngli. But the virtues of this city state were caution, justice, providence, and the defense of the positions it had won; nothing was to change.

The regularity of the rows of houses and their cleanliness soon gained for Bern the reputation of being one of the most beautiful cities in Europe. Nevertheless, a 1732 pamphlet describing the beauty of the city, entitled *Deliciae Urbis Bernae,* was proscribed. When Professor Meiner's well-meaning letters about Bern appeared in print in 1785, people grew very angry. "De qui se mêle-t-il cet impertinent? Nous n'avons point besoin de ces éloges."[22]

Bern remains a unique phenomenon. Whereas the long period of peace and the increase in wealth and freedom made it possible, in the Catholic areas of Switzerland, to build such surpassing monumental works as the monastery complexes of Einsiedeln or St. Gallen, nothing of comparable scope happened in the Calvinist or Zwinglian theocracies. The city's wealth allowed a few public buildings to be constructed (as well as many private ones) in a cautious baroque style that leaned toward the classical. Yet here, where all the power lay in the hands of the cities, no new forms of urban architecture were developed as they were, for instance, in Holland, and only a few new accents were added to the old cities. Even the two largest, Basel and Geneva, are no exception.

Chapter 3

*T*WO *POINTS OF VIEWS WERE DECISIVE* (as stated at the beginning of chapter 2) in the choice of the sea powers to be treated in this study. On the one hand, only those cities were selected in which canals or rivers afforded ships—mostly ocean-going vessels—the opportunity to dock immediately in front of residential buildings, which also served as offices and warehouses. In all these commercial centers we encounter tall, narrow buildings whose real size is apparent only when seen from the rear. In the late 19th and 20th centuries, new forms of this type of house—of enormous dimensions—were developed in Manhattan. For this reason, and only in this one instance, the frontiers of Europe have been crossed so as to include that most American of all American cities. No other city that owes its appearance to 19th and 20th century buildings was able to develop a structure of comparable, originality, beauty, and logic of form.[1]

The second characteristic developed out of the efforts of those cities to acquire possessions and rights overseas and at the same time to found settlements and colonies. Traffic was organized between bases where people could feel at home. Contacts like these opened people's eyes to a larger world than they knew of at the time. The narrowness that was part and parcel of burgher cities was

SEA POWERS

broken through in significant areas of existence: this is true of every century and in different ways of every example cited here. People were exposed to the new and frequently to the exotic.

A third characteristic of waterfront cities is of particular importance for urban design. We land in these cities, we enter them, not on their periphery but in their center. Thus, ships landed at the dam that gave Amsterdam its name and in front of which its city hall was later to be built. In Lübeck, ships unloaded their goods on the Trave as close to the marketplace as they could get. The first families of Lübeck lived in the short streets between the Trave and marketplace. In the same way, the center of Manhattan lay, and still lies, at the tip of the peninsula which can be reached on all three sides from the banks of the Hudson (fig. 52). One can only understand Venice by recognizing that it should be entered from the Molo San Marco and that the city and its network of canals must be come upon from the main square. In former times, people did not come up the canal, as we do today, from the railway station and the Piazza Roma, named for the present-day seat of power; they went down the canal from the marketplace.

Along with Venice, one might also have mentioned the small city of Ragusa (now Dubrovnik). The merchants of Ragusa managed to maintain their independence under the rule of the Venetians (1205–1358), the Hungarian kings (1358–1526), and the Turks (1526–1806). Besides Lübeck, a number of other Baltic Hanseatic cities could be singled out—above all, Danzig and Riga—and, by no means least, the North Sea river ports of Hamburg and Bremen. What I shall show in the case of Amsterdam holds good, to a lesser extent, for many other Dutch ports. Historical success and distinction in urban architecture were what ultimately determined my choice. From the latter point of view, Bruges ought also to be considered, but its heyday was concentrated into a period of less than two hundred years—from the late 13th to the 15th centuries—and its independence was constantly threatened. Do not Naples or Genoa also belong to this group? Did not cities like LaRochelle (before its humiliation at the hands of Richelieu), which kept their harbor bays enclosed, develop comparable configurations?

Genoa exemplifies what differentiates them from Venice and also from Amsterdam or Lübeck.[2] Today the city completely and densely fills the steep amphitheater formed by the surrounding hills, and on three sides descends almost to the virtually circular basin that contains the harbor. Only the fourth side is open to the sea. Genoa gradually expanded from a castle on the southern edge of the harbor until it occupied the whole semicircle. At the same time, lack of space forced the inhabitants to build farther and farther up the hillside. The limited flat land conditioned the extreme congestion of the lower quarters of the city. It was only halfway up the hillside that large-scale planning could begin. The higher up a person lived, the more wealthy that person was considered to be. The only exceptions were the princes of the house of Doria. There were few direct connections between the streets where the palaces stood—the Via Balbi, the Strada Nuova, and today the Via XX Settembre and others—and the harbor, which can be regarded as Genoa's central city square. The famous view of the city was determined on the one hand by the ring of fortresses on the hills, by means of which the municipality secured itself against attacks by land, and, on the other, by those bold streets lined with palaces built between the 16th and the 20th century, whose gardens and lofty terraces afforded them a view of the harbor. Yet people lived at a distance from the ships and the warehouses on the quays. The contrast between town and port, between the roads on the hills and the alleys down by the harbor, is as characteristic of this city as it is of Naples or Marseilles. Out of such contrast there developed a particular type of city which cannot be treated within the scope of the present work.

Venice and Amsterdam Contrasted

Before I set forth the points Venice and Amsterdam have in common, I must stress their dissimilarities. Comparison of the romantic details of these two cities leads to a misunderstanding of the conditions underlying their general structure.

Venice is a saltwater city, Amsterdam a freshwater one. Venice acquired building sites by consolidating sandbanks in the lagoon and finally succeeded in reducing the water surfaces so much that only canals remained. Even Cassiodorus tells of this.[3] Amsterdam channeled the waters of its rivers into carefully excavated canals. The waterways formed a natural network in Venice, while in Amsterdam they were an ornament that was subdivided geometrically (figs. 38 and 50).

We can go even farther: it took more than a thousand years to build Venice from the founding of the city in A.D. 421. The Amsterdam we admire so greatly developed from humble beginnings in the space of a single century.

Third, the appearance of Venice is determined by its numerous churches, the sixty-nine parish churches with their tall towers; the doge's palatinate church, St. Mark's; the many collegiate churches, among them San Giorgio Maggiore, the Franciscan church "Frari," and the Dominican church SS. Giovanni e Paolo; as well as equally important votive churches—Redentore, the Salute, Santa Maria dei Miracoli. This ship on a lagoon, so impressive a sight, is armed with an enormous ordnance of churches and towers.

Calvinist Amsterdam has few churches, although religious attitudes here had a far greater political significance, and its population of 200,000 around the year 1700 exceeded the 150,000 of the Venetian heyday around 1500. There were only two parish churches in the old city and two, the West Church and the South Church, in the new. I am not including smaller buildings. The moral order of Calvinism took the place of churches; it was an order for the social classes: the separation of rich and poor, of exaggerated cleanliness and slum conditions. Wealth was understood as a sign of probity, as proclaimed even by the rows of houses.

Still more important: Venice carried a different kind of weight politically. It ruled in Dalmatia and Greece and on the north Italian mainland as far as Udine and Bergamo. Its affairs were decided by victories. Amsterdam represented primarily an economic power. It is true that it was the only metropolis of the "Seven Northern Provinces" in the 17th century. It had more ships at its disposal than all the other cities put together in that land of cities—in its most successful years more than the combined fleets of England and France. In 1815, the new kingdom decided to make Amsterdam its capital and to elevate the 17th century city hall to the status of royal palace, though The Hague was to remain the seat of the monarchy and government. Yet the city council for all its powers was still bound by orders. Politics played second fiddle to economics.

We should here emphasize one of the most important characteristics shared by the two cities. Both were leaders in the culture of their countries at a given moment. Their art and their architecture set the standards. Both cities set their stamp upon style.

Venice manifested that unique synthesis between the imperial East, mediated first by Ravenna, and the barbaric and Romanesque North, mediated by Cividale, Verona, and Pavia, and, later, another synthesis of Gothic and Byzantine. The city was a field for experimentation which was later to translate its experience to all of its Levantine possessions, to Greece and Dalmatia, and later on, in the same way, to the Terra Firma, in Bergamo, Brescia, Padua, Verona, Vicenza, and Udine. Whenever we enter one of these cities, or whenever we go to Dubrovnik, Split, Trogir, Zadar, or to Corfu and Crete, we see immediately that they all adopted Venetian civilization. The houses and palaces all conformed to the formal canons established in Venice. The fact that Palladio, the most authoritative architectural figure in the history of Europe, was born in Vicenza, one of the cities of the Terra Firma, enabled a second representative style to be imposed, as a new cultural stratum, upon the whole Venetian state. Even the state's fortifications have their own character, as Aldo Rossi has pointed out.[4] Castelfranco, the home of Giorgione, is an example. We shall encounter it all over the Terra Firma, though least of all, significantly enough, in the model city of Palmanova (see chap. 5).

Similarly, the Dutch cities possess their own unified and at least comparable style. Amsterdam determined this style for the 17th century, particularly as The Hague and the court placed themselves outside the national culture (Huizinga). Here, however, was the source of the experience that determined the manifold use in the city's architecture of dikes, dams, and canals, the pure forms of Amsterdam classicism towering over them. There was not a city in the province of Holland that was not linked to all the others by a system of canals.

Venice, too, created such links, but they were possible only in the few completely flat parts of the Terra Firma. The development of the Brenta toward Padua is the classic example: Treviso could also be reached by ship. The river Sile was used not only as the approach to the city, and it did more than supply the city's moats. Inside the city it was divided into four canals on which the most important buildings of this small city were erected. What had proved effective in the metropolis was to be transferred to the smaller cities.

Venice

The history of the genesis of the city *ex nihilo* and on sandbanks is available and has been thoroughly researched.[5] The city of today, architectural remains, and written sources have acted as confirmation of one another. Wherever refugees, merchants, and pirates settled, in scattered colonies within the present-day urban area, parish churches were built, the names and ages of which are established, the latest dating from around 1100. It is a fascinating drama to observe—in the light of Saverio Muratori's photographs of what has been ascertained archaeologically—how at first individual islands increased in number and were more densely built up at the same time as their lake dwellings extended step by step farther into the lagoon, so that every succeeding century might claim new pieces of land from the sea until it finally took on the famous form that Jacopi Barbari represented in his woodcuts around 1500 (fig. 37). Since that time it has expanded even more.

The parish districts formed neighborhood communities. Each became a unit of urban planning with its bell tower, church, and marketplace, the whole clearly delimited first by the sea and later by the canals. From the 11th

Figure 37. Venice (after the woodcut by Jacopo dei Barbari, detail)

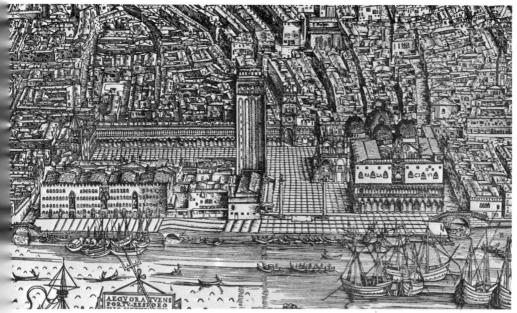

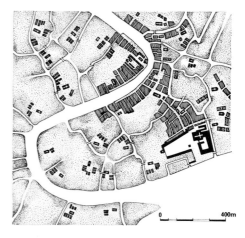

Figure 38. The first urban formation between the Rialto and St. Mark's in the 11th century (after S. Muratori) (Piazza San Marco, as it was in 1800)

century onward, the individual islands began to coalesce; bridges joined them, and footpaths and carriageways crossed their boundaries. The first pontoon bridge on the Rialto, across the Grand Canal, was built in 1181; the first wooden bridge in 1250. Midway between the Rialto and the Piazza San Marco, an enclosed city precinct was built shortly after 1100, linking the commercial center of the city to the seat of government (fig. 38). The financial departments, however, remained where the money was, on the Rialto; the Treasury remained in the Palazzo dei Dieci Savi, its president in the Palazzo dei Camerlenghi.

Only one quarter in Venice is still an island to this day—the cathedral complex of San Pietro in Castello on the extreme edge of the city. This was the site of one of the oldest settlements. It was not until 827, however, that Venice became a bishopric. The bishop's successors were later elevated to the patriarchy. But the cathedral was never the city's main church. The skeleton of the city's patron saint was buried in the palatinate chapel of the doge. A distance of this sort from the episcopal center is characteristic of most maritime towns. We shall encounter a similar arrangement in Lübeck. Cities as large and as wealthy as Bruges, Amsterdam, and Danzig in their heyday did not accept a bishop. These commercial cities rejected political interference on the part of the ecclesiastical authorities. Napoleon was taking a conscious measure to destroy the old order when he moved the seat of the patriarch of Venice to St. Mark's.

I shall here confine myself to a few facts from the rich and well-known history of Venice.[6]

In 810, the doge had moved from Malamocca at the end of the Lido to Rivalto, the island later called Venice. The first castle is believed to have been completed around 814 on the present-day site of the doge's palace. This building, too, had a predecessor as early as the 6th century—a fortification called Palacium. Even before 829, the palatinate chapel next to the castle could be dedicated to St. Theodoric. It was there, in 836, that the remains of the evangelist St. Mark were laid to rest. In the year 973, the new and larger church was dedicated to St. Mark. After 1063 the last church was built, modeled on the Church of the Apostles in Constantinople. Until the 17th century this state church was continually embellished with works of art. Its treasury was filled with unparalleled booty. Its most valuable acquisition—the four Greek horses of gilded bronze—came in 1204 from the hippodrome in Constantinople. They were erected on the facade.

We have to realize that, unlike the Piazza della Signoria in Florence, whose monuments were all made by artists active in Florence, mostly Florentines themselves, the Piazza San Marco is filled almost entirely with plunder. The first examples were the two monolithic granite columns, which are supposed to have been erected in 1172. In early times, ships tied up to them and traitors were executed between them. One of these columns bears a Chinese bronze lion endowed with wings, St. Mark's gospel set between its paws; the other, the torso of an ancient Mithridates that was transformed into the chivalric St. Theodore.

The facade of St. Mark's was decorated round about with plundered works of art, Byzantine and classical reliefs, the famous four porphyry figures of the late Roman emperors, spoils from all areas of the Mediterranean colonies, placed in niches on the walls as decoration. As trophies, these works of art acquired a political meaning whose significance was emphasized by their aesthetic perfection. Only the classical bronze feet for the three flagstaffs in front of the facade, which were made in 1505, are products of Venice itself. Yet they bore the flags of three empires that had been wrested from the Byzantine emperors—Cyprus, Moria, and Candia.

The city was continuously and systematically concerned with improving its constitution and administration. Venice was often centuries ahead of all other cities in its forms of administration, and from this administrative skill it derived part of its success. People looked the real difficulties squarely in the face and created special councils to deal with them. In 1312, a special council of twenty "wise men" for financial affairs was set up; in 1324, another one for shipping. The state establishments were completed earlier and on a grander scale than in any other city. Thus, the first arsenal was built in

1104 and was later enlarged three times. Soon after the arsenal, public warehouses are mentioned. Lodging houses were built for merchants—primarily Jews and Germans. In 1346 we hear of settlements for deserving sailors, soldiers, and employees of the arsenal.

The architectural profile of the city is well known. The various authorities worked briskly and attentively at improving the infrastructure of the city. A basically conservative attitude was constantly being relaxed in favor of well thought-out reforms. Fires led the citizenry to replace all the original wooden buildings by brick ones. Venice, where every stone had to be brought by ship, became a city of stone. Even in early times the most important buildings were faced with marble. The doge families, down the centuries, built themselves ever larger and more splendid palaces. At the same time, the palace facades were opened up toward the canals, with colonnades and windows. The city on pilings became a city on columns. Fortifications were dispensed with. The only towers were those on churches. For almost a thousand years, Venice was never attacked directly. From the 11th century onward, there were merely attempts at revolution. Every attempt at a conspiracy could be nipped in the bud. Here alone, among all the free cities, factions were proscribed. The council of ten that ruled the city with growing authority from the 15th century onward enjoyed popular support for its policies, in spite of the secrecy and cruelty of its verdicts, for it prevented encroachment by the nobles as well as domination by individual doge families.

In 1169, the thirty *quartieri* of the city were subsumed into six *sestieri,* three on each side of the Grand Canal. Administrative units were formed, each with a member of the "council of wise men" at its head. From 1206 onward, these six formed a small council, which was subordinated to a larger one with thirty-six members. Today, houses are still numbered according to *sestieri* and not by street. Even in the baroque period it was impossible to penetrate the network of small streets and canals to build larger roads in the manner of Paris or Rome. The network of waterways remained medieval.

I know of no other city that used its class structure so positively in the division of labor. The nobles took care of politics and the conduct of war as well as the running of the fleet. The middle-class merchants, who alone were called *cittadini,* provided funds, even though the great fortunes of the nobility could also be called upon. The *popolani* provided soldiers and sailors and did the manual labor. Class was also apparent in the city's architectural structure. A distinction was made between the *case,* or the palaces, of

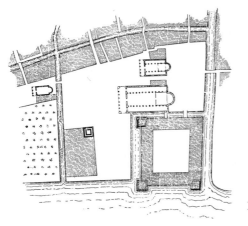

Figure 39. Piazza San Marco, ca. 1150

the nobles; the *fondachi* of the merchants—as buildings which could serve simultaneously as workshop, countinghouse, and shelter; and the extensive tenements of the common people. With the decline of the city in the 18th century, the proletariat continued its steady increase. Up to that time it had led a minimal existence in houses that were often grotesquely overcrowded. Yet, as in Florence (see chap. 2) or Turin (chap. 6), no districts were exclusively aristocratic, and only a few areas were inhabited exclusively by the common people. Whereas in Genoa an upper-class district was placed next to the old burgher city by means of the Strada Nuova, or in Edinburgh in the late 18th century an elegant new city was built on a unified plan next to a decaying royal seat, in Venice everyone was everyone else's neighbor.

Continuity and the republic's effort to achieve reform during a thousand-year period is reflected by the Piazza San Marco.[7] A political system that had built up one of the most remarkable Mediterranean systems after the Roman, the Byzantine, and the Arabian was able to create for itself the most perfect forum. Every one of its buildings illustrates, by its structure, a political function. Improvement or extension of existing buildings and complexes by means of additions, reconstruction, and new construction resulted from changes in the city's constitution, from increasing city functions, and from changing political style. The inner logic of the evolving buildings was experienced as part of their aesthetic perfection.

In the beginning was the doge's palace, which is assumed to have been a complex of four wings and was at the same time a fortress with moat and wall. Next to it, and more modest, the first palatinate and state chapel was built, dedicated to the chivalric saint, Theodore (fig. 39). Recent research is beginning to differentiate this oversimplified scheme. It is likely that this

Figure 40. Aerial view of the Piazza San Marco

most ancient city stronghold consisted, right from the start, of three buildings with different functions.

Of the buildings standing today, the oldest is the church of St. Mark—guarantor of the well-being of the state—which is also the treasury and the palatinate chapel. As we have learned, it was an imitation of the mortuary church of the Byzantine emperors, who likened themselves to the apostles. Every century has added to its wealth, and this was always regarded as a way of increasing its sacredness. It is not only the incomparable, rhythmic, early, and hence low facade of the church and its five cupolas that determine the general effect of the piazza. In order to experience the total unity of the complex we need the dignified solemnity of the inner cupolas. The classic coolness of the piazza's geometry and the symphonic mysticism of the church interior serves, by their contrast, to heighten the effect.

The site of the bell tower has never changed. The present-day brick column, almost 150 meters high and certainly not the first on this spot, was furnished with its belfry between 1156 and 1172. The building was not finished until 1517, when the statue of the Angel Gabriel was completed. This figure, standing 95 meters above the square, brings the heavenly tidings to Mary, as the second patron of St. Marks, and was intended to give visual expression to the chimes of the angelus.

Doge Sebastiano Ziani gave the piazza its present extent by filling in a canal. The arcades were also started at this time with only one upper story, in which the procurators of San Marco lived and had their offices. These officials were originally entrusted only with the administration of the palatinate chapel's ecclesiastical property and therefore lived in this atrium (fig. 40).

The same doge who, in 1177, had succeeded in bringing about a short peace between the pope and the emperor Barbarossa also opened up the state palace, which was the first building to have windows facing on to the Riva. After 1340, reconstruction was begun on the part of the present-day building that stands on the bank. Now, for the first time, the council of one thousand, which had been the legislative organ since 1172 and represented the aristocratic constitution from 1197 to 1798, acquired an appropriate space. Like all medieval council chambers, it had to be on the upper story, and its great windows facing the lagoon were designed to show the stranger from afar where the power of Venice really lay. Windows on this scale are not to be found in any earlier palace of the European Middle Ages, but no other had to contend with the problem of achieving an effect across an inlet of the sea. The history of the extension, the refurbishing and enrichments of the palace, would at the same time be a history of the Venetian state's self-understanding. The frescoes in the chamber depicted the greatness of Venice. We admire the pictorial interpretation of a myth of government. By means of a series of paintings and a series of ornaments, this maritime state removed its history and its political constitution into the realm of myth, as the Jews did with the historical books of the Bible. Today this still holds good, from the late Gothic triumphal arch, the Arco Foscari, to the revival of the painting program, following the great fires of 1574 and 1579, by Paolo Veronese and Tintoretto. Palladio himself gave some spaces a new solemnity, but the authorities did not allow him to carry out his plans for redesigning the exterior. Here, as in Vicenza, he wanted to cover the medieval structure with a new form of state architecture.

The 15th and 16th centuries brought a new impetus to the total restructuring of the Piazza (fig. 40). In 1496, plans were drawn up for the opulent clock tower (finished in 1499) that must be seen as the gateway to the city and to the Merceria, which offers the shortest route to the Rialto (fig. 38). The tower thus had a double function: to replace the old "state clock" and to serve as the city gate.[8] In 1514, the rebuilding of the Procuratorie Vecchie was begun with only one upper story; it was then extended by Sansovino around the corner of the piazza to the old parish church of St. Gimignano, after which a second story was added. The administrative tasks of this authority as a real estate office had increased. As happened later, in Florence, with the Uffizi, other administrative bodies were brought together in a series of buildings and were thus more clearly separated from the government offices in the doge's palace. The clock tower was first extended on both sides and later heightened. It assumed the semantic function of a real city gate and was thus imitated in many cities of the Terra Firma as a badge of the republic.

With the advent of Jacopo Sansovino, a Florentine, who fled to Venice in 1527 after the Sacco di Roma, the right architect had appeared on the scene—one who would play a decisive role for the whole future. He created the unity of the piazza and the piazzetta, which, besides the church of St. Mark's, includes the smaller Piazza dei Leoncini, since 1670 the site of the church of San Basso (now closed) and, since 1837, of the Palazzo Patriarcale.

The high regard accorded Sansovino for his restoration work on the cupolas of St. Mark's enabled him to begin restructuring the whole organism of the piazza with two buildings at the same time: the great library building opposite the doge's palace on the Piazzetta, the oldest such building of comparable proportions, inspired by Michelangelo's Laurenziana in Florence, and the Zecca, the Venetian mint in which sequins were coined and stored. With that first example of humanistic architecture, Sansovino created the counterpart to the doge's palace as a building representative of power, and he deliberately kept the Libreria low by building only one upper story—though this is certainly an important attic. The building demonstrates that a concern for culture and a responsibility for it, in the humanistic spirit, had been accepted as part of the state's political program. Figure 41, an engraving from the year 1571, gives some idea of what difficulties had to be overcome in order to acquire the land from private owners, especially as this was the place where butchers and other vendors offered their goods for sale. Construction could proceed only step by step from the Campanile down to the bank of the canal. With the Zecca, which retained its rustic form even when the second upper story was added in 1570, the doge's palace received an independent counterweight on the ocean side. A modest mint had stood on this spot since 1277. The monolithic columns of the entrance

Figure 41. Buildings in the Piazza (after an engraving of 1571) before the building of the Procuratie Nuovo after 1584

to St. Mark's only assumed a central position within the whole complex after the building of the Zecca and the Libreria. The huge Gothic granaries on the left of the Zecca (destroyed in 1810) also belong, in both form and function, to the plan of the whole complex.

With the building of the library, the Campanile was allowed to stand free. The library drew back from it. Sansovino had already planned to tear down the row houses bordering the main square, parallel to the Procuratorie Vecchie (fig. 41). These houses originally served as a hospice. There had to be accommodation on the city square for strangers. Scamozzi was the first to carry out the project of relinquishing these buildings to the administration and of swinging the wing of the Procuratorie Nuovo back, so that this structure, even though it had three stories, reached a fitting conclusion in the narrow frontage of the library. Since that time, every building has been related to every other from every vantage point. The Campanile was incorporated into the harmonious structure by the Loggetta, in which the leading citizens of Venice could gather on the occasion of great state ceremonies. It was built between 1536 and 1540, the same years in which Sansovino was engaged on the final plans for both the Libreria and the Zecca. The new accents thus came into being at the same time. The composition was completed on the ocean side by the move—after the ad-

Figure 42. The facade of Venice (done by Instituto Universitario di Architettura di Venezia). From left to right: Zecca; Libreria; Piazetta with the columns of the Torre di Orologio; St. Mark's; doge's palace; Bridge of Sighs, prisons.

ministration and the library—of the state prison from the doge's palace into the new prisons, the Prigioni, which were on the side of the doge's palace facing the Zecca and to which the so-called "Bridge of Sighs" led from the lawcourts (fig. 42). Planning started in 1563–66. Among the penal institutions of the Old World, those in Venice can be reckoned as among the most advanced. They were used until 1919. Again, the form of the building reveals the purpose for which it was built. The building of the prisons completed the facade of Venice. Only Venice possesses a city facade in this sense—a facade behind which the representative square of the Venetian state opens up. This relationship between city facade and representative square has remained, thanks to its symbolism and the perfection of its architectural form, unique in Europe.

Napoleon, by destroying the organism of the west side of the square—where the series of arcades of the old and new Procuratoria were interrupted and accentuated by Sansovino's facade for San Gimignano—in order to build his banqueting hall, merely reflected the same political intention as the move of the patriarchal seat to St. Mark's. In his own words, the state forum became "le plus grand salon d'Europe."

As the fruit of a development in city planning that was worked on for almost a thousand years, the Bacino of St. Mark's and its approach is the second outstanding achievement of urban architecture in Venice (fig. 43). The stranger approached the portal created by the two columns frontally from the lagoon; the native approached it by the Grand Canal from the Rialto. This approach by water constituted the most opulently appointed royal route on earth. The natural S-form of the waterway, which is between 30 and 70 meters wide, challenged every architect to provide his palace with a facade that would not only stand the test against all others but would distinguish itself from them, since each palace was seen by passersby both as part of a row of buildings and as a separate entity. At the same time, the approaches were always kept open. While in Florence a Pitti, a Medici or a Strozzi brought the fortresslike Palazzo Vecchio into a Renaissance form, Venice adapted itself to the structure of the doge's palace right down to the late rococo period.

The approach from the lagoon is accentuated by the domed churches surrounding the Bacino—Palladio's reconstruction of the old Benedictine

Figure 43. View from the Piazzetta to the Basin of St. Mark's; left, San Giorgio Maggiore. We have to complete the picture in our imagination with the Giudecca and Il Redentore, the Dogana and the entrance to Grand Canal, and Santa Maria della Salute.

church of San Giorgio Maggiore; his late work on Il Redentore (an institution endowed in thanks for delivery from the plague) on the Giudeca; and Longhena's magnificent baroque church of Santa Maria della Salute. These churches also change the lagoon optically into an inland sea fed by waterways from three sides. The very architectural forms of these churches suggest that the effect was consciously striven for. The aim was to give the city the most ceremonial approach possible. This aim had already been mentioned by Byzantine visitors. As noted, maritime cities are distinguished by the fact that they are entered at their center, not at their periphery. Venice, better than any other city and in a more significant form, exploited this fact in its urban design. One landed between the two columns, having already grasped, from a distance, the function of the closely knit composition of the Zecca, the Libreria, the doge's palace, and the prisons as the city's facade. Between the columns, the "city gate" to the Merceria and the Rialto could be seen in the background. The main work of the humanistic period, the Libreria on the left, and the main Gothic work in Venice, the state palace on the right, formed the wings of the stage upon which one now entered. Then, the portals of St. Mark's opened up on the right, and, on the left, the vast area through which numerous streets and canals provide access to the city's *quartieri*. From spaciousness and openness, from the magnificently fashioned and from that which was ennobled by political semantics, one entered the narrow spaces and a wealth of forms, in which, as on the open square, surprises and surprising sights—described in many pictures and reports—confronted the visitor, like a voyager from the "Arabian Nights," as the very principles of existence.

The eye unites the two towers of St. Mark's and San Giorgio Maggiore. From the 16th to the 18th century, vistas of the city indicate that the domes of Salute, Redentore, St. Mark's, and San Giorgio Maggiore all need to be viewed as a unit. Palladio, like Longhena, calculated the effect of his church facades when seen from a distance across the water. Yet there is no single vantage point from which this unity can be comprehended. It is only from the movement of ship traffic that it all, with constantly changing accents, comes together.

To keep the city on the lagoon flourishing required not only extraordinary political skill but a constant flow of large financial resources. The treasury had to maintain a balance, which was achieved in the centuries of Venetian preeminence by trade, booty, and tribute. There was also a highly developed fishing industry. In later periods, the financial fruits of the Terra Firma took the place of trade, and from the 17th century onward there was an exclusive tourist trade supported by the princes and the aristocracy. The festive nature of the city could be preserved until the end, though in many places it was merely a stage setting. Candor was still a method of demonstrating political security.

The fate of Venice has disturbed civilization for decades. People have rejoiced for too long in its death. The city could no more develop within the framework of Roman centralism than it could under the industrial particularism of Mestre. The lagoon, polluted and overburdened with traffic, itself became the enemy of the architecture that had protected it for a millennium. Only pieces of it can be salvaged, not the whole thing. If Venice were to become a free trade area and could be accorded a special status with its own tax system, a spontaneous recovery might be possible, though such a hope seems utopian. Just as the building up of Venice was dependent upon its political success, so its demise could only be prevented by special political privileges.

Lübeck

In contrast to all the other successful cities that have been or are to be treated in this work, the extent of the city between the Wakenitz and the Trave rivers was determined from the outset (figs. 44 and 45). Lübeck had at its disposal a site measuring about 1750 meters north to south and about 1,215 meters east to west. At the beginning, the whole area was by no means fully settled, opened up by roads, or even demarcated by walls. The disputed question whether a merchant consortium was involved in the foundation of the city or whether it was the creation of rival princes can be determined by glancing at the plan (fig. 44), for no such foundation ever took place. We are faced with a historical process which shows the clash of opposing forces.[9]

Soon after his confirmation as count of Holstein in 1142, Adolphus II of Schauenburg fortified the Slavic citadel in the northern part of the city (1). Some distance away, on the site of the later cathedral, the first merchant settlement was established (2). After this had burned down in 1157, Henry the Lion tried to take control of the area himself. He offered the merchants, in the first instance, a less favorable area on the Wakenitz for their settlement, assigning the more favorable one at the southern end—the spit of land between the confluence of the Wakenitz and the Trave (2)—to the bishop of Oldenburg. Although we have no proof, it seems that the merchants, or one of their leaders, then asked for the gently rising piece of land on which the city hall, the market, and the church of St. Mary are located today, since the most favorable site for harbor installations and warehouses was located at its foot. Then, as before, the princes' representatives—who, from 1201 to 1225, were Danes—resided in the castle. However, we do know that in the seventy years between the reestablishment of the merchant settlement, in 1158 or 1159, and the establishment of Lübeck as a free imperial city after Frederick II's victory over the Danes in 1226, the city developed with unusual rapidity as administrative center of the Hanseatic League.

Even at that time, in addition to the cathedral (2) and the city church of St. Mary (3), Lübeck boasted two further parish churches, St. Peter (5) and St. Aegidius (7), and a fourth church was built later for the lower orders. The bishop had tried to increase his sphere of influence by founding the Benedictine monastery of St. John, though this was soon forced to

Figure 44. Lübeck, ca. 1750 (after Seuter): 1, fortified gate (and convent); 2, cathedral; 3, Marien-kirche; 4, market and town hall; 5. St. Peter's; 6, St. James; 7, St. Aegidius; 8, church and convent of St. Catherine; 9, Holy Spirit almshouses; 10, convent of St. John; 11, convent of St. Anne.

Figure 45. Lübeck, 1720, from the west (after F. B. Werner). The Trave with quays and harbor was secured behind the ring of bastions.

move out of the city. As early as 1225, the Franciscans (10) had arrived, and in 1227 the Dominicans could be allocated a site in the area around the castle (8). Their church was dedicated to Mary Magdalene, for it was on her name day that the Danes were defeated and the emperor signed the agreement by which Lübeck was granted its status as a free imperial city. It was only a few years before the Reformation that the thrifty Hanseatics decided to found, as a third and final establishment, the convent of St. Anne for the care of the daughters of the nobility (11), as the duke of Magdeburg had complained that the girls who were unprovided for were being sent into convents in his duchy.

A twofold impetus favored the creation of this rich skyline: the new freedom of the city and the economic advantages of its geographical situation. In addition there was its strategic security between the two rivers. Let us take the second point first.

Between the North Sea and the Baltic, that is, between Flanders and the cities on the Rhine on the one hand and all the Scandinavian and, later, Baltic lands on the other, there were virtually no overland routes and only one sea route, which was constantly subject to attack. Lübeck, at the most secure point, and only 18 kilometers from the mouth of the Trave, became aware of the function it could assume as the turntable between East and West. The wares of the West, products of a highly developed industrial culture, could be exchanged for the wealth of the East, the fruits of hunting and fishing and of extensive grain-producing provinces. The site of the new city meant that until well into the 16th century it had little competition to fear.

Equally important was the novelty of the idea. Burgher settlements did not yet exist in the Baltic area. Landlords and farmers had earlier, each on their own behalf, tried their hands at trade. Now a new social order allowed trade to develop along solid lines, secured by Lübeck's municipal code. The merchants of Lübeck saw to it that trade proceeded in an orderly and reliable manner. This represented an enormous step forward. In 1161 we find the first burghers in Wisby, and in 1165 at the mouth of the Duna. A little later, Riga was founded. Even before 1200 there are records of Lübeck merchants' visiting fairs on Scania. Soon afterward, there is evidence of settlements in Kalmar and on the island of Rügen, and the towns of Pomerania came into being. Shortly after 1240, the castle and colony of Danzig adopted the municipal law of Lübeck. All of these new towns and settlements joined the Hanseatic League. At the height of its development the league counted 166 members, all of whom recognized Lübeck as their main center. The collection, dispatch, and receipt of goods had been regulated. Producers could rely on fixed markets and fixed times.

Of the powers that tried to rule the city of Lübeck, the lords were the first to go. Their castle became a monastery and the city's fortification. The second move was the reduction of episcopal power. From the beginning, the bishop occupied a position unique in the Holy Roman Empire. He had no rights inside the city. The construction of his Romanesque cathedral was promoted by Henry the Lion, but, as in Venice, it was situated at the extreme edge of the city, and later the bishop, as an imperial prince, had to move his residence to the distant city of Eutin. Here, too, he occupied a special position until the empire came to an end. He was the only Protestant bishop with his own territory and the rank of an imperial prince.

The city, as the third power, gave clear expression to its victory by building the church of St. Mary's and the town hall and market. Not only did the church stand on the highest point of the peninsula, but its towers, and not those of the cathedral, dominated the view (fig. 45). The dimensions of the Romanesque brick basilica, built in the early decades of the 13th century, had already exceeded those of the cathedral—itself a large building. This basilica was rebuilt around the middle of the century and made into an early Gothic hall. Even before it could be completed, however, the citizens' self-consciousness had demanded that it be rebuilt as a basilica, which was the form used for cathedrals. A start was made with the choir. From 1286 onward, the city council held the rights of patronage, enabling the council itself to appoint and dismiss the parish clergy. The nave was completed in the first half of the 14th century and the tower by 1350–51. The

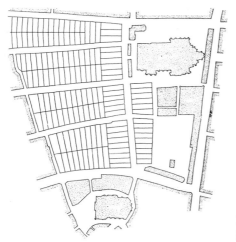

Figure 46. Lübeck: church of St. Mary, marketplace; St. Peter's; and street plan with house lots

aspiring townspeople, aided by the spirit of the age, succeeded in doing
what no bishops of the time could do, whether in Cologne, Strasbourg, or
Regensburg: they completed the building.

The main parish and city church was also the church of the city council. As in Italy, the churches in many German imperial cities also served as
the earliest assembly rooms of the city council. A chapel for the burgomasters was built opposite the first town hall and functioned as a vestibule
before each session of the council. Its upper story, the *trese* (*trésor*) served
as the treasury. The town clerks wrote their documents and contracts in
various other chapels. Almost everything that was written still fell within
the purview of the church.

The town hall and, next to it, the cloth hall, to which three large
houses were attached, stood between the marketplace and the church on
the exact spot that in a Benedictine monastery complex would be occupied
by the chapter house. As a total composition, the relationship between the
church of St. Mary and the marketplace can be compared with that of the
monastery church and the cloisters (fig. 46). After the fire of 1251, the group
of three houses was given a false facade on the side that faced the church,
and this facade was frequently altered and embellished. Between 1298 and
1308, the Danzelhaus was added on the south side: this was a ceremonial
hall for receptions and for the city council ball, a function without which
no patrician government managed to exist. The project was financed by the
rents from the goldsmiths' shops, which were accommodated in arcades on
the market side. Plans continued to be drawn up, and several decades always

elapsed before a new tract was added or a new facade built. The organism developed according to its own rules of growth. First of all, the group of three houses was extended toward the north, at the expense of the cemetery which lay between the church and the town hall (ca. 1340); then a second false front was built on the market side (ca. 1430), and a little later, about 1450, it was decided to lengthen the Danzelhaus by an extension which would accommodate the municipal weigh scale on the ground floor, with space provided on the upper floor for the War Chamber. In 1482 it was decided to continue building behind the choir of the church on the Breite Straße so as to provide accommodation for the chanceries. With the increase in administrative work, this extension was continued in the 18th century to the Mengstraße. The unity of the entire Gothic town hall complex was emphasized by the use of similar materials—glazed tiles. It was not until the Renaissance that ornamental forms in sandstone were added. In addition to what is generally found in many town halls—lawcourts, banqueting hall, council chamber, audience chamber, weigh scale, chancery—Lübeck also had the *Hansesaal* for meetings of the ambassadors to the Hanseatic League.

Equally significant from the point of view of urban design are the streets, the facades of their buildings reflecting both the legal order that the city had bestowed upon itself and their own social order. In the western part of the city, between the marketplace and the Trave, lay the district inhabited by the great merchant families, who also made up the city government. They all owned almost identically sized lots—about 9 meters wide and 36 meters deep—in the five parallel streets leading down to the quays. In Manhattan we shall find lots of similar size. In the districts inhabited by craftsmen and the lower classes, the lot size—considerably smaller—was calculated just as carefully. After the great fires of the 13th century, an ordinance was passed according to which all facades had to be built of brick. Whoever could afford it, between the 13th and the 18th century, built a facade in the style of the day, but the same size was maintained. Thus the city, in addition to a restrained bourgeois baroque, also nurtured with great care a late classicism.

In their interior arrangements, too, the merchants' houses were remarkably similar.[10] The street fronts served the business. On the ground floor, with its long hall, were the showrooms and the countinghouse. There was a large attic for storage. Living accommodations were placed in a wing at the back. Only the greatest families moved to the front of the house in the late Renaissance and baroque periods and furnished their halls with costly furniture. The merchant families were also mindful of those members of their families who were descending the social ladder. As part of a relief program, individual families always provided alleys for the poor behind their houses, cul-de-sacs with very small houses on them. The courtyards of the charitable endowments served the same purpose on larger sites, where rows of small houses faced one another.

Figure 44 obscures the fact that it was not the rows of streets running from north to south that carried the through traffic, but rather the rivers, especially the Trave, to which the main streets led down from the market area. While the Wakenitz was dammed up, thus providing protection, harbor space, fishing waters, and safe sites for mills, the Trave was used not for the defense of the city but merely as a harbor and for quays. In good times, ship after ship tied up at the quays and filled the warehouses. Between the Trave and the city there was a modest medieval fortification, and on the other side of the river the Holstein Gate (built between 1464 and 1477) with its foregate commanded the city. It was only when the river was incorporated into the city—like the Weser in Bremen and the Alster in Hamburg—that the immediate contact with ships was established which, in all the examples we have studied, made foreign trade so much easier. All the Hanseatic cities of the Baltic did the same. In Rostock, Danzig, Riga, Reval, Copenhagen, or Stockholm, ships anchored not in a harbor basin on the sea but in the totally secure area of the city, where they could serve as warehouses before they put out to sea again.

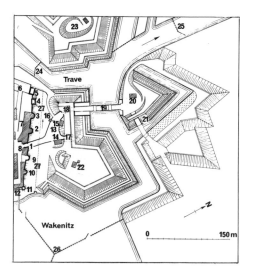

Figure 47. Lübeck: fortified gate and exit through the bastions

The aims of making the Trave run parallel to the city along its whole course and of securing both the north and south gates like the two dams across the Wakenitz presented the baroque period with the immense task of building new fortifications. The fragile Gothic city remained intact, but it was now protected by far-flung walls and bastions. Extremely complicated installations channeled the arterial roads through the area of the bastions (fig. 47). Yet trade remained profitable enough for these fortifications to be built and maintained until their fateful demolition in 1803: three years later the city suffered its one and only sack, at the hands of Napoleon's troops.

Amsterdam

To protect their cities from the sea and their building sites from flooding by rivers, the Netherlands developed dike cities, dam cities, and canal cities. These three types marked three stages in the development of the Netherlands' most successful city. In the process, the experience of older and, for a long time, larger cities could be called upon, and building techniques were borrowed from Leyden, Haarlem, Delft, and other cities.[11]

First of all, the land was secured against flooding, by means of dikes just before the Amstel flows into the Ij (an inlet of the Ijselmeer). The first groups of houses were erected on top of these dikes (fig. 48a). In a second stage of development, the Amstel was contained by a dam (attested to in 1275) in the middle of the settlement, and here the town hall and the Nieuwe Kerk were built. The dam divided the river's course into a lower, open, harbor and an upper, closed, one. Ship traffic and all the flowing water were diverted by two new canals on the left and right of the Amstel (fig. 48b). Later, two more moats were dug for defensive purposes and fed by water from the Amstel. This is the form in which the city is depicted in the famous 1544 engraving (fig. 49). The engraver emphasizes pride in the number of ships.

Representations of the city reveal that the second half of the 16th century was engaged in another extension of the fortifications. The old moat around the walls was again changed, this time into a shipping canal, which kept the name *Singel* (moat). A modern ring of fortifications strengthened by bastions was meant to encircle the greatly enlarged harbor on the east side.

Amsterdam had acquired city rights in 1300. From the beginning of the 16th century, it grew to be the largest city in the Netherlands. Occupied by Alba in 1567, it joined the anti-Spanish alliance in 1578. From then on, the city had constantly to expand. The city council and four burgomasters, as the authority which alone made the final decisions, faced the questions of how far they could extend their territory in order to keep pace with the pressures of an increasing population, and at what point costs would exceed income. Every expansion involved comprehensive works for new dams, moats, and canals. They were always carried out according to the same principle of fanning the Amstel out into a delta, the extremities of which formed the fortification moats.

From the end of the 16th century onward, the famous plan of the three canals, intended to almost triple the size of the city by some 800 hectares

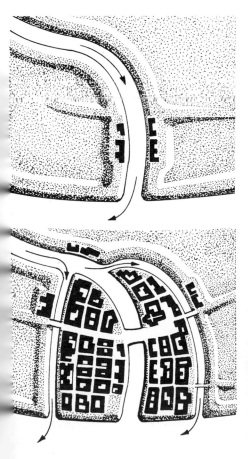

Figure 48. Amsterdam: top left, settlement around the dike; bottom left, town on the dam.

Figure 49 (below). Amsterdam: bird's-eye view, 1544 (after an engraving by Cornelis Anthoniszoon)

(fig. 50), was under discussion. Numerous voices were raised in opposition. In 1607 the project was approved, and it was begun in 1609. In the course of half a century the Herrengracht, the Kaisergracht, and the Prinsengracht were completed in turn, as well as several radial streets and canals which linked them. The principle of the star-shaped baroque fortress was adapted to the canals. The city finally lit on this brilliant idea after centuries of transforming fortification moats into shipping canals every time the city expanded. It was now possible to use the experience of new methods of constructing fortifications. The city was once more ringed round by fortifications some 8,000 meters in length, strengthened by twenty-six bastions. A highly developed system of watergates and locks served ship traffic. The Amstel was pressed into the city's service for all time.

Strict ordinances regulated house construction. A large area of the city, the Jordaan (from *jardin*), was reserved for low building, industry, craftsmen, and emigrants. On the main canals, the small lots were calculated

Figure 50. Amsterdam: city plan (after Merian, 1648)

in such a way as to leave considerable space for gardens between two houses. Although the ordinances have not been preserved, presumably because of several fires, we have to assume that the height of the houses was prescribed and their cost laid down.

The building ordinances still in force today for the expensive sites on the three canals go back to 1612 and 1663. The plans were carried out by the city architect—the person in the city council responsible for overseeing building—and by the president of the council. They were entirely the concern of the city administration. Daniel Stalpaert (1615–76), the city architect, was involved all his working life in administering the plans. In contrast to Venice, but as in Lübeck, these plans were predicated on the fact that only wealthy citizens were to have the sites on the canals, while the lower classes, Jewish emigrants from Spain and Portugal, and, later, the French Huguenots were allocated sites on the lower ground in the Jordaan. Calvinism, which understood wealth as an early sign of eternal salvation, regarded such a separation as nonnegotiable. The elegant form of architecture on the canals was also imposed upon large areas of the old city. For this reason Amsterdam is among those metropolises which have preserved in the most unified manner the architecture of a particular century—in this case the 17th. The suspension of all development from about 1680 to 1860 aided this process of preservation. All other major cities in the Netherlands retained the medieval irregularities of their urban expansion even in the 17th century. The only exceptions are the small fortified cities. Amsterdam alone made the new baroque sense of form the basis of its city plan. The experiences of the interdependence of fortifications and canal building were not neglected in the process. What was long subordinated to necessity was here emancipated into freedom of form. The expression of this new sense of self is the new, overscaled city hall, the present-day royal palace, which was started according to the plans of van Campen in 1648 and completed in 1655.

Manhattan

If the network of canals in Venice, in and around the individual parishes, was an initial stylistic phase corresponding to the sense of order of the early Middle Ages, if the regularity of Lübeck's city plan appears typical of the high Middle Ages, and if Amsterdam came up with the perfect solution for the baroque commercial city, the 1811 plan for Manhattan represented the most daring innovation of the 19th century. It is true that it only acquired its surpassing significance when the skyscrapers were built in the 20th cen-

Figure 51. New York, ca. 1810 (after an engraving by Champin)

tury. Four stylistic stages in the history of New York have been determined, dependent upon economic circumstances, the social stratification of the population, and political structures. But behind each of them there was a new conception of the city as an aesthetic event, a conception that in each instance had been formed at a different level of consciousness.

An engraving of the city of New Amsterdam dating from 1660 clearly illustrates that the architectural ideas of the mother city had been transferred to the peninsula in the New World, yet did not correspond to the topography of the site. In the spit of land between the Hudson and the East rivers, three canals were dug, in which smaller ships could anchor; the canals also served sanitary purposes. A small fortress was to serve the settlement as a protection against Indians and pirates. The settlement's success, even after the surrender to the British, was a modest one. Around 1700, it still only boasted about 5,000 inhabitants. Between 1785 and 1790 there were about 24,000. Our view of the city (fig. 51) was produced a little later. From this moment on, prosperity and population increased rapidly: by 1835 the population stood at about 200,000.

The Dutch surveyor Goerck was commissioned in 1796 to develop a new plan, which was produced in 1811 (fig. 52). The plan was laid out like a grid, 18 kilometers long, over the whole peninsula, including its hills and valleys. It provided for twelve major avenues and 150 cross streets. In order that as many people as possible might have the advantage of a site on the river bank, individual lots were kept extremely small. Access to shipping was everywhere to be kept short and unhampered. As in other maritime cities, shipping was part of the cityscape.

It was sixty years before all the streets were completed. In spite of strong opposition, at least Central Park was salvaged (it can be seen on fig. 52). The layout was bounded at its northern end by the Harlem River, a canal that joined the two branches of the river. On large stretches of the banks, jetties were provided for, and these have continually increased in number. Only in the old town, "downtown," did an irregular pattern, the legacy of historical development, have to be taken into account. There, in the most confined space, the city's commercial buildings were huddled. Battery Park was built in place of the citadel at the extreme tip of the island. Manhattan was soon too small to accommodate all the desired expansion.

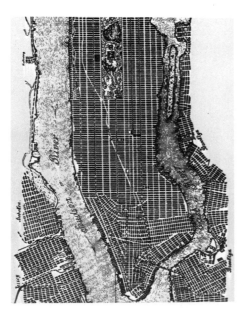

Figure 52. The 1811 plan for Manhattan

Four boroughs were added, the Bronx, Queens, Brooklyn, and Staten Island. As large and as densely populated as each of these boroughs was, they were not city centers. The main city was concentrated on Manhattan. Here, external pressures forced the buildings upward.

It is well known that the first skyscrapers were developed in Chicago. It was not until shortly before 1890 that New York took up the idea. It was there that the skyscraper first demonstrated its crucial importance to urban architecture. As decade succeeded decade, architects dared to build taller and taller buildings. This is how those office towers were built whose material, height, decoration, and name trumpet forth their claim to be representative. The Empire State Building—what office building in the Old World would have borne such a name?

Figure 53. Manhattan from Brooklyn Bridge

The iconography of New York has been treated in a famous book.[12] Yet the iconology, or symbolism, of these "cathedrals of capitalism" has, as far as I can tell, never been investigated. It was here that European styles achieved the precision of metaphors. Gothic, classical, baroque piles were built one after the other. Here, cheek by jowl, we find skyscrapers of brick, freestone, shining white marble, dark steel, or rust-colored bronze. The regularity of the street layout is creatively countered by variations in height. A cottage stands next to a colossus. The contrast amazes the beholder. Around the little plaza at Rockefeller Center, the dark steel verticals produce a vertiginous effect. Size becomes an aesthetic quality. Even the distant prospect is determined by the contrast between high and low. The quantity of gigantic buildings, not any individual building, is what creates the effect (fig. 53). Imagine what the effect would be if the building ordinances had decreed that the height of every building should be 300 or 400 feet! It is easier to imagine if we think of the fate of Stuyvesant Town, which was built by an insurance company with skyscrapers all of uniform height. The intention was to combat the degeneration into slums to which New York, as an immigrant city, had always been susceptible, and still is. While the 19th century kept strictly to the street plan in the distribution of lots, real estate being a title to wealth, it is significant that the height of a building on any lot was clearly the responsibility of the individual. The principle of freedom, which had been elevated to the political ideal of the new federation, excluded any idea of public restriction, at least until the 20th century. Thus, New York was the only city that could exploit to the limit the potential of scientific construction on a scale that determined its cityscape. Ever denser clusters developed out of free-standing skyscrapers. At the same time the needs of economic expansion were served. Skyscrapers have to be understood as monuments to entrepreneurial daring.

Comparisons with Venice are not out of place—Manhattan, too, reveals itself most completely to the seafarer. Here, too, the buildings proclaim the strength and economic power of the city and the state. However, just as in 18th century Venice, New York since about 1960 has faced a crisis situation precisely because of this principle of political freedom which today threatens the very stability of its buildings. The density of construction made the city ungovernable. The monocentric principle, out of which only one cultural center developed, began to reveal its weaknesses in ever increasing measure. Because of the prescribed form of the city, an almost automatic process was set in motion that was bound to plunge all areas of public life, as well as many areas of private existence, into new crises.

Chapter 4

*I*F "*THE HOLY ROMAN EMPIRE OF THE GERMAN NATION*" is the most medieval of all the medieval forms of state, comparable perhaps to the Kingdom of Jerusalem, then within this idealistic construct, and until it dissolved itself in 1806, the imperial cities and the free imperial cities were—apart from the bishoprics—the most remarkable structures: remarkable for their legal position rather than for their architectural form.

Imperial cities were not founded. They all came into being in the 13th and 14th centuries in power vacuums and as a result of the dissolution of the older aristocratic authorities. Most of them owe their origin to the collapse of the Hohenstaufen empire, many to the revolt of the citizenry against its bishops, and some to the extinction of the families of counts or princes. But where the territorial princes grew simultaneously stronger, the cities were unable to achieve any new charters. This was the case in old Bavaria, Austria, Saxony, and Brandenburg as well as in Bohemia. Imperial cities are found in Franconia and Swabia; along the Rhine; formerly in Alsace, Switzerland, and the Netherlands; and scattered about in the coastal regions of the North Sea and the Baltic.

The legal form of the imperial city cannot be unequivocally determined. All medieval cities

Imperial Cities

throughout Europe strove to become self-governing. City councils were formed everywhere. Step by step, many cities tried to negotiate more extensive charters from the temporal or spiritual power. The final goal of "imperial city" was by no means achieved, either de jure or de facto, by all those that bore the name. And the rights possessed by individual cities varied from city to city and from century to century.[1] The *Kölner Chronik* of 1490 names 90 imperial cities. Modern computations reckon about 105.[2] The imperial registers of the 16th century mention 146, but the compilers of these registers had an interest in keeping the numbers high, as it was the purpose of their computations to determine the contributions, in terms of troops or money, which were to be made to the imperial army. When the empire dissolved between 1789 and 1806, 51 imperial cities still remained.

In 1648, with the signing of the Peace of Westphalia, 11 of the imperial cities left the large number that then existed because they, together with the Netherlands, severed their ties with the empire. Nijmegen, Utrecht, and Antwerp were among these. In Switzerland, too, 12 cities gave up their imperial status—Basel, Geneva, Bern, Zürich, Chur, Lausanne, Lucerne, St. Gall, Schwyz, Solothurn, Winterthur, and Zug. A further 16 lost the greater part of their rights in the 17th century with the secession of Alsace, Lorraine, and Burgundy to France. The bishoprics of Metz, Toul, and Verdun were among them, as well as Besançon and Strasbourg in the French- and German-speaking areas respectively. Louis XIV had already taken over the stewardship of the 10 Alsatian imperial cities, among them Colmar (fig. 54). Within the boundaries of the empire, too, no less than 55 cities lost their old charters between 1521 and 1722, almost all of them cities which had never acquired the full rights of an imperial city. Most had been mortgaged by the emperor himself and sank to the rank of provincial city; a few became episcopal cities again or, less frequently, the seat of a temporal power. Duis-

burg, Paderborn, Quedlinburg, Freiburg-im-Breisgau, Göttingen, Halberstadt, Saarbrücken, and the beautiful city of Soest are among these. Constance became an Austrian provincial city, and Magdeburg a Prussian one.
A few, like Brunswick or Rostock, managed to protect their rights long
after 1648 until they finally fell victim to the absolutist cabinets of the territorial princes.

Of the representatives of the 51 imperial cities of 1789 or 1806, 14 sat on
the Rhenish benches and 37 on the Swabian benches at the back of the
Imperial Hall in Regensburg. In order of the number of inhabitants (according to G. Franz), not in the order in which they were seated, the Rhenish benches included:

	Population		Population
1. Hamburg	119,000	8. Mühlhausen	8,000
2. Lübeck	45,000	9. Nordhausen	8,000
3. Frankfurt	45,000	10. Dortmund	6,000
4. Cologne	43,000	11. Wetzlar	6,000
5. Bremen	30,000	12. Worms	6,000
6. Aachen	18,000	13. Speyer	6,000
7. Goslar	8,500	14. Friedberg	2,000

The Swabian benches included:

	Population		Population
1. Augsburg	36,300	8. Heilbronn	7,000
2. Nuremberg	30,000	9. Reutlingen	7,000
3. Regensburg	21,000	10. Memmingen	6,700
4. Ulm	15,000	11. Lindau	6,000
5. Nördlingen	8,000	12. Ravensburg	6,000
6. Dinkelsbühl	8,000	13. Schweinfurt	6,000
7. Kaufbeuren	7,000	14. Weissenburg	6,000

In addition, there were seats for 23 towns with fewer than 6,000 inhabitants: Aalen, Biberach, Bopfingen, Buchau, Buchhorn, Esslingen, Schwäbisch-Gmünd, Gengenbach, Schwäbisch-Hall, Isny, Kempten, Leutkirch,
Offenburg, Pfullendorf, Rothenburg ob der Tauber, Rottweil, Überlingen,
Wangen, Weil die Stadt, Zell am Hammersbach, Wimpfen, and Windsheim. To understand these figures we have to know that in some cases they

Figure 54. The imperial city of Colmar (after Merian, 1643)

refer to the city alone, and in some to the territory. Yet in 1789 only 7 imperial cities controlled a rural area of any size. These were Nuremberg with 26 square miles; Ulm with 23; Schwäbisch-Hall with 7.5; Frankfurt with 6.5; and Hamburg, Rothenburg, and Schweinfurt with about 6 each. Hamburg had a population of about 100,000 as against 19,000 in the rural area. In Ulm the situation was reversed: 15,000 lived in the city and 23,000 in the countryside.

In contrast to the Italian city-states, the German imperial cities did not carry on any immediate wars against one another. Their special position rested not on power but on rights, and it was the indissolubility of those rights that they defended. Competitive struggles were transferred to the economic sphere, and even here the security of lines of communication was more important than a position of supremacy. In cases where the imperial cities formed alliances, it was always a matter of defending their rights against the territorial princes and, at the same time, of protecting freedom of passage against robber barons. No imperial city ever incorporated another into its territory in the way Siena or Florence did.

Economically, every imperial city strove for autarky. This is why the largest among them were the most important centers for the production of works of art, certainly between the 13th and 16th centuries and, in many cases, until the dissolution of the empire. Goethe was a citizen of an imperial city and could only have developed in an imperial city. In Cologne and Nuremberg, in Lübeck and Augsburg, in Regensburg, Ulm, and Strasbourg, and in Basel, too, there were works of art which, with a few famous exceptions, had been produced in the cities themselves. Each of these cities had also supplied artworks to wide areas. In this respect, princely court cities and cathedral cities could not compare with them. Ulm exported works of art to places as far away as Landshut and Chur; and if it was not works of art that were being exported, it was artists themselves, like Veit Stoß of Nuremberg, who spent several years in Cracow. The guilds promoted competition. There was a characteristic imperial city style which developed especially in the high and late Gothic periods. It grew out of the principle that only masterpieces were to be tolerated. Perfection in craftsmanship was demanded—only what could be fashioned with the greatest diligence. Experience was gathered over the years and material and durability were tested. The tradition of producing masterpieces allowed Nuremberg and Augsburg to raise their crafts to an even higher level in the late 16th and early 17th centuries. The Thirty Years' War was unable to destroy the tradition entirely. Augsburg in the 18th century was also an artistic center, though by then it was in competition with princely court cities.

The aristocratic period from the end of the Thirty Years' War until the end of the ancien régime humbled the burgher. Aside from the Netherlands, the great achievements in urban architecture were to be found in the centers of absolutism. It was only with the Enlightenment that a change came about. It has rightly been said that the free cities had no luck politically after the middle of the 16th century.[3]

There are exceptions, however. Hamburg, Bremen, and Lübeck only completed their major fortifications at this time, permitting the areas of settlement in the former two to be almost doubled. It is hard to decide whether the Berlin of Frederick the Great or the Frankfurt of Goethe represented the greater cultural power. From the standpoint of urban design, the centers of gravity certainly moved decisively toward the capitals and the princely seats.

Self-representation as Self-interpretation

Since the Renaissance, numerous cities have depicted their physical appearance very precisely both for themselves and for strangers. The architectural profile of a city became an object of municipal pride and, at the same time,

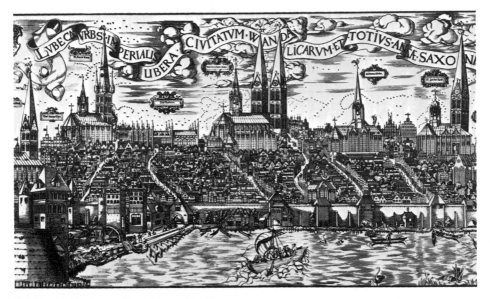

Figure 55. Lübeck, 1552, from the east (detail)

an advertisement for its greatness. Here, too, Italy was in the vanguard. Yet it is not certain whether the first large representation, the network plan of Florence (ca. 1480, 58.5 cm × 131.5 cm), does not really belong to the history of the German woodcut. Jacopo dei Barbari's famous woodcut of Venice in 1500 is supposed to have been commissioned by a Nuremberg printer. The next in the series is the view of Antwerp—at that time an imperial city—done in 1515 (53 cm × 216 cm). The plan of Venice is the immediate forerunner of Jörg Seld's depiction of Augsburg in 1521 (80 cm × 191 cm). This was followed by Woensam's view of Cologne in 1521 (62 cm × 350 cm, fig. 8), views of Amsterdam in 1544 (199.3 cm × 138 cm, fig. 49) and of Basel in the same year (40.3 cm × 89 cm), and in 1548 the curious depiction of Strasbourg by Conrad Merian, presented as a circular view from the terrace beneath the top of the cathedral tower. Bremen follows in 1550 (20 cm × 107 cm), Nuremberg and Frankfurt in 1552 (29.5 cm × 150 cm and 70 cm × 133 cm). Lübeck (fig. 55) probably produced its magnificent view of the city (73 cm × 371 cm) in the same year. *Ob singularem patriae pietatem* as Jörg Seld tells us in the inscription on his plan; "singular love of one's native land" is the reason for producing these important and large-scale works. For Woensam, a visit from Charles V was the reason for presenting the monarch with a picture of his good, solid, and holy city. At the same time,

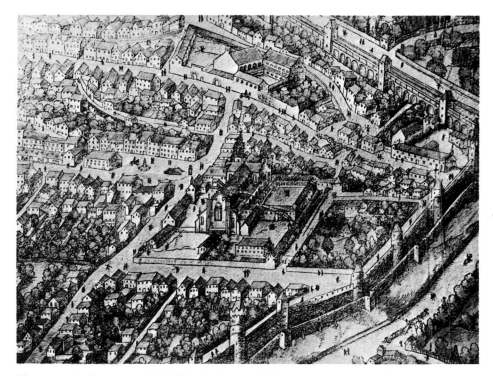

Figure 56. Augsburg, 1521 (detail of the view by Jörg Seld)

a whole series of unusually accurate city models was produced. Here too, Augsburg in 1521 was first in the field, and Sebald Behaim's model of Nuremberg followed in 1540.

The bird's-eye views in these engravings are all characterized by the fact that it was not the streets that were emphasized, but rather the clusters of houses and churches on the streets and squares (fig. 56). It was not the plan of the city that was represented but the vertical construction, and care was taken to reproduce the height of these houses in perspective shortening. One group of houses after another had to be handled as an artistic exercise. For this is how the city was seen.

This was even more true of the views of complete cities. The artist usually chose his point of view in such a way as to suggest that he was working from a captive balloon tethered at a moderate height. He aimed to include all the monumental buildings in his picture, if possible. Moreover, the churches had to be larger than life to show their importance, but at the same time he placed the buildings so close to one another that the streets and squares became almost invisible. The city was a whole, densely covered with buildings, in which there was nothing unfinished and no vacuums (fig. 56). Close quarters were considered beautiful; the unhygienic nature of this arrangement was barely understood. Height was considered a sign of power, richness of forms an expression of prosperity and craftsmanship. Every city wanted to present itself as complete, clearly defined architecturally, finished, secure, pious, and serene.[4]

We only become conscious of this particular conception of a city when we compare depictions of the 16th century with those of the 17th and 18th centuries. Princely residences are depicted in 16th century engravings as being in a state of completion which was never attained, whereas cities are shown as in a state of neglect. Decay, emptiness, and the poverty of the people are shown among the coaches of the nobility, and vegetation dominates over architecture. Guardi in Venice, or Piranesi in Florence, were not the first to depict these elements with some sort of realism. Israel Silvestre (1621–91) looked for comparable motifs in Paris, and drawings or watercolors of every imperial city can be cited in which picturesque decay is placed in the foreground as suitable for representation. Even the few short years beteen the cityscapes of Canaletto (b. 1697) and those of Guardi (b. 1712) are one more stage in the progressive loss of municipal pride. These pictures reflect cities' declining self-esteem.

Cathedral Cities as Imperial Cities

Of the fifty-one cities on the benches in Regensburg, six were former bishoprics: Cologne, Worms, Speyer, Bremen, Regensburg, and Augsburg. Only these former bishoprics were designated free imperial cities. As we have seen, Lübeck, the maritime power, was a special case. Even among those which ceased to be imperial cities in 1648 or later, several preserved the appearance of episcopal centers: Metz, Strasbourg, and, above all, Basel are three of the most important. Their topographical order was in all cases complete before they became imperial cities, as we have seen in Cologne. In these cities, it is true, many large, older ecclesiastical buildings had been renovated, like the Benedictine monastery of St. Ulrich and Afra in Augsburg between 1494 and 1506. As a rule, these cities were now developed only by the addition of secular buildings, by the strengthening of their fortified gates, by town halls, assembly rooms, or storehouses. In isolated cases, monumental buildings were erected by the Jesuits. But that was all. The only new accent in Woensam's view of Cologne (fig. 8) is the tower on the city hall, which was begun in 1396 after it had been agreed to divide the city government among representatives of the patrician merchants and of the craftsmen. For all practical purposes, construction of the cathedral had been given up. Apart from the Jesuit Church of the Assumption, no monumental work was built for almost four centuries. The mendicant orders—Dominicans, Franciscans, and Carthusians—had long since installed themselves for perpetuity. From time to time, smaller ecclesiastical institutions were established. Trade had diminished, and the old streets sufficed to carry what traffic there was. Occasionally we hear of a private citizen building a new house, or of a fugitive prince erecting his palace within the protection of the walls. The Thirty Years' War had passed Cologne by, as did every other war, leaving plagues and shortages behind it but no destruction. A condition of stasis was achieved in which it was impossible to conceive measures for city planning, until the French in 1794, and the Prussians in 1815, at last incorporated this treasure house of art into their states.

Regensburg

Regensburg offers a similar example. When Goethe saw this city, on the first day of his Italian journey, he remarked, "The spiritual lords have made good provision. Every field around the city belongs to them. In the city, church stands by church, convent by convent." The city of the perpetual Imperial Diet, which kept the council chamber of the city hall occupied from 1663 to 1803, resembles the empire itself in its diversity. Behind the constricting walls, which encompassed only 109.6 hectares, there were five institutions responsible to the emperor alone, each of which laid claim to sovereign rights: the bishop in the community of his little cathedral complex; the old Benedictine abbey of St. Emmeran; the two convents, Niedermünster and Obermünster; and the imperial city itself with its city hall. Furthermore, the duke of Bavaria could lay claim to special rights within the city. Figure 57 shows how much land belonged to these and other ecclesiastical organizations, each of which forms an independent architectural unit. Most of the houses which stood on church land were also liable for the church ground-rents or taxes. As early as the 11th century, a chronicler made the distinction between the *pagus regius,* the royal district, which at that time was probably close to St. Emmeran, the *pagus clericorum,* around the cathedral, and the *pagus mercatorum,* which was crowded into ever narrower streets leading down to the river with its storage areas.[5]

In the 11th and 12th centuries, Regensburg was the wealthiest mercantile city in southern Germany, and it flourished as such until the middle of the 14th century. Its population was between 6,000 and 10,000. The great merchants had built towers after the Italian fashion, of which about fifty can be traced. A few, some as high as nine stories, are still preserved. The new Gothic cathedral, built on the French model but with significant special features, was not begun until 1275. Open space in the city had been reduced by charitable institutions and was further reduced by numerous monasteries, not only that of the Scottish monks in the 12th century but by the Franciscans, Dominicans, Augustines, and the two chivalric orders in the 13th century. As a symbol of economic power, a stone bridge was thrown over the Danube between 1133 and 1146. Constructed on sixteen piers, it was regarded as the eighth wonder of the world. Permission for its construction had to be purchased from the emperor (*libertatem lapidei pontis*). Also contributing to the city's prosperity was a Jewish community, eventually of 5,500 souls, which had established its ghetto in the exact center of the city. The community chose this site in order to ensure the protection first of the duke in the Alte Hof, and then of the bishop. The motives for the council's political approval of the religiously inspired uprising in 1519, in which the ghetto and the synagogue were burned down and the survivors driven from the city, can be perceived. The city lacked space. First a chapel was built in the center of the new market, and a little later a Renaissance church (Zur schönen Maria). The town hall itself grew together, in the course of the centuries, out of various individual parts. Merian shows it in 1643 as a structure with several sections (fig. 58), of which the oldest, the market tower, goes back to the 13th century, while the newest, the regular complex with four wings, was added in 1661. The ballroom for patrician families—and no imperial city was prepared to forego a *Danzelhaus*—was added in 1360 and later given over to the imperial diet along with a number of other rooms, some of which were of later date. "It is like the German Empire itself, extensive, old, and decayed," wrote Friedrich Nicolai in his travel journal of 1783.

The city council of Regensburg and most of the burgher families had converted to Protestantism during the Reformation. The council had not succeeded in getting rid of the Minorite, Dominican, and Augustine monasteries or the nunneries of the Claritians and the Dominicans, which were joined, in the 17th century, by the Capucines, the Carmelites, and the Jesuits. The institutions under direct protection of the empire as well as the

Figure 57. Regensburg, ca. 1860: 1, cathedral; 2, cathedral parish church of St. Ulrich; 3, St. John; 4, St. Emmeran; 5, parish church of St. Rupert; 6, Niedermünster; 7, former parish church of SS. Peter and Paul; 8, Alte Kapelle; 9, parish church of St. Cassianus; 10, Obermünster; 11, convent of St. James; 12, St. Leonard (Order of St. John); 13, chapel of St. Goerge on the Wiedfang; 14, Dominican convent; 15, St. Aegidius (Teutonic Order); 16, Minorite convent; 17, St. Oswald; 18, city hall; 19, new parish church; 20, church of the Holy Trinity; 21, Carmelite convent; 22, St. Clara, Cupucine convent; 23, Bishop Wittmann institution (St. Salvator); 24, Dominican nunnery of the Holy Cross.

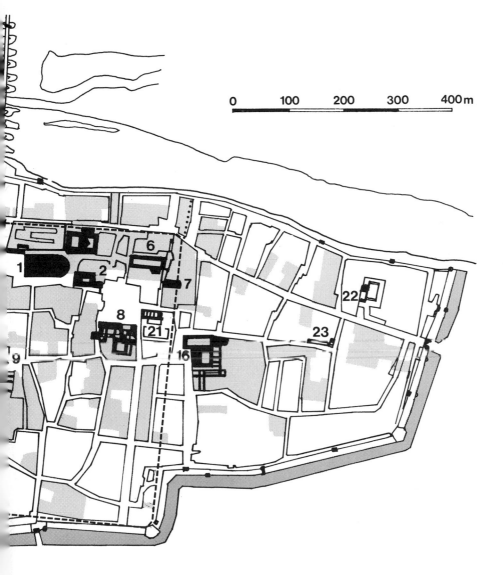

0 100 200 300 400 m

------ Roman fortification of the legion camp, A.D. 179

• • • • • • • • extension of the city in 920

extension of the city in 1300, medieval city fortifications

possessions of the imperial founders, of the knightly orders, of the convents, and of the cathedral in the Middle Ages (after Klebel)

Figure 58. The city hall in Regensburg (after Merian, 1643)

precinct around the cathedral were, in any case, beyond the reach of the imperial city ordinances. There was a whole area in which courtyards, churches, chapels, and the city quarters of outlying convents and even of imperial princes and counts were all mixed up together. Here the decorative intensity of the individual allows us to forget that there were no functional through streets.

Most of these churches, even in the 18th century, engaged leading masters of "South German" baroque to embellish their interiors with a baroque or late rococo decor, merely as a reflection of renewed self-confidence. None of the older institutions came up with major new plans, and the newer ones did not get around to it until the city was incorporated into the kingdom of Bavaria by Napoleon. Regensburg is an extreme case. The history of its urban architecture is the history of its institutions. It is incomprehensible to modern organizational theory that citizens could organize themselves into "watches" throughout the ecclesiastical complexes in order to protect the walls. There was never any question of reconstruction. People simply knew how to manage.

Augsburg

Things were quite different in Augsburg. Figure 59, 1 shows the early cathedral city. The main axis was determined by the processional route between the cathedral and the burial church of the earliest bishops, Ulrich and Afra.[6] Burial fields have been found there, indicating that the upper classes since the early 7th century had sought to be buried in the vicinity of the martyr.[7] The process of concentration, in the course of which the city absorbed both of the ecclesiastical centers and later expanded still further, need not concern us here. What does have bearing is that the processional route never turned into a through road. The two ecclesiastical buildings closed it off at the northern and southern ends. A series of markets was established along this route, the oldest dating from the 10th century, which were connected to the gates of the city by cross and diagonal streets and so on out to the arterial roads. The leading families built their palaces along this central axis. Only here were there real palaces, for Augsburg's heyday came late, in the latter half of the 15th century and the first half of the 16th, and at that time its families were among the wealthiest in the world. Jakob Fugger (1459–1525) was probably the richest of them all. His interest lay in trade, finance, mining, and many branches of industry that were just then beginning to flourish. He was the founder of the oldest social welfare settlement in the empire, the Fuggerei, still in business today, to house impoverished elderly people.[8]

In spite of a city council whose composition—equal numbers of Protestants and Catholics—was forced upon the city by Charles V, the city

Figure 59. Augsburg, the Maximilianstraße and its fountains: 1, Ulrich and Afra; 2, cathedral; 3, fountain of Augustus on the Perlach; 4, city hall; 5, fountain of Mercury; 6, Fuggerei; 7, fountain of Hercules.

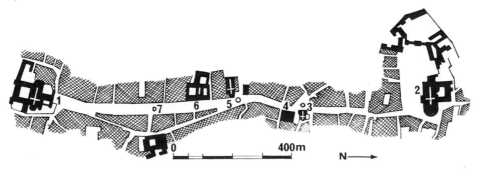

Figure 60. The city hall in Augsburg, the Perlach, and the fountain of Augustus

experienced a second heyday during the longest period of peace the empire experienced (from 1555 to 1618). The expression of this second heyday was a new humanistic architecture and an equally significant school of sculpture, whose collected works adorned the one magnificent street. The fountains were built even before the buildings. It has been shown in a recent study that the three fountains—the fountain of the city founder, Augustus; that of the god of trade, Mercury; and that of Hercules—were built according to a unified plan between 1589 and 1606.[9] In this carefully thought-out program, the city demonstrated its ideals, its achievements as well as its goals. The fountain of Augustus, commissioned from Hubert Gerhard for the celebration of the sixteen hundredth anniversary of the city, was placed diagonally across from the city hall (fig. 60). The fountain of Mercury, the model for which had been completed by Adriaen de Vries in 1596, was placed in the middle of the commercial area, while Hercules victorious over the Hydra, originally in front of the house of the city seal in the merchant district, represented the demand that the trade routes be kept secure. The choice of the site for each individual fountain was carefully calculated for its effect within the urban plan.

The ornamentation of the fountains was almost complete before Elias Holl (1573–1646) started on his enormous building activity, tackling for the last time the city as a whole, including its fortifications. I would not wish to compare him with the architects who were, at the same time, creating the new Amsterdam. The processes were too different in magnitude, and the same is true of Sir Christopher Wren's activity in London after 1666. In Germany, Balthasar Neumann was to undertake tasks of a still higher order in Würzburg. I want to emphasize just four of Holl's major works.

This urban master builder began his activity with the armory, whose steeply rising facade, with its window gables pointing upward, still retains some sense of Gothic form. Hans Reichle's St. Michael, and the cherubs with the emblems of war, reveal that the building is not just an arsenal but rather the symbol of the city's will to assert itself. It was under very different auspices that Andreas Schlüter, a century later, adorned the Berlin armory with masks of dying warriors (see chap. 6). The next documents of burgher greatness that Holl created were the facades of the butchers' hall (1609) and the Perlach tower in the marketplace (1614–16). The balance between large planes and economical decoration has given the Maximilianstraße its aesthetic character ever since. Holl's chief work was the city hall, begun in 1615 and completed shortly before the occupation of Augsburg by the Swedes in 1626. Its cubelike form was the more noticeable because the ground behind it sloped away. Its large planes were broken only by the window frames. As a work of architecture it succeeded both objectively and representationally. Its effect was increased by the triangular form and diagonal views of the square, its flat surfaces accented by the sculptured fountain of Augustus (fig. 60).

Again we must remember that, almost a thousand years before, limits had been set to the plan by the large churches, which were set diagonally to the streets, closing them off. Each century found new, partial solutions to these problems, and the long period of peace from 1555 to 1618 found the final and most perfect one. The Maximilianstraße furnishes a model solution to a precisely circumscribed problem in urban design. If we were to add the history of the delimiting churches and the origin of all the other buildings, up to the last rococo facades, we would find that an intense concern with the "where" of all construction on this street represented a challenge to the "how" of each building.

Nuremberg as a Model City

Nuremberg has always been regarded as the model of an imperial city, although its development was only completed toward the middle of the 16th century. The city plan of 1793 illustrates Nuremberg's history (fig. 61). In spite of the inevitable political and economic decline, the citizens were able to hold on to their architectural treasures and much of the art that the city owned. At the same time the city always remained small—at least in comparison with the great European centers. Its third and last wall encompassed only 126 hectares (compared with 650 in Florence and about 800 in Amsterdam). In 1806, 26,000 people were living within these walls. In Dürer's time (ca. 1500), there had been about 40,000.

The early history of the city has been reliably investigated.[10] In the beginning, Henry III's castle was located on the commanding rock. Under its protection two royal courts developed, which served as bases for the provision of reserves for service in the campaigns in the East. Around one of the courts, in the 11th and 12th centuries, a settlement of administrative officers was established, and it was they who built the first parish church, St. Sebaldus. Around the other was an early settlement of merchants and craftsmen, who chose St. Laurence as the patron saint of their church. As late as the 14th century, the Lorenz district referred to itself as *civitas,* whereas the Sebaldus district under the castle called itself *oppidum.* Each had an aristocratic monastery: St. Aegidius in the Sebaldus settlement; and to the northeast, close to the Lorenz settlement, St. Jacobus, which Henry

Figure 61. Nuremberg, city plan of 1793: 1, St. Lorenz; 2, St. Sebaldus; 3, castle; 4, church of Our Lady; 5, great marketplace; 6, St. Aegidius; 7, St. James.

- - - - - circumvallation of St. Lorenz
-----·--·-- circumvallation of St. Sebaldus
———— completion of wall in 1452

Figure 62. Nuremberg, ca. 1520 (colored drawing by Hans Wurm)

VI gave to the Teutonic Order in 1209 and which remained there until 1803—from the 16th century onward, the only Catholic enclave in the Lutheran city. In the lowlands between the two courts, the Pegnitz flowed through a wide marshy tract.

The townspeople, who gradually gained in strength from the 12th century onward, faced two specific tasks from the outset, which were of equal importance for politics and for urban planning. They had to take possession of the imperial castle and they had to unite the two districts divided by the river. They worked assiduously at both of these tasks for about two centuries.

It is astonishing to glance at old silhouettes of the city and realize that a free city could develop in the shadow of a castle 200 meters long and strongly fortified (fig. 62). When looking at these silhouettes, of course, we have to distinguish between the imperial or emperor's castle to the west and the burgrave's possessions to the east. The imperial castle with its Salic beginnings, its Hohenstaufen main structure, the two-story addition made by Frederick III, and the further extensions of 1487 and 1559 was faithfully preserved by the citizens. The burgrave's building, which the Hohenzollerns received as a fief in 1291, was actually the seat of the enemy. In 1377 the citizens built themselves the watchtower, a very high tower from which to observe this enemy. From the end of the 14th century, the council succeeded in limiting the power of the burgraves. During a siege by the duke of Bavaria, the castle collapsed. A little later, the citizens were able to buy the ruin for 125,000 guilders from its owner who became at that time margrave of Brandenburg. Nevertheless, the Hohenzollerns remained the archenemy of the city, which they kept hemmed in ever more tightly by their newly acquired possessions, Ansbach and Bayreuth.

The second task was accomplished in two separate actions. It must be assumed that both the Sebaldus district and the Lorenz district were lightly fortified. At the beginning of the 14th century, these fortifications were reinforced on the outside and linked across the Pegnitz near the island of Schütt and at the Henkersteg. Thus was founded a burgher city with two parish churches. The former fortification can still be made out on the 1793 plan (fig. 61). Even when the city area was enlarged to almost twice its size with a third ring of walls, the number of parishes was not increased. While the city of Cologne had nineteen parishes and the older maritime city of Lübeck four, two was a lot for one of the newer imperial cities. The wall took more than a century to build (1346–1452) and was secured by about a hundred towers, each within arrowshot of the other. There were only five openings in the wall, all with fortified gates. The most important of these, facing south toward Regensburg, was strengthened in the 16th century by great bastions. Italian fortification architects had recommended the addition of four powerful round towers, and these were built between 1556 and 1565. Cannons could be placed upon their platforms. The political independence of the city was demonstrated not only by the incorporation of the castle into the city's system of fortifications but by the unification of the parish areas. This unification only became effective, however, when the great marketplace was built. There, in the lowlands of the Pegnitz, lay the ghetto, which was destroyed in 1349 by agreement with Charles IV, who simultaneously endowed a lady chapel. The chapel was placed under the rule of the Augustinians of Prague and served similar functions to the palatinate chapel in Aachen. We know that the young Peter Parler was in charge of its construction. When the marketplace and the lady chapel were built, the twin cities finally acquired a center.

In this pogrom, in which the patriciate directed the energies of the rebellious craftsmen, about 562 of the approximately 1,500 Jewish inhabitants were massacred. But here, as was the case at the same time in Würzburg and in 1520 in Regensburg, the city failed to make a monumental edifice out of the market. It remained an open space in which the lady chapel and the Schöne Brunnen were the only accents. No one of any consequence built dwellings in the streets that bordered it (fig. 63).

Figure 63. The Nuremberg marketplace, 1599, with lady chapel, the Golden Fountain, and, in the background, the choir of St. Sebaldus

The unification of the two parts of the city presented the citizens with a third architectural project—the development of the banks of the Pegnitz and its numerous bridges. The river was still navigable. Special fortified gates ensured entry and exit. Mills, rows of houses, and bridges linked the two parts of the city. Large buildings like the hospital, which had been endowed by Konrad Groß, both the city's wealthiest inhabitant and its mayor, graced the river banks.

The history of Nuremberg's growth is reflected not only by the city walls but also by the addition of monasteries, the extension of the two parish churches, and a succession of three city halls. Fierce competition between the two parish churches was reflected in their furnishings from the 13th century to the Reformation. St. Sebaldus was begun in the 13th century and dedicated in 1274, but as early as 1361–79 the former Gothic choir at the east end of the nave was replaced by the lofty choir that still stands today, which soars 12 meters over the nave. St. Lorenz, which probably stood on the site of a former building, began the rebuilding of its nave at the end of the 13th century and finished its facade with the magnificent rose window toward the middle of the 14th. But here, too, a much larger choir had to replace its predecessor on the east side of the church. The way these two city churches balance one another is one of the features of Nuremberg (fig. 64). The way they interact across the Pegnitz and the market has always attracted admiration and was quite consciously striven for.

The purely patrician government was actively concerned with creating a cultivated urban existence. Precise, strict building ordinances saw to it that the building line was preserved in the rows of houses, ensured consistency in the building of facades, with precisely delimited ornamentation, and determined the number of Nuremberg oriel and bay windows that were to be permitted. In no other imperial city do we find such precise ordinances before the 18th century.[11] One effect of the ordinances was that the whole wealth of the great families had to be displayed in the inner courtyards and rooms. Another was that citizens attempted, within the limits of what was permitted, to decorate their houses with madonnas, house signs, murals, and at the same time to enrich all the churches with enormous endowments. Nuremberg in 1520 was a treasure house of art, and later that combination of artistic decoration and precision was developed even more highly in the making of watches, measuring instruments, and weapons.

In contrast to the ancient, holy cities, whose skyline—as the circumscription of a woodcut of Cologne done in the 15th century empha-

Figure 64. Nuremberg: St. Lawrence and St. Sebaldus

sizes—was colored by the blood of martyrs, Nuremberg's self-image suffered from the want of a sacral tradition of its own. The bones of St. Laurence were shared with many other cities. Recognition of the legendary figure of St. Sebaldus was not obtained from Rome until 1414 and then only with great difficulty and solely for the urban area of Nuremberg. The imperial insignia, with the blessed lance, whose procession became one of the two city festivals, offered some compensation. This paucity of symbols of its own greatness led the city, on the eve of the Reformation, to endow the church of St. Sebaldus with the most magnificent shrine and canopy boasted by any saint in Germany. It was the work of Peter Vischer and his workshop. Lacking urban semantics in the realm of the sacred, Nuremberg emphasized its position as the heart and center of the empire in diverse works of art. The Schöne Brunnen in the marketplace is a memorial to this attitude. Interlinked and superimposed on the fountain are the seven electors, the nine good heroes, and seven prophets with Moses. On the gables of the Church of the Virgin a clock was erected on which, when the hour strikes, the electors circle around the emperor.

The city was already in decline when, in 1616, it decided to erect a new city hall next to the old one, designed by Jakob Wolff, father and son, and so large that the four wings could not be completed (fig. 64). Buildings were to show the power the city no longer possessed.

Nuremberg's decline was accelerated by the extinction of the patrician families, who now in increasing numbers, were retiring into the countryside. The fourteen that remained in the city no longer wanted to carry on trade with "scale, rule, and measure" but rather to live on the proceeds of their estates and their land. "Combining domestic and botanical with artistic points of view, the famous Gardens of the Hesperides sought to force something of the magnificence of princely residences on to the Pegnitz" (M. Häussler). The lower-class citizens were burdened with taxes six times greater than those paid by their competitors in Frankfurt. The decay was unparalleled until it was transformed by the romanticism which surrounded the mastersingers and the German National Museum.

Ulm and the Small Swabian Imperial Cities

It was in Swabia that the Hohenstaufens had their earliest possessions, and here that the greatest number of small imperial cities came into being after the house was extinct. Even today the cultural physiognomy of this extensive countryside is marked—far into the Franconian countryside on the one hand and the Bavarian on the other—by the late Gothic imperial cities and by the high and late Baroque imperial monasteries. Ulm and Ottobeuren, Ravensburg and Weingarten mark two cultural epochs.

From the point of view of urban planning, these imperial cities had only two tasks: to build their fortifications with towers, citadels, moats, and walls and to build their city church. For all other urban accoutrements—market hall, city hall, market, octroi, fountain, cloth hall and all the rest—were kept within a modest framework according to the circumstances of the particular city. The 13th and 14th century settlements of the "popular orders" were often a major element. In many cities there were also older ecclesiastical and royal institutions, whose buildings had to be integrated.

Every city faced the task, as important as it was architecturally challenging, defining its shape by walls and achieving distinctness by its towers and gates. The history of these architectural undertakings is, however, completely local in character, even in places like Rothenburg ob der Tauber where the topography demanded unusual solutions. All the cities built on flat ground were circular, like Nördlingen or Ulm, even Colmar in Alsace (fig. 54), for this was regarded as the best shape for defense. It provided for the shortest routes from the center of the town to its periphery.

Much greater individuality was shown in the construction of city churches. These were often larger than would be expected in relation to the size of the city—again we may think of Ulm, Nördlingen, Dinkelsbühl, and Reutlingen—and had their own semiotic system. They were symbols of divine protection, of political and economic power, of the freedom of the municipalities. They were forms of self-representation. In the hundred or more years while the city churches were being built, rebuilt, and expanded, the building process must have been a major event, if not the most important thing going on, for the townspeople. Not only did a great number of architects, known to us by name, identify their whole lives with the one building, but the townspeople themselves would scarcely have provided such extensive funds if the building of the church had not become an existential necessity of life for them. The freedom of the city depended on the very independence of the city churches from older authorities. I offer three examples.

Esslingen

Esslingen, which in the decades before and after 1400 was the wealthiest of the smaller imperial cities, owed its prosperity to its location on the route from Ulm to Speyer. The Neckar was forded here, and then, after 1225, crossed by a stone bridge.[12] A church in Esslingen, dating from 746, was later dedicated to St. Dionysius (fig. 65, 1) and managed to acquire a large monastic possession. The burgher settlement developed under the protection of this monastery (fig. 65). The favored sites between the rows of houses on the main streets and squares were later acquired by the preaching and mendicant orders, the very best site being the oldest Dominican settlement, St. Paul (2).

Figure 65. Esslingen at the close of the Middle Ages: 1, the collegiate church of St. Dionysius; 2, Dominican convent; 3, Franciscan convent; 4, city chapel of Our Lady.

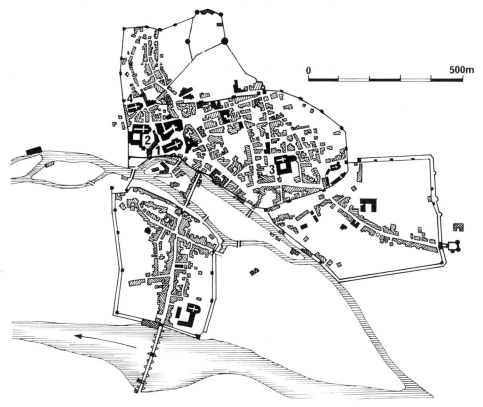

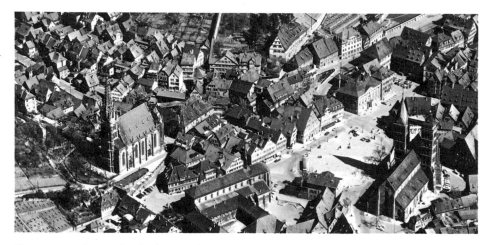

Figure 66. Esslingen: church of Our Lady, St. Paul, and St. Dionysius

When the monastery of St. Dionysius was ceded in the 12th century, the Hohenstaufens, as new lords of the city, gave the rights of patronage to the cathedral chapter in Speyer, and these new clerical lords lost no time in renovating the churches with the aid of large endowments (1). But the townspeople, who were growing stronger, were unwilling to recognize as their city church the church that had passed into the hands of strangers. One of the most remarkable city council resolutions arose from this discontent. In 1321 it was decided to build a church to the Virgin at the extreme edge of the city, on the one piece of ground still available for this purpose, even though sloping (4). The nave, which had only five cross beams, took almost a century to build, partly because of the difficulty of the site. Although the iconoclasts destroyed the ornamentation, the three glass windows of the choir still show that the city obtained the services of leading architects. This is even more true of the one west tower, which took the city another century to build; it was designed by the leading architect of the late Gothic period, Ulrich von Ensingen (d. 1419), and completed by other members of the Ensingen family and, later, Böblinger from Ulm, by 1516. It has long been considered one of the greatest works of the late Gothic period (fig. 66). It was historical pressure that made the citizens build their own church to the Virgin close by the old, but now alien, city church of St. Dionysius.

Reutlingen

The citizens of Reutlingen found themselves in a comparable situation. The city had acquired its wealth by introducing special processes for the finishing of textiles. Earlier times had bequeathed it a parish church, SS. Peter and Paul, which lay far outside the city walls and belonged at first to the monastery of Hirsau and then, from 1308 onward, to the monastery of Königsbronn, which administered it—after a fashion—by a vicar. It was a good living, for whenever there was a baptism, a marriage, or a funeral the citizens had to go out of the city to the church. During a siege which cut them off from all pastoral cure, the citizens swore that they would build their own church to the Virgin in the middle of the town. This famous building, erected between 1247 and 1343 (fig. 67) was only a chapel until the Reformation. The citizens endowed it with fourteen altars at which fourteen chaplains, mostly the sons of citizens, received a living, their only obligation being to read one mass a day. The remarkable quality of the building alone tells us how much it meant to the citizens of Reutlingen.[13] Its tower and its lofty nave became its own symbols. Circumstances favored the early victory of the Reformation, and by this means the city chapel rose in rank to be the city church, while the old parish churches outside the city gates ceased to have any importance.

In Nördlingen, Dinkelsbühl, and Rottweil, similar bases existed for equally large, or even larger, architectural undertakings. It was because of the legal situation of Rottweil's two parish churches, even though both

Figure 67. Reutlingen: church (chapel) of Our Lady, and marketplace

were within the city walls, that Rottweil built its own chapel with its famous tower. The fact that the two parish churches were within the city itself played a role in Rottweil's remaining Catholic.

Rothenburg

Even Rothenburg had its difficulties and was forced to reach a compromise. The name tells us that the market settlement was preceded by a castle, and the city plan shows the one place where it could have been located (fig. 68). The town was founded by the Hohenstaufens for the protection of their Franconian possessions. We also know that an older, 13th century town was surrounded by an extensive new town in the 14th century. While the steep slopes and the river afforded protection, on the western side, unusually strong fortified gates had to be built to protect the arterial roads that led to the east, the south, and the north. The spit of land toward the south, which was closed off by an inner gate, served primarily to protect the almshouses (6). One is struck by the fact that the few ecclesiastical buildings—the city church of St. James (2), the Franciscan church (3), and the Dominican complex (4)—were close together in the old city. Also in the center of the town

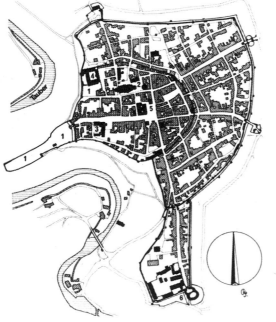

Figure 68. Rothenburg ob der Tauber: 1, castle hill; 2, city church of St. James; 3, Franciscans; 4, Dominicans; 5, town hall; 6, almshouses.

was the town hall, which was expanded and renovated several times. The town prospered only for about two centuries.

Yet Rothenburg had to come to terms with the fact that, in its main church, it was the guest of the Teutonic Order. The plan of St. James takes account of this restriction. The long west choir was reserved for the exclusive use of the Teutonic Order. The townspeople gathered in the nave of the basilica, which was added later. The reliquary of the town, the Holy Blood, for which Tilman Riemenschneider built his famous altar of the Last Supper, was therefore housed in a special double chapel on the east side of the church.

Ulm

Ulm affords the most important example of the connection between politics and church building.[14] The town grew up next door to a Frankish royal court. The settlement received city rights in 1164. In 1274 it was granted an imperial charter. In 1316, building started on the new wall, which embraced almost four times the area of the old city. The wall was finished about 1335 and, in the 15th century, was reinforced by a second wall six meters in front of the old one. The Danube allowed the city to strengthen its fortifications in 1616–23 with almost unassailable ramparts and bastions.

Ulm, too, first had a parish church outside the city walls, whose rights of patronage the emperors had transferred to the monastery of Reichenau. The War of the League of Swabian Cities against Charles IV had forced the citizens not only to give up this parish church but also to tear it down. It was difficult enough to get permission from the abbot of Reichenau to build a new church within the walls; but the negotiations over the severance of the church's dependence upon Reichenau took fifty years and were only brought to a conclusion in 1446 thanks to the intervention of Frederick II and in exchange for a sum of 25,000 guilders.

The new building, from the moment the foundation stone was laid in 1377, was regarded as the city's most intimate concern. This city church, upon which neither a chapter nor a bishop could bestow the means their position of power afforded them, grew into a cathedral according to quite different laws. Decisions were made by the city council, the citizenry bore the whole cost of the building, and many of the great families endowed columns for themselves in the building. The construction of the church symbolized the citizens' own independence. From the beginning, for example, the building was intended to be 124 meters long—its present

Figure 69. The Ulm minster

length—and 49.5 meters wide. For a whole century, those responsible for the undertaking sought the services of the best architect working at any given moment in the imperial cities. First there were two members of the Parler family, and then, in 1391, came the genius of the age, Ulrich von Ensingen, whose plan for the spire, with a projected height of 155 meters, promised the citizens the highest tower to be built in the Middle Ages. Von Ensingen's work was destined, however, to be carried out by his son-in-law, his son, and his grandson, albeit with some changes of plan. Mathias Böblinger from Esslingen and, finally, Burkhard Engelhardt from Augsburg took up the work at the end of the 15th century. Yet the spire still remained a torso and was not completed until the 19th century (fig. 69).

Every church interprets itself through its furnishings. Fortunately for Ulm, Hans Multscher (ca. 1400–67), a master and among the greatest geniuses of the late Middle Ages, became a citizen of Ulm in 1427. He founded a workshop tradition which assured Ulm's supremacy in Swabia in the realm of sculpture until about 1500. Although the greater part of the furnishings of the church in Ulm were destroyed on the "Day of the Idols" in 1531, the most important work—the choir stalls—was preserved. Jörg Syrlin and his workshops, especially the wood carver Michael Erhard, built the stalls between 1469 and 1474. The plan provided for ten sibyls and eight sages from antiquity at the foot, men on the left and women on the right. On the rear wall, about halfway up, the prophets and prophetesses of the Old Testament were depicted, and at the highest point the apostles and martyrs. Wilhelm Vöge devoted the whole of his last book to this unique plan.[15] He believed he had discovered, in many of the busts, portraits of some of Ulm's leading citizens. But how does a set of choir stalls with eighty-nine places fit into a church with only one parish priest, two vicars, and an unspecified number of chaplains? The idea was to unite all the clergy in the city into a community of worship and, furthermore, to give the minster the appearance and rank of a cathedral. The importance of the city as the center of religious life was to be made evident. The minster proclaimed the highest aspirations of the time, as did, among other things, the choir stalls within it.

The relocation of trade routes cut short the city's heyday. The Reformation stifled the desire to build. Merian's view of 1643 (fig. 70) shows how

Figure 70. Ulm during the Thirty Years' War (after Merian, 1643)

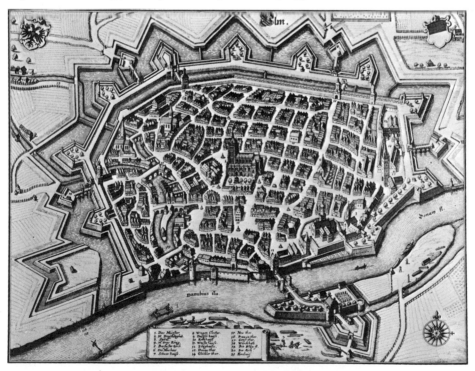

the fortifications of the 16th and 17th centuries must have exhausted the economic power of the city and its territory. With the city thus fettered, no further plans could be developed. Every effort was concentrated on the mere prolongation of existence.

Imperial Residence and Imperial City

In many later imperial cities, emperors had an imperial residential complex, if only a royal palace as in Ulm or a castle as in Nuremberg. In other, smaller imperial cities the residence and the city had grown up in a reciprocal relationship. Gelnhausen, which was soon mortgaged as an imperial city and was no longer able to redeem itself, is a well-studied example. Yet the combination of castle and market to which so many medieval cities owe their beginnings is not something to be discussed here. There is a small group of cities, in which a palace complex—preserved as a monumental set of buildings—was incorporated into a later city. Aachen, Goslar, and Frankfurt each show a different solution to this problem. In Aachen, the city grew up around the palace complex (fig. 71), in Goslar side by side with it (fig. 73), and in Frankfurt above it (fig. 74).

Figure 71. Aachen, with Charlemagne's palace (after L. Hugot)

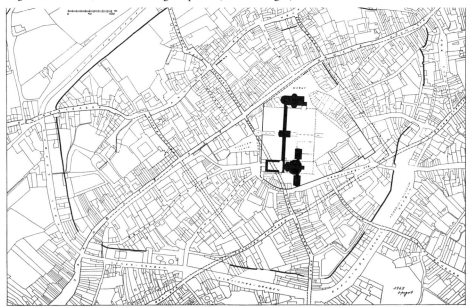

Aachen

Charlemagne's monumental palace complex was preserved practically undamaged for the Middle Ages.[16] When Charlemagne built his powerful defensive center with its palatinate chapel, its Aula Regia, and the passage that connected it to the lawcourt, he did not concern himself in the least with the street plan of the former Roman spa—a recreational center for the legions stationed along the Rhine. In front of the palace lay an older district, which the complex had already begun to surround in Carolingian times. It had only rudimentary fortifications. The craftsmen's and merchants' district, throughout all the centuries of its growth, kept to the Roman roads, which were more suitable sites. It was only after Barbarossa had bestowed the freedom of the city upon the townspeople that they built their first wall, between 1171 and 1179, and their second, between 1257 and 1357. Similar dates may be noted all over Europe.

The palatinate chapel became a provosts's church in the 11th century. The citizens had to build their own parish churches. Two monasteries were added by Otto III, but the chapel remains an independent organism. The Gothic period added the lofty choir to Charlemagne's massive octagon, as well as a number of other chapels; the baroque period added the last chapel. The church, along with the atrium in front and a cloister beside it, formed the ecclesiastical domain.

The citizens built themselves their new city hall somewhere between 1330 and 1350, on the foundations of the Aula Regia and the buildings Barbarossa had added. It was a free imperial city council that built the great arched hall in which future emperors were to hold their coronation banquet. The facade of the new city hall was turned away from the south side, with its view of the minster, toward the north side, with its view of the marketplace. Thus, the city hall, in which the council ruled under the burgomaster, and the minster with its canons and their provost, were two organisms that turned their backs on one another. But the burgher city surrounded them both in concentric circles within which no building was ever built that could compete in the city silhouette with either of these centers of municipal and ecclesiastical life. Both units preserved with care, and not without self-confidence, the heritage of a great past.

Goslar

In Goslar things were quite different. Silver had been discovered under the primeval forests in the mountains. In the valley below, Henry II started to

Figure 72. Goslar: Henry III's imperial palace and the convent of SS. Simon and Jude

build a monumental residential complex, which Henry III reconstructed on a much larger scale, and which Barbarossa restored. This complex was surrounded by woods (fig. 72). The great convent of SS. Simon and Jude, with its church, was built opposite the palace complex.[17]

The emperors were primarily concerned with developing the forest land in the Harz by founding ecclesiastical institutions. A village grew up on top of the Rammelsberg in which silver was mined. On the other bank of the Gose, opposite the palace complex, a small market settlement, complete with church, was established at the junction of the road from Halberstadt to Osterode to the Hellweg and to Hildesheim. By 1108 this market town already possessed five parish churches. By the end of the 12th century, the city wall was completed. It also enclosed the palace complex, but the palace lands remained undeveloped (fig. 73). The convent continued in existence; the palace complex was abandoned. The town occupied no more than 75 hectares until the end of the empire. Although we cannot here pursue the many-layered history of Goslar's church construction, we should note that parish churches of this size could not have been built as early in any other imperial city. The far larger parish churches of Nuremberg, Ulm, and other Southern German imperial cities are works of the late Gothic period. Social unrest, fed by political, economic, and religious factors, destroyed most of the church buildings in 1527—or, at least, emptied them.[18]

Between the 11th and the 15th centuries, the burgher city participated in the wealth generated by the mining of silver. It was the first German city to build a city hall on its marketplace. Monuments to this economic heyday of the burghers were well-groomed streets, magnificent guildhalls, large hospital buildings, and well-appointed parish churches. The citizens' houses prove that even a failing economy did not prevent the urban residential nature of the town from being kept in good order. The modern half-

Figure 73. Goslar in the High Middle Ages: 1, imperial palace; 2, convent of SS. Simon and Jude; 3, village on the hill; 4, convent of St. George; 5, market church; 6, city hall; 7, church of St. James; 8, church of St. Stephen; 9, Frankenberg church; 10, Klaus gate; 11, Vitus gate; 12, Rosen gate; 13, "broad gate."

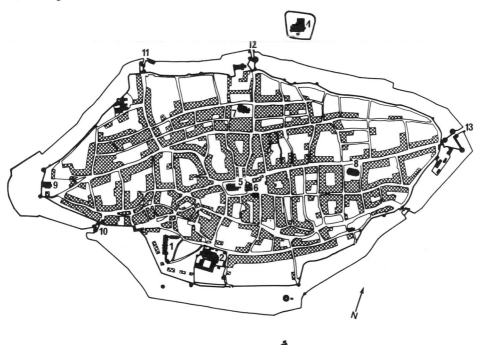

timbered buildings date only from the 16th and 17th centuries, but their appearance accords with the 12th–16th century plans. It was the only when the 19th and 20th centuries became concerned with the preservation of historic monuments that an attempt was made to give the palace complex a new role as a "historical document."

Frankfurt

The name "Franks' Ford" itself contains a piece of the history of this widely famed "free Imperial, Electoral, and Trading City," as Achilles August Lersner wrote in his chronicle of 1706. The Franks who drove the Alemanni out of the Main valley in 496 discovered the ford. Charlemagne's domain was expanded into a residential complex, first by Ludwig the Pious in 822 and then, more splendidly, by Ludwig the German in 850. The proximity of Mainz prevented the establishment of an episcopal see at this time. The site was therefore unable to acquire any importance for almost three centuries—the period of the bishops—and fell into decay, with the burgher settlement remaining insignificant. But the location of the city was bound, sooner or later, to become historically significant again.

Thus it happened that, in 1147, Henry V chose Frankfurt as the place where his son, Konrad III, was to be elected. When Barbarossa also was elected there, in 1152, a tradition had started which could be maintained.[19] Charles IV's Golden Bull elevated the tradition to law in 1356. From 1562 onward, Frankfurt replaced Aachen as the site of the imperial coronation. The monastery of St. Bartholomew was built over the palatinate chapel in the 13th century. It was not until 1405 that the city bought two houses, the Haus zum Römer and Zum goldenen Schwan, in order to use their upper stories as a city hall and as a ceremonial hall for the coronation and their ground floors for fair booths. By 1789, three more houses had been acquired. That was all the city was willing to provide for the greatest ceremony of the empire. Right down to the 18th century, when the inner rooms had been decorated in the baroque style, the emperors, on this festive day, abandoned the castles to which they were accustomed—Nymphenburg outside Munich, and Schönbrunn outside Vienna—in favor of plain burgher rooms.

From 1219 on, Frankfurt was ruled by a royal mayor. After the collapse of the Hohenstaufen regime he was assisted by a council of citizens. In 1327, patricians also became eligible for the office of mayor. From the late 14th

Figure 74. Frankfurt (after Merian, 1628, detail)

century onward, fairs were held in Frankfurt. In the 18th century, Frankfurt—after Hamburg and Leipzig—was the third wealthiest city in the empire, if we exclude Berlin and Vienna, where other standards apply. Merian's
second view of the city, done in 1628, reveals the history of its growth (fig.
74). In the foreground, on this side of the Main, is Sachsenhausen, which
is strongly fortified and is assumed to have derived its name from a colony
of Saxons forced to settle there by Charlemagne. There was a bridge here
as early as 1220. The towers of the settlement date from the heyday of the
city in the 15th century. The lens-shaped inner wall (of which sections are
still recognizable in the eastern part of the city), the sweep of the broad
streets, and the horse market date from the early 13th century. The final
circumvallation, which increased the size of the town threefold, was begun
in 1343. In 1628, Merian already shows baroque bastions around the city,
which had been reinforcing its walls since 1625. The city still looked this way
in Goethe's time. Only a few patricians had modernized the facades of their
houses in the 17th and 18th centuries, and only a few elaborate palaces had
been built. Good parts of them were still preserved until 1944.

Barbarossa had his palace in the Saalhof. Frederick II allowed the citizens to build their own parish church of St. Leonard in 1219 and gave them the site. The market church of St. Nicolai was also an imperial donation. This church was begun in 1240 or thereabouts. In 1219, the knights of the Teutonic Order settled in Sachsenhausen. In 1228, the "Order of the Penitents" founded a convent; in 1230 the Franciscans arrived, in 1236 the Antonites, in 1238 the Dominicans, in 1246 the Carmelites, and, finally, in 1259 the Knights of St. John. Their magnificent buildings can be distinguished in Merian's view of the city. Significantly, the parish church of St. Leonard, the one ecclesiastical building in the city which is still Romanesque, was situated on the Main harbor, while the mendicants settled either at or in front of the first wall. Only the Franciscans found a site in the center of the town. This "dark prison" (as Goethe described it) was torn down to make room for the Paulskirche. In 1316, the citizens managed to persuade the canons of St. Bartholomew's to make their church available as a parish church as well. This is how the imperial city acquired a city church. Frankfurt's claim to power was expressed in the west tower, begun by Madern Gertner in 1415 as a symbol of the city. Franz von Ingelheim continued work on it, but it was not completed until the 19th century.

The style of living in the comfortable houses of Frankfurt described by Goethe must already have reached a high standard in the 14th century. The prosperity of the city, with its fair and the wealth of its patricians, is reflected in the guild halls, the patrician houses, the cloth hall of 1399, the Stone House of 1464, and, even more magnificently, the Braunfels, built about 1350 by the richest resident of the city, Brune zur Weinrebe, and later inhabited by numerous princes, among them Gustavus Adolphus, until it finally became the largest of the halls to house the fair.[20] Several aristocratic families from outside Frankfurt also built houses in the city, first among them—at the behest of the emperor but entirely against the city council's will—the Thurn und Taxis. This family's palace, built according to the plans of Robert de Cotte by Hauberat, court architect of Bonn and Mannheim, is at one and the same time an architectural jewel and an alien element in the city.

Up to the end of the empire, basically until 1944, the old city of Frankfurt remained a Gothic city. Its symbol was its church tower and a series of burgher dwellings that served both as city hall and as ceremonial chambers for the imperial coronations. The greatness of this free imperial city lay in the fact that it could preserve its burgher style. People believed they could afford to invite the emperor to a banquet in a plain room. There were Gothic rooms, Renaissance rooms, baroque rooms, and classical rooms. The fifteen-year-old Goethe saw Joseph II and his consort at the banquet in 1764 in an irregular-shaped, ancient vaulted room on the top floor of the Römer. As long as the greatest secular power in Christendom could be invited to a banquet in burgher surroundings like this, so long did the Middle Ages last.

Chapter 5

*I*N ALMOST EVERY CENTURY and in most European nations, a surprising number of cities have survived that were originally planned to fulfill a specific political, military, economic, or even pedagogic function but lost their raison d'être as soon as there was no longer any need for that function. They were not planned with an eye to continuous development. Historical progress was not taken into account. Planning had to be completed before construction began. Thus they atrophied, decayed, or simply went to seed if the ensuing centuries did not give them another task to perform. Many had already lost their purpose even before completion.

I shall return to this problematic in my final chapter, "The Unplannable." Whatever is planned and designed at a certain point in time bears the essential characteristics of that time and at the same time loses its topicality. Every ideal city is the product of its moment and cannot develop with the changing course of history.

All these cities were designed from without by a superior power rather than developing from within. Their form was superimposed upon them. As I have stressed, to distinguish between the city that has grown and "become," on the one hand, and the city as founded and planned, on the other, hardly does justice to historical reality (see Introduction). Yet cities that have been conceived ex-

IDEAL CITIES

trinsically, that have been ordained, are less able to survive than those that have developed from within. It is true that many consciously planned foundings have grown into masterpieces of urban design. Bern and Lübeck are examples (see chaps. 2 and 3). However, in these cases it was only the impulse that came from the outside. Princes, as planners of the land, endowed craftsmen and merchants with settlements favored by the security of their location and the ease of communication. All later building was left to the citizens. Reason and foresight had determined the sites, economic successes promoted growth, and political self-consciousness added monumental accents to the urban complex. Many Greek colonial cities around the Mediterranean and, later, member cities of the Hanseatic League around the Baltic developed in this way. The purpose for which they were built proclaimed itself in the course of history. A process of enrichment bore testimony to the soundness of the initial conception.

No ideal city had comparable success. Pienza is the best-known example among those which were at least started (fig. 75). The fine city square with its cathedral, bishop's palace, city hall, and papal palace was still incomplete when Pope Pius II, who had commissioned it, died in 1463. Even a pope could not ensure the continued existence of his birthplace. Building went on, but the square never took on a life of its own. Art historians have pointed to it as the cradle of Renaissance urban design. It does provide a landmark in architectural history. In a history of cities it would have to count as an investment that failed—a square in the middle of a village, so laid out that the most magnificent panorama opens up to it, from the very beginning an object designed to be preserved.

The term "superimposed form"—a concept invented by Wilhelm Pinder for other purposes—can be illustrated by plans of mannerist cities. Freudenstadt in the Black Forest is an example. Heinrich Schickard was commissioned by Duke Friedrich of Württemberg to build a city in the shape of the board game of *Mühle* for the miners in the Christophtal silver mine. The commission grew out of an idea that occurred to the prince while he was playing the game and can scarcely have been intended any more seriously or profoundly than that. The board on which this game is played served as the plan of the city; the parish church and the city hall—contrary to all tradition—had to be placed at the opposite corners of a square site. A castle, which was never begun, was to be built in the empty space at the center of the board. The miners' houses framed the course of the game. They were inhabited only as long as the mines remained productive. The second heyday of the town, as a spa in the 20th century, was predicated upon the organic extension of the board into the hills and valleys outside the town. The original manneristic plan became the kernel of the city, which is now surrounded by formless new construction. As an architectural event, this city has never been more than a curiosity, and such beautifi-

Figure 75. Pienza: Piazza Piccolomini

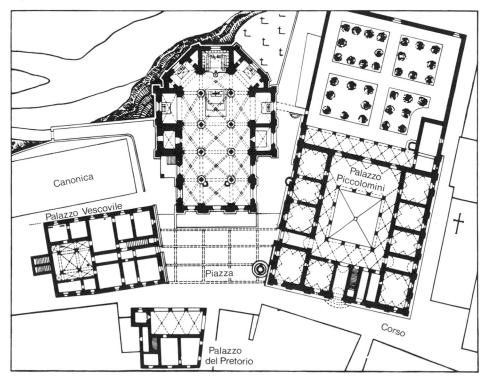

cation as has been achieved is owed entirely to the hills of the Black Forest.

Research into urban design has paid increased attention to the human game of "ideal city"—a game played by philosophers from Plato to Thomas More to Ebenezer Howard,[1] by architectural rhetoricians and builders from Filarete and Alberti to LeCorbusier, and by princes and pedagogues from the 15th century onward. Anyone could join in the game, leaving things to be completed later. The many works on urban planning in the Renaissance and the baroque period also belong to this realm, as does the modern interest in the canons of revolutionary architecture.[2] Insofar as these plans are also intended to serve a pedagogical end—the creation of the ideal state—we can speak of urban utopias. Thomas More, in 1516, used "Utopia" as the title for his book, which first appeared in Leyden. He describes a state with fifty-four cities, all built according to an identical plan, whose inhabitants were all to be educated as true Christians with a prescribed order of living. These projects had nothing to do with historical reality. We are dealing here with one of those humanist, Platonic conversational themes by means of which people distanced themselves from contemporary problems so as to be able to establish irrevocable laws. In the nature of things, there were remarkable intermediate stages along the road leading from the founding of cities, which could be realized, to ideal cities and architectural utopias, which could not.

Aigues-Mortes and Richelieu

A characteristic example of a city that was built for a temporary purpose and later fell into decay is Aigues-Mortes (fig. 76). King Louis the Holy (1226–72) began negotiations in 1240 to acquire a site with a canal and a harbor on which he could build a fortified city for mustering his armies and dispatching them to the Crusades. As is well known, an initial expedition in 1248 failed, as did the more ambitious one in 1270. The king died before the fortifications were even begun. His successor, Philip the Brave (from 1272 on), and Philip the Fair (after 1289) took up the idea. The latter finally succeeded in completing the square wall with its five gates and four towers, one at each corner, with a whole series of towers as reinforcement. In the interior, the street grid was filled up with dwelling houses. There was a market and a church. Aside from agriculture, however, it was only construction that sustained the town. The moment the royal subventions ceased to be paid, the community was bound to decay. The original reason for the founding of the town, the Crusades, no longer existed.

Figure 76. Aigues-Mortes

We now move ahead several centuries, but we remain in France. The town of Richelieu is constantly put forward as a masterpiece of urban planning, a forerunner of Versailles.[3] In a history of urban studies considered as political science, Richelieu would have to be cited as a planning failure. Its builder did not reckon with the transcendental nature of the power constellation he had built up, and even less with conditions after his death.

At the height of his success he was forced to recollect the trauma of his youth, which was spent in the direst oppression and danger at his family's ancestral castle halfway between Tours and Poitiers—not far from the site of the present-day town of Richelieu. As Louis XIII's chief minister, he was able to recover the property in 1621 and to add to it by further purchases. Ten years later, the properties were combined to create a dukedom. At that time, in 1631, his architect, Jacques le Mercier, drew up plans for a large modern castle, an extensive park, and, in the righthand corner, the town. The whole thing was a complex of about 500 by 700 meters, with a regular network of streets, precisely delimited by a wall. An academy was founded and a church built, provision was made for a handsome town square, and the officials of the small court were given modest city palaces. Dwellings were built according to a uniform plan—those on the main streets that led from one gate to another were to have a second story as well as an attic; those on the side-streets were to have an attic only. The whole project was able to be completed by 1642, the year of Richelieu's death, and remained famous. La Fontaine called it the most beautiful village in the world, remarking that its one fault was a lack of inhabitants. The court had been dissolved on the death of the cardinal, as the family lacked the means to keep the complex going. The castle was torn down during the French Revolution. The statesman who had secured France's whole future could not resist the charms of playing with a plan, which, once developed, was already a failure. The works of art that had been collected in the castle went with the people, among them Michelangelo's *Slaves,* now in the Louvre.

Terre Murate or Bastides

The high and the late Middle Ages built cities all over Europe according to regular models, which either served to defend the land owned by a city-state or a princedom, or were intended to bring in revenues from taxation. Tuscan documents of the 14th century speak of *terre murate*.[4]

The city-states of Florence, Siena, Pisa, Lucca, and Arezzo both founded and completed small towns of this kind. Monteriggioni on the borders of Siena's possessions became the most famous, for the simple reason that Dante compared its towers to the giants that loom up above the circle of a central pit in hell. The town was soon depopulated. The characteristic of these places is their regular ground plan. Most of them were built according to a uniform plan with funds from the mother city. Their own resources were never sufficient to permit an extension of their limits, however favorable individual economic circumstances might turn out to be. San Giovanni Val d'Arno, the plan of which is ascribed to Arnolfo di Cambio, and La Scarperia are among the most perfectly executed (figs. 77 and 78). In both, the palace of the podestà, who was appointed by the mother city, gives us a hint as to the circumstances in which the government found itself. The Palazzo Vecchio was imitated, but on a smaller scale. Here, as in many comparable examples, the cities were to help break the power of the barons who ruled the country—the Pazzi (among others) in San Giovanni, and primarily the Ubaldini in La Scarperia. This aim was accomplished even before the walls were finished. Later, there was no incentive to change the monumental plan of the piazza in the town center. The area already settled,

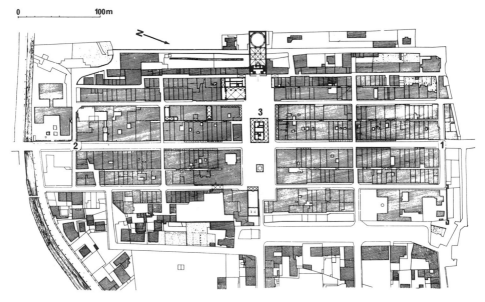

Figure 77. San Giovanni Val d'Arno, as it stands today after the removal of the walls

Figure 78. La Scarperia, as it stands today

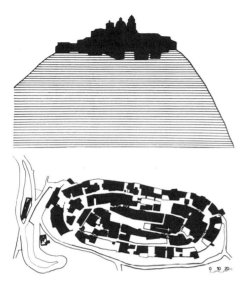

Figure 79. Nicola (after Pierotti)

surrounded by the walls, could not be filled until the Habsburg's agrarian reforms in the 18th and 19th centuries, and the town could not be extended until the Industrial Revolution. Before the Industrial Revolution the citizens never had an opportunity to exercise personal initiative. If we disregard the pillage and destruction that later wars visited on cities like this, there is only one date in their history—that of their founding.

There are some countervailing examples: Nicola, a small town near Carrara, is one suggested by Piero Pierotti (1972). Although it has shown no development for centuries, it came into existence from its citizens' own initiatives.[5] The purpose for which the town was created ensured that it would always be an active organism from the inside out (fig. 79). Nicola has been preserved intact. Its extent and the layout of its streets have remained constant. The houses and churches have always been built on the same foundations as epoch succeeded epoch. Originally, a community of farmers had settled on the summit of a steep hill, not because they feared pirates or highwaymen—the town is not fortified—nor because they were afraid of malaria. It was recognized that the shortest routes to the fields that lay around the hills met at this summit. The convenience of the site outweighed the fact that there was no natural water supply on this summit and no through traffic. The idea proved so tenable that the small community was able to exist without any help from the outside.

Compared with cities established to protect rural areas, those cities founded by princes or bishops for fiscal reasons—especially in France and

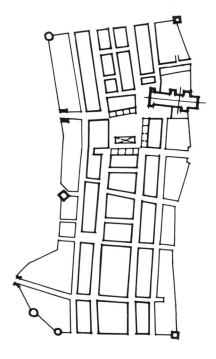

Figure 80. Beaumont du Périgord

England and, in isolated cases, Germany—have achieved considerable significance. Such cities include those built by the Zähringens—Freiburg-im-Breisgau, Bern (fig. 36), and Freiburg-im-Üchtland. The industry of the citizens was supposed to increase revenue from taxation. Thus, economic historians have paid as much attention to these cities as legal historians have done to the new merchant settlements in eastern Germany. A pioneer work in this field is Maurice Beresford's study of the founding of medieval cities in England, Wales, and those provinces of France which for a time were subject to the English crown.[6] They are *bastides,* "cities as building developments" in the modern sense.

Beresford considers only those places where planned construction immediately followed their founding. The reason for founding these towns was, in all cases, a landowner's wish to increase the earnings of his estates. Only a few of these towns, in France and on England's Scottish border, functioned to defend their country or to keep the landowner's possessions secure. Their external form does not differ from the Tuscan *terre murate.* Beaumont de Périgord may serve as one example (among many) for France (fig. 80). It was founded by Edward I's seneschal in 1272, the year he returned from the crusades, and remained famous both for its location and for the care taken in its construction. It developed no further. A picture of Flint, in Wales, done in the year 1610, clarifies the lack of success of such undertakings. This town was also founded and built by Edward I, five years after Beaumont in 1277. It could, at best, be described as a fortified village in front of the castle.[7] In England alone, between 950 and 1345, no less than 171 towns were founded with similar objectives. After the plague of 1348, only one straggler remained in 1368, and a quarter of a millennium went by before a new attempt was made with the founding of Falmouth in 1616. The idea simply had little success. Earnings were not forthcoming. Without outside subventions, these towns could scarcely exist. In any case they did not develop. It is significant that in Gutkind's choice of twenty-four of them for a history of urban planning, out of a total of 173 he could include only three that approached prosperity through functions which, though almost ignored at the outset, became their major ones.[8] These are the cathedral city of Durham; Newcastle-upon-Tyne, whose value as a defensive center near the Scottish border and its coal-exporting trade ensured its continued existence; and, finally, the port of Liverpool. Fiscal impositions, the landowner's insistence on profiting from the earnings of the townspeople's industry, paralyzed the entrepreneurial spirit. The towns remained sterile. For such vessels to be refloated would have required political charters or special privileges. Every success merely led to higher taxes. Nowhere do we find a stimulus to erect monumental buildings, which would have emphasized the taxable income even more.

These *bastides* illustrate a basic law: whatever is born of subvention needs continual subvention or new liberties if it is to develop further. The fiscal projections were never met. The only aesthetic element history has added to what was achieved in the initial planning is that which symbolizes the ancient and the idyllic, which lends value to what little there is to preserve.

Star-shaped Fortifications of the Baroque

The same is true of the many fortresses and fortified cities of the baroque period. From the beginning of the 16th century to the middle of the 18th and beyond, absolutism tried to secure borders that were threatened and areas newly conquered. The theory of defense that brought these complexes into being was known equally well to antiquity, the Middle Ages, and the modern era. Landholdings were protected by castles or cities whose inhabitants, supported and watched over by garrisons, were themselves to assume the burden of defense. The planning of such towns was a favorite occupation of all authors of military architecture handbooks from Filarete's ideal city, Sforcesca, in the mid-15th century, to the grandiose plans of the marquis de Vauban (1633–1707).[9] Vauban's last work, Neubreisach, is one of the best-preserved examples (fig. 81). Most plans for such towns begin with the circle as the basic form, with a star-shaped circle of bastions and moats surrounding it. The circular form permits roads to traverse the shortest distance from the command post at the center to the fort at the periphery. The basic idea was that each military order should correspond to a geometric one, so that aesthetic clarity would serve the effectiveness of the fortifications. The idea proved itself in those cases where towns were planned merely as garrisons and had to be sustained only as long as the political situation demanded. Gustavsburg, across from Mainz between the Rhine and the Main, provides an example. It was founded by the Swedish military. The idea also proved itself where a flourishing, free commercial city—like Bremen, Hamburg, or Lübeck—was still wealthy enough in the 17th and 18th centuries to protect itself by a circle of bastions and moats (fig. 47). But wherever plans had provided for the development of a free citizenry, side by side with the garrison, the citizens would ultimately have had to

Figure 81. Neubreisach

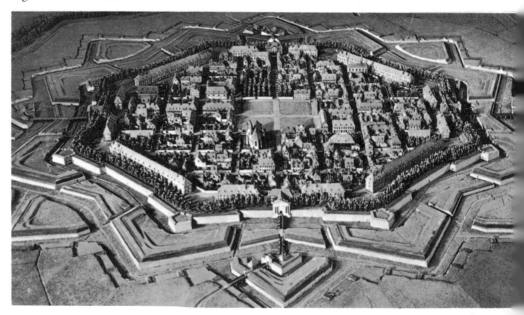

Figure 82. Palmanova (after Jean Blaeu's bird's-eye view)

bear the brunt of the whole organization. It was precisely when subventions for the garrison and fortifications were discontinued that everything started to collapse.

Palmanova, planned for the protection of the Venetian rural area against attacks from the Ottoman Empire, is an example as significant as it is famous (fig. 82).[10] Venice sought to build itself a "protective city" whose inhabitants were to sustain themselves by trade, crafts, or agriculture. Yet not a single inhabitant moved into this model city of his own accord. In 1622, the Serenissima ordered criminals to be pardoned and offered building sites and materials if they were willing to settle along the streets that had already been laid out. Yet even the prisoners did not move voluntarily. Today, the life of this small town is still determined by the military. Even where the political and military conditions for such rural fortresses were present, their success was limited to the period during which those conditions held good. A frequently cited example is that circle of towns with which, after 1542, the Spanish Habsburgs tried to secure the Netherlands against France.[11] Marienbourg, named after Maria of Hungary, the sister of Charles V, was the first. In 1545, Ville-Franche-sur-Meuse was established, and nine years later, in 1554, Philippeville, named for Philip II. Charlesville also belongs to this group. We are dealing here exclusively with central complexes which were organized entirely to suit the needs of the garrison. In the middle was a square with the town fountain and, frequently, the gallows and pillory, and streets led from this square radially to five or more

Figure 83. Philippe-Ville (after the new fortifications built in the reign of Louis XV)

bastions (fig. 83). Everything was designed to ensure that the defending troops could reach the fortifications in the shortest possible time. Anyone at all familiar with army discipline in the 16th to 18th centuries, when troops were supposed to fear their officers more than they did the enemy, knows that life in these garrisons was like living in prison. If such fortified towns ever became urban communities, it was only after the bastions had fallen and the reasons for their construction had ceased to exist.

The lethargy resulting from lack of freedom also spread to previously free organisms after they were incorporated into a larger territorial state and then designated as garrison towns. Magdeburg is characteristic of such towns.[12] The medieval town was destroyed when it was conquered by Tilly in 1631. Of the 2,000 houses, 1,700 burned down, among them all the public buildings and all the churches, with the exception of the cathedral and the convent of the Blessed Virgin. Of the approximately 35,000 inhabitants, only 2,600 were still living in the city in 1638. The council architect, and later burgomaster, Otto von Gericke (1606–86), presented a bold plan for reconstruction. In 1648, however, the city was made part of Brandenburg-Prussia. The Great Elector dismissed the last city administrator in 1666. Immediately afterward, Magdeburg was developed into the strongest fortified city in Prussia. Civil servants and officers built houses in the classical style on the old streets. A few merchants, whose prosperity derived from supplying the army, built larger palaces. The "Old Dessauer," Prince Leopold of Anhalt-Dessau, governor of the city and fortress from 1702 to 1742, promoted the extension of the carefully regulated street plan. The royal palace was built on the cathedral square as were the arsenal and the palace of the fortress architect and other officers. The largest baroque building in Magdeburg, the old Packhof, was a warehouse and storehouse. Other cathedral cities that had been destroyed were able to rebuild testimonies to their own existence, but Magdeburg was forced to become a fortress complex and was burdened with disciplinary orders. The layout of the city became a mirror of the army's discipline, its asceticism, its monotony, and its lack of freedom. Life consisted of nothing but service; architects built only according to rule. In the process, much was built that was pleasant, well proportioned, clearly defined, and cleanly constructed—the exteriors of the houses resembled the smart uniforms of the cuirassiers.

Calais and Valletta

Within the framework of this chapter, two towns should be mentioned that were built for temporary functions but maintained their importance, and thus their appearance, for a much longer period: the baroque town of Valletta, exemplary from its founding until the present day, and medieval Calais, for the whole period of English rule, 1347–1558. Extraordinary political circumstances made both of them possible.

The first thing that Edward III did after his unprecedented victory over the French-Burgundian cavalry at Crecy in 1347 was to occupy Calais, which, unprepared as it was, he was able to starve into submission in a matter of months. The city already had the shape and function of a fortress city (fig. 84)—a rectangle with a fortress in the northwest part of the city and a regular street grid. It was protected on the sea side by a sandbank and on the land side by walls and moats as well as extensive lowlands which could be flooded at any time. There were only four gates, two on the sea side (3 and 4) and two on the land side (5 and 6). The roads leading to these land gates were protected by the English kings, in the course of time, by a series of castles, for Calais developed into the "jewel" of the English crown

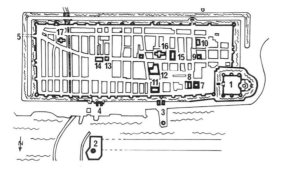

Figure 84. Calais (after the Tudor plan in the British Museum. Cotton MS. Augustus I ii 71): 1, castle; 2, watchtower; 3, "water gate"; 4, "lantern gate," 5, "milk gate"; 6, Boulogne gate; 7, royal smithy; 8, St. John's hospital; 9, Wardrobe; 10, bakery; 11, masons' lodgings; 12, wagon and carpentry workshop; 13, warehouse; 14, town hall; 15, mint; 16, St. Nicholas, 17, Our Lady (south side uppermost).

and, finally, into the last stronghold of her continental possessions and a guarantee of her hope of reconquest.[13] For this reason, the citadel (1) had to be reinforced, at great expense, and a second sea fortification, for the protection of the harbor (2), had to be built. The fortifications cost so much because the town lacked any sort of building material, except clay for bricks. Wood, stones, limestone and metal had, for the most part, all to be brought by ship from England. Walls and fortified gates had to be kept in the best repair at all times so that the final defensive measure—the flooding of the lowlands—would have to be taken as rarely as possible. Through almost unimaginable lethargy, that measure was not taken in 1558 when the duc de Guise reconquered the town for France.

The old French stronghold had lived by trading and seafaring. The patron saints of the two parish churches, St. Nicholas (16) and Our Lady (17) bear witness to the citizens' self-perception as a seafaring and burgher community. A large marketplace with a town hall (14) and a warehouse (13) formed the center of the town.

The buildings erected by order of the English crown indicate that for all practical purposes the whole western half of the city was reserved for the occupying power. There, in the shadow of the castle, a series of large buildings arose, forming the basis for the extension of the fortifications; first came the treasurer's palace opposite the church of St. Nicholas, followed by another building for lead smelting, storage chambers, the royal arsenal, the royal bakery, a weighbridge for the royal administration, a carpenter's workshop and wood storage area, and the office of the chief mason.

We can distinguish four main periods in the history of Calais.[14] During the first, 1347–85, the victorious English armies brought in enough loot to enlarge the town in a magnificent fashion. The second period brought reverses and ever greater losses of land until finally Calais itself was almost the only possession left on the Continent. At the same time, the administration, the treasury, and the building administration fell into corrupt hands. Larger and larger sums were demanded for the maintenance of the fortifications, for protective dikes, and for keeping order in the streets. Smaller and smaller sums served the purposes for which they were intended. Storm tides accompanied the military defeats. In the third period, 1422–65, more money was spent on Calais than on any other royal undertaking—and less was achieved. It is in the nature of things that an attempt should have been made to rectify these defects by means of a strict, rigid administration, aided by a bureaucracy trained in England. Once again, however, it was shown that no bureaucracy, however well trained, could reverse wrong-headed political decisions and faulty development. The collapse of Calais continued.

Finally, in 1466, the council of merchants was entrusted with administering construction. The council had already been granted, in 1363, the right to erect an office and a warehouse for the import of wool from and the export of cloth to England. The city's natural sources of income grew with these new rights and obligations. From 1466 until the reconquest in 1558, the community blossomed. Money was earned that could be used to reinforce the fortifications. Within the political and architectural framework outlined, the town grew into a important harbor. Correct economic decision making allowed the stronghold to continue to exist for another ninety years, and it was strategic indecision that was to bring about its fall. The importers and exporters had the greater advantages from belonging to England. Old views and a few remains of the original buildings confirm that this port knew how to approximate to the architectural and living style of the Flemish trading towns.

The harbor remained intact, but the fortifications were rendered unnecessary by the reconquest. Except for a few towers, the fortification material was used in the 17th century for civil buildings. Later, the harbor basin was extended and the industrial suburb of St. Pierre was incorporated into the old town—the whole once again being surrounded by a far-flung circle of fortifications. In the modern city it is difficult to make out the original street plan around the town hall and Notre-Dame.

Calais was a harbor stronghold which, because of its capture, came into the possession of foreigners and was expanded by them into a powerful urban stronghold. Valletta was built after a massive attack by the Ottoman fleets had been warded off from the island stronghold of Malta and at the moment when a still greater one—which did not in fact take place—was expected. From the day the foundation stone was laid, 28 November 1566, to the day of Napoleon's coup de main in June 1798, this important stronghold was never attacked. And, from the first, Valletta was famous in all the courts of Europe as the most perfect fortified town. It was accomplished, over the objections of the Grand Master of the Order of St. John, Jean de la Valletta (1494–1568), by an Italian, Francesco Laparelli (1521–70), who boasted that he was a pupil of Michelangelo; and the town was built according to his proposed plan.[15]

The town came into being not just because of its geographical position and its (falsely evaluated) strategic position, but because of the unique political structure of the state, which belonged to the order of St. John. It is well known that the order had fled to Rhodes in the face of the Mamelukes at the end of the 13th century and that it had made that island one of the most powerful fortresses of the Middle Ages. After a long siege by the Ottoman armies, the knights succeeded, in 1522, in securing free passage from that exposed position, and they accepted, apparently with reluctance, Charles V's offer in 1530 to give them Malta and Gozo as new strongholds in perpetuity. Both places had suffered terribly in massacres at the hands of the corsairs and the Turks. But the old capital, Medina, proves that an independent aristocracy had always been able to protect itself there. The order was to secure Christian sea-routes, at least in the western Mediterranean, especially as the knights' galleys were faster and more powerful than any other kind of ship. As soon as it arrived in Malta, the order set about defending itself. Admittedly, the retreat of the Turks after the great siege of 1565, in spite of the knights' heroism, must be ascribed in the first place to the strategic bungling of the Turkish commanders. The most valuable fortifications were also destroyed and the three old towns heavily damaged.

The plan for the new town on an uninhabited, undeveloped, rocky peninsula, between two gigantic harbor basins, demanded and drew upon the sum total of knowledge and experience from all the manuals of urban planning, from the time of Filarete and Alberti and also from the ordinances of Charles V for the planning of new towns in the Spanish colonial empire.[16] A regular street plan was imposed on a piece of land, but at the same time it had to be remembered that, contrary to all the rules, there was a tremendous variance in height to be overcome (fig. 85). Not only did the cliffs rise steeply from the sea on both the long sides, but the main roads between the narrow sides had to cross a deep valley to reach the most favorable height for a defensive position on the land side and, on the side

Figure 85. Valletta: 1, palace of the Grand Master; 2, library; 3, cathedral of St. John; 4, Italian palace; 5, palace of León; 6, palace of Aragon; 7, Bavarian palace; 8, archbishop's palace.

that thrust out into the sea, a site for at least a medium-sized position. Powerful bastions linked the cliff formation in the boldest baroque geometry. Only the inexhaustible supply of the finest stone made this enormous project feasible. Winter after winter, the galley slaves were given new and brutal tasks to perform. The settled area sufficed until the middle of the 19th century to accommodate the growth of Valletta's population.

At the same time the rule of the order, as a way of structuring the army and the state, provided sufficient stimulus for monumental construction. Constant recourse to Italian architects, mostly Neapolitans and Sicilians, and, less frequently, to Spanish designers ensured a link with the great Roman baroque traditions. These architects had to bear in mind that on this windy island, where few trees grew, wood was available only in very limited quantities, so that special systems of vaulting had to be developed for the great civil, ecclesiastical, and military buildings. Yet the aristocratic order of St. John wanted to produce buildings on a grand scale. Besides the palace of the Grand Master in the center of the town and the palaces of his government headquarters, each of the seven or sometimes eight nations, or "tongues," into which the army of the order was divided (according to the countries of origin of the knights) required a number of equally large buildings, in which each individual knight had a suite of rooms. The most important palaces were those of the knights of the Aragonian and Castilian tongues. There were twenty-one aristocratic priorates on the mainland, each responsible for providing recruits for its tongue. During the 268 years that the order ruled Malta, the competition among these usually enormous community palaces promoted architectural activity of an uncommon nature, for, in addition to the order's church of St. John the Baptist in the center of the town, most tongues had their own churches. It was not until Napoleon took over that the bishopric of the island was transferred to Valletta from the old fortified city of Vittoriosa.

Exceptional political circumstances ensured that the capital of this order should continue its organic and magnificent existence for almost 300 years. It was a chivalric order, assured in its new possessions by the last universal emperor, Charles V, supported by subventions from the whole of the West, yet it was always forced to balance its budget by means of piracy. All this must have seemed anachronistic in the 18th century. Napoleon recognized it at once. Its anachronism, however, removed the great star-shaped fortifications from the realm of a transitory experiment into that of a Christian utopia, which was forgotten by world events.

Urbanization of the Swedish Baltic Empire

The numerous city plans commissioned by the Swedish crown for the security of its Baltic empire between 1600 and 1715 make up a strange chapter in the history of ideal towns as fortresses. One of the most intelligent treatments of this subject is by Gerhard Eimer, *City Planning in the Swedish Baltic Empire* (1961). A great deal of material on these plans—Eimer mentions 30,000 pages—has been preserved. Like contemporary government ordinances, this material shows how an energetic and rapidly advancing state organism plans its use of land both as a means of securing newly conquered areas and as a means of cultural education.

The expansion of Swedish power around the Baltic and far into what were later German, Russian, and Finnish provinces, and the securing of old and new borders against Denmark and Norway, called for towns that would be fortified strongholds. Most of these areas had no existing towns. Elsewhere, especially in the Holy Roman Empire and in the Baltic areas, the old industrial towns required new fortifications as much against the inhabitants themselves as against foreign armies. Almost everywhere, popular uprisings had to be taken into account. The government faced the difficult situation of having to urbanize the land for defensive measures and as a means of promoting industry and education. In the process, architectural style was to program a new European lifestyle.

This urbanization of the North was carried out energetically and hastily by kings, their generals, and civil servants, mostly against the wishes of the population, and by rival architects, mostly with energy and often with genius. There are two characteristic elements of these large-scale undertakings. First, since there was no indigenous tradition, people had to turn for their models to Holland, France, Italy, and the empire. It was thus inevitable that, along with outstanding individual solutions from Rome, Venice, or Turin, ideal plans incorporated in architectural manuals should acquire normative significance. Utopias set the standard. These authorities were entrusted with the execution of ideal projects even when the citizens had no need of them. There were no people to fill all the space in the beautiful plans, especially as the capital, Stockholm, itself growing rapidly, attracted those who would have been most suitable, and the religious laws made large-scale immigration impossible. Thus, the urbanization of the North lacked both the people and the cultural tradition.

The dependence of architects upon collections of ideal models meant that these towns not only failed to take heed of the needs of the population and their economic potential, but were equally incapable of paying heed to the geographical data of a particular moment. Everywhere, theory called for a perfectly regular street grid, almost everywhere a closed circle of bastions and a star-shaped elevated citadel with bastions arranged so that they could fire upon the streets of the town. From a budgetary point of view, the accounts could not be balanced. The state not only had to finance these fortifications; it had to pay, even in long periods of peace, for their maintenance and for the garrisons. These new foundations were incapable of developing from within.

The monarchs and their advisers saw the town as a means of correcting nature, even as a criticism of the population's cultural level. People were forced to learn that imported classicism or baroque formed a necessary framework for every high culture. Surveyors and architects cooperated with lawmakers to integrate old towns into the grid of their geometrical measurements or to design new ones according to the idealism of the drawing board. Enormous efforts were made to gain a unified architectural hold on a whole empire. From 1691 on, a unified authority in Stockholm, *Fortifikationskontoret,* tried to give centralized guidance to all building projects. Erik Dahlberg (1633–1703), its first chief, did not hesitate to travel in person throughout the whole territory in order to inspect every building project. Discourse concerning these projects, some of which focused on a single site for decades, with plan overlaying plan, constitutes one of Sweden's great intellectual efforts. For, even if they are all good examples of a "colonial classicism" imposed upon a country, they are at the same time illustrative of a new Nordic baroque style and its enormous success when measured by former standards.

Three examples may suffice here, for the capital city does not belong in this chapter. I choose Kalmar and Landskrona in southern Sweden and the fatal plan for Carlsburg, the site of modern-day Bremerhaven.

Kalmar had a medieval nucleus. The town was long the object of political and military disputes between Sweden and Denmark. As early as 1585, an Italian, Dominicus Pahr, had drawn up a plan for a new system of bastions for its defense. After the town had been regained by Sweden in 1613, Gustavus Adolphus II wished to rebuild the settlement, which had been destroyed, and revitalize it by bringing in the textile industry from the surrounding countryside. A Dutchman, Andries Sersanders, undertook to draw up the plan, and in 1615 the king promulgated laws for its strict observance. A later survey tells us that a regular, eight-pointed star had been planned to radiate inland from the coast and that sixteen streets were to

Figure 86. Kovernholmen and Kalmar (based on Gerhard Eimer, *Die Stadtplanung im schwedischen Ostseereich* [1961], fig. 125)

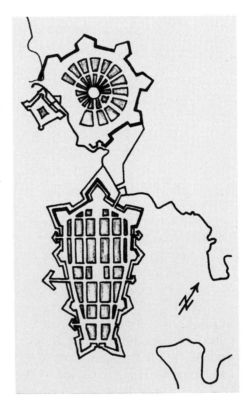

radiate from a central marketplace. The complex could not be developed for economic reasons. It continued to be threatened by uprisings against the Swedes from the mainland. However, it signifies the readiness of the North to turn ideal forms into practical ones.[17]

For a better defense, it was decided in 1647 to build a second town on the island of Kovernholmen, just off Kolmar. A Swede, Wärnskjold, drew up the preliminary plans, and Nicodemus Tessin the Elder the detailed ones (fig. 86). There was supposed to be a heptagon with three bastions directed toward the mainland. Tessin had planned gabled houses on the Hanseatic model. The town was only accessible to the mainland by a narrow bridge. In the town center a large square linked the town hall with the "cathedral." A fortified castle for the prince was planned for the little rocky islet that extends to the east. But what was to sustain the population in this isolation? Where was the market for the new textile industry? It soon had to be admitted that both towns could not be populated. The older one, Kalmar, together with its medieval stone church, was razed. In the newer town, Kovernholmen, Tessin's plan was adhered to for more than a century though the gabled houses were never built. Long before the streets could be filled up, political conditions had made the fortifications unnecessary. They were allowed to fall into decay and were later landscaped. There was no longer any reason to have a town here, nor was there any cultural stimulus for its revitalization. Thus, what had been built was left standing, and inhabitants were found who managed to eke out a modest existence in agriculture or industry. Up to the beginning of the industrial age, people lived in a town whose architectural form, modest as it was, was far beyond the needs or conditions of its inhabitants.

Landskrona suffered a harsher fate, and Carlsburg was unsuccessful from the very beginning.

After 1648, it appeared that the province of Schonen, in the south of present-day Sweden, would finally be subjected to the new empire. At that time, plans were drawn up by Nicodemus Tessin for a large city complete with its circle of bastions and a citadel; on its regular network of streets, four-winged houses were to be built for the wealthy citizens. It met with only modest success. The rebellion in Schonen in the 1670s and long partisan struggles with the supporters of Denmark threw the project into limbo. After the final reconquest of the province in 1679, rebuilding was made difficult by the fact that most of the inhabitants of the town had emigrated to Denmark. This merely led to even stronger demands by the government that all the forces of the province should be gathered together in a new town. Erik Dahlberg was commissioned to draw up a plan for a town of 5,000 fully enfranchised citizens, which would give a total population of 20,000. The idea must have seemed utopian to Dahlberg himself. But even the plan for a town of 1,500 that he presented (fig. 87) was to prove infeasible. The contradictions of the plan, by which, on the one hand, the rural population was to be forced to live in a town while being, on the other, subjected to the strictest control by a citadel, paralyzed any individual action. As early as the 18th century, the earthworks, on which work had already begun, were razed. Thanks to an inherent automatism, Swedish urban planning, having reached its zenith in Landskrona, had under the influence of Italian idealistic projects removed itself still further from any sort of reality.

Political dirigism and schematic planning based upon geometric principles suppressed all private initiative. State mercantilism itself created the economic setbacks. Baltic trade proved unprofitable precisely because of a policy of conquest. It is simply not possible to wrest areas from the empire, from Russia, or from Poland and then to carry on trade with them. Lübeck and Danzig were better partners for this sort of activity. In addition, the main trade routes had moved to the North Sea, to which Denmark, as an enemy state, could block the sea passages. This situation prompted the plan to build a town at the mouth of the Weser that could then compete with

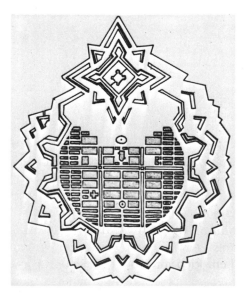

Figure 87. Landskrona: Dahlberg's plan (based on Eimer, *Stadtplanung,* fig. 309)

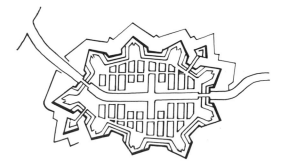

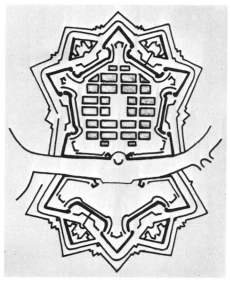

Figure 88, 89. Carlsburg: above, Dahlberg's plan, 1681; right, J von Kepten's plan, 1692 (based on Eimer, figs. 300, 302)

Bremen, Hamburg, and even Amsterdam. The town was called Carlsburg. Unsuccessful wars with Bremen accompanied the planning stage. The first sod was turned in 1672. Nikodemus Tessin and Erik Dahlberg both drew up comprehensive plans (fig. 88). The architectural theoretician Georg Rimpler developed his own proposals.[18] In 1692, Jakob von Kempten added some new proposals to the plan (fig. 89). Enormous sums of money were transferred from Stockholm. The task at hand was to use the waters of the Geeste, just upstream of its confluence with the Weser, to feed the canals in the city's harbor and the moats around its bastions. Huge earthworks were to be constructed, as much to protect the town from flooding as to defend it against the enemy city of Bremen. The architect Johann Mell had worked out a plan in 1672, which had been approved by the Royal Council on the recommendation of Field Marshal Wrangel. The town was to be oval in shape, secured by ten bastions, and within the town a T-shaped arrangement of canals was to bring ships and goods right up to the houses and workshops. The elder Tessin was commissioned to design residential and administrative buildings. Various attempts were made to channel the whole Geeste through the town. A classical solution was suggested by Erik Dahlberg in 1681 (fig. 88), whereby the canals were to form tributaries of the Geeste, which would then be filled and emptied into the fortress by means of sluices. Floods forced the abandonment of the whole scheme after 1695.

These Baltic architects had no method for controlling the North Sea tides. Apart from the unfavorable nature of the conditions of the surrounding waters, how could a free merchant community develop on such a threatened site, and under such strict military control?

Mistaken concepts lay at the root of the whole enterprise. They characterize the whole Swedish program of urbanization as a work of education and geopolitical measure. In developments of this kind, settlements might develop in fortresses but never in towns. Beautiful architectural forms were formally superimposed on the countryside, but their quality did nothing to alter the fact that the residents were required to live a life according to a program that could not be carried out. It was not just a change in the political constellation—the collapse of the empire after Peter the Great's victories over Charles XII—that caused this whole undertaking to fail; it was also the necessity, inherent in the system, for the subvention of every individual town, and this the budget of the state could not afford to provide. The fact that much survived or continued to function can be ascribed, from an outsider's point of view, to the more rapid population growth in the 18th and 19th centuries. Living space was needed. Looked at from the inside, these buildings possessed an aesthetic deadweight which has contributed to the fact that, not only in Sweden but also in Poland and Russia, the cultural incline from north to south and from east to west came into balance according to the laws that govern channels of communication. Baroque Stockholm, built by the two Tessins, is a monument to that balance.

City Plan and the Order of Salvation

There have been holy cities in many cultures and their history has frequently been treated.[19] Cities shielded and protected sacred objects. They dominated the landscape in the name of a divinity. Their power and their safety were guaranteed by divinities. Their proportions were themselves sacred. The crossing point of their main streets was regarded as a sacred symbol as people gradually became used to the idea that urban order was related to a world order (fig. 90). By dividing a town into four quarters, Gothic architecture in many places took up an idea which was fundamental to the Romans.[20] Other places were centers of pilgrimage to the divinities. Many medieval cities regarded themselves as holy cities, and, where they could not look back to any sacred tradition which justified such claims, they tried to gain possession of holy relics, placed themselves under the protection of a patron saint, and dedicated themselves to him. The sacredness of a city

Figure 90. Chichester: present-day city
plan with ancient main axes

was also a political issue. Political demands were defended in the name of
saints. But the material that has been handed down in Europe does not
permit us to isolate one particular type of city and call it a holy city.

It is a different matter with the ideal cities, in which architectural form
was supposed to educate the citizens to a new life. The cities in the land of
Utopia are themselves pedagogical institutions, assigned an educational
task which was to ensure both their earthly justification and a reward in
heaven. It was largely reform efforts that sought to substitute institutions
of this kind for the medieval holy cities. They presented their inhabitants
less with something spiritual than with an order of life. Such an order demanded a suitable architectonic framework.

There were centers of pilgrimage in which both were combined. None
of these centers can be classified as "successful" cities, for none had more
than a limited existence. I am not talking here of places like Loretto or
Altötting, which in the course of more recent developments became smaller
towns. Scherpenheuvel can perhaps serve as an example. In 1603, the governor of the Catholic Netherlands, the archduke Albert, and his wife, Isabella, promised to construct a star-shaped town, with seven arms, at a place
where there was an oak dedicated to the Virgin Mary. The duke himself
drew up the plan by which Mary, as the *stella maris,* was to be made manifest. An engraving from 1671 shows how little was achieved in more than

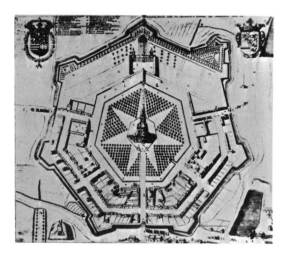

Figure 91. Scherpenheuvel
(after an engraving from Sandran,
Choreographia Brabantiae, 1671)

fifty years (fig. 91). In a garden that depicts Mary as the *hortus conclusus,* a pilgrimage chapel had been built on the site of the oak. The space between the heptagon of the garden and the heptagon of the bastions was left empty for building. Three processional routes crossed the walls and led through the gates into open country. The complex was crowned with a royal castle. At the root of all this lay the idea that the security of the complex could be enhanced by the correspondence between the symbolic form of the star and the star-shaped fortification.[21] People had similar relationships in mind at a number of places in Catholic countries.

Of more consequence are those towns in which religious refugees from foreign countries sought not only refuge but peace as well. Herrenhut was a settlement of this sort. Here people were organized according to choirs for living, working, and worshiping. When the colonial settlements in Pennsylvania and New England were built, similar ideas also played a part, though they were usually set aside because of the exigencies of everyday life. In the Mormon center of Saint Lake City in Utah, they continue to flourish and have achieved architectural expression.

The suburbs and towns which were built for the Huguenots in the Protestant areas of Germany and in England, Holland, and Switzerland, after the repeal of the Edict of Nantes in 1685, were more successful. In spite of a strict prohibition, over 200,000 Protestants succeeded in fleeing across the French border, and in all those places where fair-sized communities gathered, they founded settlements and towns, all in the same form. This consisted of a regular street grid on a square site, houses constructed to a

174

norm, generally of the same form, size, and color, a small but carefully proportioned church, and identical manufactories; the whole thing was uniformly planned and built with unsparing energy. It was seldom designed to permit growth unless new refugee communities, and thus a new settlement, necessitated the building of a new suburb or part of a town. The city administrations of Berlin, Ansbach, and Kassel sought to profit from their support of the Huguenot suburbs. Of the 20,000 inhabitants living in Berlin around 1700, one-fifth were French religious refugees, who, by their superior industry and discipline, furthered the rise of Prussia. Karlshafen, near Kassel, and Erlangen, in the territory of the Margrave of Ansbach, are the best-known Huguenot settlements in the empire.

Not only were they characterized by the regularity of their design, which was an expression of the social equality of their inhabitants,[22] but this equality was also a pedagogical principle, which was to be expressed in architecture as well as in their way of life. Puritanism here developed into a style. Ideal cities were founded that were fully planned before building could start. Every possible extension of the settlement was also planned in advance. People sought lasting peace there. They did not reckon with expansion or with further development. The Huguenots negotiated rights and liberties for themselves in an already existing political system, and they tried neither to change nor to influence it. The course of time alone was to serve the increase in prosperity. Everything else, architecturally as well as politically, was to preserve the status quo. In a foreign country there was to be as little change as there was in the language of the French in Canada or of the Germans on the Volga.

Colonial towns always have an idiosyncratic style. We have already seen this in the case of the Hanseatic foundations in the Baltic area. These communities of citizens were always culturally superior to the indigenous population. Economic success was just as assured for them in the Middle Ages as it was in the baroque period or, at the same time, in North America or Africa. Calvinism promoted, simultaneously, early capitalism and the architectural style of the Protestant settlements. History could stand still in the face of these oases just as long as their rise did not outpace the tempo with which they pursued their developmental course. When crises arose, it was always because the immigrant communities had been penetrated by, and confronted with, their hosts. The crises were always moral and political ones. Outwardly, these towns lost their form; politically, they lost their old meaning and their original function.

Chapter 6

*T*HE ONLY SUCCESSFUL "IDEAL CITIES" were the princely seats built in the age of absolutism. Versailles is the most perfect example, Nancy is one of the most charming, while Karlsruhe came closest to having the essential characteristics of an ideal city. There could scarcely be a greater contrast than that between the fortified cities or the cities built for fiscal advantage, designed by architectural theorists (as described in the preceding chapter), and these resplendent seats of government. Figures 92 and 93, showing the 17th and 18th century plans for Mannheim, illustrate such splendor. The plan for this fortress between the Rhine and the Neckar was drawn up in the Thirty Years' War. According to the plan, an impregnable citadel was to guard the town that lay before it. It was reckoned that the citizens could not only feed their protectors but also maintain the fortifications. I have already pointed out that these aims could never be achieved either politically or economically (see chap. 5), and that what was not confirmed by the realities of a situation could not succeed architecturally. From all the documents related to the planning of Mannheim in the 18th century, I show only the castle at the edge of the city in front of the bastions on the bank of the Rhine (fig. 93). The prince could draw upon his country's financial resources for the way his court was arranged, and he was confident that the absolutist

Seats of a Princely Court

theory of the state was anchored in a world order which could not be shaken by an uprising of his "subjects." He wanted to be able to move about in their midst, just as the *roi soleil* did in Versailles, and, like him, to be the sole object of attention. The castle was both open and public. Every true princely seat can be perceived as an illustration of the absolutist theory of the state, and every new interpretation of this theory is immediately reflected in the building program. Thus the various views of the state held by the French, Prussian, and Russian monarchs found their expression in the contrasts between the general structures of Versailles, Potsdam, and St. Petersburg.

Terminology at no time distinguished between a capital city and a princely seat, nor did political theory attempt to, though there were states where the two existed as separate cities. The best-known example is The Hague. The Hague was the seat of the court, while Amsterdam was always styled the capital of the Netherlands, and when the new state was founded in the 19th century, it was proclaimed as such. After Louis XIV's move to Versailles and until Louis XVI's return to Paris—a move forced on him by the French Revolution—this separation was a political reality in France as well. Historical development was to impose a similar division upon the United States. New York developed into the first city in the country. As the seat of government, Washington became the symbol at once of the unity of the new federation of states and of the independence of the individual states within that federation. In Washington, the buildings which, collectively, are a manifestation of the American constitution combine to form a court of a different kind. What came into being was not only one of the most magnificent feats of political urbanism but also a work that was compelling because of its historical logic. The architects strove to emulate the standards of the two great European metropolises, Paris and Rome.

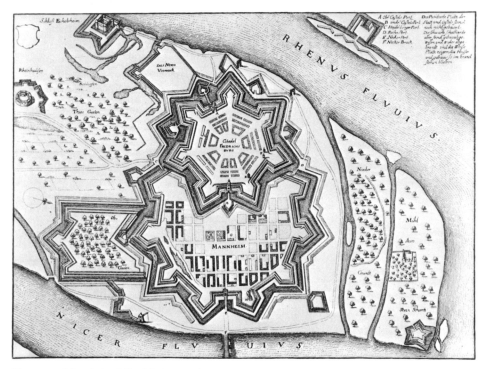

Figure 92. Mannheim (after Merian, 1645)

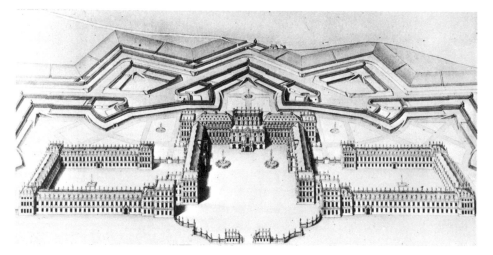

Figure 93. Mannheim castle (after a drawing in the Bibliothèque Nationale, Paris, ca. 1720)

178

European architects have tried to realize seats of government of this type by building illustrious model cities. Oskar Niemeyer's Brasília, Le Corbusier's Chandigarh, and Louis L. Kahn's Dacca, for Bangladesh, are considered the boldest achievements of 20th century planning. So far these architectural ventures have not been confirmed political successes. They are, like the White House, examples of an uncritical classicism, each showing a different view of what constitutes "modern." If Washington's Palladianism can still be understood as the expression of American puritanism, the architectural forms adopted by Niemeyer, Kahn, and Le Corbusier corresponded neither to a political program nor to a theory of what constitutes a state. They are witnesses to an age of abstract painting, and it is in this respect that they are to be criticized.

Three qualities determine the essence of a capital city as it will, in the following, be differentiated from a princely seat: (1) the masses as a political power and a political problem; (2) the special situation of such a city regarding its population, economic power, and intellectual production; and (3) its contrast to the province or the provinces. True capitals are the largest cities in their country. For this reason, Bern cannot be called the capital of Switzerland, just as Zürich could never have been. The fact that neither Rome nor Milan, in spite of their equal importance, ever became the unequivocal capital of Italy can be ascribed to their contrasting structures. Each of the four examples discussed in the next chapter—Prague, Vienna, London, and Paris—has always been the intellectual center of the country's culture at any given point in time and has set the standards for academic research as well as for art. Each had its own literature, which grew out of the detailed attention that everyone paid to everyone else, and for centuries this literature remained topical. The Holy Roman Empire, on the other hand, never had a capital, only princely seats. Berlin was the capital of Germany for scarcely seventy-five years, from 1870 to 1945, a capital of great eminence—something Bonn can never be. It is precisely that inalienable relationship to the provinces which will long be missing in this provisional solution. In Paris, to emphasize a classic example of the other extreme, all the French provinces have their own special part of the city, and each of them, by a system of give and take, achieved a special relationship to the center they all so much admired.

There are a number of princely seats that managed in the course of time to develop into capital cities. I have mentioned Berlin. I might also mention St. Petersburg, Brussels, even Munich, and, with greater justifica-

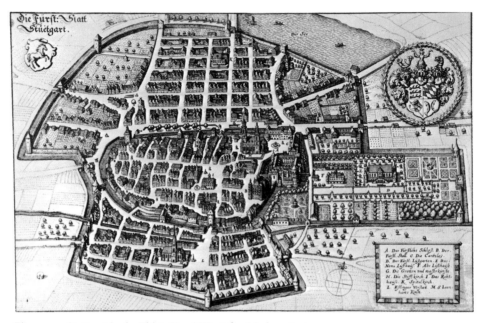

Figure 94. Stuttgart in the Thirty Years' War (after Merian, 1643)

tion, Budapest and, more recently, Athens. The so-called capitals of smaller states which did not function as a center where different people were brought together, like Turin for Piedmont, or Dresden for the Electorate of Saxony, were special cases. Numerous princely seats, like Potsdam or Versailles, lost all of their political significance once the ruler moved out of them. They often changed their architectural structure, as did Mannheim, for instance, which, deserted by the court, quickly became a modern industrial city that did not even house the main provincial authorities.

Various attempts to separate princely seat from capital city were doomed to failure because of the limited opportunities for development. Stuttgart and Ludwigsburg are examples. Württemberg was too small for two centers. Merian's depiction of Stuttgart shows us the small capital city and princely seat, the development of which is presented to us in many of its details by the townscape (fig. 94). We can make out the small, old town, which is protected by a moat. The town hall (I) is situated in the middle of the old town: to the north, and larger, is the city church (H); in a dominating position to the east is the old castle (Alte Burg) and beside it the new one, which was called the Alte Schloß from the 18th century onward. It was not until the 16th century that the city was extended on three sides. In this way new districts were built, with new churches, which were encircled by new fortifications. A fourth extension, on the east side, was reserved for the palace garden, in the middle of which lay the prince's pleasure seat, built in 1593, toward which the castle was oriented. There were about 8,000 inhabitants before the Thirty Years' War.

These conditions were regarded as unbearably restrictive by the dukes of the 18th century. Duke Eberhard Ludwig (1693–1733) retired in the year 1705 to his hunting lodge, the Erlachhof, which he then renamed Ludwigsburg.[1] Step by step, he changed and enlarged the complex. He surrounded himself more and more with alien ministers, architects, artists, and administrators, for the natives all refused to make the move. It was impossible for the members of a pietistic church community to neglect their environment in exchange for service at the ducal court. Emigrants into the new urban complex in front of the castle were granted freedom from taxes, freedom of employment, even freedom of religion, but only the court servants went there. This is not the place to go into the frequent changes of plan for the extension of the complex, drawn up by P. J. Jenisch and J. F. Nette (d. 1715) or even the larger complexes designed by D. G. Frisoni (1683–1735) and his nephew Riccardo Retti (1687–1741). On several occasions the orientation of the whole castle and its plan were changed. A situation arose in which buildings were sometimes erected, according to original plans, on sites that had long been reassigned to different uses, and the most opulent suites of rooms were built, in exquisite taste, the purpose of which was no longer clear. New plans revealed the passionate diligence, the virtuosity, and the wealth of ideas that inspired both those who commissioned the buildings and the architects themselves. More and more opulent suites of rooms, Indian and Turkish, furnished with porcelain and mirror cabinet work, all proclaim the court's ambitions. What was planned but could no longer be built was published as a series of engraving for all the world to see. Finally, a beautiful group of buildings was erected as an addition, but not as part of the whole. The castle courtyard, a space 203 meters long and 53–66 meters wide, illustrates this irresolution (fig. 95). At no point in time did the undertaking correspond to any political reality. Even compared with such a costly complex as the castle in Würzburg, vast sums had been wasted. All Eberhard Ludwig's successors turned their backs on the undertaking. Only now did they try to build a suitable castle complex in the capital, and Balthasar Neumann was engaged in 1747, along with others, to give it the right architectural form within the urban structure. Work was continued into the 19th century. The example of the far better organized plan for a court in

Munich (see below, this chapter) will make clear that it was a political failing that lent the whole Ludwigsburg undertaking the uncertainty discernible in its architectural form even today.

That France and England each has only one capital, and France only one royal court, results from the centralism of these two states. Even Nancy, when it had a court, belonged to the Holy Roman Empire. If I omit Stockholm and Copenhagen, which are both true capitals, it is not because they do not deserve to be treated. Both produced a baroque, with individual and highly significant characteristics, but both were royal seats, in which architecture illustrates no new constitutional ideas.

Poland's dependence upon foreign princes in the first half of the 18th century, and its unfortunate divisions, meant that Warsaw could not develop freely into a capital; so there is justification for omitting that city here. It might be objected that I am dealing with too few centers in Spain and Italy. In the following chapters only Turin, as far as Italy is concerned, will

Figure 95. Ludwigsburg castle

Figure 96. Milan (after a 1589 engraving)

be treated in detail, since Rome is a chapter on its own. In Florence, as we have seen, Cosimo I was able to superimpose a court program onto the medieval and Renaissance city (see chap. 2). With the completion of the Pitti, the building of the Uffizi, the series of squares, and the two fortresses above and below, he was able to achieve something truly pioneering.

A tragic fate prevented Milan, Italy's most powerful organism, from becoming a city-state, a princely seat, or a capital city. A glance at the city plan tells all (fig. 96). After the collapse of the imperial power on the death of Frederick II in 1250, it seemed that this city, which more than any other had borne the brunt of national resistance, should rise and assume the most powerful position in Italy. Around 1260 it was by far the largest and wealthiest free city in the country. Yet as early as 1287 and, finally, in 1330, it fell into the hands of the Visconti and of those whose successors provided Jakob Burkhardt, in his *Culture of the Renaissance,* with material on the most fearful oppression and fiscal exploitation of their subjects. The tyrant's castle, the Castello Sforzesco, was continually being reinforced, and it protected the regime as much against enemies within as against those without. When the French occupied it from 1499 to 1525, they had no need to fear a popular uprising; neither did the Spanish from 1536 to 1706, nor later the Austrians. Economically, the industry of the population repeatedly made recovery possible, which was expressed in individual works of architecture of very high quality. Yet no attempt was ever made to change the medieval street plan by means of new accents or large-scale demolition.

Quite different reasons were responsible for my not being able to treat either Madrid or any other Spanish city as a royal seat or as a capital. I have stressed elsewhere that the land of the Reconquista had no free cities, or, at the most, had them for very limited periods. To the very end of the great conquest, the majority of such cities were strongpoints in a battle in which neither side could do away with fortress strategy. After the fall of Granada, in 1492, an even stronger centralism developed, which afforded opportunities to the internal life of a community only because governmental power and the state's organizational talent remained limited. Almost everywhere in Spain we see a process of architectural enrichment that owes its aesthetic excellence to the desire for defense or, in some cases, fortunate improvisation. A chance decision of Philip II in the year 1561, so it is said, made possible the choice of Madrid as his capital. Its central position may have been one of the reasons for the choice. At the outset, the king ordered the Plaza Mayor to be cut out of the network of streets, for he wanted a suitable place for state occasions, which included every auto-da-fé that took place in the king's presence. Apart from this, he and his successors were concerned, at best, with completing the castle. From the moment it became capital city to the present day, Madrid has never shown itself capable of providing the living space and transportation needed for sudden increases in population. Building administrations were always behind the times, and their efforts piecemeal. The street grid was constantly expanding and growing denser and could not be sorted out. The city as a whole lacks any formal physiognomy.

If the architectural profile of the episcopal cities was determined by the church towers on their skyline, and if the city-states also boasted an opulent municipal program, the royal seats acquired their character from the court buildings. The elements of a fully developed court plan, such as we find in Munich or Turin, are, in addition to the court and the chanceries and ministeries attached to it, the court chapels and theater, the various buildings for the marshal and the guards, a series of monasteries and votive churches, special ecclesiastical buildings that served as burial places for the princes, and, last but not least, a ring of villas and castles in the surrounding countryside. Only where all other monumental buildings take second place to the development of these court buildings can we talk of a royal seat. This was true of Berlin only up to the middle of the 18th century, of St. Petersburg barely to the end. In Vienna, London, and Paris, the court buildings never, at any time, succeeded in dominating all other buildings. Conflicts arose everywhere about sites claimed by the monarch but which were occupied by citizens. This is still the case today. In the princely seats, however, the castle outshines the rest of the city. The princes arranged that all street axes should lead up to it. The plan of the court was the expression of a successful, good, and prosperous government. The city was to publicize the prince's greatness. It was only in France that this aim was stated with absolute clarity: state architecture was to serve the fame of the monarch, its raison d'être was solely *la gloire du roi*. The architectural form of every princely seat should give a clear idea of the political success of its princes.

Princely seats were at all times urban entities and received vast subventions. Absolutism summoned up the state's whole financial power when drafting representational programs. This is as true of St. Petersburg as it is of Versailles and of Turin, Munich, the Dresden of August the Strong, or the Nancy of his rival for the Polish throne, Stanislas. True, these seats were always planned from within, but it was always imperative to obtain the financial means and the artists from without. None of the masters who built Berlin, Potsdam, or St. Petersburg, and only a few of the artists who designed and decorated the court buildings in Turin, Ludwigsburg, or Dresden, were born in the cities they worked in. This, too, differentiates the royal seats from true capitals and later metropolises, Paris or London: these centers were at once the most powerful economic factors in their respective countries and the intellectual homes of their leading artists.

To this day, the bourgeoisie has never forgiven the princes of the 16th, 17th, and 18th centuries for their bad bookkeeping and for the sums spent on public display. Even their enlightened successors did not do so. The baroque aristocracy did not want to keep accounts. People relied on the fact that even artistic plans can serve economically to muster power. The building of castles developed into a historical, even a political, necessity which no one could escape. High style in architecture, as in life, was a political necessity for the liberal-Catholic and the puritan-Protestant courts alike. As symbols of successful regimes, princely seats were to shine forth above the economic misery of the land and the wretchedness and lack of freedom of its inhabitants; and even the criminal codes enacted by the guardians of such paradises were, in the eyes of their contemporaries, justified by political necessity.

When the Enlightenment began to tear aside the curtains with which the absolutist theory of the state had concealed the political conditions of the population, even architectural "high style" was no longer secure and was never again to be secure. This style was always an expression of belief in the power of the princes.

Early Forms in the 15th and 16th Centuries

Wherever castle and town combined to form an architectural unit, a clash of irreconcilable political ideas occurred, and the tensions between them could never be ironed out unless one party subjugated the other. In Nuremberg, the town succeeded in doing this when it took possession of the Imperial and, later, Hohenzollern castle (see chap. 4). In Landshut, at almost the same time, the castle was victorious. The young duke Henry had defeated the rebellious townspeople between 1408 and 1410 and, by confiscating all the patricians' property, had broken their power forever.

From the 10th to the end of the 12th centuries, we come across castles

Figure 97. The Louvre (miniature by Paul de Limburg, 1415–16, from the duc de Berry's *Très Riches Heures,* Chantilly, Musée Condé)

everywhere that were built to protect a market settlement, and markets that were organized by a castle to provision it. The growth and increasing power of these market settlements gave rise to conflicts. From the 12th century onward, the new territorial princes built themselves castles within the city limits. We shall encounter examples in Munich and Vienna. In Paris, too, the king lived at first in the Palais de la Cité and then in the Louvre, the sort of castle that was constantly being expanded with new fortifications. Contemporary drawings show that these castles appeared even mightier and more impregnable to the townspeople of the time than they do to us. See, for example, the Louvre, as portrayed by the brothers Limburg in the duc de Berry's *Book of Hours* (fig. 97). The prince often moved his castle to the periphery of the town so as to place a field of fire between himself and the people he governed. Again the Louvre is the best-known example. In Munich, too, the ducal castle was removed for these very reasons from the old court in the middle of the city to its northern edge (see below, this chapter). Sometimes princes built their castles far from their palaces, the better to protect their regime. In this connection we may think of the Tower of London or the Bastille in Paris (see chap. 7). Bishops, too, could not do without such castles to protect their regime, and, because their territorial power was small, they could only hold their own when there was an impregnable hilltop available on which to build their castles: Würzburg and Salzburg are the best examples (figs. 136 and 125). Up to the baroque period, individual princes of the Church attempted to secure their power over cities by building powerful citadels. A plan of Münster shows how difficult it was for them to assert their power there (fig. 98). Even in Rome the contrast was apparent. Without the heritage that antiquity had bestowed upon the Middle Ages and the Renaissance in the form of the impregnable Castello S. Angelo, the papal rule over the city could not have been ensured, and the Vatican, despite the tomb and church of St. Peter, could never have assumed the function of palace of government. It needed the direct protection of the castle (see chap. 8). In Vienna, as late as the end of the 15th century, the emperor Frederick III had to protect himself against a rebellious citizenry for six weeks, and the events made such a deep impression on the young Maximilian I that he hardly ever entered the city again, but instead completed the residence in Wiener Neustadt. Something similar happened in the 1640s in Paris during the rebellions of the Fronde, under Mazarin and Anna of Austria; it was one reason for Louis XIV's decision to complete Versailles.

A classic monument to the town-versus-castle conflict, and one which

Figure 98. The fortification complexes in Münster, 1763, before the destruction of the episcopal citadel

has been preserved to this day, is Heidelberg and its castle. The counts palatine had built a magnificent castle of the Renaissance and mannerist period high above the city on the Neckar (fig. 99). Later, religious conflicts also increased the tension between the inhabitants of this small town and the lord of the castle. Consequently, the original, extensive castle was not rebuilt in 1699 after the ravages of Louis XIV's armies in the War of the Palatinate, and it was thought preferable to construct a new residence in Mannheim, the plans for which we have already seen. City and castle had always existed side by side in Heidelberg. In 1719, Alberti, the court architect, drew up an imaginative plan which attempts to bring both into an organic relationship by means of a bold approach road.

We can speak of princely seats in terms of their architectural form only where a castle could open itself up toward the city, and where the city's main streets led up to the castle, the prince's territorial power having made any uprising impossible. At the same time, in many places from the 16th century onward, that new unity of castle and city arose which is the third outstanding architectural event of European urban planning—after the ecclesiastical cities of the early Middle Ages and the city-states of the late Middle Ages.

There were many intermediate stages, attempts to bring a medieval town and a burgher settlement into a single unit, increasing in number after the 15th century. In such cases, the initiatives always came from the victorious princes or from the ruler of the city, for wherever the citizens were victorious they razed every castle in a paroxysm of force, as was the case in Lucca with the fortress Agosta of the condottiere Castruccio Castracane. We have to distinguish between towns where an opening up of the castle did not result in any other architectural changes, towns where city and castle developed peacefully side by side, and a third group of towns where they achieved a direct relationship to one another.

In Landshut (fig. 100), the ducal castle, Trausnitz, remained an architectural unit of its own. Its hill site bore no relation to the valley town. After their victory over the townspeople, however, the princes felt respon-

Figure 99 The town and castle of Heidelberg, before the castle's destruction

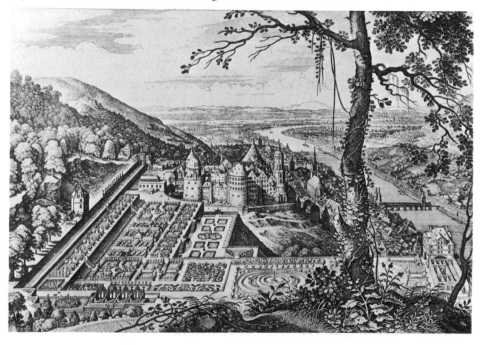

189

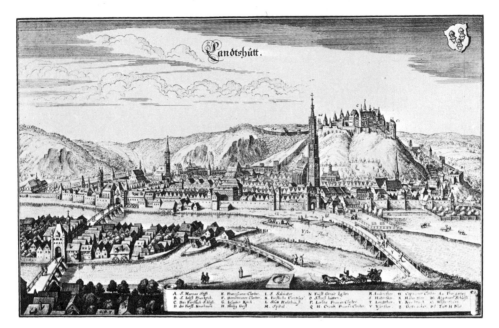

Figure 100. Landshut (after Merian, 1643)

sible for the development of the town. The massive interior of the church of St. Michael and its widely renowned brick tower, the tallest in Germany, were paid for, essentially, by the princely house. The facades of the houses on the long, broad, street market also had the princely house to thank for their constant renovation. It is significant that a Renaissance palace in the burgher town was only completed when Landshut had sunk to being the residence of the posthumous sons or heirs to the throne and when the princes' position of power no longer had to be defended inside the walls.[2]

If we look at the plan of the town of Urbino (fig. 101), we see that the duke Federigo da Montefeltro had no trouble building himself his famous unfortified Renaissance castle inside the burgher settlement: the little town never had a chance to carry on an independent political life. Yet the great palace stands like an important burgher dwelling on the main square, having made no attempt to determine the form of that square. The magnificence of the imposing courtyards only becomes evident on the inside. The topography of the place conditioned the organic unity of palace and town. The castle crowned the ridge on which it was built. But the possibility of opening up the town toward the castle, so that its rows of houses—as was

later the case in Berlin (fig. 114) or Versailles (fig. 140)—should appear to
be directed toward it and to illustrate both the prince's claim to power and
the relationship of his subordinates to the monarch, was not yet appreciated. The castle stood on a town square and merely turned one of its sides
toward it.

This is also true of the extensive complexes built by the Gonzagas in
Mantua. From 1273 onward, when the first Bonacolsi, and even more so in
1328, when the first Gonzaga, began to rule the free municipality and its
territory, the castle, which eventually contained fourteen courtyards, was
expanded, ever more opulently, into one of the finest residences in Europe
and was furnished with one of the finest art collections in Europe. Furthermore, this castle dominated the city between the three lakes because it controlled its most important point of access, the Ponte San Giorgio. Together
with the buildings of the oldest power in the city, the cathedral and the
episcopal palace, it formed that monumental group which has often been
renovated but in which no one building stands in a direct relation to another. The piazza, however, is misshapen and has no political function. It
was never a market. At best it was a place where tournaments could take
place. No one ever paid attention to it as an object of urban planning. Castle
and city stood, and stand, next to one another just as the Piazza Sordello

Figure 101. Urbino at the end of the 18th century. Montefeltro's castle at the highest point of the town
lies on the main road and unfolds toward the interior.

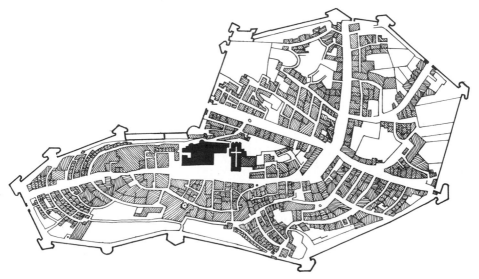

stands next to the Piazza d'Erbe, on which the municipal palace stood and still stands and where, as in many subject communities, a Madonna and a clock have replaced every other emblem of rank on the city's tower. In the heyday of the Gonzagas in the 16th century, and right up to the time of the city's defeat and pillage in 1630 at the hands of generals from Wallenstein's armies, the population grew to 30,000. Peace with its neighbors permitted Mantua to develop a certain degree of prosperity, in spite of a tremendous burden of taxation. The princely house took charge of the renovation of the most important churches, often by the finest architects in Italy. Giulio Romano, a royal architect, came to the court. His open castle in front of the town's gates, the Palazzo del Te (begun in 1624), can be considered the first unfortified castle to be built in open country. It also had a significant effect upon the arts of the courts of France and the Holy Roman Empire. It was connected with the famous stud farm, where the Mantuaner were bred, one of the main sources of income for this small princedom. There were gardens, too. We have a complete plan for the residence, but it has failed to fuse together into an urban architectural unity.

As early as the 15th century, attempts were made to integrate city and palace. Vigevano may be considered the first example (fig. 102). The extremely large castle complexes there served the Visconti and, later, the Sforzas as a summer residence. Opulently as certain wings of the castle were extended in the 15th century, however, it remained a *rocca,* with defensive wall and towers. In front of it, Ludovico il Moro enclosed the old town square on three sides with a colonnade: on the fourth stood the town church and, later, the cathedral.[3] The square was intended as an outer courtyard for the castle, to the portal of which a steep flight of steps led up under two loggia arches. Because the idea was so novel, it was ascribed to Leonardo. It is true that square and castle are a self-contained complex, but the topographical coordination was intended to point to new paths.

I am quite prepared to state that Vigevano—not Pienza—is the most perfect spatial conception of the early Italian Renaissance. It is based on a new conception of a proper program for the seat of a court. The sweeping colonnade, taken from the world of Leonardo's ideas, and the three-story gate tower, built according to one of Bramante's ideas, form an architectural group of great formal logic. When Caramuel Lobkowitz, an important architectural theoretician, was elected bishop in 1673, after Vigevano had lost all significance as a princely seat, he wanted to reorientate the castle forecourt with the aid of a new and bold cathedral facade. In this way, the complex had a double relationship. The change from a medieval street mar-

Figure 102. Vigévano (aerial photograph showing the square, castle, and cathedral)

ket into a Renaissance castle square and a baroque cathedral square can be read off as a process of lamination. The aesthetic message of the three stages of development combines into an experiential unit.

It could be said that the attempt to combine castle and town into one unit was first hazarded by Francis I with his additions to the old Louvre and, soon thereafter, by his successors' new buildings right down to Catherine de' Medici's Tuileries. The opening up of the royal castle inward toward the city and outward toward the park grounds was, from that time on, regarded as a sign of secure power. We shall discuss some individual cases later (see chap. 7). In Turin, that opening up began with the reorganization of the whole structure of the city.

Turin

The history of the city as a princely seat and as a center for the production of art began in 1599 with the return of Emmanuel Filibert of Savoy to his inheritance, which, while in the service of Spain, he had liberated from French occupation. He found a Roman city of medium size (770 m by 710 m), whose walls, gates, and street grid had been preserved through the Middle Ages (fig. 103). The Romans had placed the geometric layout of their city between the rivers Dora and Po on a spit of land from which, between the Alpine crest and the river, they could rule the fertile plain. The medieval community had established itself in the ruined area and, with its cathedral complex and its twenty-one parishes, had created some new neighborhoods, but considerable areas remained empty, which could be covered with greenery. The few new streets, like the diagonal axis that joins cathedral and market, the former Piazza d'Erbe and the present-day Piazza di Città, had developed from beaten tracks running diagonally across the ruins. At the same time, the desire of the small merchants and the craftsmen to settle near one another and near the market split up many Roman *insulae* (fig. 104). The Langobardic dukes and, later, the Frankish counts expanded the most important Roman gates into castles. Thus, the Porta Palatina became first the Palazzo and then the Porta Ducale. Not until the advent of

Figure 103. Emanuele Filiberto's Turin in 1577: the Roman city, castle, and citadel (woodcut by Giovanni Csiegher)

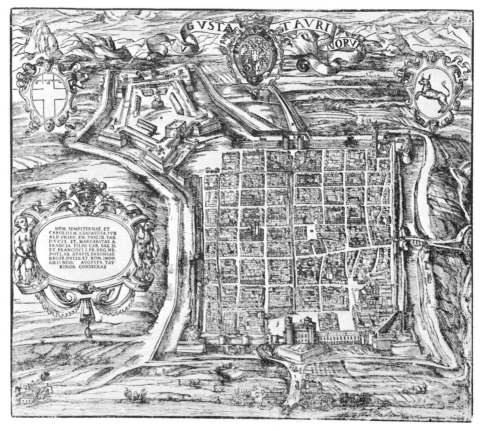

194

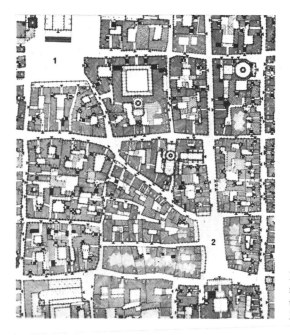

Figure 104. Turin: city center, with the medieval path from the cathedral (1) to the marketplace (2) (after A. Cavalleri-Murat)

modern archeology was the cloak of history removed to reveal the beautiful remains of the original building. The Porta Praetoria, next to which the smaller Porta Fibellona stood in the Middle Ages, was enlarged and became the castle of the city governors. Between 1348 and 1403, large areas were cleared behind it, toward the city, and in front of it, toward the Po, in order to make a field of fire for the newly developed artillery. As in many other places, Turin used the solid Roman ashlar to secure later strongpoints. Up to 1559, the Roman site was large enough for the modest increase in population. The city was never an important medieval trading center. Agriculture remained the main source of income. Although the Roman walls had been renovated, they were only reinforced at the corners with a few bastions. In 1559, Emmanuel Filibert first considered making the old castle into a fortified complex comparable with the Castello Sforcesco in Milan (fig. 96). But plans were already drawn up in 1564 for a five-pointed star-shaped citadel in front of the walls, whose cannon could protect both the city's endangered southern and western flanks and, in an emergency, the prince himself. The decision to build this citadel determined all that happened later. Turin wanted to be regarded as a fortress. The castle inside it could become the center of the city and could be opened up on all sides (fig. 105).

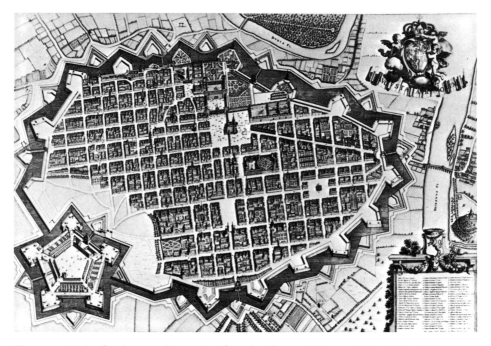

Figure 105. Turin after the second expansion (from the *Theatrum Statutum Regiae Celsitudinis Sabaudiae Ducis*, 1682)

The court buildings were completed to its north—the palace with the royal gardens behind it and extending in front of it on the bastions. The chapel of the national relic, the shroud of Christ, was integrated into the palace. This chapel became both the burial place of the princes and the choir of the cathedral. The Piazza Castello, in front of the residence, was developed into a state square, the political center of the princedom, which was later to become a kingdom (see below, fig. 108).[4]

The ruling house built and expanded the capital into an imposing residence in the most logical manner. Three characteristics distinguished all construction: (1) the old city retained its Roman street grid and developed the new districts on this grid; (2) the city area was enlarged threefold and on three sides by the addition of meticulously planned districts, which were related to the castle and the court by means of great street axes leading to the center of the city; (3) strict building statutes were enacted, which compelled the inhabitants to build similar facades for their houses and palaces on all streets of the old as well as the new cities, and these statutes were kept in force from the end of the 16th to the beginning of the 19th century.

It is of great significance that here, for the first time, all the buildings of the princely seat were supposed to adopt the high style of the prince's palace. Throughout the city, there was a desire for colonnades and monumental facades. The whole city was ordered to don an aristocratic and imposing raiment that in other cities—even in Paris—was reserved for the palaces of the nobility alone. In Versailles in the 17th century, or Potsdam in the 18th, similar attempts would be made. The city architects of Stockholm and St. Petersburg had the same thing in mind. The princely seat was to greet the visitor in a more imposing manner than the provincial cities, insofar as these themselves were not suburbs, residences, or hunting lodges like Venaria Reale (see below, fig. 110). There was, in addition, a fourth characteristic: all new towns had to be integrated with the old town and the fortress into a carefully thought-out system of fortifications. Because of its great strategic value, the little Catholic princedom on both sides of the Alpine crest had, throughout its history, to reckon with attacks from the great powers of France, Milan, and Austria and was subjected to two extremely harsh sieges, in 1639 and 1706.

Of the three outlying districts, the first to be built according to the plans of Ascanio Vittozzi (active in Turin 1584–1615) and commissioned by Carlo Emmanuel (1580–1630) was the one on the south. Its main axis, the present-day Via Roma, led from the Porta Nuova, across the Piazza San Carlo to the Piazza Castello and the residence. Its ring of fortifications was directly connected to the citadel. The plans were continued under the direction of Carlo di Castellamonte (after 1620). Engravings of the siege of 1639 show that little more than the single, large axis had then been built up. It took almost a century for the Piazza San Carlo and its two churches to be formed into that masterpiece of urban design admired by all later planners (fig. 106). But Vittozzi and his successors, the brothers Carlo and Amadeo di Castellamonte, in their capacity as first engineers and architects of the dukes, had already planned a second extension toward the east, the main axis of which, the Via Po, was to link the bridge over the river with the state square.

This expansion, which enlarged the city by almost a third, was not started until the reign of Carlo Emanuele II in 1673. After his death it was completed by his wife, Maria Giovanna. Once again, the circle of bastions had to be extended, and, as a result, the Città Nuova to the south and the old city to the north were organically linked. The princes were able to take advantage of this to extend their gardens on the bastions and their government buildings along the present-day Via Verdi. It was of great significance

Figure 106. Piazza San Carlo, looking toward the Porta Nuova (engraving, ca. 1740)

for the city organism as a whole to be able to push forward right to the Po bridge. The declivity of the river afforded architects the opportunity of laying out one of the finest squares, the present-day Piazza Vittorio Veneto.

The total project was completed when King Victor Amadeus II (1675–1730) commissioned Filippo Juvarra in 1714 to cover over the last of the flat land in the western corner of the city. Juvarra, like Guarino Guarini before him, took this opportunity to develop a newer and nobler monumental style.

With this final extension, the city acquired its well-known almond shape (fig. 105). We have to realize that, in contrast to the city-states of the Middle Ages and the Renaissance and, as we shall see, in contrast to the capital cities, the natural process of growth in Turin was directed into strictly regulated paths. Planning always ran ahead of growth. The improbable succeeded: the architecture of the city had the strength to vary the main motifs. The streets around the palace filled up with inhabitants. The individuals who had commissioned the buildings occupied only the *piani nobili* of their palaces; the ground floors and upper floors, like the courtyards in the rear, were left for the lower orders—craftsmen's families, small merchants, servants, officials, and soldiers. Thus arose that fortunate sociological admixture of population, which led in large measure to the characteristic national discipline of the Piedmontese.

Ascanio Vittozzi and his successors the two Castellamontes, and, among others, Guarino Guarini from 1668 to 1689 and Filippo Juvarra from 1714 onward, to name only the most important, preserved their plans in large-scale drawings and circulated them in the form of engravings. These go far beyond what could have been realized, and enter the realm of the utopian. Thus, the series of engravings *Theatrum Statutum Regiae Celsitudinis Sabaudiae Ducis* (Amsterdam, 1682), which contains thirty-eight plates of Turin alone, shows a princely seat in which all the buildings were designed to proclaim the fame and power of the princes. The idea transcended the reality: it had to be read in the light of the ideal. The princes of Europe, to whom this wonder was sent, gazed in astonishment at the extravagant plans of their cousins in Savoy, who were already deeply in debt. The imagination also likes to play with the idea that these plans fell into the hands of the self-confident citizens of Amsterdam in the Herren- or Prinsengracht after they had already completed, in huge numbers, their more modest, but more individual, facades. The whole difference between a wealthy commercial city and a princely seat can be made clear if we draw such a comparison. The statutes designed to realize the plans of the princes in Turin are among the most important sources of architectural thought of the 17th and 18th centuries. The two regents, Madame Royale (1638–48) and Maria Giovanna (1675–84), imposed their architectural wishes upon their subordinates with particular urgency.[5] Only in this way could the general uniformity of the streets succeed on that higher artistic level. Almost the whole body of buildings from the Middle Ages and the Renaissance was removed from the field of vision.

Every one of the "ruling" architects developed his own formal language. We can infer from the whole sweep of a street whether it was erected by Vittozzi, the two Castellamontes, Guarino Guarini, or Juvarra. The plastically mobile architectural figures of Guarini and, later, the rococo and classicism of Juvarra grew out of the sober linearism and the Palladian severity and shaftlike streets of Vittozzi and the later Castellamontes. Thus, the average height of palaces under Guarini increased from 18 to 23 meters. The larger city made monumental buildings seem a necessity. Solutions were still sought along the modish lines of Paris—the establishment of elegant tracts between a mansion and its gardens. But the espalier of the Roman street grid in the old city and its continuations in the new was retained, for it was known that the finest fruit could ripen on it. The mobile facades

Figure 107. Piazza Castello (engraving by Giambattista Borra, 1749)

of the high baroque and of Piedmontese rococo give an element of vitality against a background of the soberly horizontal and vertical lines of late mannerism. Examples of this are the facades of San Carlo and Santa Cristina, which flank the narrow side of the Piazza San Carlo (fig. 105), and the cupola ornamentation of the two Guarini churches, San Sindone and San Lorenzo, on the Piazza Castello (figs. 107, 108). Precisely because freedom of exterior design had been limited by the state, creative imagination felt compelled to achieve the boldest possible interior spaces. The city possesses its own morphology. Its churches and cupolas have often been described.[6] One is amazed at the number and variety of forms of courtyards, vestibules, outside staircases, and stairwells that open up behind the facades. The desire to beautify, the *embellissement* that the French theory of art made into a princely duty, caused many architects constantly to rethink even those streets, axes, and squares that already existed. The extension of the medieval marketplace on the site of the Roman forum and its enclosure by arcades offer one example.

More was built in Piedmont and its capital than in any other state in Italy. This building activity, which pushed economic feasibility to the limit, created a building craft of the very highest quality, permitting even the boldest architectural dreams to become reality.

This is particularly true of the court and government buildings. According to Vittozzi's plans, as transmitted by the *Theatrum Sabaudiae,* the citadel and the royal palace, with their squares and gardens, were to be combined into a unit that was to be accessible to the public or at least to any man of breeding. The plan for the state square included the bridge and the domed building from which the state relic, the shroud with the face of Christ, could be shown to the populace. The old castle was replaced and completed by a new one between 1658 and 1675 (fig. 109). Besides Guarini's brilliant solution for the dome of the reliquary, and the monumental staircase that Juvarra placed in front of the old castle (the later Palazzo Madama), additional buildings for the ministry (Segretario di Stato), the court archives, the royal theater, and other institutions were constantly required. The court area was extended by the military academy, the university, the riding school, and the mint. We get the impression that people were looking for excuses to build new buildings. Every prince wanted to prove himself by way of buildings, every architect wanted to persuade him to build

Figure 108. Piazza Castello, Via Po, and the government tracts (after the plans drawn by Ascanio Vittozzi and the brothers Castellamonte, 1674)

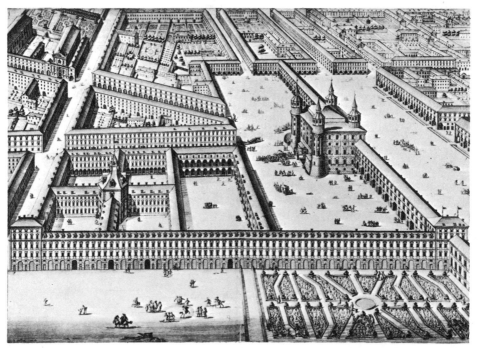

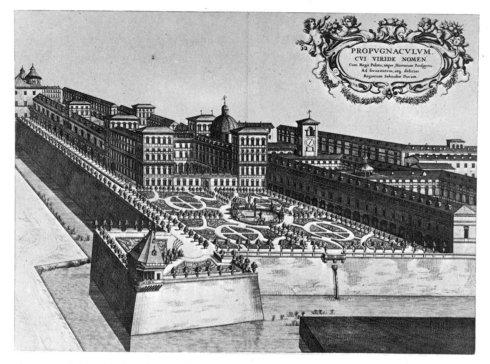

Figure 109. Palazzo Reale and the gardens on the bastions, 1692

larger ones. Planning became a duty of the state. Juvarra's decision to use an immense order of pilasters, which would have been worthy of a castle, to highlight the barracks he was asked to build at the other end of the city on the site of the former Porta Susina was but a reflection of this need to gain distinction through buildings.

Yet at no time could Turin be set beside those masterpieces of Italian planning, Florence or Venice, Siena or even Lucca. Its streets of palaces cannot be compared to those of Rome or Genoa. The royal building statutes allowed too little freedom of design either to those who commissioned buildings or those who designed them. Statutes that ordered the rapid completion of whole districts prevented loving attention to detail. Turin resembled, and still does, a manual of architecture. We feel as though we have not been accepted into an organic urban context.

The court tracts inside the city corresponded to charitable foundations—convents and churches of pilgrimage—outside the city. They were all overshadowed, both in rank and in height, by Juvarra's Superga, which had been promised by Victor Amadeus II after the siege by the French in 1706, together with a circle of hunting lodges and pleasure seats on both sides of the Po, farther out into the country. One of the essential characteristics of absolutism was that all princes, at all times, had leisure for hunting and for country parties. A do-nothing king like Philip IV of Spain, who spent most of his time hunting, was regarded as a perfect monarch. The court treasury of Piedmont sometimes had to support more than ten large complexes. The farther away from the capital the castles were built, as the supplies of game became exhausted, the larger they had to be, so as to accommodate the whole court. The highpoints were Venaria Reale to the north, begun at the same time as the new buildings in Versailles and competing with it from 1660 onward, and Juvarra's country and hunting estate, Stupinigi to the south, built when Victor Amadeus was elevated to the kingdom of Sardinia in 1729.

The magnificent layout of the town and castle of Venaria appeared in 1674 in a series of thirty-one engravings by Giorgio Tasniere (fig. 110; the castle has now fallen into total decay). Besides dwellings for the court and ceremonial sites, there were game preserves, birdhouses, fishponds, extensive stables, orangeries and lemon groves, grand avenues and ecclesiastical

Figure 110. Venaria Reale (engraving of 1740)

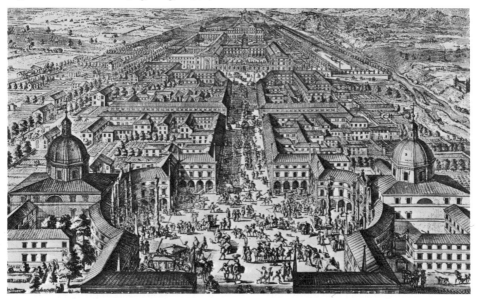

buildings, and, last but not least, the regularly laid-out suburb; every building was constructed in the highest possible style it could sustain. Venaria
was further enlarged by Juvarra, under Victor Amadeus II in 1713, when he
added the country estate and palace of La Mandria. Today there are 350 deer
and a pheasantry with 70,000 birds. It is beyond the scope of this book to
describe the continued development of the castle concept into a baroque
geometric pattern, as manifested by Venaria Reale and Juvarra's masterpiece, Stupinigi.

When, the day after his entry into the city on 22 June 1800, Napoleon
ordered the castellated fortresses of the city to be razed (only the citadel
was to be preserved), it was still not the end of Turin as a princely seat.
Using Paris as a model, Napoleon surrounded the city with huge boulevards instead of fortifications. But in 1815 the royal house moved back into
its old castles and extended them. The monumental style of the street axes
was retained, for the population increased slowly and allowed the city to
expand southward. It was not until the 1890s that the process of growth
began which turned Turin into an industrial city and has today increased
the built-up area more than tenfold. The Fiat company's Turin is gradually
stifling the princely city; the Roman *insulae* are being depopulated.

Munich

The difference in point of departure makes the Bavarian capital a striking
contrast to Turin, whether we consider the city at the end of the 16th century, at the end of the 18th, or in its present form. In Munich there has
always been a conflict between the burgher city and the royal city, a point I
shall stress in my discussion of Vienna (see chap. 7).

Commentary on the city plan at every point in its history reminds us
of this conflict (figs. 111 and 113). The state buildings of the open, northern
part of the city and the municipal buildings of the closed, southern part still
form contrasting groups today. The center of interest of the former are the
extensive court complexes, and of the latter, the Marienplatz with its old
and, later, new city hall, flanked by the two dominating parish churches, St.
Peter (der alte Peter) and the Frauenkirche, as well as by the circle of medieval monastic buildings which have today been almost entirely absorbed
into secular building complexes.

The point of departure was the fact that the burgher city preceded the
royal city and that the dukes, at least until the end of the 15th century, found
it advantageous to encourage the burgher community's industry and the

Figure III. Munich at the end of the 18th century: 1, St. Peter; 2, der Alte Hof; 3, Frauenkirche; 4, mint; 5, old city hall; 6, Franciscans; 7, Augustines; 8, Anger gate; 9, Sendlinger gate; 10, Karl gate (Neuhauser gate); 11, Schwabinger gate; 12, Isar gate; 13, Jesuits; 14, Maxburg; 15, new palace; 16, court garden; 17, Theatiner; 18, Marienplatz.

expansion of its settlement area. In the beginning, there was one settlement on the road running parallel to the Isar, with a cattle market; then there was a small town on either side of the street market, its main street the Salz-straße, which led from the ford over the Isar. South of the market street, which still today retains its character as a shopping street, stood the first parish church of St. Peter (1). An earlier building on this site was the chapel of the fortified palace of Henry the Lion.

The dukes of Bavaria erected their first castle (2) at the northeast corner of the settlement, after wresting power over the city from the bishops of Freising. As early as 1271, Bishop Konrad of Freising argued his case for approval of a second parish church, the Frauenkirche (3), by remarking that the population had grown "immeasurably." There was a population of 5,000, perhaps 6,000. The second half of the 13th century and the first half of the 14th were the true periods of growth of the burgher city. Louis the Bavarian, king from 1314, emperor from 1328 to 1347, was preoccupied with the idea of making Munich the capital of the Holy Roman Empire, an idea his successor, Charles IV, successfully carried out in the case of Prague. Under the reign of the Wittelsbacher emperor, Munich grew to the size it remained until 1789. It only expanded once more, in the northern part, to make room for the Hofgarten (Palace Garden) under Maximilian I (1591–1651). But no specifically political organizations were placed in the settlement areas to the south, east, and west. No parishes were added, only the mendicant orders. The northern district alone was an exception. The ducal court felt itself threatened by a citizenry which was gaining in strength, and in 1385 it removed its castle from the Alte Hof (2) into the area of the new palace, the Neue Residenz (15), the systematic completion of which was to take six centuries. The Frauenkirche is a monument to the power of the citizenry, its 102-meter-long nave and its twin towers, 99 meters high, were all built between 1466 and 1492. We know of no other building of comparable monumental quality that achieves such a peaceful and simple effect as this burgher cathedral. The effect comes not merely from the materials of which the cathedral is constructed but rather from the distillation of a whole cast of mind that distinguishes the brick surfaces in Munich from the luxurious stone filigrees of St. Stephen's cathedral in Vienna (see chap. 7). We are reminded neither of Nuremberg's St. Lawrence, with its free imperial city's brilliance, nor of Prague Cathedral, courtly and conscious of its rank. The modest grandeur of the Frauenkirche represents the zenith of what the citizenry of a country town could achieve.

At the same time, between 1470 and 1480, the old city hall (das Alte Rathaus [5]) was built, in whose great hall a ballroom motif by Erasmus Grasser with sixteen Morris dancers was combined with a political motif that set out to reproduce the orders of the world and of the state. The wooden ceiling, between its sun and moon, was adorned with eleven sculpted and ninety-nine painted coats of arms representing the Wittelsbach system of land and family alliances. These coats of arms were grouped around the imperial coats of arms of Louis the Bavarian, the national coats of arms of the dukes, and those of the city with its monk. Burgher power and ducal power seemed to have reached a state of equilibrium.

This was all changed by the peace treaty after the War of the Landshut Succession. The partial dukedoms were united. The court gave up all of its old residences in Ingolstadt, Landshut, Straubing, and Burghausen, though they still looked on them as secondary residences. From this moment on, the royal city began step by step to crowd out the burgher city. Characteristic of the whole situation were the three building projects of the 16th century which were developed during the longest period of peace in the empire from the Peace of Augsburg in 1555 until the start of the Thirty Years' War in 1618. The projects, all initiated and financed by the court, were the new Jesuit establishment of 1559 (13), whose church was built between 1583 and 1597 and for which thirty-six houses were sacrificed; William V's castle, the later Maxburg (14), which required the sites of fifty-six houses; and the extension of the palace (15), which became the largest in Europe. Maximilian I completed the palace in 1616 and had to be ready to extend the expensive fortifications so as to be able to build the palace garden, which extended in front of the palace on the north side. These three building projects (13–15) are all related in style. They are characteristic works of early absolutism, whose essential traits owe less to the concepts of the late Renaissance or early baroque than to the later concepts of a court art that is both humanist and mannerist.

The Jesuit church of St. Michael, too, and the convent and chapter buildings are part of this plan. It was to be perceived, at one and the same time, as the hall of fame and the mausoleum of the royal house. Statues of the Wittelsbach dynasty were placed in niches on the facade of the church above the patron saint, St. Michael, the angel of justice.

Munich's first heyday had been determined by the burghers; this second one was entirely determined by the court and was brought to an end by the uncontested surrender of the city to the Swedes in 1632 and, subse-

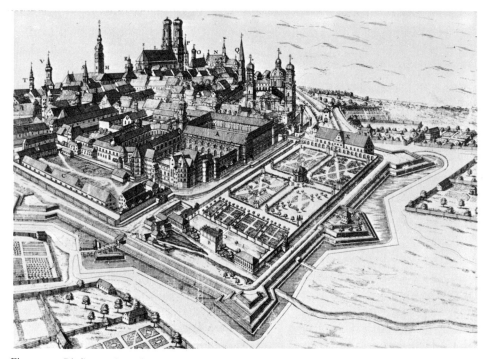

Figure 112. Bird's-eye view of Munich from the northeast, 1701 (after M. Wenig); court gardens and palace in the foreground.

quently, by the plague, which claimed more than a third of the population. Economically, the city was unable to recover from this reverse until the 19th century. Only one further large-scale royal building project was added, the Theatiner convent and church (17), which Henrietta Adelaide of Savoy commissioned in 1662 to celebrate the birth of Max Emmanuel, heir to the throne. The church was consecrated in 1675. The elder Cuvilliés did not complete the facade until 1768. This building introduced a Roman Baroque dome into the city's late Gothic skyline.

The palace was extended in the later 17th century and again in the 18th. Part of this extension are Cuvillié's "Reiche Zimmer" ("Opulent Rooms"), the apartment for Charles Albert (1735–45), which first proclaimed his aspiration to imperial dignity—a dignity he enjoyed for three unhappy years. Later, the same architect was to add his famous theater, commissioned by Max III Joseph (1745–77). Each new generation had its own apartment expensively furnished in the elegant suites. But the palace did not open up toward the city until the 19th century. It had only one frontage on a street and one garden front (fig. 112); it developed its splendor by means of additional inner courtyards, like the Gonzaga palace in Mantua. For this reason, Nicolai in 1778 compared it to a giant convent building with the statue of Mary, the patron saint of Bavaria, on the street front.

Like the dukes and kings of Savoy, the Bavarian electoral princes always sought to surround their seat with hunting lodges, in which, in the 18th century, the court mostly resided. Munich epitomizes the fact that castle building as a demonstration of a prosperous regime, demanded by theories of the state, was in the 18th century a necessity from which European states could not escape even in times of the direst need. When Max Emmanuel of Bavaria (1679–1726) returned in 1715 to his impoverished land after a humiliating defeat, he immediately felt obliged to develop and execute plans—which had been drawn up in the earlier and more successful years of his reign—for building castles. Schleißheim was completed, and Nymphenburg was enlarged to its present size. Fürstenried and Dachau were completed. Nymphenburg, with a total breadth of 685 meters, had now become the largest castle complex in the empire. Few complained of the new fiscal burdens. Most people applauded the additional credit from the court treasury, which provided work for craftsmen. Both of the main castles, Nymphenburg and Schleißheim, were so well related to the city that they could be reached in less than half a day's coach ride. They were both attached to a system of canals fed by the waters of the river Wurm, which, as an outlet of the Starnbergersee, joins this lake to the river Isar. This canal system is among the most carefully thought-out achievements of urban and land planning in the 18th century.

Yet the castles and their furnishings also reflect, as political allegories, the program of the regime and the self-image of the princes. Munich and Max Emmanuel serve as an example. When this prince returned to his capital in 1688, after his victories over the Turks, he had a suite of rooms in the palace painted with murals illustrating the successes of Alexander the Great. The "Alexander rooms," which burned down in the 18th century, depicted him as the new Alexander defending the West against the East, which he finally subjugates. In the murals at Schleißheim castle, which were also commissioned by Max Emmanuel after years of exile in the Netherlands, we see him, in another allegorical pantomime, as a severely tested, widely traveled "pius Aeneas." Everyone caught the meaning. Even the last three buildings he commissioned may be understood as a testimony to the aging prince—the Pagodenburg (1716–19), in which, catching at a plan from the time of his exile (a plan which at that time could not be carried out), he built himself his own "west-east divan," a place to escape from his cares, his Sanssouci; the Badenburg, where this aging man had pictures painted of the female playmates of his Paris years; and, finally, the Magdalene hermitage, a ruin in the forest, half Gothic, half rococo, with ceiling paintings showing Magdalene as a courtly penitent meditating on the four last things. An architectural work as a symbol of *vanitas* was to mark the end of the prince's passionate existence.

When, in the year of the French Revolution, the elector Karl Theodor realized that Munich, the seat of his court, with a population of 36,000 at that time, could no longer be regarded as a fortress, he started a new program for it. It was designed less to serve the court than to serve the citizens—primarily in their search for culture (fig. 113). The fortified walls were the first to go, so that the original palace garden could be enlarged by the English landscape garden. The most important buildings that later Bavarian kings erected on the new royal streets, the Briennerstraße and the Königsplatz (Royal Square, 14), the Ludwigsstraße (13), the Maximiliansstraße and the Josephsplatz (17), and finally the Prinzregentenstraße (19), were cultural castles built on a scale which, at that time, was only to be found in Berlin, Paris, and St. Petersburg and, a little later, in London and Vienna. These were the Glyptothek and the Propyläen on the Königsplatz, the Pinakotheken in the outer city (15), the state library and the state archive, the music academy and the university (21) between the Feldherrenhalle (Hall of the Generals), built on the model of the Loggia dei Lanzi, and the triumphal arch (Siegestor), built on the model of the arch of Constantine, on the Ludwigsstraße. King Ludwig I and his successor, Maximilian, wanted their royal seat to be seen as a "city of art." While the burgher city could expand toward the south and east, partly in an unplanned manner, partly according to the prospectuses of developers, and also, though only since 1880, according to municipal planning, the architects of the royal household developed such bold prospects as the Maximilianeum and the Friedensengel (the Angel of Peace) as the focal points of magnificent streets. They bring the range of hills on the other side of the Isar into a monumental relationship with the nucleus of the old city. They recall the concept of government of the enlightened and constitutional monarchy, in which patronage was just as great a historical necessity as was the building of castles in the 18th century. Thus a style of architecture developed in which a serious sense of decorum, together with a cultured lack of passion, had driven out the plastic strength of the baroque and the witty libertinage of the rococo. It corresponded to a changed concept of political spirituality, which, after the Wittelsbachs had abdicated in 1918, was unable to develop any convincing concepts of urban planning.

Because of the dishonesty of Nazi ideology, the buildings of the Hitler era wounded the city and did nothing to enrich it. The architectural products on the Königsplatz and the Prinzregentenstraße were meant to advertise both a national power that was only of limited reality and, at the same time, a moral order in which even its propagandists never really believed.

Figure 113. Munich: the burgher and state monumental buildings. The selection of buildings illustrates the fact that the separation between the royal city and the burgher city developed according to a law that still operates today. 1, der Alte Peter, 2, der Alte Hof; 3, Frauenkirche; 4, new city hall; 5, old city hall; 6, church of the Augustines; 7, church of the Holy Ghost; 8, Jesuit college and church; 9, Maxburg; 10, residence; 11, Theatiner convent and church; 12, court gardens; 13, Ludwigstraße; 14, Königsplatz; 15, Alte Pinakothek; 16, Neue Pinakothek; 17, Maximilianstraße; 18, Maximilianeum; 19, Prinzregentenstraße with the Bavarian National Museum; 20; Friedensengel (Angel of Peace); 21, university.

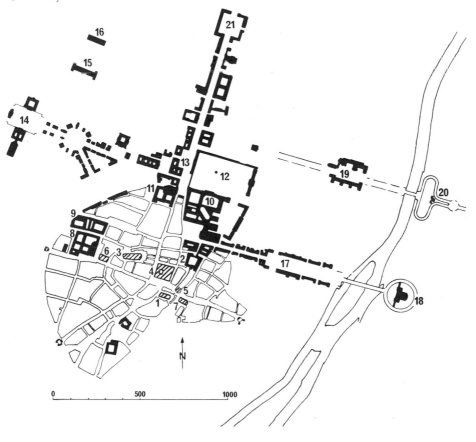

Thus, monuments were built whose semantics served political deception. That the architects themselves were victims of this deception was of no account. The size of the buildings reflected no political reality founded on an accurate understanding of the world.

Berlin as the Seat of a Princely Court

From the beginning of the period of peace ushered in by the Great Elector's victories of 1679—and even, in part, from the end of the Thirty Years' War—up to the beginning of the Seven Years' War in 1756, the capital of the new electoral state of Brandenburg (later the Kingdom of Prussia) is more comparable to Turin than to Munich or Vienna in its architectural profile, despite different points of departure. In the space of nearly a century, Berlin continued to be focused upon the castle at its center.[7] The axes that held this urban web together all led to the castle. The city was enlarged with the help of new, systematically designed towns, which formed independent administrations. The decisive difference from Turin was that soon after 1679 it ceased to regard itself as a fortress. The later walls were designed more for the purpose of making it harder for its own army's soldiers to desert than for defending itself against an enemy.

The history of Berlin can be divided into three parts, which overlap at certain points.[8] Only in the middle period, from 1500 to about 1756, did this center typify a princely seat by its architecture. Previously, Berlin had been a burgher, colonial, and Hanseatic city, in which the ruled owned a castle. Later it developed into a capital, first of the kingdom of Prussia, then, from 1871, of the Second Empire, and, from 1933, of the Third Empire. By Law 46 of the Allied Control Commission, passed on 5 February 1947, which dissolved the Prussian state, Berlin also became something of a "criticial form" in world history. We have the singular phenomenon of a city that was divided, of which every part developed along different lines. During this fourth period in its history, opposing political structures became forms of architecture, subsidized capitalism in the West, forms of dictatorial administration in the East, and between the two a new form in world history: the wall. Here we are only concerned with the second period.

Berlin is first mentioned in the latter half of the 12th century. At that time, two regularly planned colonial settlements lay on either side of the River Spree, the smaller called Cölln and the larger, Berlin. They were not united into one city until 1709. The great-grandchildren of Albert the Bear, the first Ascanian and conqueror of Brandenburg, John I and Otto III (d.

1266/67), were the first to be concerned with the extension of the city. They were also the first to reside there. After 1411, when Frederick VI, burgrave of Nuremberg, had been appointed governor of the Mark Brandenburg by the Emperor Sigismund, all eighteen princes of this dynasty down to William II had a residence in castles in Berlin. Their fortified castle was built on the Spree between 1443 and 1451. The new lords, in bitter struggles against the country gentry and the townspeople, understood how to suppress any movement toward freedom. The relations with the Hanseatic League, to which Berlin owed a rich, brick Gothic style, were dissolved by order of the Hohenzollerns as early as 1451. Berlin, together with all the free cities of Brandenburg, was forced to quit the league of free cities. The new dependence made it possible for the rulers to impose their own conception of rule upon the whole population. Now, there was only the prince, with his officers, soldiers, and subordinates.

Merian (fig. 114) shows Berlin in the first years of the Great Elector's rule (1640–88). This plan must have been drawn up shortly after 1647, the

Figure 114. Berlin (Merian's city plan of 1652)

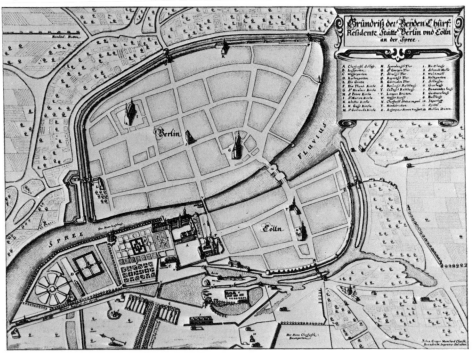

Figure 115. Berlin and Cölln with the beginnings of Unter den Linden (engraving by J. B. Schalk, 1688)

year in which the new ceremonial and processional route, Unter den Linden, was begun. We can see the principle upon which the double city at the crossing of the River Spree, the Lange Brücke (Long Bridge), was planned. The half-city, Berlin, to the east had two parishes, St. Mary and St. Nicholas. Between these parish churches lay the triumphal route of the elector, later called the Königstrasse, extending from the Königstor, past the Berlin city hall to the Lange Brücke, and across the bridge to the square in front of the castle. It ended at the choir of the Dominican church, which the electors, after their conversion to Lutheranism, called their cathedral. The Great Elector built triumphal gates on this route after his victory, and so, later on, did his son, the first king of Prussia, after his coronation in Königsberg in 1701. They gained access to their residences through these gates.

The smaller half-city, Cölln, with only one parish, had its own processional route, the Breite Strasse (Broad Street) which ran past the town hall of Cölln and also led to the cathedral and the castle. The Great Elector had observed correctly that this twin city could develop only in one direction, toward the west. There, in 1647, he laid out the monumental processional route, Unter den Linden, between the castle and the zoological gardens. Berlin was the first seat of a court to include in its architectural plan a street that doubled as a parade ground. It was essential to the calendars of these soldier princes. Unter den Linden, as a military route, became the symbol of the rise of the state (fig. 115).

While the city's three main axes, from the east, south, and west, were all directed toward the castle, the fourth side of the castle was turned toward the palace gardens and thus toward the private domain. The River Spree and its outflow ditch also protected the castle on the outside. As in Turin, the city was opened up to the eyes of its rulers from their palace, while behind it there was room for the life of the court to be carried on.

Berlin emerged from the Thirty Years' War in 1648, and from the Northern War in 1679, with tremendous casualties and impoverished to an unimaginable degree. In 1661, statistics indicate a population of only 6,500, whereas in 1618, it was reckoned at 12,000. When peace was ensured for almost eighty years by the Battle of Fehrbellin, the population was still scarcely 8,000. The four willful rulers who then succeeded one another—Frederick William I (1640–88), his son Frederick III (1688–1713), the soldier king William I (1713–40), and, to a lesser extent, Frederick the Great (1740–86)—tried, each in his own way, to promote the city. Whereas kings and governments—mostly in vain—tried to put limits upon the growth of their capitals, as in London or Paris (see chap. 7), Berlin's rulers, as was the case almost everywhere in eastern Europe, favored the immigration of whole bodies of people, mostly religious refugees, with superior professional skills. Thus, the Great Elector favored the Dutch; Frederick I, primarily the Huguenots but also the Waldensians from the valleys of Piedmont and Walloons from southern Flanders; while William I favored Protestants from Bohemia. The capital was recruited for, just like the army. The Brandenburgers even gave asylum to fifty Jewish families, whom the emperor Leopold had expelled from Austria in 1688. They multiplied rapidly. The Prussian officials were reliable bookkeepers. As early as 1700, Berlin had a population of 28,500; by 1721, 65,300; by 1785, 146,647, of whom, admittedly, 33,386 were members of the garrison if we include wives and children, though this figure does not include officers. The whole urban area was still thought of as five independent cities, with a new city having attached itself to each of the older ones (fig. 116): Berlin; Cölln and Neucölln; Friedrichswerder; Dorotheenstadt on either side of Unter den Linden, a city planned in 1673 and enlarged in 1734; and Friedrichsstadt, whose street plan was laid out in 1688 (fig. 116). It too was enlarged again in 1734. How far the plans of the first king, in particular, were ahead of the potential for the city's growth is illustrated by the fact that four further cities were almost empty a century later. These were Königstadt (1690) and the suburb of Stralau, which was sketched out in the same year; Luisenstadt (1695), whose streets were laid out in 1802, and the suburb of Spandau (1699). Aside from the expansion of Dorotheenstadt and Friedrichsstadt, which was ordered by the Soldier King, nothing more was needed until the beginning of the 19th century. In no other city within our conspectus, except for St. Peters-

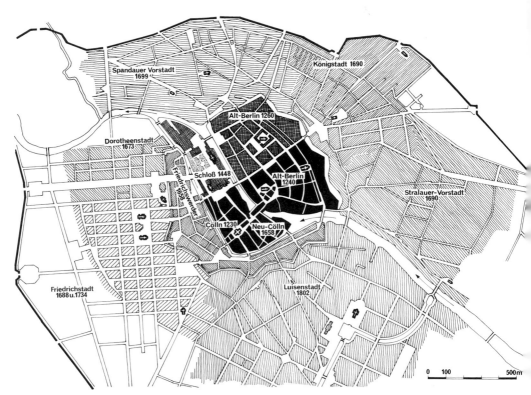

Figure 116. Berlin and its new towns, ca. 1800.

burg, were the street axes projected into the new and the open to such an extent; and in no other was additional space for settlements already identified. Public consciousness regarded new plans and growth, increase in population, growth of economic power, and elaboration of building plans as proofs of a successful regime. In each of the three editions of his description of Berlin and Potsdam as court cities (published between 1769 and 1786), Friedrich Nicolai emphasized that these cities had risen more quickly and were more neatly constructed than any others.[9] The harsh discipline imposed by the state was accepted, for everyone was participating existentially in the process of advancement. At the same time, the citizens remained true to the founding principles of the eastern cities. The older cities were enlarged, but they remained closed units. In Berlin, every extension was regarded as the addition of a new city, built next to an older one. Part of the reason is that the citizens in these large areas to the east were granted no independence of action. All planning was done officially.

The kings encouraged house construction along the new streets by every means at their disposal. We shall describe the same process in Potsdam. The style and dimensions of facades was prescribed. The ideal that all the houses of the middle classes and the palaces of the nobility should be uniform determined architectural thought. A sober, Calvinistic classicism was preferred, which was afforded a certain lightness and charm by models drawn from French architectural treatises. The new streets in Dorotheenstadt and Friedrichsstadt were painted a uniform, very light gray. As in Turin, the inhabitants felt obliged to build in a higher style than they could live in. The Soldier King and Frederick the Great spent almost the same amount of money on their streets as they did on their regiments. Public buildings and numerous churches, most of them marked by a relatively high, single steeple as the focal points of the facades, were subsidized by the kings. The order of buildings and streets was governed just as strictly as the garrison. Everything was prescribed, every house calculated beforehand and enumerated. In 1785, this city consisted of 268 streets and squares, 6,223 front premises, 3,227 back premises, and only 257 houses outside the walls and not planned in advance.[10] About the middle of the 18th century, Berlin was the tidiest royal seat in Europe; all the streets were paved, lit, cleaned, empty, and quiet. The city was a model. However, just as in Turin, a true balance could not be struck between the ordained, superimposed forms and any freely developing artistic work. The energetic and, at the same time, "elegiac" (Hubala) baroque of Andreas Schlüter's palace was pitted against a faint-hearted classicism which lacked plastic power and had virtually to renounce the decorative wealth of the baroque. There are only a few exceptions. This proper decorum of Berlin architecture characterizes the inner dependence of "Prussian" style.

Besides the plans for an increase in population, the rulers were also engaged upon their court-building program. In no other European city was the baroque phase so short. Berlin has only one palace, though there is a circle of country and suburban seats; it has essentially only one ceremonial square and one ceremonial route, admittedly a broad one, Unter den Linden. The history of the palace, the country estates, and the route illustrates not only a change in self-perception on the part of the princes but also the political rise of the city.

Even before the agreement on the new royal status could be signed, the expected elevation in rank induced Frederick I to order a rebuilding of the Alte Schloß (the Old Palace). In Andreas Schlüter (1659–1714) he had at his disposal the one outstanding baroque artist in northern Germany.

Figure 117. The palace in Berlin with the equestrian statue of the Great Elector on the Lange Brücke (from the series of engravings by J. Rosenberg)

Schlüter was a sculptor like Fischer von Erlach, not a military engineer like Lukas von Hildebrandt or Balthasar Neumann. His chef d'œuvre was the encasing of the old palace. He left the side facing the Spree in its original form and completely altered only the main facade, which faced the palace square, and the garden facade. His successor in the royal favor and in the favor of the supreme building authority, Eosander von Göthe, also adhered essentially to Schlüter's plan by designing the third facade, which could be seen from Unter den Linden. Only now was the palace emphasized as a plastic monument in the midst of the street axes, thus becoming a focal point of the old and the new cities. Its size and height, its gravity and sublime majesty gained a new meaning through the extension of the streets that led to this residence. It became a monument to royal dignity. The king's elevation in rank had forced a change in form.

Schlüter's equestrian monument is integrated into this city plan (fig. 117). It did not stand in the middle of the palace square but instead looked down, from a terrace on the Lange Brücke, onto the palace. I should like to assume that the equestrian statue of Henri IV at the Pont-Neuf in Paris was influenced by this arrangement (see below, fig. 170). When the new king made his state entry in 1701, the monument to his father had already been erected, at that time still in gilded plaster. It became the acme of an allegorical triumphal plan.

In its circle of country seats, Berlin differs from the other great princely cities. The oldest of them, Oranienburg, was built as early as 1651–55. Before its enlargement by the first king, the Great Elector built it to suit his wife's taste—as a Dutch house, using Dutch builders and furnishing it by artists brought to Berlin from the Netherlands. In private, as at the court of Peter the Great, Dutch was spoken and life was lived in Puritan style.

Frederick I built a second mansion, in the French style, for his wife, Charlotte, who came from the house of Braunschweig-Lüneburg. The engraving taken from the *Theatrum Europeanum* of 1708 shows the immense plans for this château in a countryside which is still untouched (fig. 118). Nering first built a modest central building. Then, in 1696, Siméon Godeau, a pupil of Le Nôtre's, presented his plan for the gardens, a plan that included the banks of the River Spree. These gigantic gardens forced an enlargement of the château. From 1702 onward, Eosander von Göthe was busy developing plans. They were not completed until after 1740, by Knobels-

Figure 118. Charlottenburg and its grounds (after Eosander's design of ca. 1708)

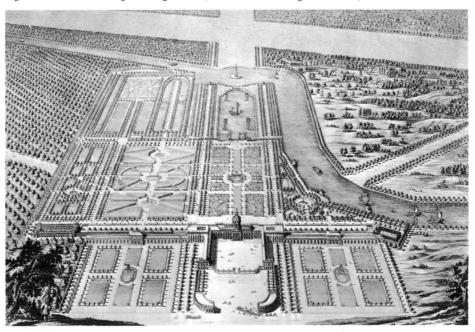

dorff. The long axes, the regularity of the layout, its strict symmetry, the emphasis on the center—achieved by means of a high dome of the sort which, in southern Europe, seemed suited only to churches—proclaim order and clarity as the virtues of this state. We have a metamorphosis of style in which Dutch and French combine with Prussian and later Frederician but which only at the end permits both to come into being. In St. Petersburg (see below, this chapter) we shall see that a Russian baroque, a Russian rococo, and a Russian classicism could be formed out of comparably alien elements.

Unter den Linden, the great avenue for parades and for military drill was, then, intended to be a royal work for the benefit of a citizenry which was gaining in strength, and a means for Berlin to acquire the character of a capital city. At the outset, Schlüter was commissioned only to build the arsenal, a building with a purely military function, to store weapons, in harmony with the original purpose of the avenue. When Frederick the Great commissioned the Catholic church of St. Hedwig, his first thought was to make it possible for Catholic soldiers in his garrison to attend their compulsory church service. The Brandenburger Tor (1783–86), designed by Langhans, was also planned as a triumphal arch for Frederick. Kaiser Wilhelm II was still the only person allowed to ride through its center arch. Yet, on either side of the avenue, more and more buildings arose that were to serve the interests of middle-class culture, among them the opera house, Humboldt University, the state library, and the Academy of Fine Arts. Even the royal pleasure gardens behind the palace on the two arms of the river Spree, into which the ceremonial route debouched, became a forecourt for these cultural buildings. Schinkel built the Alte Museum there between 1808 and 1812. The development of this route between the royal palace and the royal zoological garden from a purely processional route into one that was also a center of culture illustrates Berlin's rise from royal seat to capital city. We have seen a similar development in Munich.

Dresden and Nancy

Both Dresden and Nancy expanded into royal seats in the 18th century under princes who were Polish kings, or bore the title "King of Poland." Similar plans were drawn up for both cities. Augustus the Strong, elector of Saxony from 1695, king of Poland from 1697 to 1733, took the occasion of his elevation in rank to refurbish his residence in Dresden in the most luxurious manner. When his son, the elector Frederick Augustus III, became the Polish king Augustus II (1733–63), he enlisted the aid of Count Brühl to develop his father's program by means of further buildings and to enrich it by assembling unique collections of art and objets d'art. It was not until 1760 that Frederick II's cannon put an end to Saxony's "Augustan Age." The heyday lasted for sixty-three years.

Augustus the Strong's rival for the Polish throne was Stanislas Leszcynski (1677–1766). This Polish prince had fought for his ancestral crown before 1690, and he fought for it again in 1704 and a third time after the death of Augustus the Strong in 1734. It was the great powers, above all Austria prior to 1697 and Russia in 1704 and 1734, that blocked his candidacy. As the father-in-law of Louis XV, Stanislas received in compensation the duchy of Lorraine, which belonged de jure to the empire but de facto to France. A long life enabled Stanislas, as duke of Lorraine (1735–66), to realize his plans for a residence. Research has characterized his building activity with great accuracy.[11] It is not only the work of a disinterested Pole, an old man given over to the joys of life, nor is it merely an outstanding work of French urbanism in the rococo period. Behind everything there stands the desire of an imperial prince—who never gave up the title of king of Poland and refused to renounce his claims—to make his claims visible if only by means of a building program. In order to understand the Place Stanislas in Nancy and the Zwinger in Dresden as comparable projects, despite of differences in time and style, we have to be aware of the historical presuppositions which made both of them possible.

The electorate of Saxony had increased its power under Augustus the Strong's father, John III, because the latter had placed the imperial house under an obligation to him for his help in freeing Vienna from the Turkish army, which was beleaguering it. The expression of the increase in power was the building of the Palais im Großen Garten (the Palace in the Great Garden), which was not only the oldest baroque palace in Saxony but, more than that, the first monumental building in the German-speaking area to be built in the new "grand style." Augustus the Strong owed his elevation in rank to king of Poland, in 1697, to the support of the house of Habsburg. In 1719, his major commission as king of Poland, the Zwinger, was to be opened on the occasion of the marriage of the crown prince, later King Augustus II, to a daughter of the emperor Joseph.[12]

The difficulty that arose in this election was that a Polish king had to be Catholic, while the elector of Saxony was one of the leading Protestants. He was the hereditary president of the *corpus evangelicorum* in the Imperial Diet in Regensburg. Augustus the Strong converted. Like all his successors,

Figure 119. Dresden: the Elbe, with the court church, Brühl terrace, and Frauenkirche
(after Bernardo Belotto)

however, he succeeded in ironing out almost every conflict between the
Catholic court and the Protestant city of Dresden. Two accents determine
the general aspect of the city at the bend in the Elbe (which Augustus the
Strong tried in vain to make into another Grand Canal)—the protestant
burgher church and the Catholic court church (fig. 119). The older building,
the Protestant Church of Our Lady (Frauenkirche), built by the city council's master carpenter, Georg Bähr, between 1726 and 1736 (the lantern was
completed only in 1743), not only is the most important Protestant church
building in the Holy Roman Empire; it also became a superlative piece of
architecture. In its planning, the dual demands of divine service and of
urban planning were constantly, and always afresh, weighed against one
another. The Dôme des Invalides in Paris and Santa Maria della Salute in
Venice are two of the buildings on which it is patterned. In the midst of the
densest concentration of buildings, and built of the same stone, the *Glocke*
seems to lead the square lower story almost without transition into the lofty
dome. The court church, on the other hand, was the last building to be
built anywhere in the empire by an Italian architect. The plans drawn up by
Gaetani Chiaveri, according to which the building on the Elbe was erected,
had at first to be kept secret in this Protestant City.[13] For a long time the
talk was just of a chapel. Then, step by step, the building grew higher, and

222

the remarkable edifice was created in which facade and choir correspond to one another, so that the nave is delimited both in front and behind by semicircular arcades. On the attic, sixty-five saints were erected. The saints chosen corresponded to a conciliatory plan of the Jesuits, not to the bellicose one of the Counterreformation, and are primarily those who, like the twelve apostles, were recognized by both confessions. By their forms, each of the two churches defines the difference in religious faith. They are the expression of an existential seriousness and intellectual exactitude that characterizes the architectural styles of all great religions.

The monumentality of the churches rose up against a background of burgher architecture which was governed by strict rules and supervised by capable officials.[14] In this absolutist state, such control was true not only of the city—as in Turin—but of the whole of the electorate. The superintendent of the country's civil and military building, Count Wackerbarth (1662–1742), himself an architect and large-scale builder, supervised the collaborative efforts of the three supreme building authorities: that of the court architect; that of the rural building authority, a position occupied by Matthäus Daniel Pöppelmann; and the directorate for the issuance of building permits, whose chief administrator had to pass on all plans for middle-class buildings in the electorate. He demanded to see not only the plans themselves but also the outlines of neighboring houses and the layout of the streets. Johann Christoph Neumann, who held this last office during the heyday of the electorate, was not afraid to redraw, with his own hands, plans that had been submitted. In his treatise *Architectura practica oder die würkliche und tüchtige Baukunst* (1736), he laid down the principles that obtained in Saxon cities until about 1830. It is a simple, restrained, consciously harmonious baroque, not a style for palaces as in Turin, but rather for middle-class townhouses, a planar art which owes its effect to gentle, considered profiles and proportions. What was required was uniform restrictions on height and brightly painted facades, or, as a recommendation to the king in 1709 has it, "The houses should be of an elegance which is symmetrical and regular." Every building was considered with respect to the overall effect of the street, the square, or even the whole city. Each house served to illustrate an aesthetic conception evoked by the bright, well-tended, and serene urban environment. Such building ordinances were bound to promote the development of normative classical forms rather than the free plasticity of baroque architectural compositions.

For this reason, the court buildings were also consciously opposed to this middle-class Saxon baroque, which, incidentally, was able to develop more perfectly in the much more prosperous city of Leipzig than in Dresden.[15] Augustus the Strong and his son, Augustus II, throughout their lives, commissioned bold new plans for a residential palace which with its attendant buildings was to extend from the center of the town down to the river Elbe. Work was never begun. The kings had to content themselves with the old 16th and 17th century palace, which they tried to fix up in a sumptuous style. New apartments were built. The treasures of the princes' private exchequer were collected in the Grüne Gewölbe (the Green Vault). At the same time, building was progressing on the country seat in Pillnitz and on the hunting lodge, Moritzburg; and the "Japanese Palace" was taken over from the prime minister, Fleming, and filled with exquisite new works from the royal Meissen manufactory. The court also took over, from the same minister, Castle Übigau and, from Count Wackerbarth, the orangery and the park at Großsedlitz and built new castles in Warsaw and in other Polish centers.[16] Augustus the Strong and, later, his sons and grandsons had three castles at their disposal in Dresden for state receptions and festivities— the Palais im Großen Garten, the old residence, and the Japanese Palace. In the Dresden heath and the Elbe water meadow country were four more— Pillnitz, Moritzburg, Großsedlitz, and Übigau. The Dresden princes were almost as well off as their counterparts in Turin. In Pillnitz, the Water Palace, with a harbor for gondolas, lay on the banks of the Elbe, and, across from it, the almost identical Hill Palace. Pleasure gardens extended between the two. Both palaces are monuments to the Chinese fashion of the day— exotic pleasure palaces with roofs and fireplaces, in East Asian forms. Visitors were rowed down from Dresden in luxurious gondolas, and landed at the steps on the Elbe. The enchantment of the unreal drew the observer into its spell. The attempt to mask reality was also a political calculation, as was shown most clearly in the Zwinger (fig. 120).

The Zwinger and the orangeries were merely supposed to constitute a forecourt for a projected imperial palace, for Augustus the Strong nourished the vain hope that, on the death of Joseph II (which occurred in 1711), he would be able to seize the imperial crown. Despite opposition from his military advisers, he insisted on a building site on one of the city's bastions. In Matthäus Daniel Pöppelmann, a Westphalian (1662–1736), and the court sculptor Balthasar Permoser (1650–1732), he had two artistic personalities at his disposal with whom he could embark upon the boldest of ventures. The king himself, in numerous sketches, had assembled the thoughts on architecture that had come to him during his grand tour of Europe. He also sent Pöppelmann on tour. He was to visit Prague, Vienna, Venice, and

Figure 120. Dresden: the Zwinger, with the gallery, royal palace, and the court opera house

Rome to "look at the current way of building both palaces and gardens and, especially, to discuss with the most outstanding architects and artists the sketches he had been given for building a palace here."

The plan was drawn up in 1709. In 1710, Pöppelmann began his study trip. In 1719 the essentials seemed to have been completed. In the preceding year the whole project had been presented in a series of engravings. These show us the buildings in Watteau's misty light. The pavilions create the effect of figures "moving their limbs in dance" (Hubala). Five types of architecture revolve around the observer in this architectural ballet: the pair of oval pavilions, the quartet of the four salons with the nine axes, then the ceremonial gate as solo dancer, and the single-story galleries in the orangery as chorus. Architecture has here become plastic art, and plastic art, architecture. These buildings are at once the stage setting for a fantasy and the fantasy itself.

It has long been recognized what manifold stimuli link the Zwinger to the new age. They reach from the ruined Trianon de Porcelaine in Versailles, across the Piazza Navone in Rome, to Hildebrandt's garden temple in Göllersdorf and to Dientzenhofer's Pargue baroque. As a whole, the Zwinger is a monument to the self-confidence of Augustus the Strong, who is honored and served by all the gods in Olympus and all the muses in Parnassus. The allegorical pantomime presented by this architecture reaches its climax in the figure of the king, as "Hercules saxonicus," standing on the ramparts and holding up the orb, and, at the moat, in the gilded copper of the gate's onion-shaped roof, topped by four Polish eagles bearing the

Figure 121. Pöppelmann's crown gate
to the Dresden Zwinger

crown of Poland (fig. 121). For quality and style, the only thing comparable
to the Zwinger is Prince Eugene's Belvedere in Vienna. But in Dresden the
whole ambience is less majestic. The buildings are more richly dynamic,
more obliging in their gestures, and more indebted to a plastic form of
ornamentation than to a graphic. They are too tenderly formed to be considered works of the baroque, yet at the same time too plastic in their movements to be considered rococo. As in the Vienna Belvedere, we here encounter an "eastern" branch of that stylistic attitude which marked, at the
same time, the art of the *Régence* in Paris.

When we say "eastern," we are also talking of the Zwinger's political
significance. It was the site of tournaments and festivals for a knightly aristocracy, of a sort that continued to exist only in Poland at that time. On the
occasion of major festivals, the guests were given Polish names.

The same is true, though of course in a different way, of the Place
Stanislas in Nancy. This king's political situation was one of the most extraordinary in history. He acquired the duchy of Lorraine on condition that
after his death it would be detached from the imperial federation and united

with France. Thus, he could only build for himself by commissioning buildings solely for himself, and could only advertise a kingdom that he had lost.
Lorraine and its then capital, Nancy, which was considered one of the
strongest fortresses in the world, was occupied by French troops from 1633
to 1665, again from 1670 to 1698, and finally from 1702 to 1714, now laid to
ruins. Duke Leopold was the first to seek some sort of cure during the few
years of peace. His successor, Francis III, who had to surrender the duchy
to Stanislas in exchange for Tuscany, had from the beginning shown scant
interest in his capital. He lived in Vienna, at first as Maria Theresa's prince
consort. Duke Leopold, already before Stanislas's time, had tried to reno-
vate the court in Nancy and to build suitable summer residences in the
country. The most important of these country seats was at Lunéville and
was preserved even though all of its furnishings were looted. Boffrand himself had drawn up the plans and published them in 1709, even before building had begun. A much larger château was to be built outside Nancy—
again according to Germain Boffrand's plans—at La Malgrange. It was the
man who commissioned Nymphenburg and Schleißheim, Max Emmanuel
of Bavaria, who, during his exile in the War of the Spanish Succession,
turned the duke against the project, which had already been started. He
said it was too close to the city to be a hunting lodge but too far away to
be a residence. Leopold turned to his "Louvre," the gigantic urban palace,
which was to be a building with four wings measuring 136 by 96 meters,
but of which a single wing was built, only to be torn down by Stanislas in
1745. Here, too, the design was one of Boffrand's architectural dreams that
had already come true, as far as he was concerned, when the plans were
presented to the Académie de l'architecture in Paris and published as engravings. It is significant that this duchy, mortally threatened, should have
wanted to document its self-assertion in buildings. Nowhere in the French-
speaking area could anyone other than the king plan on such a large scale.
At the same time, Leopold's wife, the sister of the French regent, was resid-
ing in Commercy; she extended the château and furnished it at enormous
expense. Lorraine, with Nancy, Lunéville, and Commercy, was unique
among European states.

The Nancy of King Stanislas was even more remarkable. To begin
with, Stanislas was an imperial prince and king of Poland at the same time,
and he did not wish all-powerful architects in Paris to send him plans. He
was in charge of commissioning buildings himself. His architect, Emmanuel Héré, was born in Nancy in 1705, the son of a building official. He had
then been sent to Paris to work with Boffrand, before returning, in 1736, to

erect one building after another for Stanislas. There were architects in Nancy who thought they owed it to their academic architectural morality to reject the "architectural moods" of the king. A certain Jennesson came to the fore here, and French art criticism, right down to Hautecoeur's classic volumes on classical art, agreed with him.[17] Stanislas first built his burial church, Notre-Dame de Bonsecour, and there he developed a wealth of decoration inspired by the luxuriousness of Saxon architecture in the hands of the other king of Poland. Next, he rebuilt the castle of La Malgrange from the ground up and covered its wall with Delft faïence. His model was not only the Trianon de Porcelaine in Versailles but also the Japanese Palace in Dresden. Stanislas set up his main residence, just as his predecessors had done, at Lunéville. The new chapel was modeled on the chapel at the Palace of Versailles. In the park he built a number of pleasure pavilions—thus entering into competition with his Saxon rival—a Turkish and a Chinese pavilion and a cascade palace, whose flights of steps and waterfalls led down to a canal which was supposed to look like the Elbe at Pillnitz. At one end of the Lunéville estate, outside the park, Héré built the summer palace of Chanteheux, which served both as a teahouse and as a menagerie for rare animals. But this is by no means the complete list of all the buildings this prince enjoyed in his country residence. Their diversity was supposed to symbolize the cosmos. It is noteworthy that the ministers of Louis XV, after the death of his father-in-law, had all the pavilions and secondary châteaus torn down and turned the main château into a barracks. Not only had these buildings become politically meaningless, but their removal also did away with the evidence of various attempts to gain independence; such attempts were to be suppressed once and for all.

Nancy consisted of two cities, both strongly fortified but divided from one another by walls, a moat, and bastions. The old city was densely built up, the "new city" only sparsely settled, and the area on the boundary almost empty (fig. 122). Next to the ducal castle, Duke Leopold had begun his new "Louvre," to which the quarters of the nobility, on both sides of the square ("La Carrière"), were to serve as an approach. Germain Boffrand had drawn up the plans. Stanislas decided to abandon the fortifications. In place of the new palace he established the oval space, enclosed by arcades, behind which the Palais de Gouvernement was built. On the other side of the quarters already planned by Boffrand, a square was laid out, the Place Royale (now Place Stanislas) with its monument to Louix XV. The old moats now no longer served the defense of the city, only its decoration. A triumphal arch separated the Place de la Carrière from the new Place Roy-

Figure 122. The two cities of Nancy (after a 1669 engraving)

ale. It was only when these two squares were created that the city was joined into one. The diagonal axis across the new square was formed by straight roads, which Stanislas named after the patron saint of Poland, St. Catherine, and himself. Six uniform palaces surrounded the square, while the seventh, the city hall with its nineteen window axes, formed a counterpart to the distant government building. Nymphaea at the corners and the famous railings enclosed this square, just as the oval enclosed the space in front of the government buildings (fig. 123). All this was designed by Héré, with great uniformity and assuredness, within a few years after 1752, an example of the noblest French classicism in the final, spare, rococo decorative style.

More than thirty years had passed since Pöppelmann had completed the oval in front of the Zwinger. Héré had been brought up in a culture with different tastes. In his youth, Stanislas had had to face a future of inevitable renunciation. For less than five years, from 1704 to 1709, he had succeeded in clinging to the Polish throne. His relations with his son-in-law, whose marriage was a tragedy after the court had forced the seventeen-year-old king to break with his Spanish fiancée in order to marry a powerful and lackluster Polish woman, were more than reserved. Everyone could tell

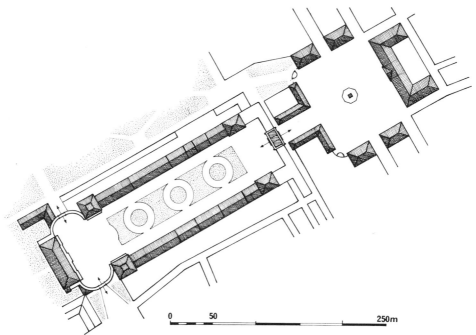

Figure 123. Nancy: Place Stanislas and Place de la Carrière

him about the magnificence of the courts in Dresden and Warsaw, which the other king of Poland had built. The goals of the sixty-year-old prince for his new residence grew out of the resentment that had marked his character. It took a life span of ninety years to realize these goals. Lunéville and Nancy were intended to demonstrate what befit a Polish king. Like the buildings surrounding the Zwinger, the palaces around the Place Stanislas characterize their purposelessness: government buildings and a city hall for a few officials, palaces without inhabitants. Whereas Versailles and Potsdam were always filled to overflowing, in Nancy we have extravagance for its own sake. An architectural pattern was constructed, as the stage on which the drama of kingship should be played out, as the symbol of the claim to the throne which had never been given up. This attempt at a synthesis of Versailles and Dresden arose out of the king's remarkably mixed character, in which idealistic radicalism was combined with senile libertinage.

Episcopal Seats in the Holy Roman Empire

Apart from Rome and the Pontifical State, it was only in this most medieval of all medieval forms of state—up to the time of the secularization in

1802—that spiritual forms of state and seats of a spiritual court were preserved. When the empire came to an end, there were still episcopal seats—four archbishoprics and twenty-two bishoprics—in which the princes of the Church, as in Prague and Vienna, had no temporal power; these are not included here. The bishops could not develop independent building programs in these episcopal seats. They possessed no political power beyond their spiritual power, and, except for their ecclesiastical tithes, they had no state incomes.

Of the four archbishoprics, three managed to keep their power over their capital—Trier, Mainz, and Salzburg. The citizens of the fourth, Cologne, had already driven their archbishop out of the city in 1262. He later took up temporary residence in Bonn, governing his diocese from there. In the case of the twenty-two bishoprics, we have to differentiate more carefully. Three of them—Chur, Basel, and Strasbourg—belonged to the empire in name only at the time of the French Revolution. Chur, the only Catholic see in Switzerland that had never changed its location, remained an episcopal seat, whose bishops, in their little castle, managed to withstand all the attacks of the townspeople. The bishops of Basel and Strasbourg also remained imperial princes. The bishop of Basel and his chapter manifested their imperial status in the modest buildings of Arlesheim and Pruntrut. The lords of Strasbourg were unable to preserve any territories which were subject to the emperor alone. The four generations of Rohan princes, as bishops of Strasbourg, built residences both there and, more luxuriously, in Saverne, to serve their needs as representatives of the Imperial Diet. Nowhere else in France do we find anything comparable.

We can divide the capitals of the remaining nineteen bishoprics into three different groups. The first consisted of centers from which the bishop governed closed territories; these, in order of magnitude, are Münster, Liège, Würzburg, Trento, Bamberg, Eichstätt, Passau, Brixen, and Freising, and also—though with certain limitations—Paderborn, that is ten, plus the three archbishoprics already mentioned. The second group consisted of states in which the bishop had lost the rights to his capital: Augsburg, Speyer, Worms, Regensburg, and, of course, Basel and Strasbourg, plus the one protestant bishopric, Lübeck, where the bishop had built himself a residence in Eutin. The third group were bishoprics that had acquired a new status as a result of the Reformation: Constance, Osnabrück, and Hildesheim. To be more accurate, we have to differentiate in the second group between such bishoprics as Cologne, where the bishop had been banned from his residence forever, and those such as Augsburg or Regensburg, in which he still had his cathedral, his palace, and certain sovereign rights but no longer possessed any temporal power in the city as such.

If we ask ourselves how a traveler, even today, could recognize from a distance whether a bishop had been driven out of his city or had managed to defend his authority over it, we find that the episcopal seats that survived were those in which the bishop, as ruler, occupied a castle on a ridge in the vicinity of the city. There were conflicts of interest everywhere between the townspeople and the bishop. But the citizens never managed to take over castles of this sort. We are thinking here of Salzburg, Würzburg, Trento, Bamberg, Eichstätt, Passau, and Freising. Chur, too, as we have noted, belongs to this group. Where, however, it was impossible to build such a

Figure 124. Trier: basilica and Palatium

Figure 125. Salzburg: view from the
Mirabell across to the cathedral and castle

castle, an imperial city arose sooner or later which expelled the bishop in
his capacity as ruler over the city or the surrounding country. Thus, Constance in 1192, Regensburg in 1245, Cologne and Strasbourg in 1262, Speyer
before 1267, and, after many uprisings, Worms in 1273, Augsburg in 1316,
and Basel shortly after 1356 all expelled their bishops. In none of these cities,
to be sure, was there a lack of powerful episcopal personalities who tried to
turn the clock back. There were exceptions, like the archbishoprics of Mainz
and Trier, where the spiritual rulers, as electors, had any number of outside
possibilities, and others, like the Westphalian bishoprics, where the citizens
succeeded in securing special rights under the crozier. Yet even in Mainz
and Trier the bishops had powerful castles at their disposal inside the
city—in Mainz, the Martinsburg on the Rhine; in Trier, the Palatium, protected by the walls of the Roman basilica (fig. 124). Figure 98 shows the
powerful citadel by means of which the bishops of Münster, in the 17th
century, managed to keep the citizens of that city in check, weakened as
they were by religious turmoil and the Thirty Years' War. It was not until
after the mid-18th century that they dared to give up the citadel and build
their new palace—today the main building of the university—which
opened up toward the city. The rule held good: only a powerful castle, like
those in Salzburg (fig. 125) or Würzburg, secured the rule of the bishops.

Wherever there was no fortress, as in Cologne or Regensburg, the position of these princes of the Church was endangered and often desperate. Within the episcopal cities, however, the castle was one of the dominant features of urban design.

All episcopal seats have their beginnings in the early Middle Ages. We have already encountered many of them (see chap. 1). The most recent is Bamberg, founded by the emperor Henry II in 1007. Only Lübeck is a more recent foundation as a bishopric. But for this very reason it never became the episcopal seat (see chap. 3). All the other episcopal seats in eastern Europe either were unable to achieve political independence, or lost it, at the very latest, when they converted to Protestantism. In none were any monumental buildings erected after the Reformation, neither in the archbishopric of Magdeburg, which finally came to Brandenburg/Prussia in 1680 (see chap. 5), nor in Brandenburg, Havelberg, Merseburg, or Naumburg, the suffragan sees which were subordinated to it, nor in the archbishopric of Hamburg/Bremen with its suffragan sees, nor in the northernmost and easternmost of the suffragan sees of Mainz and Cologne—Verden, Halberstadt, and Minden. The eastern bishoprics, in Austria, Bohemia, Moravia, and Silesia, never became immediately responsible to the emperor and could seldom undertake monumental building projects. We find this in Prague, Breslau, and Posen, as well as in the small Salzburg bishoprics—Gurk, in which a bishop resided from 1072 to 1787, Chiemsee (1215–1808), Seckau (1219–1786), and St. Andreä/Levant (1228–1859). Their building programs were even smaller than those of the Italian, Spanish, or French episcopal seats, in which, from the 16th to the 19th century, the bishop had no special political rights. From time to time, certain bishops with very large private means managed to build real residences. The bishops of the princely house of Lichtenstein, in Olmütz, provide an example.

Archbishoprics and bishoprics were elected monarchies. The cathedral chapters constituted the electoral bodies. In each case, the new prince of the Church was to be elected from their number and subsequently appointed by the pope. There were, in all, 222 noble families who, between 1500 and 1802, regularly sent their late-born sons to noble chapters in the hope that they would one day aspire to be spiritual princes of the empire. Besides members of the royal houses—primarily the Wittelsbachs and the Habsburgs but also Protestant houses like Holstein-Gottorp, which produced twelve bishops, of whom eight were bishops of Lübeck (in Eutin)—there was a whole series of noble families such as the Thuns, with twelve prince-bishops; the Metternichs, the Stadions, the Greifenclaus, the

Figure 126. The Bonn residence under Clement Augustus, ca. 1760

Hohenlohes, and the Erthals, each with four or five; and, surpassing all of them in their architectural achievements, the Schönborns, with six.

Naturally, all episcopal households between the 16th and 18th centuries built themselves palaces. Many small towns bore their stamp, for example Meersburg for Constance, or Bruchsal for Speyer. Bonn, too, may be mentioned in this connection: here the archbishops built themselves a residence with a large palace and a park and also a ring of hunting lodges, of which the nearby Poppelsdorf and Brühl were the most important. In the old city, the two original units—the convent of St. Cassius with its ancillary buildings, and the little marketplace—had for centuries turned their backs on one another. Now a third unit was added, the new palace complex, with extensive residential buildings that opened up toward the great court gardens on the south side. After secularization, they provided the quarters for the new university (fig. 126).

It is significant that even the recently established seat of government of the German Federal Republic has failed to integrate the city. The govern-

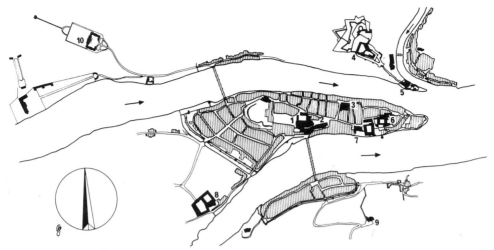

Figure 127. Passau: 1, cathedral; 2, old and new residences; 3, city hall; 4, Oberhaus castle; 5, Niederhaus castle; 6, Benedictine nuns; 7, Jesuits; 8, Augustinians; 9, Marienhilf place of pilgrimage; 10, Freudenhain palace.

ment buildings form a fourth area, which, with its centers of gravity higher up the Rhine between the old city and the castle town of Bad Godesberg, looks more like an architectural competition for office construction than a city.

Among the episcopal and archiepiscopal seats, some made virtually no changes in their architectural order, even during the period of absolutism. New buildings were erected for the most part on the foundations of previous buildings. Bamberg, Freising, and Passau belong to this group. We find enrichment but no new beginnings. In Passau, nature furnished the ideal conditions for an episcopal city with cathedral, buildings for the curia, castle, and burgher town (figs. 127 and 128). Sometimes the most charming plans were successful within a narrow compass—in Eichstätt, for example. Today, Salzburg and Würzburg can be regarded as classical episcopal seats, especially as Mainz, which approximated to them in the wealth of new buildings, lost the greater part of them in the revolutionary wars at the end of the 18th century and in the Second World War.

Salzburg

The history of Salzburg may be characterized as a process that went on for centuries, in the course of which the episcopal and clerical element crowded the burgher element more and more into the area between the cathedral

236

and the Salzach.[18] The 12th and 13th centuries were the heydays of episcopal rule. As a protection against imperial attacks during the Investiture Quarrel, the archbishops completed the fortress of Hohensalzburg, which was later enlarged and reinforced on several occasions. In the 15th century a citizenry that numbered about 5,000 developed a limited autonomy. The expression of their power is the lofty choir of the old parish church of Our Lady, which later became the church of the Franciscans. The choir was built by Hans Stethaimer, who began it in 1422. Emperor Frederick III generously accorded the inhabitants privileges, all of which Archbishop Leonhard von Keutschach took away again. During the Peasants' War, the citizens united with the rural population and besieged Archbishop Matthäus Lang von Wellenburg (1519–40)—whose features are familiar to us from a Dürer drawing—for three months on the Hohensalzburg. Retribution followed. In the course of the 16th century, the cathedral chapter changed from a monastic community to a community of aristocratic canons. In 1592, the townspeople lost even their parish church, which was given to the Franciscans. A little later, the buildings of the residence came so close to this church on two of its sides that the tall windows of the choir had to be walled up halfway on those sides (fig. 129). This kind of construction became the "critical form" of the new balance of power.

Figure 128. Passau, with Oberhaus and Niederhaus castles in the foreground (after Merian)

Wolf-Dietrich (1587–1612) and Markus Sitticus (1612–19), prelates who had been influenced in Rome by the urban planning of Sixtus V (see chap. 8), converted the old ecclesiastical and burgher city into a baroque residence for the prince bishop. Both were related to Pius IV and thus to the House of Medici. Under their rule, the cathedral cemetery was abandoned and the cathedral monastery and the burgher city reduced in size. Fifty-five of the citizens' houses were sacrificed for the square. Palazzi and piazzas cramped the winding medieval streets. As early as 1603, Wolf-Dietrich began work on Altenau, the pleasure seat that Markus Sitticus named Mirabell. In the winter of 1603–4, Vicinzo Scamozzi came to Salzburg from Venice. There was talk of a new cathedral, which was built by Santin Solari between 1614 and 1628, and of the five squares that were to surround the cathedral and the great road that was to run parallel to the river, over the Hofstallgasse, between the Franciscan monastery and the monastery of St. Peter, through

Figure 129. Salzburg: choir of
the Franciscan church surrounded by the
wings of the residence

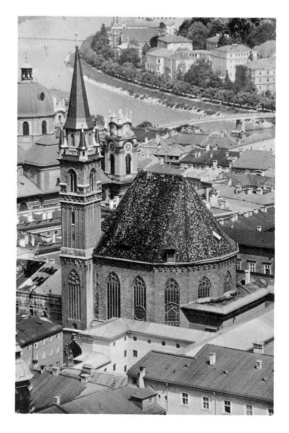

238

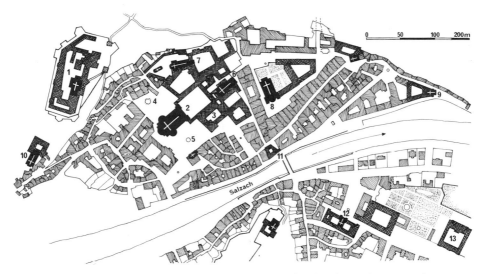

Figure 130. Salzburg. The city plan illustrates the congestion of the burgher settlement area by comparison with the possessions of the prince bishops and the church. 1, castle; 2, cathedral; 3, residence; 4, chapter square; 5, residence square (Mozartplatz); 6, Franciscans; 7, Benedictines; 8, collegiate church; 9, Ursulines; 10, St. Kajetan; 11, city hall; 12, convent of the Trinity; 13, Mirabell.

to the cathedral square and beyond it to the Kapitelplatz and the Kapitel-gasse (fig. 130). In addition to the residence by the cathedral, the pleasure seat of Mirabell, and the castle, for which a more ornate form was sought, this early baroque plan for a ceremonial city included Hellbrunn, the summer seat, which in the hands of these "Medicis" was developed as a manneristic villa outside the city on an Italian model with fosses, grottoes, and fountains.

With Roman *grandezza,* the structure of the city was to be coordinated by few axes—the street axis, of which I have spoken above, and the visual axis, which crosses it, from the Mirabell across the cathedral to the castle. Both directed the eye toward the cathedral and the residence, as the center of the city. The archbishop conceived of his work as a unit. The cathedral was given the central position, which in Berlin, for example, was occupied by the royal palace.

Everything that had been planned before the outbreak of the Thirty Years' War called for more elaborate implementation when it was over. From the point of view of urban planning, it was fortunate that the war compelled the prudent, intelligent archbishop, Paris, Count Lodron (1619–53), to turn his attention first to the fortification of the city, as his main task, a situation similar to that of the first Schönborn in Würzburg (see below, this chapter). Lodron commissioned the bold bastions which marked the boundary of the city on its one open flank, between the Salzach and the Kapuzinerring. The city gates were also his work. With the razing of the bastions and the gates, the late 19th century tore open one side of the city, and through the gap the unplanned parts of the city both moved closer and closer to the city center and out into the countryside.[19] It is characteristic of their time that Lodron's two successors, Guidobaldo, Count Thun (1654–68), and Max Gundolf, Count Kuenburg (1668–87), could only afford small building projects and decorative works. Thun, for the most part, commissioned fountains, among them the magnificent Hofbrunnen, while Kuenburg commissioned the churches of St. Erhard (1685–89) and the domed church of St. Kajetan (1685–1700), both designed by Zucalli, as well as the shrine church of Maria Plain (1671–74). Every building program in an episcopal seat, from the 17th century onwards, had to have at least one place of pilgrimage. Even in Bonn one was created, the Kreuzberg.

After the Thirty Years' War the atmosphere was dominated by Italians, and not until the victory over the Turks outside Vienna in 1687 did things change. In the Middle Ages, Salzburg had cast its eyes toward Bavaria, and in the early baroque period toward South Tyrol and Italy. It now felt compelled to draw inspiration, and recruit artists, from Vienna. For the Habsburgs, into whose homeland the archiepiscopal see penetrated deeply, it had been a long-standing and repeated political duty to place a member of the Austrian nobility on the archbishop's throne. Since the second half of the 16th century there had been no South German prince-bishop, not even a canon from a South German house.[20] Johann Ernst, Count Thun (1687–1709), was also able to assemble almost exclusively Austrian artists, foremost among them Fischer von Erlach, who built four churches in Salzburg as well as the castle of Klesheim outside the walls, the late baroque Mirabell gardens, the new Siegmundplatz, the court stables, and the summer riding school.

The arrival of this architectural specialist was the signal for extraordinary achievements. Once more, someone grasped the city as a whole. Fischer placed buildings of more imaginative monumentality next door to competent works of the Italians. The elements of Fischer's works were taken straight from the Roman source, from Borromini and Bernini, though the source was modified in the spirit of the new "peace style" (see chap. 7). The archbishops had awarded their great commissions; the cathedral, the residence, the castle, the country villa, and the pleasure seat at the edge of the

Figure 131. Salzburg (aerial photograph)

city were completed; the squares were securely established and the axes drawn. The program for the residence was closed, and the fact that a second pleasure seat, Klesheim, was added can be ascribed more to changing architectural taste and the desire to build, than to any new need. For just as Hellbrunn, at the beginning of the 17th century, had taken an Italian *villa suburbana* as a model, Klesheim wanted to be seen as a château on the model of Versailles. Hans Sedlmayr has pointed out that the Austrian synthesis of the two created something quite novel.[21] Even the late baroque and rococo did not succeed in completing much within the cathedral precincts; indeed, at the beginning of the 18th century, people were already looking back to the time of Markus Sitticus as the classic period in Salzburg's urban development. Yet the desire to beautify the princely city made much new construction possible—churches, fountains, facades, often just portals. And Fischer was the man for such abstract architecture, which went far beyond the occasion to achieve forms of great sublimity. Curves were added to planes, domes to the towers, sweeping lines to straight ones, plastic building shapes to architectural geometry (fig. 131), for it was precisely the limited space available for streets and squares that allowed new churches to achieve their effect: the sculptural power of the new collegiate church (1694–1707) for a new episcopal university, the refined elegance of the church of the Trinity (1694–1702) and of the church of the Ursulines, which, like the churches of the Piazza del Popolo (see below, fig. 183), seemed to form the figurehead of a ship (fig. 132), the row houses of two streets converging onto it. Many other small accents were created by Fischer

Figure 132. Salzburg: Ursuline convent
and its church

and, after him, by Lukas von Hildebrandt. All told, it was no misfortune that this late Viennese baroque was not followed by a rococo, even though many house fronts and some parts of churches—not least the oldest in the city, the Romanesque nave of the church of St. Peter—managed to deck themselves out in a festive garb which was lighter and more decorated. The program for this spiritual residence was completed like no other. Unity in diversity grew, on the one hand, out of the visual clarity of the whole and, on the other, out of the succession of surprises afforded by the changing scene. The coordination of architectonic motifs was accomplished at a high level of compositional consciousness.

Würzburg

It is only by comparison with Salzburg's sole rival with a similar claim to perfection that we can show the strength of the two urban personalities. There are more contrasts than similarities in the composition of Salzburg and Würzburg, as this comparison will make clear. I would like to group the contrasts in terms of four features, each of which, in its own way, has influenced the history and the appearance of Würzburg.

The first is that the city's starting point was a ducal castle (fig. 133, 1), which towered up over the steep left bank of the Main, while opposite it on the right bank lay a ducal courtly estate, in whose domain the cathedral was later to be built. Thus, the two centers of political power lay opposite one another on either side of the river, not, as in Salzburg, huddled together on one side.

It is said that the first extant stone building to be built on German soil after the departure of the Romans was erected shortly after A.D. 700 inside the castle. It was a circular chapel with huge walls round it, dedicated to the Virgin Mary. The castle passed into the possession of the church, at the latest, when the see was reorganized by Boniface in 741. The bishop managed to assume the rights of a Frankish duke and to have Barbarossa confirm those rights in 1188. The prince-bishops of Würzburg, having been forced by the growing power of the burghers to secure themselves in the Marienburg fortress during the episcopate of Bishop Hermann von Lobdeburg (1225–34), continued to live there until well into the 18th century.

Under Bishop Arno (855–92), a second cathedral was built on the site

Figure 133. Würzburg in the High Middle Ages (the shaded area is church property according to H. Bullinger): 1, Marienburg fortress; 2, cathedral; 3, town hall; 4, lady chapel; 5, Neustift ("new convent"); 6, St. Burkhard (the pentagonal walls of the city date from A.D. 1000).

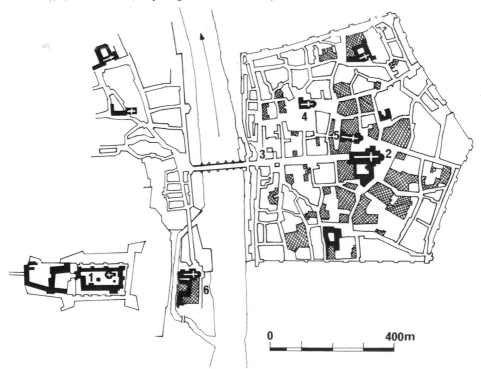

0   400m

of the present one (2). From 788 on, a Church of the Redeemer functioned
as a cathedral on the same site. The beginnings of the building that is still
standing go back to the episcopate of Bishop Bruno (1034–45). It was not
until 1188 that the nave could be dedicated. The new institutions of this
ecclesiastical city, whose wealth is represented in 16th and 17th century
views, developed around the cathedral. The polarity between castle and
cathedral, the bridge across the Main and the street axis that joined them,
presented a problem in urban design to which succeeding centuries proposed a number of different solutions.

The second characteristic feature is the rapid increase in population
since the 12th century. Würzburg had a larger and richer hinterland than
did Salzburg. Industry and trade could develop more easily. Conflicts between the bishops and the citizenry resulted in greater tensions. There were
repeated movements toward rebellion against the castle, which regularly led
to the citizens' having to assume greater burdens in order to make the castle
impregnable. The power that the castle represented to the eyes of contemporaries, in the years of the bitterest struggles, is testified to in the greatly

Figure 134. Würzburg (after Schedel's *Weltchronik*)

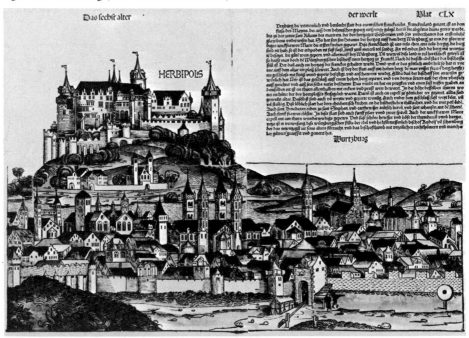

exaggerated representation of it in Schedel's *Weltchronik* of 1493 (fig. 134).
In the face of this power, even the armies of the Peasants' War under the
leadership of Götz von Berlichingen in 1525 were bound to fail, though they
were supported both by the citizens and the city council, of which Tilman
Riemenschneider was a member.

At all times, this burgher community found itself hemmed in by the
real-estate policies of the ecclesiastical city. Figure 133 shows what scanty
sites were assigned to the burghers for building their houses.[22] The center
of the citizens' life was the narrow area around the town hall (fig. 133, 3)
between the cathedral and the river, the street axis along which the main
markets were located. Even the town hall could only be completed after the
acquisition of the Grafeneckharthof in 1300. This predicament also explains
the expulsion, in 1348, of the Jewish community, which had formerly enjoyed the special protection of the bishop. In the process of expulsion, the
ghetto was burned down and the burghers' city church was built close
by—the Marienkirche, whose choir was begun in 1377 and whose nave was
not completed until 1440. Riemenschneider's sandstone figures (now in the
Mainfränkisches Museum), placed at the portal of this church, bear witness,
as the master's first commission in Würzburg, to the citizens' claims to
equal rights. The peasant armies' song "When Adam delved and Eve span,/
Who was then a gentleman?" was now enshrined in stone and finally ex-
alted. It was, at the same time, a confession of guilt that they laid upon
themselves, like the first human beings, which only Mary, through her son's
work of salvation, could atone for. We see that the empty space (4) in front
of the church was not designed but rather formed by the fire that destroyed
the ghetto. It has no form and bears no relation to other spaces, unless it is
that of proximity to the bridge and the town hall. It was only in the 17th
century that it became a farmers' market. The citizens did not dispose of
enough energy to create an integrated urban plan. The change in relations
between the citizens and the episcopal power that took place in the 16th
century as a consequence of the Counterreformation bishops' desire to
bring the people back to the old faith—first under Julius Echter von Mespelbrunn (1573–1617)—resulted in an extension of the city, in which new
episcopal centers of charitable care came into being alongside new space for
settlement (fig. 135). The main centers were the Jesuit university (7) and the
extensive buildings of the Julius Echter hospital, within the domain of
which the bishops took a second residence (8). The development has much
in common with what took place in Munich and many other cities during
this long period of peace before the outbreak of the Thirty Years' War. It

foreshadows aims of the cultural programs of the 19th century and thus emphasizes just how many developmental tendencies were interrupted by the Thirty Years' War.

A third feature leading to architectural contrasts between Würzburg and Salzburg was Würzburg's "dynasty" of bishops, members of the house of Schönborn and some of their closest relatives, like the Greifenclaus. They regarded themselves—in contrast to the rulers of Salzburg, who were obliged to comply more and more with the wishes of the Viennese court—as committed to a policy of achieving a balance between France, Austria, and, later, Prussia and were for this very reason concerned with extending the power of the imperial princes. If successful representatives of the imperial idea were to be found anywhere in the Holy Roman Empire, they were surely the Schönborns, as bishops of Mainz, Würzburg, Bamberg, Worms, Speyer, Constance, and Trier.[23]

The house of Schönborn had proved itself for centuries in the service of the bishops of Mainz, before it began its rapid rise in 1642 when Johann Philipp von Schönborn (1605–73) was elected to the bishopric of Würzburg. In 1647 he also became archbishop of Mainz and arch-chancellor of the empire and, in 1663, bishop of Worms as well. One of the three outstanding episcopal figures who had suffered through and survived the Thirty Years' War—the other two were Ferdinand von Wittelsbach in Cologne (1612–50), and Paris, Count Lodron, in Salzburg (1614–52)—Johann Philipp von Schönborn was the youngest and certainly the most important. He was known as the Great Elector of the Rhine. Although interested in all the arts, he felt constrained to turn his attention and to devote the economic power of his devastated lands primarily to the building of fortifications. The fortification of the Marienburg in Würzburg was carried out according to a conception developed by Gustavus Adolphus immediately after the capture of the city. The Swedes wanted to sacrifice all the buildings on the left bank of the Main to fortifications. A shield was designed for the whole hill, turning nature into architecture. Although the new ring of bastions and moats around the city was completed in the year of the first Schönborn's death, the uncertainty of the situation made it imperative to continue work on the walls and turrets until well into the 18th century. The city regarded itself as an imperial fortress, and the ring of bastions had to be continually modernized, although this valley city, surrounded by ranges of hills from which it could be observed and fired upon, could never be defended in the case of actual war.[24] Johann Philipp von Schönborn did the same thing for Würzburg that his contemporary, Paris, Count Lodron, did for Salzburg. A man of great political gifts, he left his sees, in spite of many reverses, economically strong again. He became the model for his nephew, Lothar Franz (1655–1729), the greatest of the Schönborns, who, together with his always cautious brother and the latter's seven sons, had created the Schönborn empire on the Main, the Rhine, and the Moselle. In 1693 he became bishop of Bamberg, in 1695 archbishop of Mainz and thus also arch-chancellor of the empire. He built the Bamberg residence, the castles of Geibach and Pommersfelden in Franconia, and the Favorite in Mainz. He also promoted the building or completion of many churches, among them

Figure 135. Würzburg in the late 18th century: 1, Marienburg fortress; 2, cathedral; 3, city hall; 4, marketplace and church of St. Mary's; 5, Neustift; 6, St. Burkhard; 7, Jesuit university; 8, Julius Echter hospital; 9, Haug foundation; 10, residence.

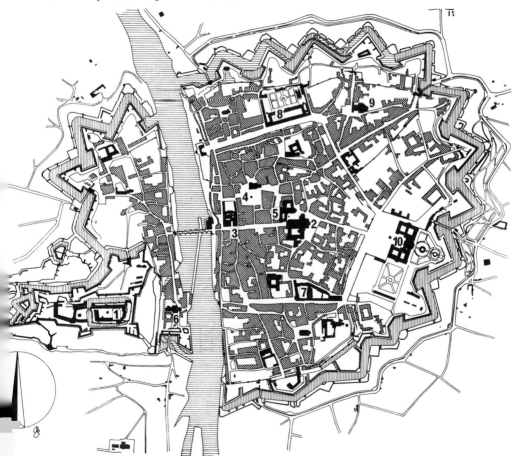

the cathedral in Würzburg. He succeeded in gaining leading spiritual and temporal positions in the empire for his seven nephews. Four of them received bishoprics, two that of the Würzburg one: first, Johann Philipp Franz (1673–1724), who was elected bishop of the Main metropolis in 1719, and second, five years after his brother's death in 1729, Friedrich Karl (1674–1746), who was also the imperial vice-chancellor in Vienna from 1705 to 1734, where he was the third great building patron—after Prince Eugene and Prince Liechtenstein—to commission buildings in the baroque style. The brothers' chief works, among many others, were the Schönborn mausoleum, which was attached (as the chapel of the Medicis is attached to the transept of San Lorenzo) to the transept of the cathedral in Würzburg, and, further, the castle in Würzburg, which, with its gardens on the bastions, was completed only after the painting of Tiepolo's ceiling frescoes in 1750–53 by the second successor of the last of the Schönborns, his sister's son, a Greifenclau. Both of these buildings were coordinated into one of the most magnificent pieces of urban design ever conceived. The actual creator of the concept was Balthasar Neumann (1685–1753). These richly endowed bishops were interested not so much in artistic goods and chattels as in large complexes, castles, extensive parks, pilgrimage churches with distant prospects, cities as a whole. These were exemplary tasks for urban planners.

Neumann's activity as a city architect was the fourth feature leading to contrasts with Salzburg. In Salzburg, one architect after another sought to differentiate the form of the city by a process of enrichment. In Würzburg, on the other hand, this one master, at the very peak of the baroque period, succeeded in balancing the antitheses between cathedral city, burgher city, and seat of the prince-bishop in a total concept.[25] This concept was itself the result of developments that characterize the planning of the Würzburg residential castle for more than sixty years, from 1719 to about 1780. Yet the plans for modernizing the fortifications were what first confronted the young artillery specialist.[26] At the age of twenty-eight, he submitted his first master plan for the city. Five years later, in 1720, he summarized his ideas in a memorandum, which, in a second version, published in 1722, he expanded to include suggestions for a set of dictatorial building ordinances. In the meantime, in the course of various journeys, he had got to know Vienna, Paris, and Milan and had worked as an engineer with Prince Eugene during the siege of Belgrade. His advancement was rapid. This officer thought in terms of spaces, internal spaces in suites of rooms, in churches and staircases, external spaces in squares, streets, gardens, castle courtyards, and bastions. He coordinated buildings with these spaces. Fortifications, street lines, pumping stations, and watermills were just as much an enduring occupation for him as building the castle, houses, or churches. He paid particular attention to the provision of wells for the city's water supply.[27] As city architect he was the most self-willed personage in the particularistic world of the Holy Roman Empire—I might also say the most important. There is more to redesigning a medieval city as a whole than just putting a Huguenot city on the drawing board to be built in open country, as the city planners of Berlin, Kassel, Ansbach, or Erlangen did (see chaps. 5 and 6). There is also more to it than simply calculating how to place a baroque ring of fortifications, with bastions and ravelins, around a Gothic wall. Whereas the older planners were busy after the Thirty Years' War rebuilding and modernizing complexes of buildings—Antonio Petrini rebuilding the collegiate church of Haug (1670–91) and the rear buildings, the Fürstenbau, of the Julius hospital (1699–1714); Joseph Greising designing the Neumünster and its facade (1710–20); and others occupied mainly with various technical buildings, essential to the maintenance even of a baroque city—Neumann was concerned with a new concept of the urban organism as a whole. He was the first architect in Germany to propose removing the medieval walls and filling in the moats to make space for promenades. The main axis from the Main bridge to the cathedral was to be given facades in accordance with a uniform plan. Neumann ordered the bridge tower to be razed and the town hall square to be redesigned. He wanted to tear down all the riverside houses on the right bank of the Main in order to create, with the houses on the left bank, a new and ceremonial baroque prospect. The cathedral and the Schönborn chapel were to be joined by a new axis to the castle with its court of honor. Later, to ensure that his plans would be carried out, Neumann designed in his own office and free of charge about thirty or forty facades a year for burgher houses. He also came to the fore as an architect himself. He designed his own house, which is of particular architectural importance and was of such large proportions that he was able to sell it immediately as a palace and could consequently build himself another to fill a gap on a critical building site. The financial means to do this came from his mirror-polishing works and his glass factory. How intensively the architect's imagination was engaged upon the task of planning a unit is evidenced by the famous thesis broadside of 1722–23 which, in accordance with the practice of the time, was commissioned after the graduation of a certain Freiherr von Reitzenstein in the Jesuit university in Würzburg (fig. 136). On this broadside Neumann presents the ideal picture of his city, in which most of the projects appear already to have been real-

Figure 136. Würzburg
(from the frontispiece to
Balthasar Neumann's thesis,
1722/23)

Figure 137. Würzburg castle and the gardens on the bastion (from a drawing by Balthasar Neumann, 1722)

ized—even the castle. The magnificent theatrical architecture, its curtain formed by the view of the city, shows the importance the 18th century accorded its architectural achievements. The pairs of columns on either side bear discs, depicting, on the left, the new university library, beneath it the projected new castle with its gardens on the bastions, and another general view of the city, and, on the right, the burial chapel of the Schönborns in plan and elevation and a plan of the fortress of Königshofen, which the bishops of Würzburg had fortified at exceptionally large cost to themselves. At the foot of the columns we see the plan and elevation of the castle.

From Lothar Franz von Schönborn's correspondence with his nephew, we know with what passion he handled the design of the castle both in its relation to the city and in the details of its architecture.[28] Up to ten architects from Mainz, Vienna, and Prague were engaged in making designs for it all at the same time. Many of their suggestions became part of a development which ended up in Neumann's hands again. The fundamental idea had already been established in 1719, when Lothar Franz was still talking of an "architectural abortion" (fig. 137). Aside from Neumann, Lukas von Hildebrandt was the main influence on the detailed design of the body of the building and its decoration. Three generations of artists and craftsmen were schooled at this task. The long work of planning, like the sincerity of the architects' efforts to produce a design, found its expression in the consummately balanced composition, both interior and exterior. In the process, the problem had been posed as to how to create a "Versailles," within the fortifications that already existed, with its gardens and its axes of squares and streets, and how to solve this problem better than in any of the cities we have been considering—better than in Berlin, Turin, or Vienna, better than in Stuttgart or Rome. At the same time the residence building program as a whole was extended by the addition of the summer palace of Veitshöchheim, begun as early as 1680 and extended by Neumann between 1748 and 1753, although the final appointments of the park were not completed until 1780. The city's pilgrimage church, the chapel on the hill, on the left bank of the Main, was also finally completed by Neumann. The last of the prince-bishops, a Seinsheim from 1754 to 1779 and an Erthal from 1779 to 1794, whose mode of governing was a source of admiration to Karl August of Weimar, continued to promote the city's environment. That architecture should correspond to political constitution was a concept that was not only preserved but was understood as necessary.

Versailles

To read the residence of Louis XIV as a political document is unlikely to offer new insights.[29] From the day building began, both palace and town were the object of reports in which attention was paid to every detail. Contemporary attention was directed both to the observation of royal psychology—the rivalry between the king's advisers and his artists—and to the real architectural measures and their significance as a mirror of a theory of statecraft. Saint-Simon was the most comprehensive reporter but not always the most reliable witness, for Versailles from the very beginning was planned as an illustration of absolutism and was understood in this light.

The psychology of the king and his theory of statecraft were interdependent. Such interdependence characterizes the 17th century mentality. This is something we shall discuss in connection with the popes (see chap. 8). The popes felt themselves to be the representatives of Christ not only by virtue of their office but in their own person. The king not only bore the royal office but, because of his blood and his being, was the only one who could.

Versailles grew out of the understanding that distance from the capital, and from the irrational attitude of the masses who lived there, was a prerequisite for the preservation of royal power and its sacred dignity. Louis XIV had to be unapproachable, surrounded by a higher glory, and yet at the same time be visible. The experience of the Fronde, the flight from the Louvre and the Tuileries, the news of the execution of the English king, Charles I, the humiliation of the confrontation with the enemies of the central power, had all made ineradicable impressions on Louis as a boy. For this reason, the nobility, each of its members in his own person, was to be made totally dependent upon the grace of the monarch in whose service he had to wear himself out. The twenty-year-old's lively attention to every word and every gesture made everyone subservient. The taste of the new master had been molded by the magical, inaccessible elegance of his mother, Anne of Austria, her luxury, her valuables, her wardrobe, her perfumes, that combination of feminine gentility and sensuality which revealed itself in his mother as characteristic of all kingship. In his tutor, Cardinal Mazarin, he had a model in whom a sense of power and a sense for art revealed themselves as characteristic of the same thing. In the 17th century the power of the state appeared in the guise of art more than it did in any other century. This combination is understood in the concept of *gloire*. Versailles was its definition. Palace and park were built for the glory of the king, a glory they illustrated and manifested in themselves. *Rome dans un palais*—"Rome, the metropolis of the ancient world, in a palace"—this the caption to an early engraving of the palace, which was itself to be understood as political propaganda for the king.

We know that Louis XIII liked to hunt in the forests around Versailles. He first built a small château and then a larger one, though still modest, on this domain, which he had purchased not without difficulty from Jean François de Gondi of Florence, the first archbishop of Paris and a favorite of the king's mother, Maria de' Medici. He later rounded the domain off. Louis XIV first left his father's château intact but surrounded it with other buildings in his initial building campaign (see fig. 138) and appointed the park more splendidly. These early building projects were completed in 1665. For the twenty-four-year-old king it was the supreme confirmation of his selfhood to be able to show his mother, in May 1664, the new *île enchantée* in a series of splendid festivals, which, for their magnificence and elegance, surpassed everything his court had done up to that moment. In 1668, Le Vau and others began replacing the old château with a much larger one. Mansard built the present mammoth structure, which included and extended Le Vau's château, between 1677 and 1688 (fig. 139). Each time, care had to be taken not to disturb the life of the court or the functioning of

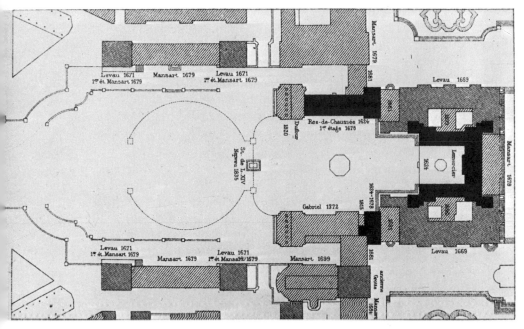

Figure 138. Versailles: schematic representation of its building history (after M. Questel)

Figure 139. Versailles: castle and Communs (aerial photograph)

government in the old châteaus, while the new ones were built rapidly with the same solidity of construction and of the same materials. Louis XV and Louis XVI also commissioned extensions to the building. Louis XIV's energy and imagination were constantly engaged upon plans for building and equipping, and in the course of this planning the gardens and park, with their three approach avenues, swallowed up far greater sums than did the palace itself. The work could only be carried out by huge contingents of troops, for the draining of the marshes, on the one hand, and the supply of enormous quantities of water, on the other, presented almost insuperable difficulties to the royal undertaking. Nature opposed this metamorphosis into geometry, a change that was to be animated by an unheard-of outlay for rare trees and flowers that would bloom at every season of the year and an even larger outlay for standing and running water, waterfalls and fountains, which on the occasion of the great festivals consumed 5,000 cubic meters of water an hour. We know what the curve of expenditure was for each year: it rose steeply in times of peace and fell just as steeply in times of war. At its highest point, in 1686–87, it reached more than 10 percent of the total state expenditure. The total was 80 million livres, the equivalent of more than 1½ billion working hours, or 500,000 working years.

At the same time, we must bear in mind that it was a palace with a large, active household, which from 1682 onward was the official seat of the government, and also that new pavilions and wings were constantly being added, additional suites of rooms in which Olympus circling around the ever-present king, as Phoebus-Apollo, was to be understood now as an allegory of the state, now as an erotic pantomime. It was only in the reign of Louis XV that Venus and her retinue expelled her brother Apollo and his people.

Hardouin-Mansard completed the third project, but not until 1690. It was only in 1699 that the king moved into the bedroom in the middle of the marble court on the east side of the palace, the room that had hitherto been his salon. Here his aim was to liken his waking-up to the rising of the sun and his going to sleep to its setting (fig. 139). The last building, the chapel, was completed in 1710.

"Il n'y a rien dans cette superbe maison, qui n'ait rapport à cette divinité," writes Félibien in the first detailed description of Versailles in 1676. By divinity he means Apollo and the king. People delighted in the allegories of the four elements, the twelve months, the four seasons, all parts of the earth that served the king. The domain of heaven and earth, and especially the aquatic world, was present everywhere. This erotic pantomime consummated itself above all in the aquatic areas. Beneath the king's apartments was the equally ornate *appartement des bains,* the center of which was a gigantic, monolithic bath. In the garden one could visit the grotto of Thetis, the bath of the nymphs, and the water avenue and then proceed to the bath of Diana, the fountain of Apollo in the very center of the park in front of the palace, the water pavilion, the water theater, the water cradle (*Bassin des Enfants*), the pool of the four seasons, the island of delight, and much more. New ideas were constantly causing older installations to be abandoned, but these have been preserved for us in engravings. Each renovation involved a process of clarification. Every festive arrangement—fireworks, ballet, theater—emphasized this clarification in constantly changing forms. Art was the medium by which eroticism and the theory of statecraft joined hands. The enormous and intelligent energy of the ministers, primarily Colbert, and the king's equally progidious industry, even ruthlessness, nonetheless left room for allegorical manifestations of omnipotence.

It was only after thirty years that the king let things stand. There were still alterations to be made, but they no longer expressed changes in his theory of the state. Louis and the court had to suffer the discomforts of this daily presence in a divine paradise for twenty-five years until the revolt of the nobles, led by the regent, on the very day of the great king's death, forced a move into Paris. The young king, Louis XV, had to set things right in his own way.

Versailles can only be understood by someone who knows the history of its genesis and the dependence of that genesis upon the business of government, the family, the king's *affaires amoureuses,* and, last but not least, the composition of the court.[30] Nothing can be more misleading than to try to do justice to the facades for their own sake. Every tract of land, every space, had a function. The imaginative power of the king and of his ministers and architects was constantly engaged in dealing architecturally with changes in the royal family as a result of births, marriages, and deaths, and of changes in the composition of the cabinet or the court offices. Each of the great *maîtresses en titre* influenced the erotic pantomime of decoration, just as every external success could alter the political pantomime. Architecture and the program of furnishing the buildings was to indicate to everyone what was suited to his rank, and to exalt everyone the king wished to honor. The palace, as a historical document, reflects in its genesis, in its alterations and extensions, the fate of the court and the regime.

Thus it is significant that two wings were already added in front of Le Vau's original building, in whose four corner pavilions resided the four

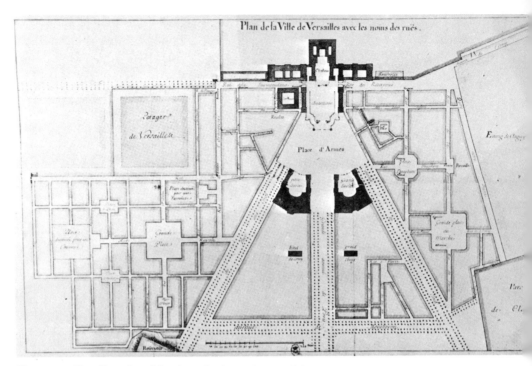

Figure 140. Versailles: plan of the city and palace (after Langlois)

secretaries of state, who at that time formed the entire royal cabinet. The pavilion closest to the main building was Colbert's, and, in the long tracts which joined the pavilions, the quarters of the French and Swiss guards faced one another (fig. 138). The ministers, like the guards, were always at hand and were only a few steps from the royal audience chamber. On the left, near the forecourt on the city side, the Grands Communs were joined to the palace—these were the residences of many of the court servants, among them the landscape architect Le Nôtre, and here, too, kitchen complexes for more than 2,000 people were planned. Mansard's Communs formed a block measuring 86 by 79 meters. Another custom of Louis XIV's was to accommodate his overlapping amours—and the children that issued from them—by developing satellite châteaus.

The king's creative talent was such that he was constantly planning such châteaus even though bearing the immense burden of government. One of the most famous examples is the Trianon de Porcelaine, which Le Vau built for Madame Montespan in the far north of the park. It is a group of five buildings, set in an elegantly appointed garden, which, according to one of Félibien's sayings, were built in a single winter (1670–71) and, to everyone's delight, appeared in the following May like a full-blown flower. We know the château from a series of engravings. Planned on a much more generous scale was Jules Hardouin-Mansard's first work, Clagny, scarcely a half-hour away from Versailles, which Louis XIV commissioned to be built for his illegitimate children, two of them the survivors of six born to Madame La Vallière, and five of them the children of Madame de Montespan. Madame de Maintenon was chosen to educate these seven children: she later became Louis XIV's third great mistress and, finally, his wife.

Clagny is one of the most important works of French classicism. The intertwining of private life and politics is characteristic of royal life in the 17th century. The stratification of improvisations for the everyday needs of so many people, as well as court etiquette, lent the charm of the picturesque to these noble châteaus.

One of the great urban design ideas that emerged from the conversations between Colbert and Hardouin-Mansard was that of placing the extensive stable buildings, the Petite Ecurie and the Grande Ecurie, at the junction of the three approach routes (fig. 140). The routes themselves had already been built by Louis XIII. Châteaus and parks had been built for close relatives of the king on the empty space between them. The stables are architectonic masterpieces *sui generis*. We can still see today, when we look at the portals, the windows, and the vaulting above the stalls, that they were built for visitors of the highest rank. Lower forms of the high style in which the château itself was built were orchestrated in such a way as to form a conscious contrast between the rustic solidity of individual forms and the tenderest decorative systems of the Trianon de Porcelaine and the later garden buildings, which are only slightly older. In bad weather, festivities could be shifted into these vast complexes, which were completed by Mansard in 1679, though not fully paid for until 1692.

The building of the town followed closely upon that of the palace. The town was to be built on either side of the three main axes, on a series of uniform squares and according to precise regulations.[31] In 1669, the double avenues of these axes were planted with large trees. In 1671 the first privileges were promulgated for new inhabitants, with more added in 1672. Parish churches, charitable institutions, and a prison were built. The height, breadth, number of floors, color, and building materials of the houses were all prescribed. A bright, lively, and uniform town was to be built as a reflection of the prosperous regime. The townspeople had to pave the streets and keep them clean; they were to put up lamps in front of their houses and provide candles for them. In spite of these rigid conditions, almost five hundred building applications were approved between 1682 and 1708. Soon both town and palace were hopelessly overcrowded—every attic was occupied. At the time of Louis XIV's death, Versailles had a population of some 25,000. During the regency the number declined by about one-half. By the eve of the Revolution it had risen to 40,000, according to Necker's register, making Versailles the sixth largest town in France. Until the very end the town was ruled by a governor. There was no self-government. People lived for, and by, the court. Everything was clean and uniform, ensconced in a park landscape in which the royal complexes grew closer and closer together. It was less than two hours by coach to Saint-Cloud, and another hour to Saint-Germain-en-Laye. The king's insistence on order made use of the geometry of the gardens to push nature into the background. It was not until the pioneers of the Revolution began to spread their message, Rousseau chief among them, that people were taught to see the countryside again.

Both palace and park were public. Anyone who had been presented had access to the palace, and anyone properly dressed had access to the park. What people did not want to see were poverty and misery. The royal family lived its life in public. On the occasion of state receptions, marriages, and births, the halls were unable to accommodate the masses of people. The king and the court gathered in the midwife's room. The cries of enthusiasm that were raised around the crown princess's bed at the birth of the heir to the throne were heard in the court and transmitted from there to Paris. The park too was overcrowded. There was no way of stopping the theft of small works of art. The king wanted the palace to be public, for this was the way his greatness, his success, and his fortune could be measured. The enormous costs involved were defended in Paris because they provided work for artists and craftsmen. It was only by being public that the palace became a political force in the promotion of a theory of state.

Potsdam

Sanssouci, outside Potsdam, was not public (fig. 141). It was always the private dwelling of the highest officer in the state, which is how Frederick the Great wished to be regarded. Only friends and officials, on official business, were admitted. Even Frederick's wife never set foot in Sanssouci. The building was hidden, and no approach road led directly to it. This work of the late rococo—a point stressed by Voltaire—was built between 1744 and

Figure 141. Sanssouci palace

1747, that is, about eighty years after Louis XIV's palace. It was neither the central point of a town nor the focal point of vistas in a park. It was simply not meant to be noticed.

The history of Potsdam exists in the form of autobiographies, yet reflects not only the characters and inclinations of each of the two kings primarily responsible for creating the town and its châteaus, Frederick William I (1713–40) and Frederick the Great (1740–86), but also their understanding of the state.

There was an earlier settlement on the island in the Havel. Potsdam is first referred to as a town in 1317. It ranked last on the list of towns in Brandenburg by which the princes made known their possessions. In 1661, the same year in which Louis XIV turned his attention to Versailles, the Great Elector began building a palace to which gardens were to be added later. Small pleasure and hunting lodges were also to be built on the periphery. In front of the palace lay the pleasure garden with its view of the Havel basin.

A few months after the death of his father, the twenty-four-year-old Frederick I decided that his royal guards, with whom he had performed military exercises for years, having brought together, at great expense, "tall fellows" literally from all over the world, should be moved to Potsdam. The town had fewer than 200 houses and scarcely 1,500 inhabitants; the troop consisted of 750 men, all of whom were to be comfortably accommodated in private billets. They were to be well looked after, and the owners of the houses in which they were billeted, together with their servants, were responsible, under the threat of extreme punishment, for seeing that none of them absconded. The reason for moving the troop and the king's household has to be sought in the fact that any escape from Potsdam, which was surrounded by rivers and marshes, was practically impossible. The Soldier King also arranged for 600 lamps, which his father had acquired to light the road from Berlin to Charlottenburg, to be brought to Potsdam in order to make escape under the cover of darkness impossible. A canal that surrounded the oldest part of the town on the land side was a further means of promoting security.

The increase in the number of troops forced the king to extend the town.[32] The settlement areas were increased according to a prearranged plan in 1722 and again in 1733 and 1737 (fig. 142). The king subsidized anyone who was willing to build. "Potsdam is being built up as a great grenadier barracks, and it is only because the soldiers have to live in civilian quarters that houses have to be built for civilians too."[33] Peter the Great, who, while a guest in Potsdam, could tell Frederick William I of his success in St. Petersburg despite great difficulties, was the source of inspiration for using the marshes behind the town to enlarge the living areas. In 1717, the town contained 198 houses. On the death of the Soldier King there were 860. Between 1748 and 1786, Frederick the Great approved the construction of 621 civilian houses, no less than 99 barracks and 29 manufactories. Friedrich Mielke has catalogued the new buildings, according to year, in his exemplary studies. The king adhered to a large-scale building program. Only a few of his father's unpretentious rows of houses were kept. In time, Potsdam turned into a model town, with houses patterned on Vicenza, Nancy, and Paris. Behind the Palladian facades, the roll of inhabitants mentions grooms and innkeepers as the first residents. To walk through Potsdam was to walk through a collection of models for an architectural manifesto on buildings for the middle class. At the same time, the clean lines followed the changing tastes every five years or so, yet kept to exactly prescribed measurements. Visitors noticed that, apart from soldiers and officers, almost no one was to be seen on these neat streets or among the architectural scenery. Model styles of architecture matched the model regiments. What has been preserved, especially drawings and photographs, which have now become irreplaceable[34] since more than two-thirds of the town was destroyed in the Second World War and the ruins were later removed, speak to us of the charm, the discipline, and the craftsmanship in these differing styles of architecture.

Frederick William I did not alter his father's château. It was not until the reign of Frederick the Great that Knobelsdorff was commissioned to enlarge it and furnish it more luxuriously. Frederick I replanted the pleasure garden that his father had partially turned into a parade ground. But he did not reform the life of the château, which was still governed by the clock on the garrison church.

At the time of his death, Potsdam's population stood at 18,503, in addition to 6,539 soldiers, all of whom were billeted in only 1,207 private houses. Earlier, the rule had been two soldiers to every inhabitant. Every apartment had to billet at least two soldiers, and every house at least four, if we include the barracks, which were certainly not very large.

Outside this garrison town, but not annexed or related to it and approachable only through the vegetable gardens and greenhouses, was the palace in which Frederick was to live. The site he settled on was an orchard on a row of hills. He drew up the plan for the whole complex himself. He forced his informal rococo style on his friend and architect Knobelsdorff, who himself cultivated a restrained elegiac, early classical style (fig. 141). Frederick also had to insist upon the building's opening up to the terrace gardens at ground level. Knobelsdorff would rather have raised it up on a socle.

The king loved to plan and to build. The gardens were constantly being extended toward the west. Chinese and Japanese houses were built, also a picture gallery, a mock ruin, and, finally, far to the east and after the Seven Years' War, as the culmination of the whole project, the new palace itself and the structures in front of it, the colonnades of the Communs—whose name and function were taken from the comparable building in Versailles (see above; see fig. 143). There were 322 windows in the main building, 240 monumental pilasters, and 428 statues. No king was ever to live in such magnificence. The rooms were at the disposal of friends and relatives; they included ten state rooms, a ballroom, a marble gallery, and a grotto, but there were only side staircases, no grand central one. Frederick the Great called the whole complex Fanfaronade or "victory fanfare." The allegorical sculptures proclaimed Prussia's greatness with enormous pathos.

Frederick the Great answered those who criticized him by saying that

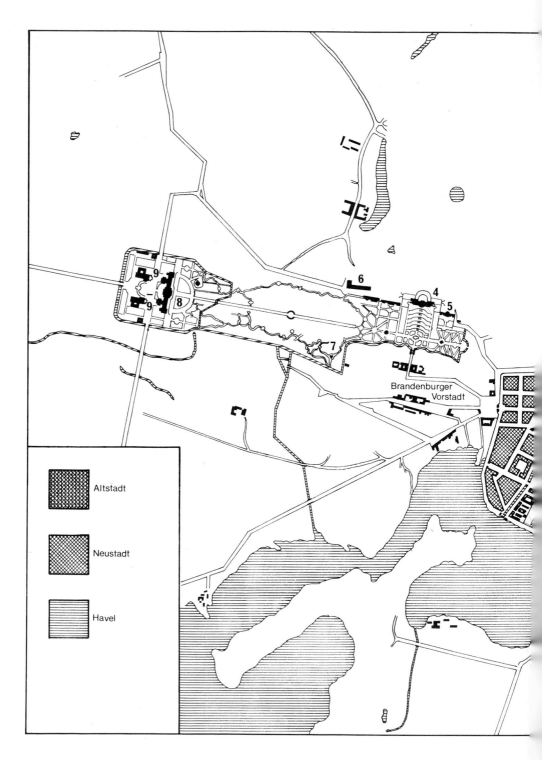

Altstadt

Neustadt

Havel

Brandenburger
Vorstadt

Berlin →

Teltower
Vorstadt

Figure 142. Potsdam, plan of the town and palace complexes (after drawings by S. D. Schleuen, 1770, and Friedrich Mielke): 1, old castle; 2, pleasure gardens; 3, town hall; 4, Sanssouci; 5, art gallery; 6, greenhouse; 7, Chinese house; 8, new palais; 9, Communs.

Figure 143. Potsdam: new palace

architecture was the dolls he played with. This was a totally unbaroque way of thinking. Anyone who enters Sanssouci steals a glance into the king's private life. Everything is select, tasteful, brilliant, and artistic. It is not a form of architecture that illustrates an order of state. The allegorical program for the gardens may be well thought out but lacks sense of necessity and interprets neither the king nor the cosmos. As far as Frederick was concerned, architecture could no longer fulfill this task.

The contrast between the parade ground and the pietistic garrison church on the one hand, and this idyll of taste and intelligence in the hills on the other, is still a burdensome one. It also reminds us of the contradictions in Frederick's character. For twenty-three years after the Seven Years' War, the old king dwelt in this edifice, erected when he was a young man, without altering anything. The king had no desire to illustrate his politics in buildings. Sanssouci was merely a negative reflection of his view of the state. It proclaimed that the monarch was no longer the state, as Louis XIV had insisted, but rather its highest servant, who has to live in a more refined style than all the others. Whatever was refined or tasteful could still be built with this motto in mind, but it was not great architecture. The new palace remained a monument to itself, Sanssouci, fully consistent, but a building of high artistic merit in a style suited to a lower branch of the art—the orangery.[35]

St. Petersburg

The last of the princely seats in our survey was the most successful city created by absolutism from the ground up. Just as Versailles illustrates Louis XIV's theory of the state, and Potsdam that of Frederick the Great, so St. Petersburg illustrates Russian despotism in all its severity and greatness and with all its efforts at reform.

It began with Peter the Great's (1689–1725) decision to open Russia up to the sea and to the West.[36] The young czar wanted to turn his back on the old Russian conservatism, and on Moscow, where his predecessors had ruled in close concert with the patriarch of the Orthodox Church. He now placed the patriarch under a synod. St. Petersburg became a symbolic form, in which this desire for progress is expressed. Progress, however, meant a connection with Western culture and economy, with the Netherlands, Germany, France, and soon with England as well. The Russia that had formerly been closed off was to be opened up to a stream of alien culture. In the process, what was indigenous was also reawakened. A European synthesis was created that was completely Russian in style. This synthesis succeeded in architecture earlier than it did in literature, music, or science. Whereas Moscow and the older Russian art had always looked toward Byzantium and the East, St. Petersburg became Russia's first Western city.

For a few years, Peter the Great could not decide whether to build the new residence in the North or in the South on the Sea of Azov. There, too, at the mouth of the Don, harbor installations and fortifications had already been built. Military reverses in the war against the Turks and a series of victories in the war against Sweden had caused him to decide in favor of the Neva delta and its island areas. The czar wanted to build a new Amsterdam, a city that had impressed him on his journey to the West in 1697. The forks of the Neva and new canal systems were to divide up the city. The city was first given a Dutch name, Sankt Pieter Burck. The first sod was turned on St. Peter's Day 1703; from 1712 it bore the German name of St. Petersburg, which was changed at the beginning of the First World War to Petrograd, and it was not until 1924 that Stalin renamed it Leningrad. That was a misnomer, for it never looked as though it was Lenin's city.

There was still no plan ready in 1703. A start was made on the Peter-Paul fortress, on an island (fig. 144). On the mainland opposite, the harbor installations and the Admiralty were built, designed to serve as a second fortress. The new Amsterdam was to be built, with its streets bordering canals, as a third fortress on Vasilyevsky Island. After his victory over

Figure 144. St. Petersburg (after an engraving by M. J. Machejev, 1753). In the center bottom of the picture the Peter-Paul fortress as well as the Admiralty fortress and its harbor basin.

Charles XII at Poltava, in 1712, Peter the Great decided to move his residence there. The first buildings for the court were built in a simple Dutch style. Model houses were designed, and all inhabitants—court, nobility, merchants, and ordinary people—were ordered to build according to their means. Le Blond, a pupil of Le Nôtre, arrived in 1716 and was dismayed by the whole thing. He came up with an ideal plan, which could, however, not be executed; it was a huge oval surrounded by bastions and divided up like a garden.

The beginnings of the city are like the beginnings of a colonial settlement in an uncharted land. Peter the Great had at first been concerned only with military security. The fortress of Kronburg was built on an island in the Gulf of Finland beyond the mouth of the Neva; at the other end, where the Neva flows out of Lake Ladoga, the Schlüsselburg fortress was built, with St. Petersburg in between. Yet this emphasis on security and the enormous expenditure on fortifications were unnecessary. Charles XII's Swedish imperial adventure was bound to fail, after some initial successes, and, years before peace in the Great Northern War was finally made in 1721, Sweden had already ceased to be Russia's adversary.[37]

The city in the huge marshy areas faced enormous difficulties. The wide river overflowed its banks every year and could not yet be bridged. The climate in the 60th degree of latitude, the long winters and short summers without transitional seasons, decimated the army of workers—prisoners-of-war, convicts, and peasants.[38] Everything had to be built on piles. The only material available was wood, and the first buildings, as in colonial settlements, were made of wood. Then Peter ordered buildings to be built of clay with wooden and sometimes brick supports. From 1714 onward, stone buildings were prescribed for the city, while building with stone was forbidden, under pain of punishment, in all the rest of Russia so that stones already quarried could be brought to St. Petersburg.

Vasilyevsky Island was to form the center. The chief minister, Menshi-kov, built his palace there; it was costly, though modest and simple when compared with later ones. The building for the twelve councils of the chief administrative authorities was also built on the island (fig. 145), as was the Stock Exchange, the main building of the commercial city. Yet even this plan was doomed to miscarry. It was too difficult to cross the river to get to the interior of the country. In time, history corrected these planning failures, and most of the new buildings were withdrawn from active life. They, or the buildings that succeeded them, today serve in a magnificently fitting manner as the university. On the other hand, the settlement around the Admiralty developed initially without a plan. The first row of palaces and the first and second Winter Palace were built on the bank of the Neva. From this point, the grid of very broad, straight roads was driven into the wooded countryside; after 1717, the Nevsky Prospekt and parts of the present-day Voznessenic Prospekt were created, and not until 1740 did the third axis, the Garoschovaya, come into being (fig. 146). The Nevsky Prospekt was to serve for the transportation of building materials. After a visit to France in 1717, Peter the Great had new ideas: the ideal picture of Versailles superseded the ideal picture of Amsterdam. By now it had already been decided to leave the new capital unfortified. There was no external enemy to be feared, and the czars were protected against domestic enemies by the Fort Peter and Paul and the admiralty.

After Peter the Great's death in 1725, the whole undertaking collapsed. More than half the population and all the nobility fled. The merchants could not be persuaded to return in spite of threats of punishment. The young Peter II had to be taken to Moscow. In 1729, Petersburg was so empty of people that its continued existence was in question. Clay huts and wooden buildings decayed or simply fell down. Only the very poorest people remained. Political considerations moved Anya Ivanovna to return in 1732. A new plan was developed. "Police architects," as they styled themselves, were supposed to carry out the plan. Vasilyevsky Island was abandoned as the center of the city. In the proper place, around the Admiralty, a new city was built, which extended along the roads leading into the interior. In 1736 and 1737, two large fires in this area, probably set by enemies of the czarina, provided the necessary free space for new planning. The

Figure 145. St. Petersburg: administrative building (left) and market hall at the end of the 18th century

proletariat lost its huts and was forced out to the periphery. Now the city could assume the architectural form suited to its function. The capital was to be to the south and west, on the mainland, delimited by the main branch of the Neva. In front of the capital was the island area, providing the most varied sites for castle complexes in a broad circle around the center, which was shaped by the tower of the Admiralty and, later, by the new Winter Palace and the gigantic, semicircular, enclosed square in front with the Montferrand columns (fig. 147). One has the impression that, after the first few years of the reign of the Czarina Elizabeth, the army of slave workers succeeded in controlling the water and in using the various branches of the Neva, the lakes, and the bay itself to enhance the architectonic situation. New canals were built, and the broad surfaces of the water were opened up to view. Versailles was the model, but nature provided St. Petersburg, even if only for a few summer months, what had to be wrested from it in Versailles. Until the beginning of the 19th century, only the Admiralty and the harbor were left isolated by walls and a moat.

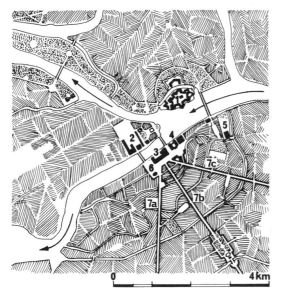

Figure 146. St. Petersburg, schematic drawing: 1, Peter-Paul fortress; 2, Vassily island with the twelve-council administrative building and Menschikov Palace; 3, Admiralty; 4, Winter Palace and Hermitage; 5, Summer Palace; 6, St. Isaac cathedral; 7 a, b, c, main axes.

Figure 147. Rastrelli's Winter Palace with a view of the Admiralty

After the right topographical site had been found some thirty years after the founding of the city, and after many new starts, which were the fruit of the interaction of planning and development, everything else developed as of necessity. The building of the city was fostered by determined royal personages and their ministers, and by a series of great architects. One after another, outstanding monarchs commissioned buildings: Elizabeth, a daughter of Peter the Great (1741–62); Catherine the Great (1762–96); Alexander I (1801–25); and Nicholas I (1825–55). The latter finally relaxed the despotic building ordinances and, as a price for granting this new freedom, had to contend with formless growth in the city. In each of these rulers, individual personality and character tied in with the stylistic climate of the epoch. Peter the Great promoted the classicism of a Dutch colonial puritanism; Elizabeth, who, like her contemporary and ideal, Louis XV, was given over to the sensual pleasures, favored a magnificent Russian rococo; and Alexander I favored the Russian form of *Empire*. For just as characteristic as the interaction of personality and style in the works commissioned by these architectural despots is the fact that, even though many of the architects were foreigners and even though they all used one formal canon, which was imported from Holland, Germany, France, and Italy, the result corresponded precisely to the Russian feeling for form. Not only this city but its architecture could not have come about in any other place on earth. It defines, as a whole and with each of its forms, a political situation—the relationship of the giant Russian empire to the West. It demonstrates its dependence and its enormous self-consciousness, in which Oriental extravagance combines with true greatness in its commitment to life, and unites this with a charm, especially in the palaces in the park, that no one can resist. This is as true of the cautious, dainty colonial style of the early period as it is of the monumental works built after the middle of the century. Here are buildings of wood, stone, and stucco, colorfully painted in bright colors and adorned in a totally untectonic manner with enormous decorative pieces, so that an amorphous plasticity blends with a musical polyphony of forms (fig. 147). Both Russian and, with more rigor, Western research have sought to classify the style.[39]

To divide the styles of the architects who carried out the work into Russian and foreign is just as unproductive for our purposes as to describe the life's work and development of each individual. Peter the Great sent for Germans, like Schlüter, Italians, like Trezzini, Frenchmen, like Le Blond, and many others, as well as numerous Russians from Moscow. His successors all went about things in the same way. Under Elizabeth, the greatest

Figure 148. Rastrelli's Smolny convent

personality was Rastrelli (1700–1770), who came to St. Petersburg with his father when he was only sixteen. He was a master of late Russian baroque, the creator of the Winter Palace, the Great Palace, and many secondary buildings in the Russian Versailles of the Tsarskoye Selo. Just how independently this all came about can be seen most clearly in his chef d'oeuvre, the cathedral of the Smolny convent. The luxuriousness of Czarina Elizabeth's life-style finds expression equally in the gigantic palace (fig. 147) in which she entertained on festive occasions, as in the convent (fig. 148), to which she considered retiring as a penitent. Under Catherine the Great, things had reached the point where Siberian marble could be imported for the Marble Palace, built by Antonio Rinaldi between 1768 and 1785, and the same czarina was able to build a major building, the Academy of Fine Arts, in the face of which even the sober French encyclopedists had to suppress their criticism. No other architect of the 18th century or, indeed, of any other century until the 20th, has designed so large an enclosed space as did this Italian, who was born in France and raised in Russia. Moreover, no one else determined the style of St. Petersburg more precisely.

Extensive urban planning measures were part of the czars' style of government. The czars were equally concerned with the planning of new palaces and their coordination into the structure of the city or country, and with the new burgher settlement areas. Subsequently, even Vasilyevsky Island was given its street grid and canals, just as Peter the Great had dreamed of them. Later, suggestions were carried out for the uniform development of the area around the Admiralty. These were worked out by an energetic and important "police architect," Jetropkin, and the Commission for St. Petersburg, which was founded in 1737. The Field of Mars and the Summer Garden, with Peter the Great's Summer Palace and the Marble Palace, were all developed into a new monumental center—on the model of the development of banks of the Seine in Paris—along with the Peter-Paul fortress, the tip of Vasilyevsky Island, and, beyond that, the city center with the Admiralty and the Winter Palace. For those parts of the city lying further afield and for the island areas, for example the Kolomna district, plans were only gradually realized. The three straight roads radiating from the Admiralty were first laid out in the 19th century when the fortifications in the Admiralty area were abandoned.

It is the gigantic nature of the axes, the squares, and the palaces that finally determined the city's countenance. The despotic will of the czars, as well as the enormous dead weight of their empire, were concentrated in St. Petersburg for more than two centuries. Such concentration of power led to extravagant expenditures. The empire defined, in its royal seat, the new form of the state and its cultural program.

The architectural significance of St. Petersburg is the result of very conscious planning. From 1760 until 1796 there was a city architectural commission. In 1763 it announced its first competition. Regional plans were drawn up, which were combined into a total plan. The quays of the Neva, the main roads, the canals, the composition of the great squares (Senate Square, Admiralty Square, Rozvodny Square, and Palace Square) were laid out with the aim of beautifying the city and representing the greatness of the czars. From 1816 onward, a building committee submitted the most important plans to the czar for his approval. Time and again a czar had the courage to stop work on large complexes, even on churches such as the Cathedral of St. Isaac, in order to build even larger ones. The St. Petersburg of Catherine the Great therefore overlaps that of the czarina Elizabeth, which in turn overlapped that of Alexander I, in which plans drawn up by Napoleon's architects for Paris were realized in St. Petersburg. Thus the victory over the West in 1812 assumed a more clearly architectural form here than in any other city, even more than in the Moscow, which had been destroyed.

It was only in the 19th century that the city lost some of its original character as a royal seat, harbor, and fortified city, when more and more industries were relocated in St. Petersburg. By 1914, almost one-third of Russian industry was there, and the work force was large enough to form the basis for the overthrow of the old order. Consequently, not only did St. Petersburg forfeit its character as royal seat, but the population declined between 1917 and 1920 from 2,400,000 to 750,000—a loss, however, that had been made up again by 1926. The city's monumental architecture, the mansions of the nobility, the ministries and the palaces of the czars lost all relation to the structure of the population. It is only since the 1950s that they have been rediscovered as national monuments.

Chapter 7

*M*OST OF THE TWENTY-ONE CULTURES CLASSIFIED by Arnold Toynbee possessed a capital city. In these capitals, all the political, economic, and religious forces of large empires were concentrated. The Ur of Sumeria, Babylon as the capital of overlapping empires, Persepolis, Carthage, and, above all, Rome and Constantinople are all examples. Ancient Greece is almost the only exception, but there, too, in the 5th century, Athens took over the leadership of Hellenic culture in all areas. Science and literature flourished in these cities because of the critical attention everyone paid to everyone else. The refinement of life-style, which was also served by the fine arts, grew out of competition among the elite and also out of their competition in making sacrifices to the gods. Every talent, of any consequence, from all the provinces of these empires strove to prove itself in the capital city. The development of trade, the influx of financial resources, the development of the means of production of ever more refined goods created employment for larger and larger numbers of people. The Constantinople of the late Paleologi, in the century before its capture, shows that the continued existence of the capital city is more important for the life of a culture than the continued existence of the empire.

This thesis can also be proved in reverse. As long as a state had several or even many cultural

Capital Cities

centers, of equal value or perhaps rivaling one another, it had no capital city. This was the case in the Holy Roman Empire and in Italy until late in the 19th century. Even Paris and London did not become capitals until the end of the 12th century, or, at least, they were only beginning to develop into capitals at that time. The monastic and cathedral cultures of both countries developed independently of them (see below, this chapter). By contrast, ancient Rome exercised a normative influence, just as Paris did in the century of French classicism, which set the standard for the cultural output of all the Roman provinces. The proximity of those who held the political reins developed the political understanding of the citizens of every capital city. The rational handling of all the tasks associated with the state was present in these cities in contrast to the irrational mass movements which were repeatedly to prevent the further development of capital cities. The heyday and the decline of empires was tied in with the prosperity and destruction of their capital cities. The terrors that accompanied the death of great cities—the burning of Babylon, the sack of Jerusalem, the fall of Carthage, the conquest of Constantinople—all reflected in historical memory, the excessive self-esteem that marked those cities. Each one formed a world of its own.

This greatness was always translated into architecture. The architectural structure of the city became its made-to-measure suit, the Sunday best of the city's personality, the means by which its individuality could best be illustrated. Capital cities developed according to a special set of laws. Their essence and their architectural profile were taken very seriously. Capitals became the symbols of human greatness and political behavior. Paris, London, Vienna, and Prague all have an attitude toward life that is admired and, in a remarkable manner, beloved. Their appearance is not merely an outward one. It reflects an essence that cannot be denominated because relationships and intellectual currents have entered into it on a number of different levels. Only a part of it could be planned; a somewhat larger part may be inferred from the appearance of the city. But the whole defies precise classification.

Prague

The plan of Prague (fig. 149) reflects the history and the fate of this capital city, which was still a capital even when no longer the seat of an independent regime.[1] Because of the varied problems presented to planners and designers by the multiplicity of political, geographic, and ethnographic con-

Figure 149. Prague, ca. 1640 (after Merian): 1, Hradcany; 2, Vyschehrad; 3, old town, 4, lesser quarter; 5, Hradcany-town; 6, new town.

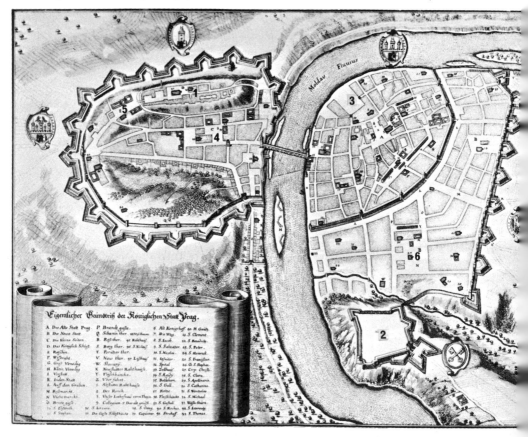

ditions, Prague has justifiably been called the Holy Roman Empire's most important achievement in urban planning.

From its beginnings, the city was destined to be the center of a country that the lozenge-shaped form of its mountains had provided with unalterable boundaries. All roads necessarily led from the border to this one center. The high hill, topped by a castle, on the meandering course of the Moldau, with its secure ford, was bound to attract princes as well as merchants. The river had as many advantages as a waterway as the castle hill did as a fortress. To protect this traffic junction, another castle, the Vysehrad, was built in the 11th century on the opposite bank, with a wooden bridge between the two. This was replaced by a stone bridge as early as 1167. Large-scale conditions were to be repeated on a small scale. The stone bridge, which was renewed on several occasions, was protected at one end by a bishop's castle and at the other by the castle and hospital of the Order of St. John. The general downward slope of culture from West to East led to the formation of a German middle class (between the lower Slavic class and an aristocracy that looked increasingly for international connections) of craftsmen and merchants, who found an opportunity of using their experience in the building of cities. A large Jewish community constituted a fourth element from the 11th century onward. In this way, medieval history acquired its accents through the dates of the founding of the castle and the four cities that constitute Prague.

The first royal seat was built on the Hradcany in the 9th century, and a church was built in the early 10th century. Duke Wenceslas, who was killed by his own brother in 929, is supposed to have commissioned it. In 973, Prague became a bishopric. By about 1000, there were three churches in the castle precinct. Around 1050, the precinct was fortified within an area 453 meters long and between 70 and 140 meters wide—at first, as was usual, by palisades, then by a stone wall, and, as early as the 12th century, by pretentious ashlar architecture, of which only the 40-foot-high "Black Tower" was preserved.

Beginning in the 10th century, merchant settlements formed in the valley on either side of the Moldau. We have an Arab geographer's description—he had a Jewish informant—which, already in 965, stresses the extent of trade in Prague and the diversity of commercial activity. At that time Prague is thought to have been a city built of clay and stone.[2] The first rows of houses grew up on the little ring road. The Jewish community had a synagogue from 1127 onward. In 1178, the German merchants were accorded

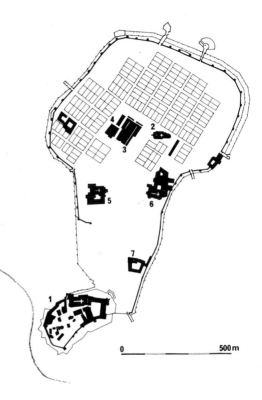

Figure 150. Cracow, the Polish royal castle and the German colonial town: 1, castle and cathedral; 2, St. Mary's market church; 3, cloth hall; 4, city hall; 5, Franciscans; 6, Dominicans; 7, Augustinians.

0   500 m

the famous privilege of being allowed to live according to their own laws and system of justice. At least thirty-six widely dispersed churches stood on this large, open settlement.

Before continuing my detailed account of Prague, I must digress for a moment.

Outside the Roman Empire, as we have seen, castle, church, and market were the elements of early towns.[3] That was the case in Magdeburg, the imperial city of the Ottonian Empire, and in Cracow, later the royal city of Poland. It was only the polarity of those basic elements that caused the rulers of the high and late Middle Ages to add a fourth element, the burgher town, which was planned in all its parts, secured by walls, and accorded its own rights.

All over eastern Europe the burgher cities were the work of colonists, craftsmen, and merchants who were more civilized than the native population. Bohemian and Polish kings sought to raise the general cultural level of their countries by favoring the immigration of those classes. The plan of Cracow (fig. 150) illustrates the circumstances more clearly than does that of Prague. In Cracow, too, there was first a castle and an episcopal seat on the hill above the settlements, and a market on the low ground near the river.[4] Ten such settlements, some already with a church, have been excavated.[5] In 1275, the king proclaimed privileges for the colonists within their area. German craftsmen and merchants were to build the city; serfs and free Poles from the country were not, at first, allowed to move in. This colonial city was fortified. A marketplace was laid out in its center, on which the market halls, the town hall, and the church of St. Maria were erected. Uniform blocks of houses, each with eight or, later, sixteen courts (*curiae*) were built along the regularly laid-out streets. All new building was subordinated to this checkerboard pattern. Only in the space between the castle hill and the city could individual buildings be built to a free design. It was here that the most important convents were built. In 1335, Casimir the Great is supposed to have built a second city, also with walls, a market, and regular plots for houses. There are still plans from the 18th century for a third, very similar, city.

It has often been pointed out that, in eastern European cities, individual foundations were permitted little opportunity for growth. Wherever a ruler or a coalition of townspeople tried to do something on a larger scale, they ended up founding a second or third functional city, with wall, marketplace, and town hall, next to the original unit. The new town then crystallized into the old one.

Four such towns were to be started in Prague, one after the other. It is revealing, in this connection, that the king had not gained sufficient organizing ability, until shortly before the middle of the 13th century, to channel a natural growth into the proposed plan. Soon after 1230, Wenceslas I commissioned his mint master, Eberhard, to draw up plans for streets and housing sites for a new colonial city to be imposed on the older settlements. Apparently the mint master was the only expert at the king's disposal for such a task. Elsewhere we come across goldsmiths who were city planners—for example, in London at the same time (see below, this chapter). Brunelleschi belongs to this group.

In 1253, Prague was enclosed by a circular wall. The merchants and craftsmen, mainly Franks, who governed their affairs according to Nuremberg's municipal law, received further privileges. This old town is the first of the four cities of Prague.

In 1257, Ottokar II ordered a second city, to be built on the other bank of the Moldau (the left bank), which was called the "Lesser Quarter" (Malà Strana). Here too, Czech peasants and craftsmen had to make room for the colonists from northern Germany. The latter, following the model of the Hanseatic League, created a square marketplace for themselves (fig. 151), and adopted Magdeburg's municipal law. These were the two cities joined by the bridge. Charles IV was to give each of them special rights. They were given a council and could elect their own consuls, and each had its own jurisdiction and its own town hall. We can envisage the slowly unfolding process as a kind of drama, where planning and the law, faced with the diversity of free settlement, delimited ever new zones of architectural order.

In the meantime, on the other side of the castle, a third urban community had been formed, the Hradcany city, where those many diverse elements settled who found it advantageous to be connected to the court. The planning of the fourth Prague city, starting 1348, was a major feat of

Figure 151. Hradcany and lesser quarter (after an engraving by Ägidius Sadeler, 1606, detail)

urban design. The walls of this city were 3.5 kilometers long and surrounded the old and the new cities in a wide arc, starting at Vysehrad. Figure 149 gives us a general view of the way things were. Recent Czech research has demonstrated that Charles IV and his architects planned the new city with great care. In their siting of the church squares, they reverted to the Ottonian example and made them cruciform. Certain details suggest that Rome and Avignon also served as models.[6] Three large markets were separated in the new plans; among these, Charles Square measured 152 by 550 meters. Imposing plots for houses and significant tax advantages were intended to attract settlers. A few craft guilds were forced to move from the old city. The king, who was later to become emperor, built two parish churches and six convents in the new city. Like the old town and the "Lesser Quarter," the new city also had an independent administration and its own town hall. Besides these four Christian cities, the Bohemian kings, from the time of the Premyslids onward, also accorded the inalienable privileges to the Jewish city that were essential if it was to flourish. Between the 14th and 18th centuries, the Jewish city frequently numbered more than 5,000 inhabitants. Illustrative of 13th and 14th century thought was the fact that the kings, who had decisively ordered the various sets of plans, secured by charter all the freedoms needed for self-development; for only the frameworks of the four Prague cities had been predetermined by the wall. Their street plans, of necessity, grew out of the application of a particular law on a prescribed site. The municipalities remained free as far as details of design were concerned. This tension between large-scale planning and freedom of detailed design gave the creative spirit the developmental possibilities suited to it.

The urban composition on either side of the bend in the Moldau remained unique. All other large capital cities—Vienna, Berlin, London, Paris, Moscow, even Munich, Turin, Brussels, Copenhagen, or Stockholm—lie on broad plains or on the banks of a river. The challenge presented by Prague's geographical situation, with the castle hill, the bend in the river, and the plain, corresponded to the challenge presented by the competition between peoples and classes. Prague was a capital with three different peoples. In no other capital was Jewry able to develop so fruitfully. In addition, the competition between the monarchy, the nobility, and the patricians, and, at times, that between different religions in the city, encouraged architectural monumentality.

The age of Charles IV, as urban planning's first heyday in Prague, is characterized by two large-scale plans, both of a high order. I have already stressed the boldness with which the broad strip of the new city was laid around the old. Charles IV manifested the same enthusiasm for planning in the design of the Hradcany castle. We should bear in mind that the young ruler had taken over the Romanesque royal castle in a state of decay, and, as the old ruler, left it behind as a Gothic imperial castle in the middle of which stood the archbishop's new cathedral. In this process, large-scale planning and individual works complemented one another, not just architectural works but paintings and sculptures which served to illustrate and, indeed, to define the new political aims.

It was a stratified process. King John of Luxembourg (1311–46) had at first given his son and heir the name of the Czech patron saint, Wenceslas. On the occasion of his confirmation by Charles IV of France, the boy assumed the name of that king—one that no German king had borne since Carolingian times. In 1433, at the age of eighteen, Charles returned from his studies in France as his father's representative. The centralism of the French kingdom had set the seal on his way of thinking. The Premyslid idea of the sacred nature of their royal dignity and power had been passed on to him by his mother. From the diversity of the structure of the empire, a mission was formed that he, as emperor, not only had to deal with in the political arena but had to make manifest in his architectural projects. In 1344, by dint of clever negotiations, he arranged with his teacher, who was reigning in Avignon as Pope Clement VI, to have the city in which he resided elevated to an archbishropic. In 1348 a university was founded, which was subject to the archbishop and quickly developed into the largest in the empire. In the same year the king laid the foundation stone of the city's new wall. Four years previously, in 1344, Matthieu d'Arras had already presented him with a plan for a cathedral patterned after French ones. The ground floor of the choir and eight of the eleven chapels that were planned in the choir aisles were completed when the Frenchman died in 1352. His cathedral was to symbolize the independence of the metropolitan from the old archdiocese of Mainz, and at the same time was to serve as a place of pilgrimage to the remains of the patron saint of the country. It is characteristic of the change in the political view of life that in 1356 the new emperor appointed as successor to d'Arras a young member of the rising generation of architects from one of his own imperial German cities, twenty-three-year-old Peter Parler, a son of Heinrich Parler, from Schwäbisch Gmünd.

In conversations between this intelligent, daring, active young architect and his patron there developed a new iconological program for further construction which corresponded more to the monarch's assessment of himself than to the needs of the archbishop and his chapter. This new plan was realized by three measures taken for new construction and two taken for furnishing the cathedral. All these measures took into account the new political theology that Charles IV derived from his dual position as German emperor and king of Bohemia. They have therefore to be mentioned in any description of the planning of capital cities, for they characterize most clearly the political ideals that combined the cathedral and the royal residence on the Hradcany into a single unit, the like of which we encounter only in the City of Westminster in London before 1534, where the king's partner was not an archbishop but an abbot (see below, this chapter).

The first measure, and Peter Parler's first job, was to build a chapel for Wenceslas, the patron saint of the country. Because of the predetermined site and the prescribed architectural form for this chapel it was impossible to coordinate it with the doctrinaire Gothic style of the cathedral (fig. 152, 1). Its four pillars were to be seen as bearers of the baldachin over the saint's tomb. The second measure consisted in reorienting the whole of the cathedral to accommodate to the new south portal, which was now the main entrance and faced the royal palace. By the way these portals were arranged (152, 2) and even more by the iconographic program of its mosaics, the whole cathedral was reinterpreted as the chapel of the emperor's palace. Opposite the chapel of Wenceslas on the other side of the portal, as the third work in this series of new orientations, Peter Parler started work on the massive south tower, which was calculated—when viewed from the city—to look as much like the tower of the imperial residence as that of the cathedral. Towers of this size and in this situation were quite foreign to Gothic architecture. The same idea was subsequently taken up in Vienna. Parler's sons raised the tower to its present height, and the baroque period merely added the tall, steep, sweeping roof, which rises up in three steps. These three works, the chapel of Wenceslas, the south portal, and the south tower (figs. 152 and 153) not only form a unified, very richly designed group but arise out of the same architectural iconology.

The same is true of the sculptural program that Peter Parler and his workshop completed at the same time. As memorials to the Premyslid kings, six tombs were built for the cathedral's choir chapels, among them the tomb of Ottokar III, crafted by the master himself. Three of the kings were represented in their royal regalia, three in armor. These ancestral tombs have to be seen as a group, along with the twenty-one busts over the corridors of the lower triforium and the ten busts of the saints in the upper triforium, by means of which Charles provided a monument to himself, his father, his brothers, and his son, each with his wife, and to the archbishop and the architects as well.[7] In this context there is no need to speak of Parler's most important achievement, the clerestory of the choir itself.

Despite all the work going on in the palace, on the cathedral, and on the Hradcany, Charles IV never neglected to support construction in the four cities. Peter Parler's great engineering achievement, the bridge with sixteen arches and a total length of 520 meters, justifiably bears the name of the monarch. With its towered gateways it made possible and, at the same time, secured communications between the cities, the castle, and the old city (fig. 154).

Figure 152. Prague: plan of the cathedral

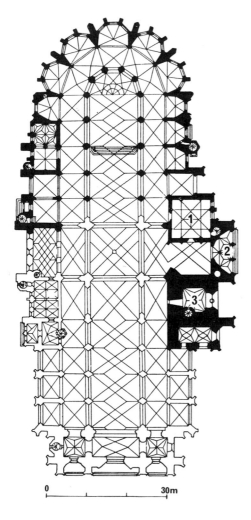

0   30m

Figure 153. Prague Cathedral (engraving of 1791)

There are religious and political grounds for the fact that the Gothic building was abandoned in the 15th century and not, as in many places, the 16th, and was left with its torso uncompleted until the 19th century. The unity of the imperial seat and the cathedral broke up as early as 1410 on the death of Wenceslas. Such an eminently aristocratic work no longer had a function in Hussite Prague. People had to come to terms with the fact that the Hradcany could no longer be experienced as a whole. The four cities led their own lives. The castle and the cathedral remained a problem which was constantly readdressed by the individual monarchs, but to which no permanent solution responsive to the needs of every century was ever found.

This becomes especially clear when we recall the architectural provisions which the "alien" kings made for the Hradcany in the humanist period. Between the reign of Charles IV and Vladislav II (1471–1516), no buildings of outstanding merit were commissioned in the capital, nor did any outstanding architect work there between the time of Peter Parler (d. 1399) and Benedikt Ried (in Prague from 1448). The Hussites put an end to the fragile art of courtly Gothic. Georg von Podebrad, a mediating figure, regent in Bohemia from 1448 and king from 1458 to 1471, could add

287

only a few accents to the cityscape. Vladislav II, who had at first taken up residence in the late Gothic royal city palace, was forced by rebel movements to embattle himself on the Hradcany in 1484. Because of the political situation, Benedikt Ried (1454–1534), a fortification architect, was summoned from Landshut. His first task was to enclose the Hradcany by a ring of fortifications with a total length of 2,500 meters, with walls, towers, and fortified gates designed for the needs of the new artillery warfare.[8] Ried then received commissions for completion work in the palace itself, the ceremonial staircase and the Vladislav Hall (1493–1502), which is among

Figure 154. The Charles bridge and its fortified towers (engraving by Ägidius Sadeler, 1606, detail)

the largest and certainly the boldest interiors designed in the Middle Ages. It measures 62 by 16 meters and is 12 meters high. We have to remember that this hall was built above the Romanesque barrel-vaulted palace of Dobeslav II and the Gothic hall of Charles IV and thus represents the third and final point in a development of which the extent and unity can only be perceived from the castle garden. The composition of the palace was completed by the tract built between 1502 and 1509, which bears the name of the king's son, Louis. The windows and doors of Vladislav Hall are framed with Renaissance columns and gables. The whole of the south front is similar in decor, though not in proportions, to a Renaissance palace. The celebrated interior consists of five cupolas, which give the effect of full-blown sails, while the curved course of the ribs, with their five-times-recurring pattern, serves to illustrate the unity of the space—the parts that are load-bearing and the parts that are not. This vault creates a light, buoyant, lively, and transparent effect. It is worth dwelling on here because the hall is the expression of a political situation. In 1490 a Polish prince, elevated to the kingship of Bohemia and shortly before his election to the Hungarian crown as well, commissioned a German architect to erect in his castle a throne room and tournament hall of unusual height, in which late Gothic architectural graphics were combined with the Italian feeling for architectural space and with Renaissance decorative forms. This clever monarch wished to balance his preferment in Buda by manifesting his presence in buildings in Prague. His Prague residence was to be comparable to the one in Buda, where his predecessor, Matthias Corvinus, had already helped Italian humanism and the Italian Renaissance make a breakthrough.

Later kings of Bohemia and the leaders of the court aristocracy in their service made similar efforts. While a new political climate forced these monarchs to set even tighter limits to the freedom of the citizens, new Renaissance buildings filled the castle hill and the castle itself. In 1535, Giovanni Spatio began to build the Belvedere (fig. 151, extreme right) for the wife of Ferdinand I of Habsburg, who was awarded the Bohemian crown in 1526. The leading families of the nobility bought large plots on the Hradcany: for example, the Rosenbergs and the Lobkovitzs, whose palace—built between 1545 and 1563 and later acquired by the Schwarzenbergs—represents a high point of manneristic architecture in Prague. At the same time, the rooms in the royal residence were being filled up with works of art. Rudolph II (1576–1612) gathered the greatest collection of the day there. Dwelling space for the citizens was further reduced to make room for the palaces of the aristocracy. Wallenstein had twenty-six townhouses razed in

1624 to make room for his palace with its loggias and its terrace before he could entrust Andrea Spezza to build his royal seat, which he did with military expedition.

The third heyday of urban construction in Prague began with this palace and lasted until 1784, when the destruction of the old city units permitted the building of the new metropolis. After the Habsburgs' victory in the Thirty Years' War, the formerly predominantly Protestant citizens declined in numbers as against the Catholic nobility. Rudolph II was the last king to maintain his permanent residence in Prague; he lived there from 1583 until 1612. A new architecture now developed which was both aristo-

Figure 155. Hradcany and lesser quarter

cratic and ecclesiastical, superimposing itself on the Gothic city and on both the Renaissance and mannerist royal buildings. The palaces of the nobility, built in the latter half of the 17th century and in the 18th, together with the rebuilt imperial castle on the Hradcany (1756–75, fig. 155), introduced into the cityscape regular, dominant, horizontal lines. They formed a dynamic and tense relationship with the vertical lines of the Gothic architecture and at the same time changed the scale of the whole city structure. Characteristic of this new style of architecture were the immense palace buildings. Old established families like the Lichtensteins, the Schwarzenbergs, the Czernins, the Kinskys, the Lobkovitzs, and the Waldsteins began to compete

Figure 156. Prague: Czernin palace

with the new families who had made their money in the war—the Piccolominis, the Colloredos, and the Thun-Hohensteins. Bernini himself was
occupied with plans for Count Czernin's palace. The massive facade built
by Francesco Carotti (of Ticino) and others between 1667 and 1697 is the
largest that any private person ever built in Bohemia (fig. 156). Many of
these magnates took the bestowal of high government office as the occasion
for building in the high style. After his appointment as Marshal of Bohemia, Johann Wenceslas, Count Gallas, commissioned Fischer von Erlach to
build him his famous Prague city palace. In the process of changing the
Gothic burgher city into an aristocratic baroque city, the ecclesiastical institutions, first among them the Jesuits, took on the same significance as the
leading aristocratic families. Even the archbishop came into prominence for
the last time. He commissioned the building of a new residence on the
model of Fischer von Erlach's Palais Trautson opposite the new imperial
palace. It was precisely these official buildings, in contrast to the baroque
churches of the city, that cultivated a conservatism betraying the lack of
independence even of the institutions. Once again, they documented the

fact that those institutions which do not promote future projects cling to old and tried models even in their architecture.

What remained was the variety of conditions that characterize Prague baroque. The city has retained the diversity that was bound to develop from three different levels of competition, which were also the source of its creative energies: first, the struggle between the different peoples—Germans, Czechs and Jews; second, the struggle between the classes—monarchy, nobility, middle classes, and clergy, in which the rebel movements of the lower classes had constantly been involved; and, third, the struggle between religious confessions, which was only superficially resolved by the victory of the Roman Catholic Counterreformation. The Hussite countermovements, which have to be regarded as nationalist movements, could never be completely stifled.

The multitude of architectonic ideas, reflecting the manifold political movements, combined with the favorable nature of the site to give the city its extraordinarily rich personality. The political fate that burdened the city throughout the many epochs of its history, and still burdens it today, has left its traces everywhere, but at the same time it has presented a remarkable challenge to Prague's creative powers. It is beyond the scope of this work to characterize the special nature of Bohemian baroque.[9] A process by which Gothic was overlaid by baroque also acted as the setting for the city units in Prague. We encountered the same situation in Amsterdam, Turin, Potsdam, and St. Petersburg. Every one of these cities, and many others, had to cut out the baroque costume that suited it. In this costume the cities not only displayed their own particular attitude to the world and their conception of existence but also proclaimed their assessment of themselves, which always involved a political program.

At no time after 1784 did the city of Prague find the strength to undertake extensive new planning. Unity was utopian; diversity remained. True, significant attempts were made, in the period of promoterism and *art nouveau,* to monumentalize the ring roads that had been built when the walls dividing the cities had been razed. Here, too, Czech nationalism found expression. There were also programs for slum clearance; in one such program, a terribly run-down ghetto was replaced with uniform new buildings. But until 1918 that creative freedom which had made its mark upon Munich or Vienna was lacking in Prague, and between 1918 and 1939 Prague lacked the power to guide its own growth. Since 1939, subjection in new guises at first prevented any planning at all and then, to the present day, demeaned planning to the point where planning itself documented the city's lack of freedom.

Vienna: The Conflict

As far back as 1237, the walls of Vienna surrounded an area that was to remain the same size for over 620 years, until 1857. From the 15th century onward, 40,000 to 50,000 people lived within these walls.[10] Between the first siege of Vienna by the Turks in 1529 and the last in 1683, the fortifications were continually being strengthened and modernized. This meant that the glacis (the area in front of the bastions) had to be repeatedly enlarged as a field of fire. In 1529 it was 90 meters wide, and after 1683 it was broadened to 450 meters. Until 1858, nothing was built on it at all (figs. 157 and 158).

On the other side of the glacis were several small towns. These were mainly destroyed during the siege of 1683, and terrible massacres took place in them. After the siege was lifted, the Viennese population was seized with the flush of victory, which allowed them to rebuild the city rapidly. This was the time when the numerous garden palaces were built on the high ground outside the city. Fischer von Erlach made the first start with the plans for the imperial palace of Schönbrunn. By 1720, 200 country seats had been erected. By 1740, 400 aristocratic and 1,000 burgher country villas are reckoned to have been in existence. Prince Eugene had acquired one of the most beautiful estates—and one of the largest—with the first funds he received. There, over a period of forty years, he built the Lower and the Upper Belvedere with their extensive gardens.[11] The fortified city could be seen from his terraces. The bold architecture of the facade of the Karlskirche, as a pictorial structure made up of symbols, can only be explained by the fact that the facade, in turn, was intended to be visible as a distant prospect from the bastions of the city.[12]

Between 1683 and 1857, the circle of country seats and the suburbs of the city developed into a densely built-up architectural network, which continued to grow until 1918. Hans Sedlmayr has compared this Vienna to the planet Saturn: the fortress and the old city as the planet, the country seats and the suburbs as the rings. When on 12 December 1857 the emperor Francis Joseph I was finally ready to demolish the ring of fortifications, the resulting space provided the city with an opportunity to build a ring road with a perfect plan for building on both sides of it: a plan in which governmental, administrative, and cultural buildings complement each other (see below, fig. 163). But more of that later.

Within the ring of fortifications, a conflict arose between the court and the imperial castle, on the one hand, and the citizens' need for space, on the other. The history of the construction of St. Stephen's cathedral as center of the burgher city and the history of the building and the architecture of the *Hofburg* (the court castle) both reflect this conflict.

Vienna had been a Roman encampment city.[13] The ravages of the pe-

Figure 157. View of Vienna from the south (engraving by Georg M. Fischer, 1675). St. Stephen's was placed in the center of the picture; on the left, the Alte Burg and the Leopold tract.

Figure 158. Bird's-eye view of Vienna from the West (by Folbert von Alten-Alten, 1683). In the year of the Turkish siege, the engraver stresses the strength of the city's bastions.

riod of the great migrations, the rule of the Avari, and the attacks of the Huns delayed every attempt to make a fresh start. There was little continuity. Only the very poorest elements of the population dared to go on living in settlements inside the walls. The patron saints of the two parish churches, St. Rupert and St. Peter, point to the fact that Vienna was visited by missionaries from Salzburg. They are the patron saints of Salzburg cathedral. Step by step, the Babenberger margraves approached the city and advanced their seat from Melk, via Tulln and Klosterneuburg, into Vienna. The city came into their hands under Leopold III (1125–30). It was not until after 1150, however, that Heinrich Jasomirgott was to build a castle there. It lay *am Hof* (at the court), not yet on the periphery of the city. But the Babenbergers reached the city too late. In contrast to Prague, where the dukes were the first to arrive and had quickly brought a bishop along before establishing the three burgher cities in a planned and regular fashion around the older marketplaces, Vienna did not become an episcopal seat until 1474, its townspeople having already held power before the rulers entered the city. The margraves first sought to gain an advantage by promoting the citizenry and their foreign trade to such an extent that in the 13th century the citizens often thought of expelling the duke, with the emperor's approval, and thus acquiring the status of a free imperial city. As late as 1462, the emperor Frederick III had to defend himself in his castle for six weeks against the rebellious citizenry. He was forced back into a later castle on the outskirts of the city. That is why he planned to move to Wiener Neustadt.

Until all building ceased in 1514, the history of the building of St. Stephen's clearly reflects this struggle for power.[14] After Ferdinand I's bloody purge of the citizenry and the city council in 1521, building the royal castle became a major project, for up to that point the Habsburgs, too, had had to make do with the medieval castle, where living quarters looked out onto the narrow courtyard today called the Swiss Courtyard (Schweizer Hof). Later, and then for a period of 200 years, the common fear of attack by the Turks and the consequent efforts to build fortifications united citizens and court. The founding of a new parish church prior to 1137 by Regunmar, bishop of Passau, during a power vacuum was connected with the taking over of the city by the Babenburg margraves, who were made dukes in 1156. This church, located outside the original medieval walls of the city, was dedicated to the patron saint of the bishop's own cathedral, St. Stephen. All other parish churches in the city were subordinated to this new one in 1137. It was not until 1200 that the church was included within a new city wall. The size of even the first church of St. Stephen was amazing.

The parish church, completed around 1160, was 83 meters long and had the proportions of a cathedral. It was intended to be seen as symbolic of the aspirations to power of the bishops of Passau and of their rivalry with the Babenberg rulers of the city. The second Romanesque building, started around 1240 and dedicated in 1263, and whose west facade with its huge door has been preserved, was already essentially promoted by the new forces, the citizens and the ducal house. After his victory over the rebellious citizens, Frederick II had, with great self-confidence, arrogated to himself the rights of the city church, in opposition to the bishop, and had appointed his own chancellor as vicar.

The Gothic rebuilding of St. Stephen's, which was started in 1304, reflects in its construction and its furnishings both the rivalry and the cooperation of the three powers—the duke, the bishops of Passau, and the citizens. The great nave, one of the widest in Europe, attests that the citizens were in a position to play the decisive role in this struggle (fig. 159). The choir was built between 1304 and 1344. Work was begun in 1359 on the side walls of the nave, which surrounded the old Romanesque nave like a sheath. It was not until 1446 that the final vaulting beneath the huge roof

Figure 159. St. Stephen's from the south

was completed. From 1359 until 1433, work was in progress on the south spire. It was the model of Prague that prompted the architect to build two spires at the end of the apse, which embraced the church between them. The nave, the uniformly high roof, the south spire as the badge of the city, are the expression of the citizens' pride and power. The enormous expenditure of craftsmanship and effort on the stone filigree of the gables of the nave and, rising above, the most perfect of all Gothic spires, is to be seen as a demonstration of the citizens' virtues. A member of the city council, as master of the church, was responsible for the provision of building materials.

St. Stephen's became, nonetheless, the ducal, the royal, and, finally, the imperial church. The open space in front of the huge door was the site of the royal court of justice. The loft of the west choir served as an oratory for the ruler. The chapter of the palatinate chapel had moved from the castle chapel into this burgher cathedral. The Habsburgs gave their provost the rank of prince and occasionally of arch-chancellor. The parish was finally subordinated to the provost. Even later bishops did not succeed in subordinating these provosts and their chapter, the *capella regia*. Although the citizens had to bear the bulk of the building costs, every one of the Habsburgs took part in the building process by making generous contributions. Up to the end of the Gothic period, most of the rulers and their consorts were commemorated in statues on the exterior. The "gallery of dukes" is comparable to the royal galleries in French cathedrals. The ducal chapel, too, as a double chapel, annexed on the righthand side to one of the towers of the Romanesque facade, is a court addition inside the building.

When building was stopped on St. Stephen's in 1511, the "Gothic" chapter of Viennese history came to an end. But the new chapter—"the city of the aristocracy and the baroque"—did not begin for a while. At first there were no changes in the castle around the Schweizerhof that had been laid out by Ottokar II (1247–78) and built by Albrecht between 1283 and 1308 in a form that was to last for 200 years. The court first established itself in Wiener Neustadt, then from time to time in the castle of Ambras near Innsbruck, later in Graz, and then in Prague. In 1559, some of the most important imperial authorities moved to Vienna, but it was not until the death of Rudolph II in 1612 that the city became the seat of the Holy Roman emperors.

After the second half of the 16th century, the old castle no longer met the demands even of a much more modest court.[15] Private houses had to be rented in increasing numbers for state offices. The imperial architects tried

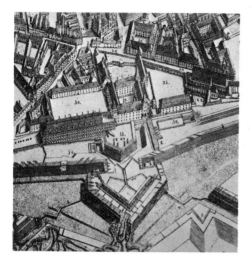

Figure 160. The Viennese Hofburg (from D. Suttinger's view of the city, 1683): foreground, from left to right, The Amalienburg as the left end of the tournament court; Leopold tract; the old Hofburg; and the ball house.

to open up the walls of the old castle. Gardens were built on the land on either side of the moats on the southwest. In 1575, the open space in the northeast, which had always been available to the court for tournaments, was completed by Rudolph II in a monumental way with the Amalienburg (fig. 160), which has been preserved to this day. It was left to the future to give shape to the great court "in the castle." Time and again in the 17th and 18th centuries the imperial architects rattled the chains with which the bastions of the fortress outside, and the burgher city inside, tried to prevent the imperial castle's erupting into monumental proportions. How could a suitably large, ceremonial, and regularly articulated imperial residence be built for the Habsburgs when there was no room anywhere, when old and venerable buildings had to be preserved, and when imperial ceremony could never be interrupted by construction? When faced with this problem, even the greatest architects failed—the two Fischer von Erlachs and Lukas von Hildebrandt under Joseph I and Charles VI; Jadot de Ville, Issey, Balthasar Neumann, and others under Maria Theresa and Joseph II. They all presented master plans for a symmetrical residence on a scale that would have been suited to the empire (fig. 161), but none could succeed in coordinating his plan with the available space. There was no site available in Vienna on which a Louvre extending down to the Tuileries could be built. The architects had to be content with a patchwork in the north toward the city, in the east toward the Augustinerkirche, and on the west toward the Amalienburg (fig. 162). Despite these restrictions some great architecture was produced—such as Lukas von Hildebrandt's south wing in the castle courtyard and Fischer von Erlach's court library—but there is no general unity. Schönbrunn, which is outside the city, was still a country seat rather than a city residence.

The nobility was more successful than the court. Like Prague, Vienna at the end of the 17th century changed from a burgher city to a city of aristocrats. With the victory over the Turks, ever larger areas of the Balkans were opened up to the imperial power. Again and again we hear that mem-

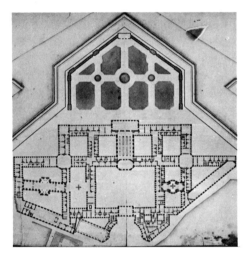

Figure 161. Balthasar Neumann's conceptual plan for the Hofburg. Apart from Fischer von Erlach's library, all the older buildings were to be torn down; the great staircase occupies the center.

Figure 162 (below). Plan of the Hofburg, upper story: 1, Schweizer Hof (Swiss courtyard); 2, Amalienburg; 3, Leopold tract; 4, winter riding school; 5, court library.

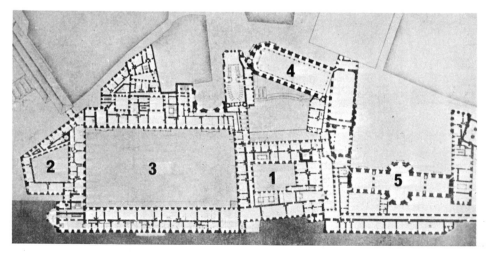

bers of the houses of Lichtenstein, Starhemberg, Mansfeld-Fondi, Lobkowitz, Harrach, Schönborn, Althan, and Schwarzenberg were commissioned
to equip armies and administer provinces. Whereas in centralist France,
Louis XIV forced his nobles to ruin themselves in their service to the court,
decentralized Austria offered the great houses enormous opportunities to
amass wealth in a liberality which had been acquired by a long process of
education. The net profits could be expended in monumental architecture
and collections of art. While the aristocracy was conducting campaigns or
building up an administrative hierarchy in Naples, Milan, or Mantua, in
Brussels, Prague, or Budapest, in Belgrade or in the lands of Greater Austria, on the Rhine, in Swabia, Banat or Wallachia, they were also building
their mansions in Vienna and endowing churches in the capital and convents in the country. There was almost always a new building being commissioned in connection with a new distribution of offices in the court or
the imperial administration. In the 17th century, Vienna was still a Gothic
city whose irrational principles of order only the most recent research into
urban design has attempted to determine.[16] Today, in the narrow streets,
we often perceive the great horizontal lines of the baroque palaces as they
replace the vertical lines of the old gabled houses. Even at the time the
palaces were built, people complained that they could not be seen properly
on those narrow streets. It was not long before the palaces of the nobility
inside the walls were matched by extensive castle and garden complexes on
the hilly country beyond the open space surrounding the bastions. What in
Paris could only be afforded by the king and a few princes of the blood
royal, namely, a city palace and a summer palace outside the city, was the
dream of everyone in Vienna, for there was no room in the inner city for
new aristocratic districts. The only complexes on the outskirts of the city
that were preserved were the narrow sector that contains Prince Eugene's
Belvedere and Prince Mansfeld-Fondi's summer palace (known as Schwarzenberg from 1716 on); the Palais Lichtenstein in the Rossau; and the Palais
Trautson with its gardens. It was Vienna's finest hour. There had never been
a period of comparable splendor. The victory of 1683 had transformed the
world. Vienna changed from frontier city to central city. The country
opened up. The political horizons of the great families grew ever wider,
their journeys ever longer.

This great hour in Vienna was also a great hour for architecture. Architecture, like music, became a social passion. It was a part of culture. A
generation of native architects replaced the Italians. Fischer von Erlach the
Elder and Lukas von Hildebrandt were the most successful among them.

The man of the moment was Prince Eugene of Savoy. His palace in the city and the Belvedere outside the wall became models. These buildings symbolize a new political self-confidence. Hans Sedlmayr has spoken of an "imperial style," Otto Brunner of an "emperor's style."[17] In the 18th century sense these are good designations, but they narrow the processes down. It was not a style that sought to dominate an empire. It created no forms of government. I would describe Viennese baroque as the first "peace style." The castles shed their armor, and fortified walls and towers disappeared from the land. The castle complexes, with their gardens, spread into the outskirts of the city, unprotected, open, and with extravagant charm. People had had to protect themselves from foreign armies for too long—they now wanted to demonstrate that they were free.

The Vienna of Prince Eugene and of the latter years of Maria Theresa's reign was like St. Petersburg, London, or Paris in the 18th century—a dynamic city. Buildings were erected on the grand scale, not only because of population growth and the desire for aristocratic pomp, but because buildings were forms of self-assertion and of the mastery of existence. People believed that by building they were promoting economic growth and technical progress. Prince Eugene saw the construction of the Belvedere as a way of employing his army veterans. The hydraulic works used in constructing the water terraces in his grounds provided experience which could later be applied to the creation of the capital's water supply system. Such castle buildings assembled economic forces and supported technological progress.

Engravings of the period represent the capital as a closed entity. They reflect the contemporary admiration for what the builders had achieved. In 1769, Maria Theresa herself commissioned Joseph Daniel Hopfer to draw up a total picture of Vienna, surrounded by its satellite towns, and to preserve it with all the details in a monumental engraving. The high point had been reached.

Neither the shortage of space inside the ring of fortifications, nor the traffic problems attendant upon the connection of the city with its suburbs, could be solved in the 18th century. The closing of several convents by Joseph II and the use of their gardens for the building of dwellings and manufactories did no more to resolve the conflictual situation in Vienna than it did in Paris after 1789 or in Munich after 1802.[18] Parts of the lungs of these cities were taken away without bringing the living space and the traffic, the needs of the state and the citizens, into any sort of balance. After the conquest of Vienna in 1809, Napoleon ordered the bastions to be opened up.

The castle gate (Burgtor) was projected. But it was only when the railroad network was planned and the first railroad stations built that the road to a radically new organization of the body of the city was suggested.

This road was taken immediately after Joseph I promulgated his famous decree in December 1857: "It is my will that the extension of the inner city of Vienna, in view of the relationship between it and the suburbs, should be undertaken as soon as possible and that, at the same time, thought should be given to the regulation and embellishment of my imperial capital and the seat of my court. . . ." Vienna could now begin to do what Paris had been doing since 1664, what Berlin had already done in 1734, Hanover in 1763, and Graz in 1784, and what Frankfurt and Turin had done on Napoleon's orders. The broad space formed an ideal challenge for the design of monumental buildings on each side of the new ring road (Ringstraße). No other European capital undertook a comparable task at so late a date. The Prussian administration placed too many limits on the possibilities in Cologne, whose walls did not come down until 1882. As a whole, the success of the Viennese Ringstraße results from a conception of a capital that corresponded to the personal view of the emperor Franz Joseph (1830–1916). It can also be called a testimony to the self-confidence of the Danubian monarchy. Native and foreign architects, among them Friedrich von Schmidt from Cologne, Theophil Hansen from Denmark, and, foremost among them, Gottfried Semper from Dresden, all participated in the massive undertaking. Among the Viennese architects, Eduard van der Null has pride of place as the designer of the opera house in conjunction with Heinrich von Ferstel, who at the age of twenty-seven had already won the competition for the Votivkirche and was later to build the nearby university as well as a number of other buildings (fig. 163).

The whole project went back to suggestions made by Ludwig Forster of Bayreuth. Already in the 18th century, repeated demands had been made for the walls to be razed. Joseph II had built roads through the deserted land, and here and there trees had been planted; there were also open spaces which served as parade grounds. After the building of the Votivkirche in 1856—it was endowed as a thank offering after an unsuccessful attempt on the emperor's life—work could be started on the project. After 1858, work was begun simultaneously at a number of places. The whole area of the Ring was divided into zones, each to serve a different purpose. Besides culture and administration, they were to serve trade, finance, traffic, individual branches of industry, and last but by no means least, the leading families of the nobility, with elegant new districts and palaces. Recent research into the Ringstraße has revealed the extent of the political self-confidence that proclaimed itself in these diverse building programs.[19]

The rhythm of the building process can also be discerned from surviving statistical surveys, which show that, until 1872, the unfavorable political situation repeatedly hindered the execution of the major projects. At the outset, only the Votivkirche (1853–79) and the opera house (1861–69) were standing; the latter called forth such vehement criticism that its architect, van der Nüll, committed suicide. The three determinative complexes were

Figure 163. Schematic drawing of the Viennese Ringstraße and its buildings: A, St. Stephen's; B, Hofburg; 1, Votivkirche; 2, opera house; 3, Neue Hofburg; 4, courthouse; 5, museum of art history; 6, Museum of natural history; 7, Parliament; 8, city hall; 9, university; 10, Burgtheater; 11, banking union; 12, stock exchange; 13, barracks; 14, school for arts and crafts.

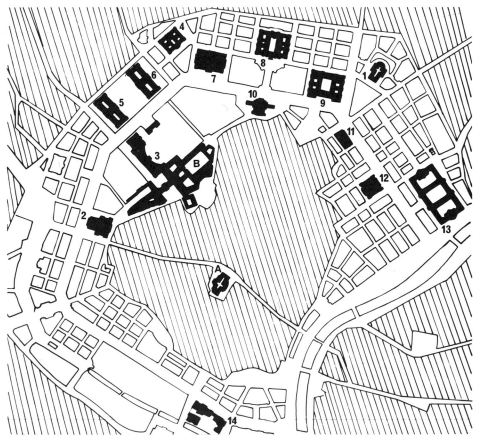

built simultaneously between 1872 and 1883, the period of "promoterism": the great cruciform complex with the city hall (fig. 163, 8) between Parliament (7) and the university (9), with the Burgtheater (10) opposite; the two court museums (5 and 6) opposite the Burg (3); and the financial district. The last piece of building was the extension to the Hofburg in 1913. The period of the Danubian monarchy and of imperial Vienna was drawing to a close.

Three characteristics mark the enterprise. First, the most important monumental buildings are free-standing in parks and gardens. The city park (Stadtpark), the Kursalon, monuments, and conservatories were all part of the program. People were to be able to wander among the buildings, to look at them from a distance, and at the same time to recall the great figures in the intellectual life of the city and the state—Beethoven, Brahms, Schubert, Maria Theresa and her fieldmarshals, and many others. This was a quite conscious development. Second, the composition of all sections of the Ring and of the buildings in each of them has a topology which takes into account the political and social functions of the building. This is true not only of the group of the three largest buildings—Parliament (7), the university (9), and the city hall (8), which is flanked by the other two, thus emphasizing its importance for the city. It is true also of the relationship of the Hofburg (3) to the two court museums, the museum of art history (Kunsthistorisches Museum) (5) and the museum of natural history (Naturhistorisches Museum) (6). We must also bear in mind at this point that, for good reasons, the opera (2), the Burgtheater (10), and the stock exchange (Börse) (12) lie on the city side of the Ringstraße and are thus in the right spot from the point of view of traffic patterns, while Parliament, the city hall, and the museums all lie on the country side. The districts in which the nobility lived were also, as they were in the baroque period, in the neighborhood of the Hofburg, while the upper middle classes built their mansions in the neighborhood of the Stock Exchange.[20]

A third factor seems even more important. The historical styles in which the different buildings are built vary and are at the same time closely related to the political function of the building in question. It was this relationship that was discussed most extensively by architects, by those commissioning the buildings, and by critics. Which styles corresponded to the different political, sociological, and economic functions of the buildings? Each of the historical styles contains a precise iconological statement about this heyday of historicism. An instructive significance was assigned to each style, just as it was assigned to orders of columns in the 16th and

17th centuries. For, like every other period, the period of promoterism had only one style—historicism—but this style was elevated to the height of luxury by its opposite pole, belief in progress. The different historical forms were merely its *modi*. Thus Hansen was fully aware that the language of neoclassicism must be used when building Parliament, so as to remind us of the land where democracy originated. The men who commissioned the city hall recognized from the beginning that the only person who could build it was the cathedral architect, Schmidt, for he alone was capable of developing a luxurious style out of Gothic forms. Gothic was the language of a self-confident bourgeoisie. On the other hand, for those buildings that served cultural ends—the university, the museums, the Opera, the Burg-theater, and many others—only Renaissance forms in the humanistic tra-dition could be considered, though the extravagance of the baroque also seemed suitable. It is notable that, in the case of the new Hofburg (3), it was decided to place the basic style of the Péristyle du Louvre inside a semicircle and to embellish it with baroque forms—using motifs from the Würzburg residence—in the Corps du Logis. This topological harmony must be perceived as the decisive characteristic of the Ringstraße with its optimistic attitude. Its complete execution before 1900 and before the dam-age done by automotive traffic can be compared to the symphonic works of Brahms and Wagner; here too was a total work of art, in which conserva-tism, historicism, and belief in progress were linked to worlds of contiguous feeling.

The effect of the complexes depended upon that enlivening optimism which had seized the Danubian monarchy in the first years of the Triple Alliance, entered into in 1872.

Yet, even before 1900, unpolitical, even antipolitical, lines of stylistic thought had been superimposed upon the "Ringstraße period," among them Viennese *art nouveau*. As far as the expressionist critics were con-cerned, these imperial buildings were, at best, symbols of *vanitas*. The re-discovery of the Ringstraße in the 1960s and 1970s was coupled with a re-jection of its program, for both political and social reasons.

From 1918 onward, Vienna has been an invalid, kept alive by blood transfusions. The capital of the Danubian monarchy no longer had tasks to fulfill which were suited to its size. There was no lack of attempts by the Social Democratic government to give the city new and suitable accents by building extensive projects for the workers. But a status quo could never be maintained in the tension that resulted from restoration and decay. As in Istanbul after the collapse of the Ottoman Empire and the move of the capital to Ankara, as in Leningrad in the new Soviet Union, or as in Berlin in 1945, the clothes of this urban personality seemed to have been cut too large. The representational program of the empire was too grand for the little republic. People move around in spaces which can no longer be filled with political vitality.

Paris as a Model City

In their *Orbis Pictus* of 1575, Braun and Hogenberg included a view of Paris titled "the city of three personalities" (*la ville aux trois personnalités*, fig. 164). What was meant by this was, first, the island in the Seine, which is still called *la Cité*, second, the merchant city on the right bank around the *hôtel de ville*, which was simply called *la ville*; and, third, the left bank, which was called *l'université*, or the Latin Quarter. Under Henry IV, Paris was divided into sixteen districts of which the Cité was only one. There were two more

Figure 164. Paris, *la ville des trois personnalités*, ca. 1530–1550 (from Braun's city atlas, 1575)

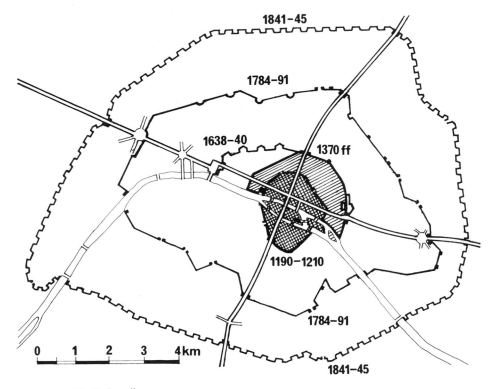

Figure 165. The Paris walls

on the left bank, while the city on the right bank was divided into thirteen, in which the pillars of economic and municipal growth lived—the citizenry in the narrower sense. Two through routes from north to south linked the three cities first by four and then, as early as 1556, five bridges. These main routes led from the Portes Saint-Denis and Saint-Martin to roads on the opposite side, Gibard and Saint-Jacques. Apart from the Seine itself, the east-west route from the Porte Saint-Antoine to the Porte Saint-Honoré was the most important cross axis. The clarity of the city's structure is admirable.

From the end of the 16th century, the city on the left bank expanded more rapidly than that on the right. It became oval in shape. Within the customs wall of the Fermiers Généraux, which were built between 1784 and 1791 (fig. 165), there were fifty-three parishes, of which thirteen lay in the Cité, thirteen on the left bank, and seventeen on the right bank, with ten others in the *faubourgs*. These numbers also reveal that a network of streets of terrifying density had grown up in the Cité, while on both sides of it, working outward, the network had grown increasingly widely meshed.

The political forces that shaped Paris can be regarded from four points of view, of which the first is the great mass of the population itself, whose growth is indicated by the various walls and attempts to delimit the city. Attempts to contain the city were just as unsuccessful between the reign of Henry II (1547–59) and 1765 as they are under today's republic. The second point of view is that of the "Royal Axis," which developed from the palace on the island in the Seine, through the old Louvre and the Tuileries out of the city, across the Place de la Concorde, up the Champs-Elysées to the Etoile, now the Place Charles de Gaulle. As a third point of view, I would point to the formation of the bank of the Seine, the bridges over the river, and the monumental buildings that delimit this cross axis. Figure 166 isolates these second and third elements.[21] Symmetry and axiality are obviously their main characteristics. Yet there is a fourth point of view that must be considered along with the other three—the attempts to beautify the city, the *embellissement* of Paris, which was, and still is, a political element inasmuch as these works were regarded as existing with the conscious aim of extolling the fame of the king, of the emperor, even of France itself.[22]

France more than any other country regarded its capital as a monument to its greatness, to the state, and to the level of its culture. Napoleon gave classic expression to this desire for *embellissement* while traveling from Toulon to Malta. "If I ruled France, I would make Paris not only the most beautiful city there is, the most beautiful there ever has been, but also the most beautiful there can be."[23] The desire to design the city according to aesthetic principles had, from the 17th century, been separated from the needs and functions of its buildings and streets. In the face of enormous pressure from the population of the city, the state carried out a ceremonial program that has remained a political fact until this day. No other head of state in Europe could officiate in front of an urban backdrop that emphasized his rank so positively. The entry to the city along the Champs-Elysées remained, as a manifestation of grandeur, just as unattainable as a reception at Versailles. Only the pope pronouncing his blessing from the balcony in St. Peter's Square in Rome can be compared to it.

The history of each of the four points of view depends on the entire history of France, its political development, the differences in the governmental structure of its constitutions, its monarchs' views of the state; it depends on the history of great ideas as well as on intellectual history. In the alchemy of the city's development, everything is linked to everything else, and over and over again this interlinking has prevented the isolated observation of individual elements in the process. Thus it is impossible to "narrate" Paris. Since the 12th century, not only has more been written *in* Paris than in any other city in the world but more has been written *about* Paris.[24] Every principle of selection raises a new set of problems in this close intertwining of political, economic, and intellectual life. Even taking stock and reproducing it in map form occupied the municipality more intensively than it did any other city of comparable size before the 20th century. These efforts reached their climax in the relief map of Paris that was made in the 18th century in the great gallery of the Louvre before it became a museum, and also in the maps commissioned from more than sixty artists by the administrators of the "Plans for the Embellishment of Paris" project. (Many

Figure 166. Schematic drawing of the royal axis and the cross axes across the Seine: 1, Louvre; 2, Palais Royal; 3, Place de la Concorde; 4, Etoile; 5, Institut de France; 6, Luxembourg; 7, Parliament; 8, Madeleine; 9, Invalides; 10, Grand Palais and Petit Palais; 11, Ecole Militaire; 12, Eiffel tower; 13, Trocadéro.

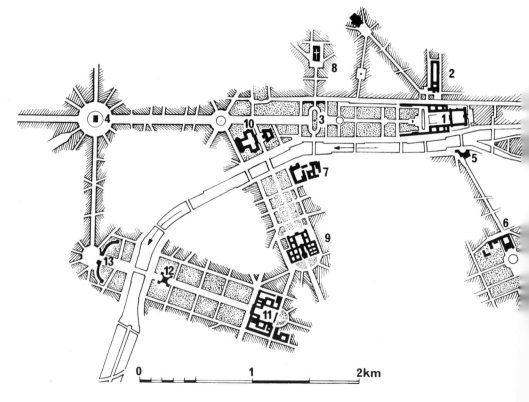

visitors to the Couvent des Cordelliers have followed the creation of those maps with eager attention.)

Before attempting to characterize these four points of view, I must first refer to two stages in the prehistory of Paris, for they determined much of what happened later: the Roman city, and the episcopal, ecclesiastical city of the Middle Ages.

Unlike London, Paris did not grow out of the needs of geopolitics or of traffic that was more than local. Common to both capitals was the fact that they were built at precisely the same point on their respective rivers, the Thames and the Seine—the farthest point at which the rivers were navigable for sea-going traffic, and the point at which the island, in Paris, and the tributaries, in London, offered favorable places to tie up ships. Yet neither the first settlement of the Celtic Parisi on the island between the two arms of the river, nor the later Roman Lutetia, was a capital; it was not even one of the largest cities in Gaul, though the Romans did build one of their luxurious colonial cities on the left bank, extending far beyond the slopes—later to become the site of the convents and church of the patron saint of the city, Saint Genevieve.

Chlodwig's decision in 508 to build his main residence among the Roman ruins on the left bank was governed by military considerations. These Frankish kings were certainly experienced in capturing land but not in building cities, nor were they even interested in doing so. They merely wanted to build their palace in the midst of their newly conquered territory on the site of a Roman palace. In this way, the conditions for the city's later rise to the status of capital were created. Not all of Chlodwig's successors regarded Paris as their main seat. For the Carolingians, Saint-Denis later became an important center both as a convent and a burial place, but not Paris itself. Charlemagne can only be shown to have been there once. Down to the 10th century, the kind of deurbanization that took place in and around Paris is characteristic of a greater temporal distance from the Mediterranean centers of culture.

Here, too, ecclesiastical institutions started a countermovement. This was the second stage. At the beginning of the 11th century, the bishop of Paris was still the largest property owner in the city, as well as being regent of the country. From the 6th century on, the conventual institutions had continued to grow on the secure ranges of hills on both sides of the river. Many of the convents had extensive land holdings outside the Cité, which, as the only fortified place, was the only one in which a modest urban existence could be led. Saint-Germain des Prés and Saint-Martin des Champs

Figure 167. The Cité of Paris (after an engraving by Merian, 1615)

were among the most important convents outside the city. Until the expansion of the city after the 13th century and, finally, the French Revolution caused the convents to turn country property into development property, their expenses had been defrayed by the income from their real estate holdings.

As we have seen, there were thirteen parishes on the little Cité clustered around their churches. In addition, the deck of this "ship," between the two arms of the river, carried on its stern the large area with the bishop's palace, the cemetery, and Notre-Dame and, on its bow, the royal palace (fig. 167). Since the 18th century, the congestion of this unhealthy labyrinth of streets, which also housed the workrooms of numerous craftsmen, has been a constant source of complaint.[25] This part of the city must have been thickly settled in the 12th century. All the greater, then, as a feat of urban planning, was the clearance of the site by Bishop Maurice de Sully (1160–96) for the building of the new cathedral. The great building forced everything subordinate to it to one side, and even its forecourt was extended. Such an undertaking could only succeed with the cooperation of all the political forces—the church, the monarchy, and the citizens imbued with the new intellectual goals of the scholarly world. The measure of significance replaces that of function. The enormous size of the cathedral and, later, of the royal palace contrasted with the smallness of the townspeople's cramped living area.

The city continued its rise from the middle of the 11th century until the end of the 13th and, in many areas, almost until the mid-14th. In the Hundred Years' War with England, the French monarchy was forced to the brink of the abyss on more than one occasion. In 1347, the flower of French chivalry fell in the Battle of Crécy. In 1348, the Black Death is said to have reduced the population of the city by one-third. Before the Black Death, the population was reckoned to be 200,000, but by 1400, no more than 60,000 to 80,000. The decline continued until the last third of the 15th century. The kings had left the capital and held court in castles in the country. At night, in the city's swamplike streets, people ran the danger of being torn apart by wolves. In large cities, forces that conditioned decline were always locked in an unequal struggle with the forces of progress. In times of crisis, the cost of the upkeep of roads and buildings exceeded the income from the economy. If the forces of decline kept regaining the upper hand in Paris between 1348 and the time of Louis XIV, it was the forces of expansion and renewal that dominated from the 11th century through the classical 13th.

The city's advancement was fostered by a series of resolute rulers, whose aims repeatedly coincided with those of the church and of the citizens with their increasing strength. There were terrifying reverses as well, but each of the kings was able to add essential features to the life of the city. Thus, Louis the Fat, who reigned for fifty-seven years, from 1080 to 1137, built the second important bridge, the Pont au Change. Louis VII, who reigned 43 years (1137–80), left the citizens the Place Grève for their main market, storage place, and seat of justice. Later, the city hall was erected there. Another forty-three years (1180–1223) constituted the reign of Philip Augustus—albeit a reign constantly threatened by war—to whom Paris owes the completion of the royal palace, the new city wall, and the new fortress (the old Louvre, fig. 97). This new encircling wall, the second to be built on the right bank but probably the first ever on the left bank, was being constructed at the same time as Cologne's third wall (see chap. 1), from 1180 until 1210 or 1212. We may assume that it was the threat posed by the area over which the English ruled—an area that had come closer by twenty miles—that led the king and the citizens to make the wall as short as possible. It was built so that it could be extended only at a few points—how different from the contemporary wall in Cologne (fig. 6) or the Florentine wall built a hundred years later (fig. 21).

Under the successor of that ruthless and energetic king, Louis IX, who ascended the throne in 1226 and held it for another forty-four years, until 1270, Paris developed into the most perfect city of the Gothic period. The new wall, with its small compass, its gates, and its towers, must even then have been numbered among the best-designed works of the time because of the unity of its execution. It demarcated not only living space but, to an even greater extent, space for 13th century creative endeavor. The few ecclesiastical buildings, the sculptures, the goldsmiths' work and miniatures that have been preserved in Paris from that time, and, later, the two apsidal facades of Notre-Dame, the Sainte-Chapelle with its windows and the apostle cycle, the refectory of Saint-Martin des Champs by Pierre de Montreuil, the remains of the Chapelle de la Vierge in Saint-Germain (admittedly outside the city gates) by the same architect, who was buried there in 1266—all these works lay claim, for the first time in the history of the West, to classical and courtly perfection as a part of a capital city. Such perfection had previously been encountered only in the great capitals of antiquity and in Constantinople, which preserved it at least until its capture in 1204. Many of the masters of Chartres, Reims, or Amiens also hailed from Paris.[26] The imagination boggles at the attempt to realize, on the basis of what little is left to us, the totality of this Early and High Gothic order of a capital city. It was a royal and, at the same time, a burgher city. As early as the reign of Louis IX, Paris can be described as a city with three personalities. The royal city was the third stage in the development of Paris after the Roman and the convent city. Here, too, for the first time, those four characteristics are to be found which were henceforth to put their stamp on Paris.

1. *The masses as power and as problem.* The building of the wall under Philip Augustus and his building of the Louvre represent the first attempt to come to terms with the masses as a political power, though those works were started with quite different political aims (fig. 165).

However, the citizens of Paris soon ceased to take the fortifications seriously. The new wall had only seven fortified gates to protect the main roads on the right bank and only four to protect those on the left bank. The local inhabitants soon began to make little gaps in the wall, the more conveniently to reach their properties outside the city. A few mendicant orders that had settled on the edge of the city, but inside the wall, resorted to similar measures so as to be able to expand. The Dominicans built a refectory on the Rue Saint-Jacques that went right through the wall.[27] Many cities saw similar outgrowths, whereby an irrational element opposed the rational forces of order. In Prague and Vienna we have seen how an attempt was made to restrain that very element, and we shall be discussing quite different measures for the maintenance of order in London. Among the capitals of Europe, Moscow can be most readily compared to Paris with its growth in concentric circles. When, after 1367, Charles V doubled the length of the walls by adding a new encircling wall, he included several districts on the outskirts that had grown up partly around convents and partly along the roads, but each one according to its own rules. Later, between 1633 and 1636, Louis XIII was to wall in two further districts to the west, which permitted the inclusion of the court gardens of the Tuileries.

From the time of Henry II until 1765, a constant increase in the severity of the penal provisions forbade any building, first outside the walls and later outside the boulevards. The kings, recognizing the danger posed by the masses, were terrorized by them over and over again. Yet they felt bound to take account of ever widening boundaries. When Louix XIV razed all the city walls in 1664—Paris was the first city in Europe to lose them—and replaced them by laying out his famous boulevards with their wide rows of trees, he wanted his action to show that his capital, in contrast to the Vienna of his great opponents, no longer needed protection of this sort. At the same time, he tightened up the laws governing movement into the city. The meaning of the undertaking is made clear by those triumphal arches which, on Colbert's orders, Blondel was to erect in place of the old city gates. Despite all the regulations limiting the size of the city, however, it grew without ceasing. Soon after 1500, the population probably exceeded 300,000, and by 1700 it was as high as 700,000.[28] The Revolution and the Revolutionary Wars brought the number down to 550,000 before it rose again to 1,000,000 as a result of the Industrial Revolution and control of disease. Napoleon I was the only ruler who felt strong enough to promote systematic growth in Paris. His successors recognized anew the resultant dangers. To this day, the size of Paris is a burden to the life within it. Even though ten million people live in the city and the surrounding area, it is believed that further immigration cannot be prevented.

The rapid growth outside the city was matched by the concentration of streets within it. As a result of overcrowding, some sections became un-inhabitable. I have already mentioned Restif's categorization of the Cité at the end of the 18th century (see chap. 7, note 25). Similar conditions pre-vailed around the Hôtel de Ville and in the quartiers Saint-Denis and Saint-Martin, as described by Balzac. In 1848, M. DuChamp stressed the fact that "Paris was about to become uninhabitable. Its population was suffocating in putrid, narrow, tangled alleys, packed in them without any choice."[29] Warnings were given of dangers to health, safety, and morals. It was not until they were forced to live together in such close proximity that the townspeople turned into the masses in whose political attitude the rational and the irrational complemented one another. The French Revolution was also sparked at the borders of the city by the customs walls of the Fermiers Généraux.

This explosion, which was to change the course of world history, was a Parisian revolution. The process had already taken place several times be-fore, but in a smaller framework. Earlier examples are the uprising of the townspeople against the crown under Etienne Marcel in 1358; the religious struggles that led to the St. Bartholomew's Eve Massacre in 1572; and the insurrection of the nobles, la Fronde, against the supremacy of the king in 1648. The rebellion of 1358, like the threat to the young Louis XIV, had caused the monarch to retreat from the city for almost a century and a half. In the meantime, the townspeople managed to gather so much strength that in the second period they even considered making the Louvre into the city hall. Robert de Cotte suggested it during Louis XIV's reign, and the city made an official petition to Louis XV to that end in 1749. The Revolution performed consistently by immediately forcing the king to return to Paris, so that he could be kept under control in the Tuileries. The whole of the 19th century was filled with the after-shocks of the earthquake in 1789. Among them are the uprising of 1831 in the course of which the bishop's palace was sacrificed, and the more radical one of the Commune in 1871 when the Tuileries and the Hôtel de Ville were burned down. The fuel for smaller explosions could always prove dangerous under such a pressure from the masses. The unrest that took place in the city in the spring of 1968 should still be regarded in this light.

After the 13th century, it was not until the second half of the 18th and the second half of the 19th centuries that measures adopted for administrative and architectural control of growth on the edges of the city and overcrowding in the inner city met with even relative success. The Age of Enlightenment was more aware of the problem than any preceding period and for this reason fostered more building. We read of 600 mansions and 30,000 houses for ordinary citizens being built in rather less than forty years. The architects of the Enlightenment and of the new rational classicism, from Gabriel to Ledoux and Boullée—unlike the architects of the Revolution, whose many projects were matched by virtually no actual buildings between 1789 and the rise of Napoleon—tried to solve the problem of overpopulation by building enormous complexes commissioned either by the royal house or by the government. As a result, larger and larger sections of the population were, as in Turin and Potsdam, forced to live in a manner that was beyond their means. The uniform blocks of houses of the Île Saint-Louis, a development sponsored by a building board, are the best illustration of the aims of those measures. The Revolution deceived itself with the hope that the expropriation of all Church property, the dissolution of the monasteries and convents, and the destruction of numerous churches would provide the space necessary for building. Such measures had their roots in the same kind of irrational emotions as the destruction of all monuments that might remind people of the monarchy, the nobility, or the rule of the Church. The gaps were closed before they became apparent, and they merely made it easier to cut streets through later on. The state, too, had confiscated most of the plots for its own programs.

After 1848, increased attempts were made to clear the inner city and to include the outer districts in a general traffic scheme. We may lament the destruction of the old Cité and many other districts by Haussmann (Prefect of Paris, 1853–70) and his successors. Politically, however, it was just as right to do this as it was to cut new streets, place a second set of boulevards round the now obsolete customs barriers of the Fermiers Généraux, and complete the twelve boulevards which radiate from the Etoile. Opening up the inner city in this way was as successful as the final ring of fortifications was unsuccessful, for by 1870–71 that ring no longer related in any way to strategic developments. It merely afforded an opportunity to build yet a third outer ring of streets around the city (fig. 165).

If we bear in mind that, in Napoleon III's Paris, communication with the outside was now by rail, and that from 1900 much of the local traffic was taken away by the underground railroads, while automobile traffic was still insignificant, then the boldness of the concept of cutting new streets in the second half of the 19th century soon becomes clear. It seemed as if the *belle époque*'s belief in progress had some hope of solving the problem of the masses as a political power by means of city planning.

2. *The royal axis*. Napoleon I and Haussman's Place de l'Etoile form the final and culminating point of that ceremonial axis, the beginning of which had been established when Philip Augustus built the Louvre around 1200 (fig. 166). The Louvre, as a whole, represents one of those developments which in the course of seven centuries was borne forward by a constant series of new architectonic ideas (fig. 168). Every stage in this development was conditioned by the attitude of the king and, later, the emperor toward Paris and their conception of the monarchy itself.[30]

The point of departure was, as we have pointed out, the castle at the bow of the island in the Seine. The Grand Châtelet on the right bank and the Petit Châtelet on the left bank secured the river crossings (fig. 167). The necessary consequence of Philip Augustus's city walls was the building of fortifications in front of the castle—the later Louvre. The representation in the Duc de Berry's *Book of Hours* reveals how impregnable this demonstration of the king's power appeared to contemporaries around 1400 (fig. 97).[31] It is true that Charles V had placed a residence, one suited to the time, inside the Louvre, but at the same time he had also built, in the shadow of the Bastille and of his new wall, a second, unfortified castle, the Hôtel Saint-Pol, in which, until the reign of Henry II (d. 1559), kings usually stayed while in Paris. Thus the Louvre in the West and the Bastille in the East, like the Tower of London or the Castello S. Angelo in Rome, secured the power of the state (fig. 172). Francis I, Henry II, and Henry III made significant additions to the old Louvre, which have been preserved.

After the unfortunate death of her husband, Henry II, in a tournament, Catherine de Médici no longer wished to live in the Louvre. For this

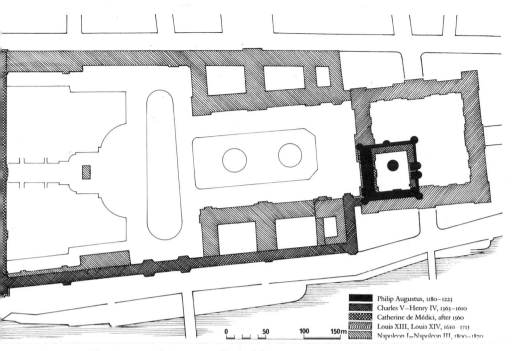

Philip Augustus, 1180–1223
Charles V–Henry IV, 1363–1610
Catherine de Médici, after 1560
Louis XIII, Louis XIV, 1610–1715
Napoleon I–Napoleon III, 1800–1870

0   50   100   150m

Figure 168. The Louvre and the stages of its building.

reason, plans were drawn up for the garden seat of the Tuileries, which, thanks both to its position at the edge of the city and to its coordination into a manneristic court garden, corresponded exactly to the taste of the time as proclaimed in Munich, Salzburg, or Stuttgart. From 1563 on, purchases of land and planning projects followed hard upon one another. Later, the more distant summer seat necessitated the construction of the long connecting tract that Catherine had planned but that was not built until the reign of Henry IV, which joined the Louvre to the Tuileries (fig. 168).

Under Louis XIII, the idea arose of breaking up the old fortified square of the Louvre. The larger square, which Louis XIV built as a continuation of the magnificent rooms occupied by his mother, was then planned. The architects were Le Vau and, later, Perrault. The colonnades of the Louvre, which Perrault was allowed to build after a dishonest contest with Bernini, were supposed to demonstrate the superiority of French classicism over Roman baroque. These columns reflect the king's intention to use the Louvre largely for ceremonial purposes and no longer as a dwelling. Yet we have to bear in mind that the famous Péristyle du Louvre, which

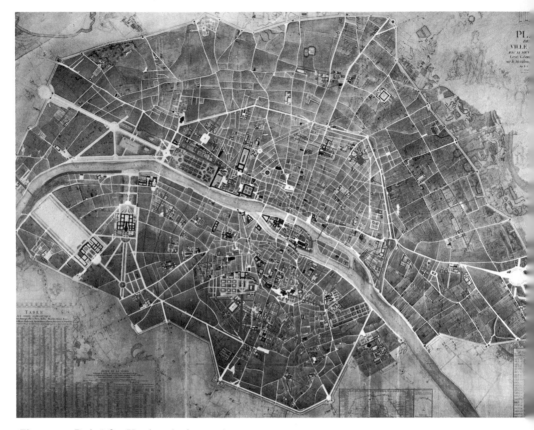

Figure 169. Paris (after Verniquet's plan, 1791)

was certainly designed to be seen from a distance, was enclosed on all sides until the 19th century (fig. 169).

What Napoleon I, the Second Republic, Napoleon II, and, finally, the Third Republic added surpasses in volume all that was built in the earlier periods, yet reveals itself as merely the logical completion of the symmetrical axis. We have to realize that, up to the time of the Revolution, a number of burgher buildings had been packed between Louis XIV's great square and the Tuileries. The plan of 1791 shows the situation at that time (fig. 169). There was no lack of plans under Louis XV, any more than under Napoleon I, to open up this great area and line it with monumental buildings. Napoleon's Arc de Triomphe du Carrousel is a monument to those attempts. But what all the new wings and the new tracts had lacked since the days of Louis XIV was a suitable purpose. They became offices, dwellings for higher civil servants, and then, to an ever larger extent, a museum, a demonstration of the grandeur of the state without reference to the office and person of the monarch.

The design of the great axis, including the layout of the Place de la Concorde, was drawn up under Louis XV. The plans for this new Place Royale occupied a generation of architects, who, however, considered only the cross axis to the Seine. It is characteristic of a change in basic attitude that Henry IV was still able to surround his Place des Vosges with individual houses, whereas J. A. Gabriel in his plans for the Place de la Concorde thought only in terms of axes and facades, which were to be placed in front of blocks of houses of a different architectural structure and with a different social use. At the same time, the love of nature that typified the late 18th century caused these city planners to open up the city to the park-like streets of the Champs-Elysées.

The whole complex did not acquire a political meaning until the Arc de Triomphe was built at its crown.[32] Napoleon, seizing upon Roman models and not without reference to the triumphal arches built by Louis XIV, wanted to be commemorated by the greatest monument ever built. He was unable to complete it, and the later Bourbon kings changed its semantics. Yet it still bore an obvious relation to the royal seat, the Tuileries, across the Place de la Concorde.

The destruction of the Tuileries changed the nature of the whole axis. It was given a new meaning when the triumphal arch was changed into the tomb of the Unknown Warrior, and thus of all those who had fallen in service to their country. Napoleon himself had already named the continuation of the axis the Avenue de la Grande Armée. The renaming of the Place de l'Etoile as the Place Charles de Gaulle shows that, in a living state organism, people are always trying to reinterpret political symbolism. In intention and architectural form, this axis did for Paris what the Ringstraße was later to do for Vienna.

3. *The river banks and their cross axes.* If we compare Braun's plan of 1575 or Merian's of 1615 with Turgot's plan of 1740, we can see how the Seine was brought under control in the course of these 150 years (figs. 164, 167, 172). In both views of the city the river appears as its most important traffic axis. The ships seem to have increased in number with the population. But the river, which in 1575—with the exception of the makeshift quays between the Pont au Change and the Tuileries—was still open, its sandy banks threatened by repeated flooding, had by 1740 been contained between high

walls at all points. Francis I had ordered the city to build the first quays, as far as the Louvre, in 1528, and these were not extended to the Tuileries until 1538. They are a work that reflects the Renaissance sense of order. Medieval indolence had regarded it as inevitable that the bridges leading to the island in the Seine should be destroyed by flooding. Henry III finally decided to build a new bridge, which Henry IV completed in 1606. This, too, was supported by the tip of the island. Originally, it was intended that this Pont-Neuf should finance itself, as did all the other bridges, by the rental of the houses and shops to be built on it. However, Henry IV decided that the bridge should not be built upon so that the view of the Louvre could be left open. He wanted to draw the attention of passersby to the magnificence of the royal residence. The only exception was the Samaritaine, the pumping station that provided water for the royal gardens. Robert de Cotte further embellished this building in 1719. An engraving made in that same year also shows the oldest bridge, the Pont Royal, which crossed the whole river by the Tuileries (fig. 170). The walls of the quays were lengthened and the number of bridges increased to keep pace with the growth of the city.

While the Middle Ages had kept their bridges closed by the Grand Châtelet on the Cité side and the Petit Châtelet on the Université side, there was an increasing sense, at least after the building of the Collège des Quatre Nations, of the interaction of monumental buildings across the river. The Collège was built between 1661 and 1667 (fig. 171). The Hôtel and Dôme des Invalides took up this idea but on a much larger scale. A broad garden opened up toward the Seine in front of this architectural composition, thus placing the dome at a suitable distance from the river. The 18th century repeated the 17th century motif with the Ecole Militaire, commissioned by Madame de Pompadour. The Champ de Mars—where later the Eiffel Tower was to be erected—was designed as the approach to this building. The Palais de Chaillot and the garden of the Trocadéro, on the other side of the Seine, complemented the Ecole Militaire. Napoleon I gave clearer emphasis to a further axis across the Seine when he commissioned the same classical facade for the Palais Bourbon, which from that time on has been the home of the French parliament, as for the Madeleine on the right bank beyond the Place de la Concorde. In the final years of his empire, the course of the Seine was like a single building site, especially as its architects, Percier and Fontaine, wanted to build more monumental buildings between the Invalides and the Champ de Mars on the left bank, while planning a massive imperial palace on the site of the later Trocadéro for the right bank. This palace was to be open on one side to the river, and on the other side its gardens were to end in the Bois de Boulogne. These Napoleonic plans form a chapter of history for themselves, a chapter that was closed by the sudden fall of the emperor.[33]

That sense of symmetry and axiality which distinguishes French classicism used the architectonic possibilities of a river flowing through the middle of a city better here than in any other city. The 19th and even the 20th centuries have given even more variety in their buildings on both banks. In contrast to London, Cologne, or even Prague, building on the banks of the river became one of the greatest events in the history of architecture.

4. *Measures for the "embellissement" of Paris*. If we ignore the great axes and their monumental buildings, the numerous monuments and fountains, the chief means of beautification was to carry over the principle of all ideal

Figure 170. Pont-Neuf and Samaritaine, looking toward the Louvre, 1719

Figure 171. Collège des Quatre Nations (Institut de France) (engraving by G. Perelle, ca. 1670)

cities—regular rows of houses for the citizens—into the design of individual, mostly new, squares and streets. Certainly those who commissioned every splendid palace, those who endowed every church and monastery, and even the city and state as commissioners of public buildings developed their plans in concert with the architects in the full consciousness that they were enriching and embellishing Paris as a whole. In many cases, individual buildings achieved a significance which transcended their simple function. In the most important aristocratic districts, the Marais in the 16th and 17th centuries, the Faubourg Saint-Germain in the 18th, a series of architectural masterpieces, in close proximity to one another, left their mark on the overall character of the streets. At the same time, each of these buildings sought to display its own individuality—the churches as well as the palace facades. The ordinary citizens, on the other hand, were ordered to build houses with uniform facades for the *embellissement* of Paris. These houses create the effect of strophic divisions in a strict metrical form.

This principle of similarity was first developed on the bridges, which had been the property of the monarch since time immemorial. As has been mentioned, Louis VII (1137–80) commissioned the rebuilding in stone of the second, upper bridge on the right side, with a mill wheel suspended between each of fifteen of the sixteen piers. Ships could pass only between the fourth and fifth piers, which were set farther apart than the others. Above these two piers, there was division in the rows of houses, leaving a clear view of the river. In the 14th century, this Grand Pont had sixty-eight goldsmiths' shops and workshops on one side and seventy-two money-changing stalls on the other—hence it was known as the Pont au Change. In the Middle Ages, the townspeople tried to settle everywhere on the smallest sites. Even the lower bridge, the Pont Notre Dame, had buildings on it. After being destroyed by flood, it was rebuilt between 1502 and 1510 by Fra Giocondo, who had come to Paris in Charles VIII's retinue. The houses, thirty-four on each side, were built uniformly of brick with stone corners and were decorated with the statues of saints and the city coat of arms. The whole was accepted as an outstanding achievement in urban design. As a result, the neighboring streets, too, had to be better paved and built upon more uniformly (fig. 167).

Henry IV made use of these experiences when he built the Place Dauphin on the stern of the island and the Place des Vosges in the Marais. Figure 172 shows that the geometric form of a square has been created

Figure 172. Place des Vosges, Bastille, and Ile-Saint-Louis (from Turgot's plan of 1740, detail)

among a network of streets. In the earliest stages of planning, the king had wanted to build settlements for the workers from a Milanese silk-weaving mill. However, it was quickly decided to design this square as an image of the state itself. A Pavillon du Roi and a Pavillon de la Reine were framed by uniform houses, while in the middle of the square an equestrian statue of the king was to be erected. This was the prototype of the Place Royale, which was widely imitated both in Paris and the provinces. Under Louis XIV, the Place Vendôme and the Place des Victoires took their place among such imitations. In contrast to the London squares, which in their basic design resemble the Place des Vosges, the point of departure for the Place Royale was not the housing needs of a class that could be expected to buy or rent there, but rather the wish to erect a monument to the king in front of a suitable backdrop of houses.[34] Building companies were allowed to execute the buildings, while the authorities determined the facades, which, as in Turin or Potsdam (see chap. 6), bore no relationship to the lifestyle of the people. They overreached themselves. In building the two palace facades in the Place de la Concorde in the 18th century, J. A. Gabriel completely ignored the social structure of the people living in the buildings behind them; the facades were simply a sham. Later, Napoleon I was to enforce the use of a regular design for house fronts in a few streets in the inner city (Rues de Rivoli, Castiglione, de la Paix, and des Pyramides). Again and again, building ordinances achieved comparable uniformity for individual parts of the city. Axiality, symmetry, uniformity of all facades remained the aim of the *embellissement,* clearly indicating what a subordinate position the inhabitants occupied in Paris, while at the same time making it possible to gain an overall view of the city.

Napoleon III, whose economic policies were as successful as his foreign policy was unsuccessful, managed to give the French capital that appearance which was to be understood as the documentation of its political greatness. He did this by means of magnificent buildings, parks, cultural palaces for libraries, the Opéra, theaters, the university, great international expositions, and the numerous fountains proclaiming success in the supply of water. The new opera house, like Haussmann's boulevards, especially the twelve that radiate from the Etoile, became the symbol of the ideals of this capital city. Until 1914, and in individual cases until the present day, that same spirit has prevailed. "Paris advertises France"—such a thought would never have occurred to anyone in London. Magnificence was consumed as the expression of *gloire.* The wretchedness of the suburbs was not to be noticed, while a particular sense of connoisseurship could be developed for the zones of neglect—in the shadow of the monumental plan—as centers of a more real existence and a more secret history.

London

The encircling walls and the royal axis—these are the characteristics with which I tried to encompass the history of Paris. If I wished to emphasize comparable characteristics in London, I should have to mention the "City of London" and the "City of Westminster," two cities that lay next to each other but three kilometers apart on the north bank of the Thames. In addition to these two cities there were the outlying districts, or boroughs. In the 19th century, London had become the largest city in the world, without ever looking upon itself as a unity. As late as 1855, it was calculated that London was governed by as many as 300 different authorities, whose jurisdictions overlapped one another and whose development projects were seldom harmonized.[35] Whereas in Paris, ever since the 13th century, repeated attempts had been made to set some rational limits on the size and organization of the city, London clung to its traditional diversity. Thus, the "City of London" was the only large city in Europe whose wall had never been lengthened from Roman times until it was taken down in the 17th and 18th centuries (fig. 173). Diversity was treasured and size was unimportant. As early as the 18th century, the complaint was heard, "London is inconvenient, inelegant, without the least pretension to magnificence or grandeur."[36]

I have stressed elsewhere in this work that no one was ever able to write the "novel" of Versailles in all its diversity (see chap. 6, note 30) and that it is impossible to "narrate" Paris (see above, this chapter). The novel "London" has at least been sketched out by Steen Eiler Rasmussen in his *London: The Unique City*.[37] This Danish town planner at first wanted to call his book "The Lesson of London." The last chapter is entitled "A Most Unhappy Ending." Steen saw the construction of continental-style tenements as the beginning of the destruction of the city's personality, and today he would lament even more the way in which the city's general appearance has been changed by American-style skyscrapers. Rasmussen compares London, as a "scattered town," with closed cities like Paris, Cologne, or Milan—cityscapes in which several historical centers have developed freely side by side. The fact that his attention was focused mainly on the present and the future allowed him to ignore almost entirely the process which had led to the fragmentation. The modern city of London appears to the reader as a sprawling commercial and residential metropolis in which the political

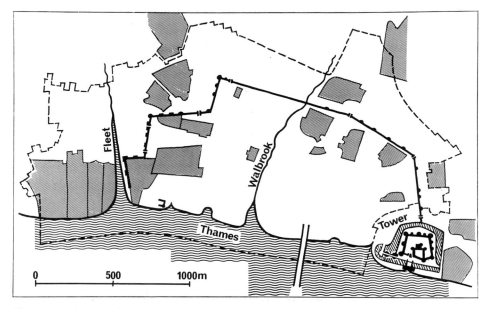

Figure 173. The City of London in the Middle Ages. The shaded area represents church property before 1539.

conditions of its growth are hidden by the present demands of its being. Nonetheless, they have remained fully legible.

The Romans deliberated very carefully before making "Londinium," of all the settlements in the newly conquered island, the storage place for their reserves and the distribution center for their commerce. It was the exact spot to which seagoing ships could still ply, at which there was a slight eminence upon which a citadel could be built, and where the tributaries of the Thames, the Fleet and the Walbrook, allowed landing stages to be built where ships could tie up. It was also the farthest down site at which the Thames could still be bridged. The Romans built six main roads from the two bridgeheads, thus opening up the whole country. The roads led to the Channel ports and to Chester, Silchester, York, and Colchester. London was neither the capital of the colony nor one of its provincial capitals, but it became the largest Roman city in Britain.[38]

By choosing this location, the Romans made a geopolitical choice whose universal historical success is still apparent. The one waterway to the sea was more important than all the roads. It made London a "port." No port, no landlocked city, no other river in England, and no other point on the Thames would have been anything like as suited to the tasks that fell to the lot of this capital. From the 17th century on, and downstream from the original harbors on the river, larger and larger channels were dug from the Thames into the open country. In this way, the largest harbor complexes and the most extensive docks in history were built. With the choice of this site, the conditions for the conquest of the later maritime and world empire were created.

The Romans gave up the city in 410. The history of the early medieval resettlement cannot be reliably reconstructed. By the 10th century it was once again the most populous town in the island. William the Conqueror held his armies back from it. The wealth of the merchants was respected and made use of, and from that time on they had repeatedly to purchase their freedom and their rights from the crown. In 1086, London is said to have had a population of 17,850; in 1377, 35,000, compared with only 11,000 in York, 9,500 in Bristol, 7,000 in Coventry and Plymouth, 6,000 in Norwich, about 3,500 in Lincoln, and scarcely 2,500 in Oxford.[39] The cities in England all remained small, their independent development curbed. Their value to the crown was, on the one hand, their fiscal yield and, on the other, the fact that they formed a political counterweight to the barons in the counties. For this reason, the legislature was later split into the House of Commons and the House of Lords. The monarchy permitted each individual city to buy from it, piecemeal, the privileges necessary for survival. London always produced by far the largest yield. There were no rebel movements in the city, for citizens and rulers always came to terms. Cromwell's

Figure 174. The City of Westminster, 1647 (after Wenzel Hollar). The buildings that stand out are St. Stephen's Chapel (the seat of Parliament), the Norman Hall (with Gothic additions), and the Abbey.

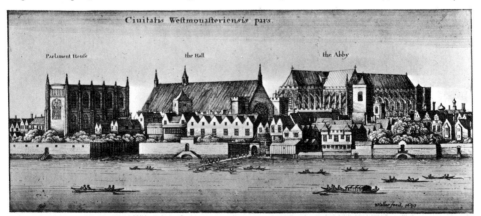

revolution was a country revolution, not, like the revolutions in France, a city revolution.

Like most large medieval cities, London was surrounded by monasteries with large landholdings. Edward the Confessor (1044–62) transferred his residence to one of these. William the Conqueror started construction of the largest Norman hall known to us. Kings continued to build upstream for centuries. A multipartite castle complex was built (fig. 174), but the city of Westminster remained unfortified.

The Tower—which William started building in order to secure his power after 1066—at the other end of the city and on the exact site of the Roman citadel, struck the balance. The Tower was enlarged by William's successor in 1097, who built in light-colored stone. The first building in the complex was the "White Tower," by means of which the kings kept the city under control. Succeeding monarchs extended the Tower and made it into a fortress, which no one ever succeeded in storming (fig. 173). It was at once a royal castle, a prison, a treasure house, and barracks. Its functions were comparable to those of the Bastille and the Castello S. Angelo. Each of the three royal complexes—the City of Westminster, with the royal residence, the commercial City of London, and the Tower—had its individual history in the Middle Ages. The Thames served as the most important route between them. The burgher city was bounded by two seats of royal power: the Tower to the east and Westminster to the west.

In contrast to Prague, the commercial city did not develop at the door of the castle; in contrast to Paris, the royal residence did not develop from the heart of the burgher city, and in contrast to Vienna it did not develop on the periphery. London's topographical conditions, which were much more complicated than the conditions in those three cities, corresponded to an equally complex and stratified political structure.

Let us look first at the history of the royal residence.[40] In the 11th century it was not at all unusual for a monarch to establish his household in a monastery close to his burial place. Because of London's proximity, Edward the Confessor had decided to move there from the small town of Winchester. In the same way, it was quite consistent with the Norman style of government for William the Conqueror and his successors to build their royal hall there—the largest in Europe at that time. Gundolf, bishop of Rochester, is traditionally regarded as its architect. Later, he also built the Tower and the new London bridge. His contemporaries admired his art but deplored the severity with which he compelled the population to do their compulsory labor.[41] In 1099, the first assembly was held in the hall.

Subsequently, building activity alternated between the church and the monastery, on the one hand, and the residence on the other. Henry III (1216–72) and his goldsmith, Odo, created a large ceremonial complex on the Thames, part of which was the king's "Great Chamber," filled with frescoes; the edifice was preserved until 1834. In 1254 the great abbey church was begun, which still stands today. It was not until the reign of Edward I (1272–1307) that people began to talk of the "City of Westminster" as the opposite pole to the "City of London." Edward also built St. Stephen's chapel, in which parliament was later to meet. Simon de Montfort gathered the representatives of the counties and cities together in Westminster for the first time in 1265.

The special situation of the royal seat was such that the monarchs felt constrained to place the body which controlled their finances at their own doorstep. When this body was divided, a century later, into an upper and a lower chamber, the one met in St. Stephen's chapel, the other in the chapter house of the abbey. The kings of England reigned for almost 500 years in

Figure 175. London—the public buildings and their functional relationships; 1, Tower of London; 2, Bank of England, 3, Guildhall; 4, St. Paul's; 5, Temple; 5a, Royal Courts of Justice; 6, Lincoln's Inn Fields; 7, Trafalgar Square; 8, St. James's Palace; 9, Buckingham Palace; 10, Admiralty; 11, War Office, 12, Horse Guards; 13, New Scotland Yard (the old building); 14, Parliament and Westminster Hall; 15, Westminster Abbey; 16, Archbishop's Park; 17, British Museum.

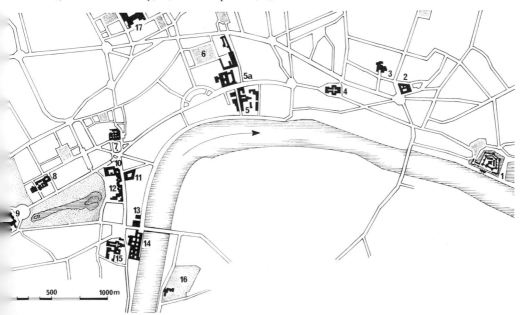

Westminster, more than half of that time sharing accommodations with the various parliaments.

It was in Westminster, too, that the supreme court made its decisions. After the order of the Knights Templar had been disbanded in the 14th century, as it had been in France also, and its possessions taken over, the judges and lawyers settled around the extensive cloisters of their vast complexes, outside the walls of the City but not too far from Westminster. There they developed their own little city in which they have stayed until today (fig. 175, 5). The site itself was intended to demonstrate their independence both from the city and from the crown. Later, when Westminster ceased to be the seat of the courts of justice, the lawyers took the royal courts into their own area. The Royal Courts of Justice (5a) were built in the immediate vicinity of the Temple.

The nationalization of church property between 1538 and 1540 gave Henry VIII the chance to remove the court from its proximity to Parliament. Parliament and the law courts stayed where they were. The abbey church retained its function as the church in which monarchs were crowned (a function it has to this day) and used to be buried. The kings themselves began their strange peregrination through their newly acquired ecclesiastical possessions, the course of which corresponded to their changed constitutional position. This peregrination led across Whitehall and St. James's Palace to Buckingham Palace, having gone even farther afield, for a short time, to Kensington Palace.

Henry VIII moved into the grand palace of the archbishops of York, about 500 meters downriver on the main road from Westminster to the City, after putting Cardinal Wolsey, its proprietor, to death. Previous princes of the Church had owned a residence on this site from 1245: a site on which the War Office (11) was later to be built. The palace was enlarged by Henry VIII and by all his successors down to Charles II (1660–85). The only building in the whole residential complex in Whitehall that has survived is the Banqueting Hall, designed by Inigo Jones in 1619, with ceiling frescoes painted by Rubens in 1630, depicting the apotheosis of the Stuart dynasty. In the second half of the 17th century, the king's architects toyed with the idea of enlarging the whole complex into a huge city palace comparable to the Louvre. The size of the main courtyard was to be double that of the Louvre. However, William III (1689–1702), who suffered from asthma, was forced to leave Whitehall and move to Kensington Palace. Shortly thereafter, in 1698, Whitehall burned down. The king had finally left the road from Westminster to the City. But his government remained there; from the 17th century to the present day, new buildings for ministries succeeded one another on this site. Among the oldest is the Admiralty, built between 1722 and 1726, with its pillared vestibule by the younger Adam (1759) (10) and William Kent's "Horse Guards" building (12), built between 1750 and 1760. The tall, late Victorian buildings for the Foreign Office and the War Office dominated the scene. The police headquarters that William Shaw built in 1891, New Scotland Yard, is one of the symbols of Victorian order. It stands at exactly the right spot, between Parliament and the executive district. Earlier, in 1875, consideration had been given to building an opera house on this site. Political intrigues prevented its construction, and, in any case, it certainly did not belong there.

Charles II resided in Whitehall after the Restoration in 1660 with some vestiges of luxury. At the same time, he began construction on his new residence on either side of the little hunting lodge of St. James, built for Henry VIII (8). As mentioned, William of Orange preferred Kensington because the air was better in the outlying districts. The area around St. James was completed under the Hanoverians in the 18th century. The spot was exactly right for the king. There, above all, the elegance of the age could be developed. George III had the sense to buy the Duke of Buckingham's city palace in 1762 (9). The St. James residential area was completed with Buckingham Palace and its parks. But it was only after John Nash had redesigned the interior of the palace in 1824 that it could serve Queen Victoria, on her accession in 1837, as the monarch's residence. It was not until Edward VII's reign that the exterior was designed in its present form. Sir Aston Webb created the right ceremonial axis to the city by his completion of the Mall as a street of great magnificence.

We must stress at this point that the Mall and, parallel to it, Pall Mall were designed and used for royal games of bowls by both the Stuarts and the Hanoverians, unlike Unter den Linden in Berlin, which was designed as a ceremonial route, or the Champs-Elysées in Paris, designed as an avenue to reflect the glory of the monarch on his way to the Parnasse Français, which had been planned in the 18th century and was intended to stand on what is now the site of the Arc de Triomphe.

A few decades after the acquisition of Buckingham Palace, Parliament was given a new building (14) commensurate with its function. A fire was the outward cause. All that was left of the old complex was the Hall of Justice, Westminster Hall. In contrast to Paris, Vienna, and Prague, the Houses of Parliament and not the royal castle became the symbol of the city and the state. The Houses of Parliament themselves were built between 1840 and 1852; the clock tower was erected only in 1858 and the Victoria Tower in 1860. Figure 175 shows that now the legislature, the executive, and the constitutional monarch have achieved precisely the topographical relationship corresponding to their constitutional tasks.

One final thing is deserving of attention. St. Paul's, as the cathedral church of the bishops of London, was the main church in the city. The royal church, Westminster Abbey, was presided over by an abbot, later a prior, and finally, a dean.[42] The primate of England, in Catholic and in Protestant times, was the Archbishop of Canterbury, who was rarely bishop of London as well. In any case, the two offices had no immediate connection, and so it was no easy task to find an official residence for this prince of the Church that was suited to his courtly duties. The solution was discovered as early as the 13th century. Although Westminster Bridge, only the second bridge anywhere in London, was not built until 1739, the archbishop decided (and he was the only person to do so) that he would build his palace on the south bank of the Thames and surround it with extensive parks—Lambeth Palace and the Archbishop's Park (16). Thus he went outside the confines of London. Yet he was as close as possible to, and in full view of, the royal residence, separated from it by the river alone but at a distance which, at that time, was hard to cover.

The City at first had no part in this development. Where in Cologne, Florence, and Paris, space for a settlement would either have been furnished in advance by a new wall or at least have been secured afterward, the merchants of London at no time felt any pressure to replace their costly wall with a larger one. The congestion was accepted all the more readily because the wall represented a jurisdictional boundary. The Lord Mayor of London's special rights did not extend beyond it. New arrivals felt obliged to settle in outlying districts, in the "wards without," which corresponded to the "wards within." As early as 1598, in his *Survey of London,* John Stow had characterized the indissoluble enmeshment of these two areas.[43] On the other hand, the City administration was concerned, from the 16th century onward, with its own green belt areas outside the wall. Most of these extended in front of inns. Lincoln's Inn Fields (fig. 175, 6) is an example.

As in Paris, Parliament and the crown tried to make it hard to move into London. In a proclamation by Queen Elizabeth I in 1580, which was made into a parliamentary decree in 1592, it became illegal for more than one family to rent a new building or for any new buildings to be erected within three miles of the town.[44] That decree has influenced house design in London, and consequently in the whole country, to this day. Single-family houses pushed farther and farther away from the town. The royal hunting grounds, which later formed London's parks, had in any case to remain open spaces. It is to the nationalization of monastery property in the early 16th century, rather than in the 18th and 19th centuries as in the rest of Europe, that London owes not only its unique parks but also the development of many field games, from tennis to cricket, football, and golf. According to an account dating from the second half of the 17th century, long before "English gardens" were recognized as a new style of garden in their mother country, a plan for a castle garden in St. James was rejected on the grounds that an open hunting ground would be aesthetically preferable.[45]

I can find no precise information about the population of the Greater London area before the Great Plague of 1665, in which some 69,000 perished, or before the Great Fire of 1666, which destroyed 13,700 houses, among them four guildhalls, St. Paul's Cathedral, eighty-seven churches, the Customs House, and the Exchange. The fire burned for eight days. Descriptions of the city before the Great Fire tell us that it was intolerably overpopulated, unhealthy, and dirty. Up to the time of the fire, life was lived in a totally medieval commercial city, like Lübeck or Nuremberg, and even after the fire the strict building ordinances imposed by the king were just as ineffective as the plans for reconstruction presented by Sir Christopher Wren and others. Every citizen built his house on the same spot as the old. The regulations gearing the number of stories to the width of the street were seldom, if ever, heeded. Monumental accents were changed only in Wren's classical churches, St. Paul's Cathedral (4), and many other buildings such as his new Exchange. London remained congested. The plans were too "ideal" ever to be realized. They were engraved, printed, and admired but not implemented.[46] The size and form of St. Paul's (1675–1710), the largest church after St. Peter's in Rome, tell us that a nation that could realize plans of this sort so optimistically was on its way to becoming a world empire.

The large area between the City and the royal parks—St. James's Park, Green Park, Hyde Park, and Regent's Park—was completed in the 17th century as a new and very large town. These extensive developments alternate between older, low buildings and elegantly designed newer structures. The upper classes built themselves districts in a form that was possible only in London—in squares consisting of townhouses for the aristocracy with a garden in the middle to which only residents of the square had keys (fig. 176). Inigo Jones's Covent Garden, begun in 1631, is the oldest example.

Francis Russell, the fourth earl of Bedford, collaborated with a developer in order to derive more profit from the old abbey garden that his ancestors had acquired in 1552 from the huge quantities of secularized property. And so the *piazza* was built that was soon to be imitated by any number of others (fig. 177). The notion of these townhouses on a rectangular, square, or circular site, even along roads with sweeping curves, has influenced urban planning in England more than that of any other European nation to this day. A high point was reached when the John Woods, father and son, drew up their plans for Bath. Erwin Gutkind has called Bath the first large modern city in Europe.[47] As I pointed out earlier in this chapter, whereas the Places Royales in France were framed with rows of houses, like stage scenery, all of them looking toward a royal monument but designed with no concern for the residential requirements of the tenants or buyers, such a concern was the very point of departure for the English square.[48]

Until the middle of the 18th century, even the biggest streets and traffic axes related, in their archtectonic design, to their inhabitants. The most

Figure 176. St. James's Square, 1755 (after Sutton Nicholls)

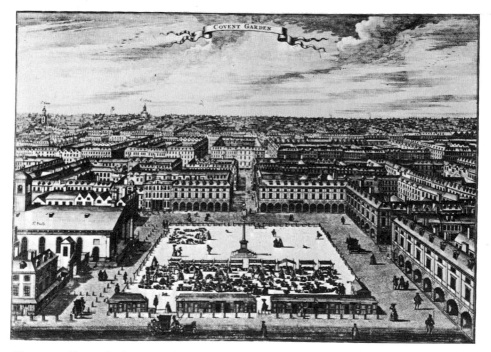

Figure 177. Covent Garden, 1720 (after Sutton Nicholls)

famous example is Regent's Street, designed by John Nash (1765–1835). Plans for this route from the center to the northern part of the city and on to Regent's Park were developed in the mid-18th century. The great axes designed by Napoleon I for Paris moved the Prince of Wales (later King George IV), who became regent in 1810, to build this street in spite of the enormous costs involved. A statute providing for a uniform style for both residential and commercial buildings was enacted in 1813. Photographs taken at the end of the 19th century illustrate the breadth of the undertaking as well as its restraint.[49] The construction of the winding street has proved itself from the points of view both of architecture and of traffic, even if the 20th century has renounced the simple architectural form in favor of a more pompous one—especially in the quadrant which is the nucleus of the whole undertaking. The sense of an appropriate architectural language fell into abeyance. No answer was sought to the question posed by the old rhyme: "Care colonne, che state quà? / Non lo sappiamo in verità."

In the early 19th century, London's extended urban complex had still managed to maintain a center. The great streets of Westminster and the

337

City—Whitehall and the Strand—had met from time immemorial at Charing Cross, the last of the monuments erected in 1291 at the twelve resting
places along the route of Queen Eleanor's funeral procession from Notting-
ham to Westminster. It was also the end point of the old and the new axes
toward the north, the street now called Charing Cross Road and the later
Regent's Street (via the Haymarket). The former recreational road—which
had served since the 17th century as a place for kings to play their ballgame
"Palle Maille"—also began at Charing Cross. This road, the Mall, was later
to become the ceremonial approach to Buckingham Palace. Until the beginning of the 19th century Charing Cross was devoid of monumental buildings because it was the site of the Great Mews, the royal stables and coach
houses (fig. 178). The memorial cross was moved in 1633 to make room for
an equestrian statue of Charles I, which was replaced in 1675. In the early
19th century the coach houses were moved in order to create a national
square, Trafalgar Square (fig. 175, 7), which would form a unit with the
Nelson column and, a little later, the National Gallery (fig. 179). It should
be noted that this gallery, the richest in Europe after the Prado and the
Louvre, does not contain royal collections. It was first stocked from private
collections but was increasingly given state support. The relatively modest

Figure 178. Charing Cross:
1, equestrian statue of Charles I;
2, Whitehall;
3, Haymarket;
4, the Strand;
5, stables.

Figure 179. Charing Cross with the National Gallery, ca. 1840 (the naval monument in the middle of the square was never built).

design of its facade, with classical motifs, as well as its later construction on the site reserved for it historically, testifies to its origin in a political situation upon which a number of forces were acting: the government and, to a lesser extent, the royal house and the City. What was decisive, however, was the new self-confidence that the victories over Napoleon had engendered in the nation.

Today all roads from London are measured from the site of the old Charing Cross. It is impossible to imagine a greater contrast than that between the modest national monument to Nelson and the Arc de Triomphe on the Place Charles de Gaulle. Trafalgar Square merely functions as the center of a city. There are no ceremonial approaches to it. Here, everything was even more confined than around the Bank of England (fig. 175, 2) or St. Paul's (4), as the poles of the City of London; around Westminster Abbey (15) and the Houses of Parliament (14), as the center of the legislature; around Buckingham Palace (9), with its grand approach route, the Mall; or even around the Admiralty and the other government buildings (10–12). But precisely because of its modesty, Trafalgar Square became a symbol of national political self-confidence. It wished to be regarded neither as the only square in the city nor as the principal one. London remained a city of many centers, and the last one to be built refused to take on monumental dimensions. The greatness of the empire documented itself only in part by the buildings of its capital.

Chapter 8

A<small>S AN URBAN PERSONALITY,</small> Rome surpasses all other capitals. There is nothing to compare with the first, imperial Rome as the capital of that most perfect world empire which ruled all the coasts surrounding the Mediterranean. Nor is there anything to compare with the papal city of the Renaissance and the baroque period, *Roma secunda*. This is just as true of Rome's political activity as of the architectural physiognomy that was formed in its service. In no other city do we find elements of order and chaos, of creation and decay, intermixed in so many different forms.

Faced with the scholarship and literature on Rome, it is more essential than in the case of any other city that brevity should be striven for in describing its urban growth. Research on Rome simply cannot be surveyed in toto. The culture of Rome is a subject to which a lifetime of study could be devoted. As with research on Paris, but in a different way, we get lost in a jungle of information and pictures. Writings about Paris became a part of French literature: about Rome they remained chronicle, accusation or glorification fostered by the ideology of Rome, hampered by the knowledge that the first and second Romes were increasingly destroyed by the third Rome after 1870.[1] Rome was not a success as the capital of a unified

THE SECOND AND THIRD ROME

Italy. The population grew from 220,000 in 1871 to 2,630,000 by 1971—a twelvefold increase, of which about a million came in the twenty years between 1951 and 1971. In the meantime, the three million mark may have been passed. In the same time period, the population of the inner city was reduced from 146,000 to 72,000. Life became intolerable in many districts. The destruction of almost one-third of all the historical buildings or ruins to make way for road traffic or for new ministries or, in one case, for the monument to King Victor Emmanuel II (which is also a self-representation of the new national consciousness) proved to have been unnecessary. The new through roads can no longer cope with the traffic, and the dimensions and pathos of the monument are felt to be offensive. The demand for the removal of the central administrative offices to the periphery of the city is repeated more and more urgently. The growth of the city on the other side of the Aurelian walls, with its disregard for any plan, proves humiliating to the citizens. The city has become incapable of functioning. By the autumn of 1973, the cost of its debt service was about $16 billion—almost one-half of all tax revenue—and could only be extended with the aid of state guarantees.

A utopian program was developed, in which the old Rome would be restored by tearing down the new one and a new Rome would be built far outside the old walls; between the two there would be a broad green belt.[2] Ancient road maps confirm that these requirements were "objectively correct." They could never be realized, however.

There are three major reasons why Rome could not succeed as the capital of a reunited Italy after 1871.

1. The city is in the wrong place. Bologna or even, perhaps, Milan should have been chosen.[3] For centuries Rome was in the right place as the

center of an empire which it had created itself and to which it gave its name—as right as a spider in the middle of a web of traffic routes, which were primarily searoutes. This was the best place from which to conquer, first, southern and central Italy; then, simultaneously, Africa, Carthage, and northern Italy; after that Spain, the whole of the East, and Egypt; and, finally, Gaul, parts of Germania, Britain, and the Balkans. Around the Mediterranean, 5,627 towns can be counted that were either founded or settled by this, the most perfect empire. Seneca (*Dialogues* XI, 7) stressed the fact that whatever the Romans conquered they also settled (*ubicumque vincit Romanus habitat*).

From the 2d century B.C., Rome no longer tried to feed its growing population from its own resources. It lived on conquests: the greater part of the population did little or no work. Under Claudius, there were 159 holidays, on 93 of which games were held. In 354 A.D., there were more than 200 holidays, on 175 of which games were held that regularly included all sorts of mortal ordeals. Long before the decision was made, in 324, to move to Constantinople, the emperor and his civil servants had recognized that this capital could no longer fulfill its task.[4] We are again aware of this today, but a move is no longer possible.

2. The city's own traditions, coupled with the fact that it was in the wrong place, made it almost impossible for a citizenry to develop that would have been capable of supporting the life of the city. The city was peopled with administrative officials, clerks, artists, speculators, the unemployed, prostitutes (who had been there from the days of antiquity), and beggars. Just as in Washington, D.C., where, because of its position between the northern and southern states, the black population is constantly increasing, so people from southern Italy seek refuge in Rome. In order to find them employment, the number of central administrative authorities has become inflated. Self-support by industry, crafts, and trade, which is an intrinsic part of every capital, is guaranteed only to a limited extent in both Washington and Rome. Rome lives off blood transfusions, and this has been the case since the second century B.C. Even in the glorious days of the Renaissance and the baroque there was no expansive citizenry to occupy the place between the cardinal and papal families on the one hand and the lower classes and servants on the other.

3. After centuries of fractionalization, which permitted the most diverse forms of state to flourish on the Apennine peninsula—city-states, maritime states, princedoms—but which also saw the surrender of large tracts to foreign rule, the new reform movement of 1870–71 demanded the

sort of centralism for Italy that had proved its worth in Piedmont but did not correspond historically to what Italians had been educated to for a thousand years. This centralism functioned only incompletely under the kings, only at fearful cost in the period of fascism, and since 1945 it has functioned worse with each succeeding year. The attempt to centralize Rome as a city was bound to fail. It did not succeed in coordinating the different walks of life with one another as London did (see above). There are central authorities throughout the city. The rate of growth gave the planners no chance to create paths for developmental tendencies. All attempts at the self-representation of Rome as the capital of the new Italy led to destruction of the city's substance—for example, the new Corso Vittorio Emanuele with the old Via del Corso in front of the national monument on the Piazza Venezia, or Mussolini's Via del Impero through the monumental areas of ancient Rome, or the papal Via della Conciliazione, which was built in the style of Hitler's Imperial Chancellery, and for which the old Borgo had to be sacrificed.[5]

These three factors—the unsuitability of location, the unbalanced structure of the population, and an exaggerated centralism—together wrecked all attempts at solving the problem by means of urban planning. Furthermore, in the path of every plan, history placed stumbling blocks that proved insurmountable because of the ever-present deadweight of intellectual, artistic, and even ethical traditions. The third Rome could not flourish on the site of the first, imperial Rome or on that of the second, papal Rome. The conflict not only determines and burdens the impression the city makes on us: its solution became a political problem upon which every government would inevitably founder.

The Second Rome

The ancient city within the Aurelian walls, which was built in A.D. 264, encompassed 1,330 hectares—compared with only 132 in Roman London, 34 in Roman Florence, and little more in Roman Cologne or Turin inside their original walls, 264 hectares in Nîmes, and 285 in Trier. An inventory made between A.D. 312 and 315 records 1,790 *domi,* large single-family dwellings, and 46,602 *insulae,* blocks of dwellings consisting mainly of tenements which are described as being inhumanly overcrowded.[6] The population must have been far more than a million, probably closer to 1½ million.[7] The image of the city on the hills on either side of the Tiber was marked by a wide diversity of buildings—temples, imperial palaces, forums, amphitheaters, racecourses—and by aquatic luxury. The inventory lists 9 canals, 11 public baths, 5 aquatic areas for the theatrical representation of sea battles, 926 private baths, 500 fountains, and 700 basins and ponds. Rome's indolence is illustrated in its theaters and baths. When the water supply to the Caracalla baths failed in A.D. 537, the death struggle of the first Rome was over.

Before that, however, for rather more than two centuries, the city had succeeded in bringing about a remarkable renewal of its architectural structure. With Constantine's victory in 312 and the raising of Christianity to the status of state religion, the path was cleared for the design of new ecclesiastical centers with monumental buildings. In spite of the capital's move to Constantinople, and in spite of the constant defensive battles waged against the spearheads of the migratory armies, Rome managed to add many new accents to the antique composition of the city. These included Constantine's basilicas and those of his successors, primarily the city's four churches, San Pietro, San Giovanni in the Lateran, Santa Maria Maggiore, and San Paolo fuori la mura. There are records of more than thirty-five places of worship, many of which have monumental buildings—not only churches—left behind by those two centuries of late antiquity as administrative problems for the Middle Ages. Such buildings had arisen, in part, from the destruction of imperial monumentality, the more so as many of them lay outside the Aurelian walls in the area of the old necropolises. The architectural feats necessitated by the Christianization of pagan Rome form one of the outstanding chapters in the whole history of urban design.

The history of the second Rome did not begin until after the collapse of the Rome of Constantine, his successors, and the early popes. That history can be divided into two parts. In the first, the Roman Middle Ages, the forces of renewal were in every century subordinated to the forces hastening decay. The failure of the water supply meant that the population was crowded into the narrow area around the bend in the Tiber. Only a few robber barons nested in the Roman ruins on the hills. Widely dispersed both within the Aurelian wall and in front of it, ecclesiastical institutions on the memorial sites of early Christianity continued to vegetate, now blooming, now dying down. The sacralization of monuments by history and legend concealed from the visitor to the *mirabilia urbis Romae* the disproportionate relationship between decay and rebuilding. The efforts of individual popes to create zones of new architectural order were successful only to the extent that every religious endowment in the sacral area received indissoluble rights. At no time did the Romans undertake—as many of the smallest towns in Tuscany or Umbria did—to unite themselves into a functional municipality that could sustain itself economically. Even medieval Rome had to depend upon subventions, and the whole spiritual power of the papacy did not suffice to ensure their continued existence. Circumstances became so unbearable that the princes of the Church finally abandoned their city and moved to Avignon under the protection of the French crown. Yet the Middle Ages bequeathed to the modern era the task of integrating into the city the new ecclesiastical centers, which lay for the most part outside the area of settlement around the bend in the Tiber. These are, first, the seven great pilgrimage centers: St. Peter's and the Vatican, Santa Maria Maggiore, San Giovanni and the Lateran, San Paolo fuori le mura, and, further, Santa Croce in Gerusalemme, San Lorenzo and San Sebastiano on the Appian Way (see below, fig. 184).

The second part of the history of papal Rome did not even begin with the return of the pope from Avignon, for the Great Schism meant more than a quarter of a century of decay. It was only with the election of Oddo Colonna as Pope Martin V in 1417, and after his return to Rome, with the earliest Bull (1495) dealing with building, that reconstruction could begin, step by step and with many a hindrance and reversal. As a city, Rome had collapsed. There remained a population of only 19,000 or even, according to some reports, 17,000 in the area surrounded by the Aurelian wall,[8] and these were robber barons, thieves, a totally impoverished clergy, and a people subsisting on the extreme edge of poverty. Even by 1800, in comparison with London or Vienna, Rome was still a small city with a population of 120,000.[9] In 1420 it was not to be compared with flourishing municipalities like Florence, Siena, Venice, Milan, and others, not even with the royal seats and provincial capitals, Naples and Palermo.

In this second period of its history, however, papal Rome developed into a unique structure as regards both its politics and its architectural form. Again, we may subsume the reasons for this development into three main groups.

1. The power of the popes over the city of Rome was unlimited. As in almost all capitals or princely seats, all organizational forms of municipal self-government atrophied after brief periods of existence.[10] From Martin V (1417–31) to Pius VI (1775–99), forty-five popes ruled over Rome. Most of them were old men: their term of office averaged 8½ years. Almost every one of these popes faced three different architectural tasks: first, the extension of the papal residence, consisting of the Vatican, the Lateran, and later the summer residence on the Quirinal; second, the building of a family

residence, generally with a city palace and a villa, often also with a family church; and, third, the opening up of the city itself by means of new streets and its resuscitation by a water supply. The majority of these absolute rulers had had to wait a long time for their high office, and the uncertainty of each candidacy, the surprise element in the election itself, as well as the unshakable belief of many of them that they really were Christ's successors, led to the development of some very obstinate personalities. As a result, Rome became the only city with numerous and very large family residences that exceed in monumentality and luxury the aristocratic palaces of all other cities. At the same time, we must bear in mind that all the popes proceeded from a college of cardinals, the members of which had royal rank and often built in a regal manner. Many of them were, in their turn, supported by papal nepotism and were assisted in their building plans by both public and church funds.

2. Because the popes were the spiritual shepherds of the Roman Catholic world, extraordinary resources flowed into their coffers. Their state, the *patrimonium Petri,* and the city were not supported by their own incomes, but, like ancient Rome, by resources from the outside. Most of the cardinals, too, drew large incomes from ecclesiastical tithes which originated outside Rome. The city was further enriched by the fact that all the monastic orders had main branches in Rome and maintained them at considerable expense. Another source of income was the only form of mass tourism known to those centuries—pilgrimages. For this reason most countries maintained national churches in Rome as meeting places for their pilgrims, often with hostels where they could stay, for example, Santa Maria dell' Anima for the Germans, and San Luigi dei Francesi for the French. Thus the economic bases of the second Rome differ from those of all the other cities in the West because of the variety of forms of subvention it enjoyed. Earnings from crafts and foreign trade were of small importance in comparison with these other sources. A shipowner and a banker as important as Agostino Chigi, a patron of Raphael, was an exceptional phenomenon in Rome. Apart from this, the provision of resources in the form of grants and endowments created a sense of the ideal, which sought expression in monumental buildings whose aesthetic perfection proclaimed their cause.

3. What is known as the "idea of Rome" imparts a special character to this sense of the ideal at the very highest political level. The city not only considered itself eternal and unique; it also believed in its function as savior and orderer of the world. The city, not just the papacy, identified with this

function. People lived in the large ruined area secure in the belief that they had a heritage and a mission that were defined in monumental buildings. In the Renaissance and the baroque, this mission released creative energies that were uniquely structured. In contrast to all other cities, the artists who have illustrated the importance of the papal office and the idea of Rome in buildings and pictures were never Romans, and yet they all later became Romans: Bramante, Raphael, Michelangelo, and later Vignola della Porta and Fontana, Bernini, Borromini, Maderna, and many others. Not merely the resources but also the artists came from outside, as did two-thirds of the popes. People met in the service of a problem, and everyone—pope, cardinal, artist or financier—finally proved himself by the understanding that he brought to this problem and the form in which he solved it.

The Vatican as Seat of Government

The popes did not move into the Vatican until after their return from Avignon. Hadrian's tomb, which later became the Castello S. Angelo, had been preserved as an impregnable fortress and could be extended and reinforced. In the same way, St. Peter's and parts of the palace had also been preserved. The renovation, the extension, and the furnishing of this residence occupied popes for more than three centuries. The Vatican and its Borgo formed their own city, with its own fortifications, which had only one entrance to the burgher city on the other side of the Tiber, the Ponte S. Angelo, the arches of which were supported by those of the old pons Adriana, which led straight up to the gate of the mausoleum. The completion of this papal residence, and of the roads that were to connect it to the city on the Tiber, was the first piece of town planning to be undertaken by the popes (fig. 180).

It started with the fantastic project of a spiritual residence with a new St. Peter's cathedral and a new papal castle of enormous dimensions, for which the humanist pope, Nicholas V (1447–55), was able to secure the services of Leo Battista Alberti.[11] We know these plans solely by descriptions of them. The new choir around the tomb of St. Peter was the only thing begun by Alberti's master-builder Rossellini. An open residence was to be built, guarded by the impregnable Castello S. Angelo and supplied by the services of the Borgo. Space prevents our tracing the process, which started with Nicholas V's projects and ended with Bernini's colonnades (fig. 181). Again and again a master plan was made—often a utopian papal residence with a gigantic cathedral and an enormous square which was to be surrounded by palaces of incomparable size and beauty. The idea was that this complex should illustrate the predominance of the pope as the representative of Christ. Yet only parts of the plan were ever started; almost nothing was completed. Thus, especially at the beginning, starts were made by Alberti and Rossellini, then by Bramante, Peruzzi, and Raphael. Later, the closer they came to being completed, the more realistic the projects for the improvement of the complex became. In no other place has the factor of time proved more productive. The completion of the palace, the rebuilding of the church up to Michelangelo's dome and out to Maderna's facade, the layout of the Belvedere gardens by Bramante and his successors, the ordering of the space in the square and its accentuation by fountains and an obelisk, the redesigning of the Castello S. Angelo, not to speak of the interpretations of the whole, its coordination into world history and into the ideology of Rome, represented in Raphael's and Michelangelo's frescoes, in

Figure 180. St. Peter's Square and the Vatican, 1694

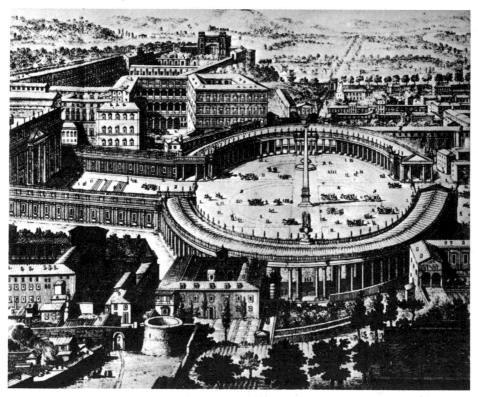

Figure 181. St. Peter's Square, ca. 1930

the decoration of the altars, the series of tapestries, and the rows of sculptures—all this, and much more, creates at the highest level the most perfect unity attainable by the Renaissance and the baroque.

And not only that. In its constantly self-revitalizing inception, the late antique composition of St. Peter's, the papal palace, the atrium, and the cemetery found a topological design of the highest political and aesthetic order. Thus, it made sense for people to assemble in front of a church and not, as with a secular ruler, in front of a palace. It made sense that immediately on leaving this square one was led through the church to the tomb of St. Peter, the justification of the papal office. It was just as fitting that the palace should be seen to be at one side and significantly elevated. The palace had been started under Sixtus IV at the same time as the Sistine Chapel. Julius II and Bramante had extended it, and Sixtus V had completed it with Fontana's new palace.[12] Farther to the right and behind the palace, the same harmony is achieved by Bramante's gardens with the Belvedere, in which famous antiquities were given the role of symbolizing human attitudes.[13] In this whole building complex, scale corresponds to importance. Frescoes and statues interpret the higher, the universal, historical sense of the whole.

The Opening Up of the City and Its Hills

Rome, which had used the paved road to conquer an empire, was by 1424, in the eyes of a pope, a vast area of ruins in which there were no roads. Pilgrims had to find their way over muddy paths to the shrines. However, roads were, and still are, a political factor, as emphasized by the decree that ordered the reinstatement of the *magister viarum*. They also serve in the fight against crime.[14] Inside the city it is only with the help of roads that private property can be demarcated from public property. Roads guarantee building ordinances. We have repeatedly stressed that the function of roads was to bring different political centers into a relationship with one another. For a city to function, its traffic must be safe and there must be roads for it.

In the 16th century, three measures were taken, one after another, to get rid of the inconveniences, and these measures were further developed in the 17th and 18th centuries. In the 15th we already encounter some modest beginnings: (1) the opening up of the city on the Tiber from the Vatican and the Ponte S. Angelo (fig. 182); (2) the opening up of the city to the main stream of traffic from the north, from the Porta and the Piazza del Popolo (fig. 183); (3) the opening up of the rising country (fig. 185) on the seven hills of Rome, from which the population had retired in antiquity, after the water supply had failed.

The most important route to this capital city was then, as now, the Tiber. At first the only crossing was the Ponte S. Angelo, on which the heads of criminals who had been condemned by the princes of the Church were displayed. After the Jubilee Year of 1475, there was also the new Ponte Sisto, built as a relief route. On one side of the new bridge, the narrow approach was guarded by the Castello S. Angelo. On the other side, a large square opened up—the Platea Pontis (now the Piazza S. Angelo), from which streets fanned out into the thickly settled area of the Tiber city. These roads were built by popes in the second half of the 15th and in the early 16th centuries (fig. 182). The names of the streets on the extreme right to the south, which was reached by the Via Paola, the Strada Julia, and the street on the extreme left to the north, the Torre di Nono, were retained. Only these streets could run in a more or less straight line.[15] On the most important street, the Strada di Banchi (today Via Banco Santo Spirito), the great

Figure 182. Castello San Angelo and the Tiber city, 1676 (after G. B. Falda)

Figure 183. Piazza del Popolo, ca. 1750 (after G. B. Piranesi)

banks of Tuscany were erected on the square in front of the papal mint. Only one of these streets, today the Via dei Carbonari, follows the route of its ancient predecessor. The popes conferred special privileges on all who built palaces here. Some of these streets had to be built, others merely extended, paved, and opened up. The ordinances that drew dividing lines between private and public property were very strictly enforced. Until about 1560, almost all the palaces were erected in the old, overpopulated center of the city, many of them on new streets, though some were built in the Borgo, in front of the Vatican, and in Trastavere.[16]

I have constantly reiterated the point that main roads must radiate out from castles to a city or into the country, in the shape of a webfoot (Versailles is the most important example). This was precisely the solution Rome was forced to adopt because of the topographical situation of the city on the Tiber and the Vatican, with the Castello S. Angelo as "sentry-box" and the Ponte S. Angelo as the one link between them. The first task facing the Renaissance popes was to link the new seat of government in the Vatican with the city architecturally, in such a manner that politico-strategic aims as well as religious and economic ones would be served.

The second task arose out of the understanding that most travelers, couriers, ambassadors, and, above all, pilgrims, as well as goods, came from the north and arrived in the city by way of the Via Flaminia through the Porto del Popolo. The natural extension of the Via Flaminia was the Via Lata, which led to the capitol, but this street had not yet been designed in the 16th century. It appears that Raphael, as the first person to hold office as the city architect and curator of Roman antiquities, proposed some new solutions, for under Leo IX (1513–21) a plan was drawn up whereby three streets would fan out from this square and run into the city. The old Via Lata was to be leveled and widened; to its right, the Via di Ripetta (originally as a counterpart to the Via Giulia and called the Via Leonina) was to be built; and, to its left, the Via Babuino, which was commissioned by Clement VII (1523–34). It was not until Sixtus V was pope (1585–90) that the erection of an obelisk created a center for the whole plan. It was only in the 17th century that the two churches were built at the wedge-shaped intersection of the streets; these churches drew strangers' attention to the fact that they were walking in a holy city (fig. 183).

The inner city was opened up by means of these two fan-shaped street layouts, built in the 15th and 16th centuries. There still remained the task of making roads out of the pilgrimage paths leading to the seven and, later, nine main churches that had to be visited in order for pilgrims to be granted the Roman indulgence (fig. 184). This marked the start of the activity of the greatest city planner among all the popes, Sixtus V, who, in the five years of his reign, took hold of Rome in its entirety and redesigned it. This was the third step, in the course of which the hill country inside the Aurelian wall was opened up.

This pope's unique achievement was widely recognized.[17] We have to imagine an extremely energetic, robust, and tough personality of peasant origin, who had been brought up from the age of twelve in the tradition of Franciscan asceticism and had developed into one of the leading theologians and preachers of his time. As cardinal he had been condemned to inactivity by his predecessor, Gregory XIII (1572–85), from the age of fifty-one to sixty-four. At that time his main concerns were the gardens and buildings of his Villa Montalto on the other side of Santa Maria Maggiore, and it was

Figure 184. The seven main churches of Rome (after a propaganda leaflet for the Holy Year in 1575)

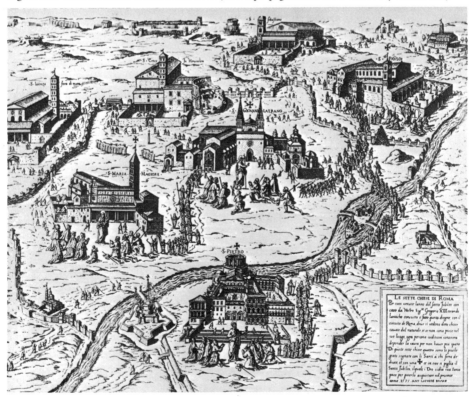

during this period that plans for the reorganization of the city and the Roman hills—which had been neglected since late antiquity because of the failure of the water supply—began to ripen in this countryman's mind. Immediately after his election, he put his own and his predecessor's plans to work. In Domenico Fontana, the oldest of the Ticino architects in Rome, he had at his side an engineer of equal energy. His ascetic lifestyle, enormous energy, and astute administrative measures made it possible for this pope, in spite of the enormous costs of his buildings, to hand the papal treasury over to his successor twenty times richer than it was when he took it over. Among his administrative measures was the amalgamation of uncontrollable small parishes, throughout the city, into a few large ones. His passionate and rigid rationalism turned at first to the urgent reordering of the whole urban area. Four different, but complementary, plans were realized at the same time.

1. A new basis was established for Rome's water supply. The old *congregatio sopra la fonte* was given greater responsibility. Apart from a few other sources, the Middle Ages had relied entirely upon the Tiber. Of the fourteen water intakes of antiquity, only one, which was renovated by the Renaissance popes, was still occasionally in use. This was Agrippa's Aqua Virgo, later the Acqua Vergine, which flowed into the inner city to the Trevi fountain: its daily output could be raised to 63,000 cubic meters. Sixtus repaired and rebuilt a second conduit from Palestrina, which was over 20 kilometers in length and made use of aqueducts built in antiquity. This conduit—called Acqua Felice after the pope's first name, Felix—could supply water to the whole of the hilly country on the left bank of the Tiber—primarily to his own extensive gardens. It debouched into the fountain of Moses, and he wished to be regarded as a second Moses, striking water out of a rock. Even though Acqua Felice had an output of only 24,000 cubic meters a day, it changed the city. This example prompted Paul V (1605–21) to build the more abundant Acqua Paola, which supplied Trastavere, the Vatican, and the Gianicolo on the right bank of the Tiber, with an output of 95,000 cubic meters a day. The three supplies sufficed until 1870. Whereas Gregory XIII had not yet succeeded in realizing the first great plan for distributing water through eighteen fountains, Rome could now afford to revive its squares with numerous new fountains. There were no longer any obstacles to having gardens within the walls.

2. The street grid was extended into the districts which had been revived by the welcome abundance of water. The central point of the new street system was Santa Maria Maggiore: the object now was to make the

paths connecting the individual churches of pilgrimage usable for vehicles (fig. 185). Thus, the great axis was built, 2,780 meters long, that joined Santa Maria Maggiore with S. Croce in Gerusalemme to the south and, by way of the Via Babuino, with the Piazza del Popolo to the north. Part of this route, however, involved a detour, as the section from the Trinità dei Monti to the Piazza del Popolo had not yet been built. At the same time, it brought traffic from the Porto del Popolo south to the Via Appia by making a detour around the inner city.

Figure 185. Rome, new streets and regulations in the 16th century: 1, Piazza Sant' Angelo; 1a. Via Paola; 1b, Via Banco di Santo Spirito; 1c, Via Panico; 2, Via Giulia; 3, Piazza del Popolo; 3a, Via di Ripetta; 3b, Via del Corso; 3c, Via del Babuino; 4, Piazza di Spagna; 5, Piazza Navona; 6, Capitol; 7, Quirinal; 7a, Via del Quirinale; 7b, Porta Pia; 8, Santa Maria Maggiore; 8a, Via di Quattro Fontane; 8b, Via Sistina; 8c, Via Merulana; 8d, San Giovanni in Laterano; 8e, Santa Croce in Gerusalemme; 9, Colosseum.

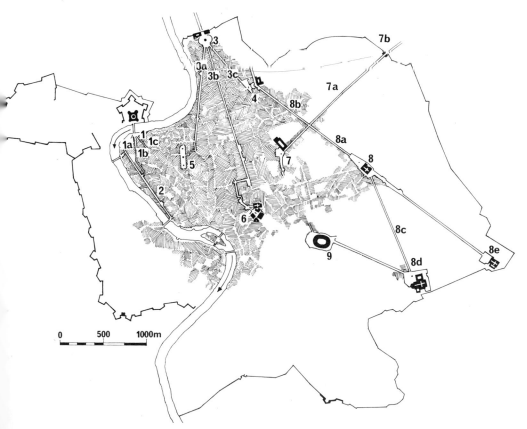

With this axis as a starting point, and in each case close to Santa Maria Maggiore at the center, the pope built four more roads, one to the Porta Pia; one to S. Croce in Gerasulemme; one, which his predecessors had already started, to San Giovanni in the Lateran; and the fourth to the center of the city and Trajan's column. Contemporary descriptions of Rome testify to the fact that this Franciscan pope intended to elevate Santa Maria Maggiore to the sacral centerpiece of the city (fig. 184). The pope had repeatedly walked these stretches in person. In doing so he was primarily concerned with improving the pilgrimage routes to the main churches, but for him a secondary consideration was always the appearance of the city. The customary privileges were intended to promote building on all of these roads. The laws of the Constitutio Gregoriana were revived and made stricter. According to these laws, small gardens and low buildings could be expropriated to make way for monumental buildings, even for private owners.[18] Besides building these new axes, Sixtus V is said to have repaved a total of 125 streets. One of the characteristics of this new opening up of the city was that the streets did not proceed in straight lines but had a regular series of bends in them to modify the climb into the hilly country, which enabled them to accommodate to steeper gradients along their course. Sixtus had outlined the problem for all his successors; its solution would open up anew the whole city within the Aurelian wall.

The pope has been reproached with neglecting ancient monuments in the process of opening up these roads. Fontana, it seems, proceeded with ruthless haste. The pope is said to have defended himself, in the language of modern radicals, with the words of his favorite writer, St. Jerome, "These works are woven out of the sorrows of the unfortunate and the labor of the condemned."[19] Fontana even wanted to turn the Colosseum into a wool-weaving mill, in which Rome's beggars could find work and shelter. At the same time, the city was to be rid of the monstrous number of robbers—under no other regime had so many heads been seen on the Ponte S. Angelo en route to St. Peter's—as well as the equally monstrous number of beggars. It was not just a matter of security: in the eyes of an age stamped with the imprint of the Counterreformation, it was a matter of appearances for a good city that misery should be removed—even if it meant compulsorily placing the poor in a workhouse which could be guarded like a prison. The pope died at the age of sixty-nine before the plan could be set in motion, and Fontana was exiled from Rome.

The Papal Squares

Apart from creating the street axes, which enlarged the area of settlement, one of the most important measures undertaken by the popes was that of turning crossroads, hill sites on the periphery, and empty sites in the inner city into squares. Rome has more such squares than other cities, and each one, in contrast to the Places Royales in Paris or the London squares, was designed as a completely separate architectural organism. We saw this in the case of St. Peter's Square, and we shall come across the same diversity of design in the Capitol Square or the Piazza Navona. Many others—like the Piazza del Popolo, the Quirinal Square, the Piazza Barbarini, the Piazza di Spagna, and, formerly, the Piazza Venezia—join the ranks. The late Renaissance and baroque squares surprise us precisely because of their diversity, and this element of surprise is intensified by the fact that many of them take up less space than they appear to.[20]

Sixtus V also built a number of new squares and improved some older ones. Among his most important commissions were Fontana's new palaces for the Vatican and the Lateran, and the reacquisition and completion of the Quirinal as a summer palace. This last undertaking was only made possible by the new water supply.

The victory of Christianity over paganism was to be illustrated by a new interpretation of the ancient monuments in many of the city's squares. Fontana restored and opened up Trajan's column and the column of Marcus Aurelius, and the pope had them adorned with bronze statues of the apostles Peter and Paul. A famous engraving of Rome, sold as a memento for pilgrims, includes, besides the seven main churches, only these two columns with their representation of the Roman claim to the primacy of the papacy. No fewer than four obelisks were moved by this pope and made into monuments to the Counterreformation by the addition of a cross. Thus the Piazza del Popolo acquired a new centerpiece with the obelisk near the fountain; the Piazza San Giovanni, the piazza in front of the choir of Santa Maria Maggiore, and, above all, St. Peter's Square itself each received its obelisk. The pope's workers managed to take down, lay flat, and transport the 25.5-meter-high red granite monolith that Caligula had brought to Rome from Heliopolis to place in Nero's Circus. Even Michelangelo and Bramante—and this was given special emphasis—as well as all the pope's advisers had considered the undertaking impossible. Sixtus V alone was to carry the day, and Fontana knew what to do. Moreover, the timetable was strictly adhered to. The stone was erected on 10 September 1586 so that it could be dedicated on the Feast of the Exaltation of the Cross, 14 September. Everyone understood the new significance of the Egyptian sun symbol, a significance stressed by the inscriptions on it.

By means of these obelisks, the evolving design of the Piazza San Pietro, the Piazza San Giovanni, the Piazza Santa Maria Maggiore, and the Piazza del Popolo acquired an accent that was later to challenge the new creations of the baroque. At the same time, each of these undertakings served the same political religiosity. They had a higher meaning and promoted the *interpretatio christiana* of the city. Christian Rome was to draw abreast of ancient Rome; the old monuments were to document anew the victory of Christianity over paganism. The pilgrim was everywhere to be strengthened in his belief in salvation by comparable and comprehensible signs. The measures taken during the short reign of this energetic Franciscan were to point the way for the following two centuries.

It is characteristic that these plans were completed during the depression between two waves of artistic creativity. Fontana's period cannot be compared either to Michelangelo's before him or to Bernini's after him. In architecture, too, planning had triumphed over the creation of forms. Fontana's palaces for the Lateran and the Vatican look like sober institutions, outstanding only for their monumentality and clean proportions. First, only the framework was laid out, in which the popes and their nepotic protégés could build their villas in the 17th and 18th centuries. The palaces of the Barberini, Pamphili, and Borghese are examples, as are the villas of the Colonna, Ludovisi, Borghese, and Giustianini. Each of the great papal personalities of the 17th century developed his own policy for city planning or, rather, for the city's improvement. Urban VII Barberini (1633–44), who erected his palace in the area opened up by the Via Felice, surrounded the Gianicolo and Trastevere with their new bastions. Innocent X Pamphili (1644–55) created the Piazza Navona. Alexander VI (1655–77) turned his attention not only to the Piazza San Pietro and the Piazza del Popolo but also to the redesigning of Santa Maria della Pace. The Chigi pope, Alexander VII, set up a wooden model of Rome so that he could at all times see the current state of building activity in the city.

In all these programs, we see that this city, which was supported by the whole of the West, exhausted itself proclaiming its political goals and its political greatness in monuments. Only incipient efforts were made toward attaining those goals. There was no political reality corresponding to the ideality of baroque Rome. Nor can we dismiss the thought that, since it was impossible to realize plans for the salvation of the world or for universal education and healing, flight into earthly paradises offered an alternative, and this is how the villas, palaces, squares, and churches are depicted in contemporary engravings.

The Piazza Navona is one example among many. The interior of Domitian's stadium remained empty throughout the Middle Ages, while in the tiers around the arena only the lowest possible buildings could be erected. The square was the most popular in Rome and served as a market. Innocent X Pamphili, who had been born there, purchased the land for his family palace. The building of this palace served him as an excuse for completely rebuilding the church of Sant' Agnese, which was next to it, and for opening it up to the square through its main portal. Thus the Piazza Navona became the papal square and, at the same time, the forecourt of a church. In the center of the square, the same pope commissioned Bernini to build that fourfold fountain by which the papacy's claims to spiritual and temporal power (which are embodied in the ruling pope) had been made manifest.[21] Innocent X felt that he was the center of the world, not only because of his office as vicar of Christ but because, in his own eyes and in those of his contemporaries, he was its center in his own person. As with Louix XIV, the person was the standard for the office's claim to power. Contemporaries have given us precise accounts of the semantics of the fountain.[22] The point of departure was a 16-meter-high obelisk which the pope wished to have erected over a fountain. Out of conversations of the pope with his advisers and the artist, a work emerged which, when unveiled in 1651, generated enormous enthusiasm with its virtuosity of form and its cosmological significance (fig. 186). Bernini set the obelisk on a cross-shaped, split rock, from beneath which water streamed forth. Resting on the rock are four river gods, who, with the four corners of the earth, incorporate the whole world. The rivers Nile, Danube, Rio de la Plata, and Ganges are symbolized by animals or trees. They indicate the directions in which the new efforts of the *propaganda fidei* were to achieve success. The combination of the elements of rock and water proclaims the papal claim to authority over the whole globe. The obelisk itself was interpreted as a "figural allegory of the macrocosm and of the immaterial world which sinks down into the material world."[23] Instead of a cross, a dove—the coat of arms of the Pamphili and the symbol of the *pax Christi* rather than of the Holy Ghost—was placed on top of the obelisk. Everyone understood this political allegory. It contains the self-interpretation of the Pamphili pope and of the function of the city of Rome. Sculptors never grew tired of repeating the motif in many forms on other monuments. The diversity of the building as plastic bodies in space, like the diversity of the sculptures as accents in urban planning, also arose out of a desire to lend this one doctrine, over and over again in ever new beginnings, the reality and spirituality of symbols.

The Capitol as Political Utopia

We have not yet thought about the major achievement in design of a Roman square, Michelangelo's Capitol, which not only surpasses all other squares as a work of art but also, and to a greater extent, by its own political symbolism. In it, a claim to authority can be discerned to which no actual power ever corresponded. Out of the material of history itself, a new reality was formed, which spent, in the aesthetic sphere, what was really not its to spend.[24] The pretext was the knowledge of the sacred meaning of the ancient capitol as the center of power. In an awakening that was soon followed by an even deeper sleep, a group of Roman citizens decided, in 1144, to summon a new senate in the old city archives, the tabularium, in which the

Figure 186. Piazza Navona, 1697 (after an engraving by S. B. Sluyter)

Figure 187. The Capitol, ca. 1552 (after a drawing in the Cabinet des Dessins du Louvre)

Corsini had taken up residence. The front of the building—which had previously faced the forum—was altered, and oriented toward the Capitoline Hill. It is among the remarkable facts of Roman history that the forum itself was left untouched (except for the few churches that had evolved from temples) and served as a *campus vaccarum,* a cow pasture, until the archaeologists took it over in the 19th century. None of the Renaissance or baroque popes even tried to design a square on the site. In one corner, diagonally across from the senate building, the city erected its guild court in the mid-14th century, and renovated it in 1520. The square also served as a place for the bestowal of honors that were the city's to confer: strange coronations of poets and the bestowal of Roman citizenship, which Michelangelo himself received there in 1537. Figure 187 shows how little there was there and how neglected this rubbish dump was, when Pope Paul III transferred the equestrian statue of Marcus Aurelius from the Lateran to this site in 1538 or even after Michelangelo had completed his double flight of steps in 1552. This was what the middle of Rome as a municipality looked like. When we think of the Piazza San Marco in Venice or the Piazza della Signoria in Florence, the decline in Roman power is emphasized. Even on this site, the

Figure 188. Michelangelo's Capitol (after an engraving by Etienne Dupérac, 1569)

flights of steps and the statue had been placed there by the pope, not by the municipality.

Michelangelo's new master plan, the execution of which took more than a century, is handed down to us in two engravings, made in 1569 by Étienne Dupérac (fig. 188). A square was designed which was to include three palaces and a balustrade. Five roads or flights of steps lead into this square. The buildings form a harmonious architectural unity but do not close the square off. They are the backdrop and wings of a stage, which the city of Rome can use for bestowing its honors. The emperor, Marcus Aurelius, rides over the hill. Inscriptions on the base of the statue point to the change in power between imperial and Christian Rome. The oval in which this statue stands was also intended, by its form, to illustrate the Capitoline Hill. The pattern, which, according to Dupérac's engravings, did not replace the old pavement until 400 years after it was designed, forms a twelve-pointed star, surrounded by marble paths that are also twelve-pointed and are to be understood as symbols of the twelve signs of the zodiac: the center is the head and navel of the world—*caput et umbilicus mundi.*

Originally, Paul III had demanded that the two horse breakers be moved here from the Quirinal. Michelangelo successfully opposed this move, mainly because they could not be coordinated into his plans. On the other hand, he had seen to it that two smaller (also ancient) figures holding horses should be erected on the balustrade that demarcates the square. Here he was probably referring to Dante's interpretation of the dioscuri as the symbols and leaders of popular rebellion against tyrants.[25]

Michelangelo moved the two river gods, Nile and Tigris, to the foot of the steps leading to the palace of the senate: these two statues had already been transferred to the Capitoline square with other antiquities. The Tigris was now interpreted as the Tiber. Between the two, a statue of Jupiter was to recall the sacred nature of the square. However, the Counterreformation did not want to see Jupiter as the allegory of the highest God. Dante had

Figure 189. The Capitol (after an engraving of Domenico dei Rossi, 1692)

Figure 190. National monument and Capitol

still glorified God the Father, in the highest circle of Paradise, as *sommo giove*. For this reason a statue of Minerva was placed in the niche, to which Sixtus V added a cross as an attribute. In front of this statue, the basin of a fountain with running water was to proclaim Minerva's domination over the elements. In 1593, this Minerva was replaced by the smaller one that is still there today. The rivers too were understood as symbols of the Roman claim to dominion over the world.

The Capitol is a work of the popes for the Roman municipality but can also be interpreted as Michelangelo's personal political confession.[26] In it he expressed his rejection of the proto-absolutist rule of the Medici in Florence. The unreality of the claim to world dominion, coupled with the demand for a republican city government in papal Rome—the city without citizens—gave art the opportunity of illustrating political conditions in a world in which historical tradition mingled with utopian demands for the future. Only the intellect of a Michelangelo could make a unity out of such disparate elements—a unity in which ideality and tragedy work together. Michelangelo's plan for the Capitol, according to Dupérac's testimony, could not be carried out after his death as period succeeded period and as styles changed. Della Porta and his successors in the building administration had to change the rigidity of the formal language into a sense of baroque harmony. An engraving made in 1692 illustrates the reinterpretation (fig. 189). Research should constantly remind itself of such changes.[27] The showpiece side, as seen from the flights of steps that led up to it, was further emphasized; the decorative forms were embellished; a prominent new axis was created between the facing palaces. We experience a festive baroque backdrop, the change from architecture as political utopia into architecture as theatrical allegoresis. Compared to the Capitol, even St. Peter's Square is still a symbol of real power. This finds expression in the different proportionality of the two city centers. St. Peter's Square is the largest of the Roman squares, the Capitol the smallest. The limitations and the utopian, fatalistic nature of this sacred hill became even clearer after the *tertia Roma* placed its gigantic national monument beside it: this too, in a new rhetorical style, was to conceal the limitations of the state (fig. 190). The two together are documents which, with the greatest precision, illustrate and interpret political situations and weigh their power.

Epilogue: The Unplannable

Europe is a continent of urban personalities. Wherever a human community sought to establish itself as best it might, there it established a town. Towns were the prerequisite for the existence of all the world's major cultures. Towns formed the field of experimentation out of which the main achievements of civilization have sprung. The versatility of urban individualities and their diversity, from Amsterdam to Rome, from St. Petersburg to Venice, from London to Vienna, are manifestations of uniquely successful creative activities.

The architectural form and physical appearance of all the towns we have treated here emerged from planning processes that for centuries, sometimes for a millennium, constantly made fresh starts and quickened imaginative and creative powers. Only the "ideal cities," created in the main for temporary purposes, are exceptions. No successful capital came into being according to a plan that was complete when the city was founded. No major plan was continued beyond the life of the generation that had drawn it up. New political, economic, sociological, and religious conditions generally represented new design challenges, as, indeed, did changes in style, which were at the same time conditioned by a change in the ideal conception of what a town should be. Wherever a grand design was carried out with despotic rigidity, according to a suggestion made long before, a model was created which, in the final analysis, petrified into the gigantic.

This law knows of no exceptions. We have seen it in Rome and in Versailles, in the Piazza San Marco and the Louvre, in the castle complexes of Potsdam and the Vienna Ringstraße. As long as the creative spirit was actively involved with cities, they continued to change. Only what the centuries had set their seal upon could continue to exist for centuries. Cities that do not go on developing either petrify or die. In the best case, they can—like Venice today, or imperial Vienna—be kept alive by blood transfusions.

Descartes complained that not all French cities were built according to the same well-thought-out plan. From Plato to Ebenezer Howard (1850–1928), philosophers and urban planners have been preoccupied with the perfect city and have replaced continuous creative design with a mode of thought that attempts to preprogram life. This game playing has little to do with reality. History has given scant honor to such optimism. Its hubris is offensive. Le Corbusier's plans for the inner city in Paris are part of this new tradition of *homo ludens* playing at planning.

What is the boundary between necessary planning and the unplannable? The answer can be given only by history, not by theory. Our comparative investigation of many successful towns and their creative developments leads to three principal conclusions.

1. The freedom to participate in the design of one's own urban living environment has been a prerequisite for the success of towns. One cannot plan for strangers. Nor can architectural and living styles be determined by ordinances, unless, as in the case of princely seats, such ordinances served a total work of art that grew out of political constraints imposed from above. There, too, the execution generally lacked inspiration in its detail, and such inspiration cannot be enjoined. It is part of the freedom in question that, as in many early episcopal cities, the architect and the person commissioning the building were either one and the same person or, as later, at least equal partners. We have discussed towns in which the citizens, as builders, determined the plans, and others in which a superior architectural personality made a city council or a prince understand what was suited to their rank, their needs, and the future expectations of the city. Both parties always felt integrated into the productive process. On the other hand, wherever something already completed was put at the disposal of alien or recruited users, it remained empty and fell into decay unless it was later reinterpreted and altered.

2. History cannot be planned in advance. Changed conditions always demanded new programs. These changed conditions were a part of the material that planning had to shape.

This is true of the large buildings that dominate a city and of the city as a whole. Urban planning has more to do with land planning than with building houses. The Romans, as the greatest land planners of all time, knew precisely in which places towns could be established, and so did Charlemagne (see chap. 1). London, Florence, Cologne, and Regensburg were on the right sites. The sites of the Westphalian bishoprics Münster, Osnabrück, Paderborn, and Minden were carefully considered. It would hardly have been possible to find better sites for the Hanseatic cities of the Baltic or for the Zähringen towns in Switzerland. Nuclei were created which could later be developed. Only where nature itself offered no alternative did these towns grow into the form that had been designed at the outset. Lübeck is an example.

Even a castle and an urban organism as precisely ordered as Versailles was constantly being rebuilt, enlarged, and reinterpreted in the hundred years that marked its heyday (1660–1760). As rigidly as the structure of Gothic cathedrals was determined, their plans were always changed by every later generation of architects. Only what could be completed immediately after its inception was built as planned. When the design for the facade and spires of Cologne Cathedral, which had been drawn up in 1320, was redis-covered in the 19th century and a start was made a few decades later to com-plete the building, it was discovered that the late 14th century had already decided not to follow the original design. An attempt was made to correct these new, late-medieval developments, and finally a compromise was agreed upon. The result was called—with justification—a "petrified model."[1]

It was Adolf Hildebrand who insisted that a sculptor, when working on a piece of stone, must always reserve enough material and enough form to enable him to work productively until the last blow of the mallet, even while he is still polishing and smoothing. Nothing must remain to be com-pleted mechanically.[2] This insistence applies even more to the total structure of cities. It was always necessary to have elbow room for planning if the buildings were to be good ones.

Peter Paul Rubens published the series of engravings *Palazzi moderni di Genova* in order to show his fellow citizens in Antwerp the style in which they should build in a new palace district. His model was the Strada Nuova in the northern part of Genoa, in which one noble family after another had built themselves town residences exactly reflecting their lifestyle and aspi-rations. It was not only the fact that Antwerp had, in the meantime, surren-dered to Amsterdam its superior position as a harbor that made the great painter's suggestions utopian. The plan for such a street, built according to a previously existing model, would not have succeeded in any other city either. When James Craig, in 1767, undertook something comparable in Edinburgh, a second, Palladian city came into being—side by side with the old "colonial city"—for an upper crust which was now English rather than Scottish.

In a very large group of towns the fulfillment of our first requirement ensured, in a peculiar way, an apparent breach of the second. I refer to those colonial towns, from the end of the 6th century A.D. to the end of the 18th century, which were founded and built by groups of emigrants as a new home. Here, street grids and uniform houses could prove their worth. The Greeks had imposed similar patterns on all the coasts of the Mediterranean. The Romans assigned such sites to the veterans of their legions for settlement. The merchants and craftsmen migrating eastward in the German Middle Ages realized a similar idea in the new Hanseatic cities. Numerous American cities suggest, by their names, that the early settlers wished to transplant their hometowns into the New World—New Amsterdam, New Orleans, New Glasgow, and many others. The Huguenots, religious refugees, were even more aggressive in building cities that were preplanned in this way and in which they avoided any sort of monumental expense. As we have seen, in many places in eastern Europe, in Prague, Cracow, Danzig, Reval, and Berlin, the in-migration of new citizens did not bring about an enlargement of the city but, rather, the building of new organisms centered upon themselves. The alien townspeople brought their own town plan with them.

3. In every century, anyone who planned only for necessity did not even achieve what was necessary. Humanity had need of an emotional relationship to its dwelling places; it demanded aesthetic uplift, a creative culture that could lend more than polish to the everyday.

Modern lines of research, information aesthetics and semiotics, have concerned themselves with variety in form as a factor in the well-being of all classes of society. Preservationists defend traditional buildings by pointing to the "quality of life" they transmit. We attempt to preserve an environment that has already been shaped. Cities need symbols for the definition of their individuality. What is aesthetically beautiful defines the ideals. The wealth of the urban personality is constructed from all levels of the historical past. Age itself is part of its title to fame. The existential seriousness of every good church, its unchanging size, becomes a force that leaves its imprint on existence. The ceremonial quality of castles translates the optimism of former ages into the present. The facades of the townhouses and palaces of Amsterdam and Venice, Siena and Florence, Lübeck and Bruges, even the last remains of Nuremberg or Barcelona, carry over the principles of their ordering, as postulates, to the whole city. In city centers, the accents bestowed by a city palace or a city hall, a cloth hall or a fountain in the marketplace, are experienced as witnesses to the mastering of life and are perceived as standards for the whole future. Cities in their general appearance remain the expression of fundamental political attitudes which have, above all, advertised their own ideality by means of buildings. They are the field where past and present meet, and, with individual works ranking as artistic achievements, this encounter has gained in both earnestness and splendor.

To sum up: one cannot build for strangers; history cannot be planned in advance; what is necessary needs aesthetic exaggeration. Successful urban compositions have always fulfilled these three premises. Yet there is a point of view from which the third claim seems to run counter to the first two. As we have seen, in many places far more comprehensive plans than one generation could ever hope to complete have not only been prepared prior to any construction, but have also predetermined the artistic rank of every building actually erected. This has been true of numerous architectural projects, including cathedrals, courts, every stage of the new plans for the Vatican from the time of L. B. Alberti onward, every design suggestion for the Piazza San Marco, the traffic axis between the Palazzo Vecchio and the cathedral in Florence, the "royal axis" in Paris, and the Maximiliansstraße in Augsburg. The spirit of planning has always felt bound to reach out beyond what could be realized. The rulers of the baroque period published engravings of castle and park layouts far more magnificent than they ever dared to build. From disdain for the possible arose the intellectual energy for what was still capable of being accomplished.

That is the paradox of urbanization. The whole is projected, its dimensions are staked out, plans are published, and the model is exhibited. Then perhaps one epoch lacks the creative power, another the economic power, and another the political stability to carry out the plan. Only parts are completed. The next or a later generation takes up the idea. Again plans are developed, parts completed. But each part, throughout the future, will speak of the whole from which it has sprung. As centuries pass, the totality unites into an image of the centuries—multiform, burdened and tested by history, a work of succeeding ages, a dwelling place that could, and still can, convey the forces that formed it.

NOTES

Introductory Note

Urban studies are conducted in ten disciplines: (1) Documentation of materials by archaeology, pictures of buildings, views of a town, city plans; (2) the general history of cities; (3) legal and constitutional history; (4) economic history; (5) sociology; (6) political science; (7) geography and historical geography; (8) art history; (9) preservation of monuments in theory and practice; (10) the study of "urban planning" as a contemporary task. The boundaries between these disciplines cannot be drawn. We could increase their number if we were to isolate more recent research goals the semantics of monumental groups, information theory, structuralism, etc. The literature on these subjects has, of necessity, become an immense one. E. Ennen, *Die europäische Stadt des Mittelalters* (Göttingen, 1972), lists 952 titles. The number can be multiplied at will, especially if we attempt to mention everything that has been written about individual cities—Rome, Paris, Florence, Cologne, for example. Much is constantly being repeated. Only on a few points can we perceive any scholarly consensus. When the individual problem is pursued, we lose sight of the whole. Movements to differentiate research on modern town planning and design (*urbanistica*) from that of the historial disciplines (*storia urbana*) have failed. Particularly in research respecting a future-directed realization of town planning, we find an overlap of investigation, theories, and design projects. Literature in one language takes little account of what has been written in another. Anyone selecting from among primary sources or recent literature on a subject should be under no illusions about their conditional nature. The following notes take this situation into account. I cite only what I was able to use directly, and among the works cited there are many of which I could use only a few pages. At the same time, there are references to works that go much more deeply into a topic, especially in the history of individual towns and of their architecture. Here, too, the choice was conditioned by what was more easily available to me.

Introduction

1. This view is confirmed by Fritz Rörig, "Die Stadt in der deutschen Geschichte," in *Die Stadt des Mittelalters,* ed. Carl Haase, vol. 1 (Darmstadt, 1969), pp. 31ff.
2. "Domus miserorum poenis et damnatorum labore vestitiae," Hieronymus, *Episto-*

lae, 46 (Pauli et Eustachi ad Marcellam) n. 10, in *Corp. script. eccl. lat.* LIV 341; cf. L. von Pastor, *Geschichte der Päpste,* X, p. 450.

3. The significance of castle, vic, and market for the genesis of towns—as against the overwhelmingly political reasons for their genesis—is overemphasized by historians with respect to developments in northern France. This is also stated by E. Ennen, *Frühgeschichte der europäischen Stadt* (Bonn, 1953), and in his masterly survey *Die europäische Stadt im Mittelalter* (Göttingen, 1972), which contains a good bibliography. H. Pirenne, *Medieval Cities: Their Origins and the Revival of Trade* (Princeton, 1924), remains the fundamental work.

4. On the Crusades and the "cult of the cart," see H. Sedlmayr, *Die Entstehung der Kathedrale* (Zürich, 1950), pp. 363 ff. The few reports about auxiliary services in the building of cathedrals out of religious enthusiasm run the danger of being romantically transfigured. Much more sober are the concrete records of labor conditions in Florence, Siena, or Cologne.

5. These trains of thought are present in W. Braunfels, "Institutions and Their Corresponding Ideals: An Essay on Architectonic Form and Social Institutions," in *Smithsonian Annual II: The Fitness of Man's Environment* (Washington D.C., 1968), pp. 63–75.

6. Fundamental to this question is G. Bandmann, *Mittelalterliche Architektur als Bedeutungsträger* (Berlin, 1951); for a more recent summing up, see Chr. Norberg-Schulz, *Significato nell'architettura occidentale* (Milan, 1974).

7. See chap. 7, note 6, below.

8. See chap. 7, note 14, below.

9. The rise of the lower forms of architecture in the 18th century was repeatedly discussed by H. Sedlmayr in lectures and talks.

10. See W. Braunfels, *Mittelalterliche Stadtbaukunst in der Toskana* (Berlin, 1951), pp. 10ff. In this connection I do not touch upon the mostly small and undevelopable *terre murate* in Italy or the *bastides* in France (see chap. 5).

11. The great importance, though with other aims, of C. Sitte's *Der Städtebau nach seinen künstlerischen Grundsätzen* (Vienna, 1889), and P. Lavedan's *Histoire de l'urbanisme,* 2 vols. (Paris, 1926), is not to be diminished by what is said here. New research on the aesthetics of information and the history of formal structures in old towns build upon the fundamental insights of these works.

12. Jane Jacobs, *The Death and Life of Great American Cities* (New York, 1961), especially the final chapter, "The Categories of the Problem a City Is."

13. Historical research necessarily emphasizes these beginnings; art-historical research, however, emphasizes the results of monumental design. See the extensive bibliography in E. Ennen, *Frühgeschichte,* with its numerous titles on the history of origins.

Chapter One

1. *Studien zu den Anfängen des europäischen Städtewesens: Vorträge und Forschungen,* published by the Institut für geschichtliche Landesforschung des Bodenseegebietes in Constance, under the direction of Theodor Mayer, vol. 4 (Lindau and Constance, 1958), especially the articles by Ernst Klebel, "Regensburg," pp. 87–104; Franz Petri, "Die Anfänge des mittelalterlichen Städtewesens in den Niederlanden und dem angrenzenden Frank-

reich," pp. 227–96; Walter Schlesinger, "Städtische Frühformen zwischen Rhein und Elbe," pp. 297–362; Herbert Ludat, "Frühformen des Städtewesens in Osteuropa," pp. 527–53.

2. Summary in Jean Hubert, "Evolution de la topographie et de l'aspect des villes de Gaulle du Ve au Xe siècle," in *La città nell'alto Medioevo* (Spoleto, 1959), pp. 529–58 (*Settimana di Studio del centro Italiano di Studi sull'alto Medioevo VI*). The hastiness of the accompanying sketches shows that we do not have precise measurements.

3. Braunfels, *Mittelalterliche Stadtbaukunst*, pp. 139–43.

4. Aldo Rossi, *Die Architektur der Stadt: Skizze zu einer grundlegenden Theorie des Urbanen* (Düsseldorf, 1973), pp. 13 ff. The original edition appeared as *L'architettura della città*, vol. 8 in the series, Biblioteca di Architettura e Urbanistica (Milan, 1966).

5. Albrecht Mann, "Großbauten vorkarlischer Zeit und aus der Epoche von Karl dem Großen bis zu Lothar I," in *Karl der Große*, vol. 3, *Karolingische Kunst* (Düsseldorf, 1965), pp. 320ff.

6. See Eugenio Dupré Theseider, "Problemi della Città," in *La città nell'alto Medioevo* (Spoleto, 1959), pp. 37–38.

7. The fundamental work on the *Genossenschaften* and their conflicts with the rulers is Walter Schlesinger, *Beiträge zur deutschen Verfassungsgeschichte des Mittelalters*, 2 vols. (Göttingen, 1963); further, by the same author, "Frühgeschichte des deutschen Städtewesens," *Lüneburger Blätter* 17 (1966).

8. Unexcelled and unsurpassable: H. Keussen, *Topographie der Stadt Köln im Mittelalter*, 2 vols. (Bonn, 1912).

9. The importance of these fourteen units in the minds of contemporaries was made clear in 1075 by the fact that the eight-day-long funeral procession, with the skeleton of St. Anno, rested in each of these churches—the final one being St. Heribert—but not in any of the parish churches. See the catalog of the exhibition, *Monumenta Annonis* (Cologne, 1975), "Itinerarium mortui," p. 41—with an illustrative map. These fourteen centers are emphasized in all pictorial representations; see W. Braunfels, "Anton Woensam's Kölnprospekt von 1530," *Wallraf-Richartz-Jahrbuch* 12 (1960): 115–36.

10. cf. Klaus Goethert, *Zur Stadtbaukunst von Köln* (Cologne, Düsseldorf, 1958), and "Mittelalterliche Bauten in der Achse des Kölner Doms," *Kölner Domblatt* 18/19 (1960): 139–50.

11. W. Meyer-Barkhausen, *Das große Jahrhundert Kölnischer Kirchenbaukunst 1150–1250* (Cologne, 1952).

12. Most recently in the catalog of the exhibition, *Monumenta Annonis* pp. 30–31.

13. Among the conditions for this symbol of burgher self-government were, first, the expulsion of the Jews in 1348 (the ghetto made room for the town hall square) and, second, the union in 1396 of the guilds with the patriciate documented in the *Verbundbrief*. In accordance with a resolution, the tower was completed in the seven years between 1406 and 1413, and in the year of its completion the emperor Sigismund was shown his loyal imperial city from the top of the tower.

14. Eugen Ewig, "Trier in Merowingerreich," *Trierer Zeitschrift* 21 (1953) and, as a book, *Trier* (1945); Erich Herzog, *Die ottonische Stadt* (Berlin, 1964), pp. 125ff.

15. Most recently, Willy Weyres, "Die Domgrabungen," XVI: "Die frühchristlichen Bischofskirchen und Baptisterien," *Kölner Domblatt* 30 (1968): 121–30.

16. Eberhard Zahn, "Die Porta Nigra, die Simeonskirche, das Simeonsstift," in

Rheinische Kunststätten (Neuss, 1974). Erich Kubach, "Zur romanischen Simeonskirche," in *Festschrift Graf Wolff-Metternich* (Neuss, 1973), pp. 122–30.

17. There are model studies of the early history of Magdeburg and its topology: H. J. Mrusek, *Magdeburg* (Leipzig, 1966); W. Schlesinger, "Zur Geschichte der Magdeburger Königspfalz," *Blätter für deutsche Landesgeschichte* 104 (1968): 1–31.

18. Herzog, *Die ottonische Stadt* pp. 242ff; J. Lindenberg, *Stadt und Kirche im spätmittelalterlichen Hildesheim* (Hildesheim, 1964).

19. Thangmar, "Das Leben des Bischofs Bernward von Hildesheim," in *Geschichtsschriften der deutschen Vorzeit* (1859). There is a more recent translation by B. Gerlach, "Thangmars Lebensbeschreibung des heiligen Bischofs Bernward," *Unsere Diözese in Vergangenheit und Gegenwart, Zeitschrift des Vereins für Heimatkunde im Bistum Hildesheim* 15, (1941). F. J. Tschan, *Saint Bernward of Hildesheim*, 3 vols. (South Bend, Ind., 1972).

20. I was unable to determine, from the literature available to me, when all the districts of the city were enclosed by a wall. The wall was reinforced with ramparts in 1575, as Merian shows us in his view of the city. Cf. J. H. Gebauer, *Geschichte der Stadt Hildesheim*, 2 vols (Hildesheim/Leipzig, 1922/24); Heinrich Viss., *Die Entstehung und Entwicklung des Grundrißes der Stadt Hildesheim* (Hildesheim, 1928); *Althildesheims Werden und Untergang*, ed. H. A. Gerstenberg (1966).

21. Herzog, p. 113.

22. The reading of the most diverse treatments of urban constitutional history forces us to take this view. See Hans Strahm, "Zur Verfassungsgeschichte der mittelalterlichen Stadt," *Zeitschrift für Schweizerische Geschichte* 30 (1950): 373ff; W. Schlesinger, "Zur Frühgeschichte des norddeutschen Städtewesens," *Lüneburger Blätter* 17 (1966), and his "Herrschaft und Gefolgschaft in der germanisch-deutschen Verfassungsgeschichte," *Historische Zeitschrift* 176 (1953).

23. Harald Keller, *Bamberg* (Munich/Berlin, 1950); Herzog, *Die ottonische Stadt*, pp. 171ff.

24. The first results of the new excavations are reported by Walter Sage, "Burg und Bischofskirche, Gewinne und Verluste," in *Ausgrabungen aus Bayern* (1974), part 1.

25. Hans Sedlmayr, *Die Entstehung der Kathedrale* (Zürich, 1950), pp. 359–63, 466–75.

26. Otto von Simson, *The Gothic Cathedral: Origins of Gothic Architecture and the Medieval Concept of Order* (New York, 1962); see the same author in *Propyläen Kunstgeschichte: Das Mittelalter II* (Berlin, 1972).

27. Jürgen Paul, *Die Stadt im Aufbruch der perspektivischen Welt* (Berlin, 1963), pp. 69ff.

28. Hans Fiedler, *Dome und Politik* (Bremen/Berlin, 1937).

29. The rejection of exaggerations in the above-mentioned work followed immediately in Kunze, "Dome und Politik," in *Sachsen und Anhalt: Jahrbuch der Landesgeschichte für die Provinzen Sachsen und Anhalt* 13 (1937): 1–72.

Chapter Two

1. Modern research into urban planning sprang, in large measure, from legal history; see, e.g., Siegfried Rietschel, *Markt und Stadt in ihrem rechtlichen Verhältnis* (Leipzig, 1897); summarized later in Hans Planitz, *Die deutsche Stadt im Mittelalter von der Römerzeit bis zu*

den Zunftkämpfen (Graz/Cologne, 1954); further, W. Schlesinger, *Beiträge zur Verfassungs-geschichte,* 2 vols. (Göttingen, 1963).

2. Dietrich W. H. Schwarz, "Die Stadt in der Schweiz im 15. Jahrhundert," in *Die Stadt am Ausgang des Mittelalters,* ed. W. Rausch (Linz, 1974), pp. 45ff.

3. P. J. Maier, *Der Grundriß der deutschen Stadt des Mittelalters in seiner Bedeutung als geschichtliche Quelle,* Korrespondenzblatt des Gesamtvereins, 57 (1908); and *Fortschritte in der Frage der Anfänge und Grundrißbildung der deutschen Stadt* (ibid, 1912), cols. 222ff. Hans Strahm, "Zur Verfassungstopographie der mittelalterlichen Stadt," *Zeitschrift für Schweizer-ische Geschichte* 30 (1950): 373ff.

4. The best compilation of the material on Florence (particularly the volume contain-ing tables) is Giovanni Fanelli's *Firenze: Architettura e città,* 2 vols. (Florence, 1973).

5. It is significant that Florence, for a short while the capital of a united Italy, replaced the Mercato Vecchio and the Roman forum with a new forum, Piazza Vittorio Emanuele, but this was never accepted beside the Piazza della Signoria as a city center, nor was it used as such. The idea of renaming it, in 1945, Piazza della Repubblica is contradicted by the architecture.

6. Giovanni Villani, IX, p. 256.

7. L. Ginori-Lisci, *I palazzi di Firenze* (Florence, 1972), p. 13.

8. Later Italian research has confirmed this fundamental idea of my *Mittelalterliche Stadtbaukunst* (1952), though it has been made more precise at some points.

9. A comprehensive treatment of history and architectural history is Giuseppe Cach-iagi's *Pisa,* 4 vols. (Pisa, 1970–72); still of use is G. Rohault de Fleury, *Les monuments de Pise au Moyen Age* (Paris, 1866); more recent and basic, Emilio Toalini, *Forma Pisana* (Pisa, 1967); a good survey of the state of research—in spite of its unnecessary polemics—is Piero San Paolesi, *Il Duomo di Pisa* (Pisa, 1975), especially, "La Formazione della Piazza del Duomo," pp. 147–57.

10. The photographs in *Il Centro Storico di Pistoia: Atti del Convegno* (Pistoia, 1968) are an excellent record of what was originally in the town, its stratification and the new programs of slum clearance. For the economic and demographic development of the city, see David Herlihy, *Medieval and Renaissance Pistoia: The Social History of an Italian Town, 1300–1430* (New Haven and London, 1967).

11. This material is to be found in the reports of the conference: *Il Romanico Pistoiese: Atti del I. Congresso* (1964), and *Il Gotico a Pistoia* (1966).

12. Piero Pierotti, *Lucca edilizia urbanistica medioevale* (Milan, 1965); Manlio Fulvio, *Lucca le sue corti, le sue strade, le sue Piazze* (Lucca, 1968). The two volumes *Lucca nelle imagini,* and *Lucca, Centro Internazionale per lo studio delle cerchie urbane* (1974 and 1975), contain useful illustrative material.

13. Braunfels, *Mittelalterliche Stadtbaukunst,* p. 94.

14. There is no comprehensive treatment of the urbanistics of Siena, although Siena is cited in all the authoritative works as an example. There are monographs on most of the buildings and complexes. V. Lusini, "Note storiche sulla topografia di Siena nel sc. XIII," in *Dante e Siena* (Siena, 1901), is still of use. An impressive treatment, though starting out from a different point of view, is Enrico Guidoni, *Arte e urbanistica in Toscana 1000–1315* (Rome, 1967), pp. 85ff. For the richest collection of medieval building ordinances, see A. Lisini, *Il constituto del Comune di Siena volgarizzato nel 1309–1310* (Siena, 1903). Further, Aldo

Cairola and Enzo Carli, *Il Palazzo Pubblico di Siena* (Siena, 1963); Enrico Guidoni, *Il Campo di Siena* (Rome, 1970); G. Pruinai et al. *Il Palazzo Tolomei a Siena* (Cassa di Risparmi di Firenze, 1971).

15. A thorough study of all these ordinances and decrees, which goes further than the suggestions I make in *Mittelalterliche Stadtbaukunst,* pp. 87ff., has yet to be written.

16. Edward Wright, *Some Observations made in travelling through France, Italy &c, in the years MDCCXX, MDCCXXI, MDCCXXII,* 2 vols. in 1, 2d ed. (London, 1764).

17. G. Kauffmann, "Das Forum von Florenze," in *Studies in Renaissance and Baroque Art, presented to Anthony Blunt on his 60th Birthday* (London and New York, 1967).

18. Reference in W. H. Schwartz, op. cit. (see chap. 2, note 2, above).

19. A. Largiader, *Geschichte von Stadt und Landschaft Zürich,* 2 vols (Zürich, 1945), vol. 2, *Das Stadtbild Zürich,* pp. 79–88; Wolfgang Naegeli, *Die bauliche Entwicklung der Stadt Zürich von der Römerzeit bis zum 14. Jahrhundert* (Zürich, 1960). For details, see Konrad Escher's *Kunstdenkmäler der Schweiz,* vol. 10 (Basel, 1939), vol. 22 (Basel, 1949), and vol. 27 (Basel, 1952) (*Kanton Zürich IV, V, VI*).

20. H. Strahm, *Der Zähringer Gründungsplan der Stadt Bern,* Archiv des historischen Vereins des Kantons Bern, 39 (1948), pp. 371ff.; summary accounts by Paul Hofer in *Ausstellungskatalog Zähringerstädte* (Thun, 1964); also the volumes of the *Kunstdenkmäler der Schweiz* for Bern, ed. Paul Höfer: *Kanton Bern I* (1952), *Das Stadtbild II* (1959), *Die Staatsbauten III* (1969). For an unexcelled survey, *Historisches Biographisches Lexikon der Schweiz,* vol. 1 (1921), pp. 126–84.

21. Paul Hofer, "Bauvorschriften im alten Bern," in Paul Hofer, *Fundplätze–Bauplätze: Aufsätze zur Archäologie, Architektur und Städtebau* (Basel and Stuttgart, 1970), pp. 70ff.

22. Hofer, pp. 96ff. The works which were proscribed in Bern are Johann Rudolf Gruner, *Deliciae Urbis Bernae: Merkwürdigkeiten der hochlöblichen Stadt Bern* (Zürich, 1732), and the Göttingen professor of philosophy, (*Weltweisheit*), Christoph Meiner, *Briefe über die Schweiz,* 3 vols. (Berlin, 1784–90). See also Michael Stettner, *Neues Bernerlob* (Bern, 1967), pp. 67–68.

Chapter Three

1. What we admire in Mexico City does not dominate the whole city but has, rather, a decorative function, and what was achieved in Brasilia is about to be reduced in stature by the building of excrescences. Chandigarh is an architectural masterpiece, which was bound to fail as an experiment in urban planning because its style did not correspond to the form of the state that was to be ruled from it.

2. Eduardo Mazzini and Teofilo Ossian de Negri, *Il Centro Storico di Genova,* 3d. ed. (Genoa, 1974), illustrates well enough, thanks to its plans, the development of the city. The bibliography gives the extensive literature up to 1966. See also Ennio Poleggi, *Strada Nuova: Una lottazione del Cinquecento a Genova* (Genoa, 1968).

3. "In this area, where sea and land vie with each other, you have built your houses like the nests of aquatic birds, you have joined your dwellings by fascines and artificial dams, you pile up the sand of the sea to break the raging of the waves, and the apparently feeble wall defies the strength of the waters." Cassiodorus, *Variae* XII, 4 (written in 537 in *Monu-*

menta Germaniae Historica, Auctores Antiguissimi, XII, pp. 379–80 (1894 ed.). See H. Keller, *Die Kunstlandschaften Italiens* (Munich, 1960), p. 273.

4. A. Rossi, "Caratteri urbani delle città venete," in *La città di Padova* (Rome, 1970), pp. 431ff.

5. Matchless; S. Muratori, *Studi per una operante Storia urbana di Venezia* (Rome 1959), and P. Maretto, *L'edilizia Gotica Veneziana* (Rome 1960). Still of use: G. B. Paganuzzi, *Iconografia della trenta parrocchie di Venezia* (Venice, 1822). A model publication is G. Mazzarial and T. Pignatti, *La Pianta prospettica disegnata da Jacopo de' Barbari* (Venice, 1962). Reliable: E. Hubala, "Venedig," in *Oberitalien-Ost,* Reclams Kunstführer (Stuttgart, 1956).

6. H. Kretschmayr, *Geschichte Venedigs,* 3 vols. (Gotha, 1905, 1920, and Stuttgart, 1934); E. Miozzi, *Venezia nel Secoli,* vol. 2 (Venice, 1967).

7. G. Samona et al., *Piazza San Marco* (Padua, 1970). W. Lotz, "Sansovino's Bibliothek von San Marco und die Stadtbaukunst der Renaissance," in *Kunst des Mittelalters in Sachsen, Festschrift W. Schubert* (Weimar, 1962), and "La transformazione Sansoviniana di Piazza San Marco e l'urbanistica del Cinquecento," *Bollettino del Centro internazionale di Studi di Andrea Palladio,* 1966.

8. The point of view has already been chosen on de Barbari's woodcut of 1500, so that we look through the pillars of this gate and onto the Merceria as the main trading street (see fig. 37).

9. The question was carefully examined in Fritz Rörig, "Heinrich der Löwe und die Gründung Lübecks: Grundsätzliche Erörterung zur stadtischen Ostseesiedlung," *Deutsches Archiv* I (1937). Rörig also summarizes the question in "Die Stadt in der deutchen Geschichte" (1952), in *Die Stadt des Mittelalters,* ed. Carl Haase (Darmstadt, 1969), pp. 14ff. See ibid., Heinrich Reincke, "Über Städtegründungen: Betrachtungen und Phantasien," pp. 331–51.

10. Hans Hübler, "Das Lübecker Bürgerhaus," in *Das deutsche Bürgerhaus,* vol. 10 (Tübingen, 1968). Cf. also Michael Brix and Jan Meissner, "Lübeck als Kulturdenkmal," in *Lübeck: die Altstadt als Denkmal* (Munich, 1975).

11. Gerald L. Burke, *The Making of Dutch Towns: A Study in Urban Development from the Tenth to the Seventeenth Centuries* (London, 1956), pp. 32ff., 242–53.

12. I. N. Phelps Stokes, *The Inconography of Manhattan Island, 1498–1909,* 6 vols (New York, 1915–1928; reprint 1967); H. Jackson, *New York Architecture 1659–1952* (New York, 1952); W. Weisman, "New York and the Problem of the First Skyscraper," *Journal of the Society of Architectural Historians* I (1953): 13–21; *Municipal Art Society of New York, Index of Architectural Historic Structures in New York City* (New York, 1957).

Chapter Four

1. The literature on the question of the definition of the imperial city and its relation to the emperor and the empire is extensive. There is a clear survey in G. Pfeiffer, "Stadtherr und Gemeinde in den spätmittelalterlichen Reichsstädten," in *Die Stadt am Ausgang des Mittelalters: Beiträge zur Geschichte der Städte Mitteleuropas,* III (Linz, 1974), pp. 202–23.

2. See Günther Franz, *Deutschland im Jahre 1789, Staats- und Verwaltungsgrenzen, im Auftrag der Akademie für Raumforschung und Landesplanung, Erläuterungshefte* (Munich, 1952). I have taken this number from a manuscript on population statistics in the Holy

Roman Empire written in 1966 which was kindly placed at my disposal by Günther Franz. Surveys of the number of imperial cities are to be found in Götz Landwehr, "Die Verpfändung der deutschen Reichsstädte im Mittelalter," in *Forschungen zur deutschen Reichsgeschichte*, vol. 5 (Cologne/Graz, 1967).

3. This is the opinion of Erich Maschke, "Deutsche Städte am Ausgang des Mittelalters" in *Die Stadt am Ausgang des Mittelalters* (Linz, 1974), p. 2.

4. Cf. W. Braunfels, "Anton Woensams Kölnprospekt in der Geschichte des Sehens," *Wallraf-Richartz-Jahrbuch* 22 (1960): 115–56.

5. The limits of the church's property (fig. 57) are taken from the measurements made by E. Klebel (see chap. 1, note 1, above). The most comprehensive summary of history and topographical development is to be found in Heinz Stroop, *Deutscher Städteatlas*, I. Lieferung, Nr. 8 (Dortmund, 1973), with bibliography and precise cartographic information.

6. Survey of medieval urban development in Erich Herzog, "Werden und Wesen der mittelalterlichen Stadt," in *Augusta 955–1955* (Munich, 1955), pp. 83ff., and, by the same author, *Ottonische Stadtbaukunst*, pp. 182–96.

7. The results of Joachim Werner's (Munich) excavations, which have been made known through lectures, have still to be published.

8. The Augsburger *Fuggerei* (1516–25) marks the beginning of the history of social settlements inside a large city. The originality of the thought and its architectural form should not distract us from the fact that it was designed as a living area for old people only and was set apart from any commercial or political activity.

9. Helmut Friedel, *Die Bronzebildmonumente in Augsburg, 1589–1606: Bild und Urbanität* (Augsburg, 1974).

10. Werner Schultheiß, *Kleine Geschichte der Stadt Nürnberg* (Nuremberg, 1957); Karl Bosl, "Frühgeschichte der Reichsstädte in Franken und Oberschwaben," in *Jahrbuch für Geschichte der oberdeutschen Reichsstädte*, Eßlinger Studien, vol. 14 (1968). Gerhard Pfeiffer, *Nürnberg—Geschichte einer europäischen Stadt* (Munich, 1971).

11. Andreas Urshlechter, *Das Baurecht der Stadt Nürnberg*, diss. Erlangen (Erlangen, 1940); Wilhelm Schwemmer, *Das Bürgerhaus in Nürnberg*, vol. 16 of *Das deutsche Bürgerhaus* (Tübingen, 1972), with bibliography.

12. Erich Keyser, *Württemberg: Städtebuch* (Stuttgart, 1962), pp. 68ff. Otto Borst, *Die Eßlinger Altstadt* (Stuttgart, Berlin, Cologne, 1972), contains excellent cartographical material but no biliography.

13. Wolfgang Jäger, *Die freie Reichsstadt Reutlingen* (Würzburg, 1940); Werner Gross, "Die Marienkirche in Reutlingen," in *Schwäbische Heimat* III (Stuttgart, 1952), pp. 64–73; E. von Knorre, *Die Marienkirche in Reutlingen* (Munich 1963).

14. Michael Ernst, *Die älteste Geschichte Ulms* (Ulm, 1937); Herbert Pée, *Ulm: Deutsche Lande—Deutsche Kunst*, 2d. ed. (Munich, 1967).

15. Wilhelm Vöge, *Jörg Syrlin der Ältere und seine Bildwerke* (Berlin, 1960); Herbert Pée, *Jörg Syrlin der Ältere: Das Ulmer Chorgestühl* (Stuttgart, 1962); Reinhard Wortmann, *Das Ulmer Münster* (Stuttgart, 1972).

16. B. Poll summarizes the state of affairs in *Geschichte Aachens in Daten* (Aachen, 1960); Leo Hugot, "Die Pfalz Karls des Grossen in Aachen," in *Karl der Grosse*, vol. 3, *Karolingische Kunst* (Düsseldorf, 1965), pp. 534–72.

17. Ernst von Niebelschütz, *Das Kaiserhaus in Goslar* (Munich, 1949); Hans-Günther

Griess, "Goslars Pfalzbezirk und die Domkurien," *Harz-Zeitschrift* 19/20 (1967/68): 205–52.

18. Hans Günther Grub, "das Bürgerhaus in Goslar," in *Das Deutsche Bürgerhaus* (Tübingen, 1959). Cf. Gundermar Blume, *Goslar und der Schmalkaldische Bund* (Goslar, 1965); the imperial action against the dukes of Brunswick-Lüneburg because of the enforced treaty of Reichenberg in 1552, which gave the town its independence, was still unsettled in 1802. See Wolfram Werner, *Goslar am Ende seiner reichsstädtischen Freiheit* (Goslar, 1967).

19. Baldemar von Patterweil, *Beschreibung von Frankfurt am Main; Archiv für Frankfurter Geschichte und Kunst,* 3, folio 5 (1896), pp. 1ff.; Adolf Feulner, *Frankfurt am Main: Deutsche Lande—Deutsche Kunst* (Munich, 1964); Erich Keyser, *Hessisches Städtebuch* (Stuttgart, 1957), pp. 122ff.

20. Walter Sage, "Das Bürgerhaus in Frankfurt am Main bis zum Ausgang des Dreißigjährigen Krieges," in *Das Deutsche Bürgerhaus,* (Tübingen, 1959).

Chapter Five

1. The material is collected in S. Lang, "The Ideal City from Plato to Howard," *Architectural Review* 112 (1952): 9ff.; Georg Münter, *Idealstädte: Ihre Geschichte vom 15. bis zum 17. Jahrhundert* (Berlin, 1957); Gerhard Eimer, *Die Stadtplanung im schwedischen Ostseereich, 1600–1715* (Stockholm, 1961), pp. 43–148; Erwin A. Gutkind, *International History of City Development*, 8 vols (New York, 1964–72), vol. 2 (1967), pp. 111–28.

2. Emil Kaufmann, *Revolutionary Architects. Boullée, Ledoux, and Lequeu* (Philadelphia, 1952), is fundamental for the study of revolutionary architecture. The exhibition catalog, *Revolutionsarchitektur: Boullée, Ledoux, Lequeu* (Baden-Baden, 1970), is comprehensive, with bibliography. Its historical significance is presented in an unexcelled manner by Hans Sedlmayr, *Verlust der Mitte* (Salzburg, 1949), pp. 25ff.

3. The city of Richelieu as a work of art has attracted the attention of most historians of urban planning—Brinckmann (1920), pp. 35ff.; Lavedan (1959), pp. 228–33; Egli III (1967), pp. 557–58; Gutkind V (1970), pp. 11ff.

4. See Maria Richter, "Die 'Terra Murata' im Florentinischen Gebiet," *Mitteilungen des Kunsthistorischen Instituts in Florenz* 5 (1937): 351–86. The material was presented by E. Detti, G. Di Pietro, and G. Fanello in *Città murate e sviluppo contemporaneo, 42 centri della Toscana* (Lucca, 1968), a richly illustrated volume; see the critical review in P. Pierotti, *Urbanistica: Storia e Prassi* (Florence, 1972), pp. 37–108. David Friedmann, "Le Terre Nuove Florentine," *Archeologia Mediovale* 1 (1974): 31–47.

5. Piero Pierotti, *Città spontanee e città fondata* (1972), pp. 25–36.

6. Maurice Beresford, *New Towns of the Middle Ages: Town-Plantation in England, Wales and Gascony* (London, 1967), with extensive bibliography. There are numerous bastides in the Netherlands as well. See T. F. Tout, *Medieval Town Planning* (London, 1934); A. Giry, the article "Bastides" in *La grande encyclopédie française,* V, pp. 664ff. In this article, Montpazier (Dordogne) is represented as a prime example. Pierre Lavedan and Jean Hugneney, *L'urbanisme médiéval* (Geneva, 1974), present several ground plans of unsuccessful founder cities.

7. Beresford, *New Towns,* pp. 39–41, fig. 6.

8. Gutkind, *City Development* vol. 5 (1970).

9. The majority of ideal cities from the 16th to the 18th centuries were fortified cities,

mainly citadels, and new fortified cities became, of necessity, ideal cities. "L'urbanistica militare" (see L. Grodecki, "Vauban Urbaniste," in *Etudes sur l'art au XVIIe siècle*, Paris, 1957) made it possible to realize geometrical layouts. From Filarete, Alberti, and Dürer onward, the formative imagination of most artists in the service of a prince was engaged with the *ars militaris*, into which far higher sums were invested than were invested even in the building of castles and about which far more treatises have been written. Cf. Horst DeLaCroix, "Military Architecture and the Radial City Plan in Sixteenth Century Italy, *Art Bulletin* 42 (1960): 263–90. See G. Eimer, *Die Stadtplanung im schwedischen Ostseereich, 1600–1715* (Stockholm, 1961), pp. 43–141.

10. L. Rosenfels, *Palmanova* (Udine, 1888); Eimer, *Stadtplanung*, pp. 84ff; Rossi, *La città di Padova*, pp. 431ff.

11. Lavedan, *Histoire de l'urbanisme*, vol. 2, p. 128; Eimer, *Stadtplanung*, pp. 100ff; Gutkind, *City Development*, vol. 5 (1970), p. 460.

12. The failure to rebuild is illustrated in Alfred Hentzen, *Magdeburger Barockarchitektur: Bildung und Verfall eines Bürgerhaustypus und des Stadtbildes einer mitteldeutschen Großstadt vom Dreissigjährigen Krieg bis zum Ende des Barock*, diss. Leipzig (Dessau, 1927). More recent research is reflected in Sigrid Hinz, *Das Magdeburger Stadtbild in sechs Jahrhunderten*, exhibition catalog (Magdeburg, 1960), and Hans-Joachim Mrusek, *Magdeburg* (Leipzig, 1966).

13. The details are presented in a model way by H. M. Calvin, *The History of the King's Works*, vol. 1 (London, 1963), pp. 423ff.

14. I have taken all the references from Calvin, *History*, who, as the editor of the comprehensive work on buildings by the English crown in the Middle Ages and the modern period, was personally responsible for the section "Calais."

15. Comprehensive bibliography in the catalog of the European exhibition, *The Order of St. John in Malta* (Valletta, 1970); a reliable summary of the architectural history of the city is also to be found in Quentin Hughes, *Military Architecture* (London, 1974). Laparelli's collection of plans is in a codex of the Biblioteca Communale in Cortona, but is as yet unpublished.

16. These decrees were subsumed in statutes dating from 3 July 1573—*Real Ordenanzas para Nuevos Poblaciones* etc.—now in the National Archives in Madrid. They form a compendium for the replanning of cities; essential parts of it were taken into consideration during the planning of Valletta.

17. Eimer, *Stadtplanung*, p. 233

18. Eimer, *Stadtplanung*, pp. 446ff.

19. W. Müller, *Die heilige Stadt* (Stuttgart, 1961), with good bibliography.

20. Ibid., pp. 64–65.

21. Antonius Sanderus, *Chorographie sacra Brabantiae* (Brussels, 1659). History in A. Boni, *Scherpenheuvel, Basiliek en gemeente in het kader van de vaderlandse geschiednis* (Louvain, 1953); Eimer, *Stadtplanung*, pp. 100–104; Gutkind, *City Development*, vol. 5 (1970), p. 40.

22. I am unaware of any comprehensive treatment of the Huguenot cities. Cf. Eimer, *Stadtplanung*, pp. 143ff.

Chapter Six

1. Werner Fleischhauer, *Barock im Herzogtum Württemberg* (Stuttgart, 1958), pp. 137–255.

2. "Landshut," in *Kunstdenkmäler Bayerns, Niederbayern*, XVI, (Munich 1927); Karl Otmar von Aretin, *Landshut* (Bildband) (Munich 1955).

3. Vittorio Ramella, *Storia della città di Vigévano* (Banco Popolare di Vigévano, 1972), is valuable mainly for the plans, which give a detailed reproduction of the Castello but, unfortunately, not of the Piazza.

4. The works of A. Cavalleri-Murat and his associates on the urban planning of Turin are unexcelled as to method and detail; A. Cavalleri-Murat, *Ritratto urbanistica di Torino* (Turin, 1956); "Breve Storia dell'urbanistica in Piemont," in *Storia del Piemonte* (Turin, 1960); but most important of all, A. Cavalleri-Murat and others, *Forma urbana ed architettura nella Torino Barocca*, 3 vols. (Turin, 1968). This is a work of some 1,500 pages, of three columns each, with about 1,800 illustrations. The collection of representations of Turin in A. Peyrot's *Torino nel Secoli* is useful.

5. The chief building ordinances are reprinted in Cavalleri-Murat, *Forma urbana*, vol. 2, pp. 463–84.

6. The great theme of Turin baroque is summarized in the exhibition catalog *Mostra del Barocco Piemontese*, 3 vols. (Turin, 1963), with extensive bibliography. There are further the more recent monographs by N. Carbonesi, *Ascania Vitozzi* (Rome 1966); *Guarino Guarini e l'internazionalità del Barocco: Atti del Convento Internazionale*, 2 vols. (Turin, 1970); S. Bascarino, *Juvarra architetto* (Rome, 1973).

7. Bibliography of Berlin in *Veröffentlichungen der Historischen Kommission zu Berlin*, vol. 15 (1965). The bibliography in *Bau- und Kunstdenkmäler von Berlin: Berlin seit 1955* gives an idea of the mass of literature. There is a good summary in Paul Ortwin Rave, *Berlin in der Geschichte seiner Bauten: Deutsche Lande—Deutsche Kunst*, 2d ed. (Berlin and Munich, 1966); Goerd Peschgen, "Die städtebauliche Einordnung des Berliner Schlosses zur Zeit des preußischen Absolutismus," in *Gedenkschrift Ernst Gall* (Munich, Berlin, 1968), pp. 345–70; Hans Reuther, *Barock in Berlin, 1640–1786* (Berlin 1969).

8. Further Werner Hagemann, *Das steinerne Berlin* (Berlin, 1930; new ed., 1963).

9. Friedrich Nicolai, *Beschreibung der königlichen Residenzstädte*, 3d ed. (Berlin and Potsdam, 1786), vol. 1, pp. Lff.

10. Ibid., p. LXIX

11. The best source for learning about what was intended to be built is the series of engravings in Emmanuel Héré, *Recueil des plans, élévations et coupes . . . des châteaux que le Roy de Pologne occupe en Lorraine*, 3 vols. (Paris, 1753); a basic work is Christian Pfister, *Histoire de Nancy*, 3 vols. (Nancy, 1902–9); also Pierre Lavedan, "Les palaces de Louis XVI," *La vie urbaine*, 1958, pp. 1–38; further, as a survey, Pierre Morot, *Le vieux Nancy* (Nancy 1970), with bibliography; Reginald Bloomfield, *A History of French Architecture from the Death of Mazarin till the Death of Louis XVI, 1660–1792* (New York, 1973), p. 112–20.

12. Mathes Daniel Pöppelmann, *L'Orangerie Royale de Dresden* (Dresden 1718), a series of engravings; unexcelled is Eberhard Hempel, *Der Zwinger zu Dresden* (Berlin, 1961).

13. Eberhard Hempel, Gaetano Chiaveri, *Der Architect der katholischen Hofkirche zu Dresden* (Dresden, 1955), and *Die Hofkirche zu Dresden* (Berlin, 1966).

14. Fritz Löffler, *Das alte Dresden* (Dresden, 1955), pp. 39ff.

15. Nikolaus Pevsner, *Leipziger Barock* (Dresden, 1928).

16. Walter Henschel, *Die sächsische Baukunst im Polen des 18. Jahrhunderts,* 2 vols. (Berlin, 1967).

17. Louis Hautecoeur, *Histoire de l'architecture classique en France,* vol. 3 (Paris, 1950), p. 488.

18. Because of its rank as an achievement in urban planning, Salzburg has been the subject of numerous studies, descriptions, and characterizations. The introduction to Franz Fuhrmann's *Salzburg in alten Ansichten* (Salzburg, 1963), contains one of the best summaries of the city's architectural history (with bibliography).

19. On the ravages to the architectural profile and structure of the city, see Hans Sedlmayr, *Die demolierte Schönheit: Ein Aufruf zur Rettung der Alstadt von Salzburg* (Salzburg, 1965); and *Stadt und Landschaft: Salzburgs Schicksal morgen?* (Salzburg, 1970). Meanwhile, the process of devaluing the architectural substance of the city by mindless and immoderate new construction continues without cease.

20. See Johannes Graf Moy, "Die historischen und soziologischen Grundlagen der Salzburger Schloßkulter," *Mitteilungen der Gesellschaft für Salzburger Landeskunde* 107 (1967): 253–75.

21. The characterization of this synthesis can be found in Hans Sedlmayr, *Österreichische Barockarchitektur 1690–1740* (Vienna, 1930), pp. 22ff., an unexcelled study.

22. H. Bullinger, "Area, Straßenführung und Besitzgrenzungen im früh- und hochmittelalterlichen Würzburg," *Mainfränkisches Jahrbuch* 15 (1963): 118–64; A. Scheuerbach, *Südwestdeutsche Stadttypen und Städtegruppen bis zum frühen 19. Jahrhundert* (Heidelberg, 1972), fig. 9 (see also its bibliography).

23. No comprehensive work on the political and politico-cultural significance of the Schönborns has yet been written. Significantly enough, their name does not appear in the five volumes by Theodor Heuss and W. Heimpel on the "Great Germans." There is no shortage of studies on individual processes and works. A fundamental work is H. Hantsch, A. Scherf, and M. von Freeden, *Quellen zur Geschichte des Barocks in Franken unter dem Einfluß des Hauses Schönborn,* vol. 1, parts 1 and 2, (Würzburg, 1931, 1955). Further, *Katalog der Ausstellung Kurfürst Lothar Franz von Schönborn* (Bamberg, 1955); O. Meyer, *Kurfürst Lothar Franz von Schönborn,* (Bamberg, 1961); R. Kömstedt and H. Reuther, *Von Bauten und Baumeistern des fränkischen Barocks* (Berlin, 1963); A. Graf von und zu Egloffstein, *Schlösser und Burgen in Oberfranken* (Frankfurt, 1972); *Ausstellungskatalog, Balthasar Neumann in Baden-Württemberg* (Stuttgart, 1975).

24. Franz Seberich, in *Die Stadtbefestigung Würzburgs,* Mainfränkische Hefte 39 and 40 (1962, 1963), with numerous references to sources, and a bibliography, vol. 2, pp. 157ff, points out that those who commissioned the extensive fortifications were well aware of their weaknesses.

25. Further, M. von Freeden, *Balthasar Neumann als Stadtbaumeister* (Berlin, 1937), and *Balthasar Neumann: Leben und Werk* (Munich/Berlin, 1953; 2d ed. 1963).

26. There are reports of how frequently the bishops rode around the bastions with their engineers and considered possible improvements. More depressing are the documents about the grueling work of excavation for which soldiers, convicts in chains, vagabonds, and even prostitutes were conscripted. See Seberich, *Stadtbefestigung,* vol. 2, p. 73.

27. On Neumann's work in supplying water to the city and the moats, see ibid., pp. 104ff.

28. Richard Sedlmaier and Rudolf Pfister, *Die Fürstbischöfliche Residenz in Würzburg* (Munich, 1923). This is still a basic work.

29. The standard work on Versailles remained Pierre de Nolhac, *Histore du château de Versailles*, 2 vols. (Paris, 1911). A survey of half a century of literature on the subject appears in *Revue de l'histoire de Versailles*, 1962. The most recent work to which I had access, and which can be considered scholarly, is Alfred Marie, *Naissance de Versailles*, 2 vols. (Paris, 1972). Outstanding among the source works are Mlle de Scudéry, *La Promenade de Versailles* (Paris, 1669), and A. Felibien, *Description de la Grotte de Versailles* (Paris, 1676).

30. There have been repeated attempts to write the "novel" of Versailles, e.g., Pierre Verler, *Versailles* (Paris, 1961). The extent of the material, which is constantly being added to by scholarly research (see note 29 above), and the fact that each of these attempts also aimed to serve as a guide to the contemporary state of affairs, prevented any of them from becoming a classic.

31. Exemplary, and with a wealth of bibliography, Jacques Levron, *Versailles, Ville Royale* (Paris, 1965).

32. I am using the material provided by Friedrich Milke in his model essay, "Das Bürgerhaus in Potsdam," in *Das deutsche Bürgerhaus,* ed. G. Binding, 2 vols. (Tübingen, 1972). The data for fig. 142 were also put together, in part, from the drawings in Milke.

33. J. Hackel, *Geschichte der Stadt Potsdam* (Potsdam, 1912, cited in Milke, "Bürgerhaus," note 7).

34. Once more I would point to Milke's comprehensive documentation. The graphic depictions represent a life's work which today has to take the place of what has been lost.

35. This is an idea repeatedly developed in Hans Sedlmayr's lectures.

36. One of the most beautiful books about the city is L. Réau, *Saint-Pétersbourg* (Paris, 1913). The work is interesting too because of its date of publication. Réau was director of the French Cultural Institute in St. Petersburg. He still found it possible to believe that the circumstances that had seen the rise of the city still existed. See his "Urbanisme et architecture française en Russie," in *Etudes écrites et publiées en l'honneur de Pierre Lavedan* (Paris, 1954). Still of use: Brinckmann, *Stadtbaukunst*, pp. 77–88; see also Lavedan, *Urbanisme*, vol. 3, pp. 266–73. Fundamental because of his characterizations of style: G. H. Hamilton, "St. Petersburg," in *The Pelican History of Art: The Art and Architecture of Russia* (Harmondsworth, 1945), pp. 163–233. The Russian literature on the subject was accessible only through J. E. Grabar et al., *Geschichte der russischen Kunst*, vols. 5 and 6 (Dresden, 1970).

37. Because of its almost contemporary concern, the summary of conditions in Voltaire's *Histoire du Charles XII* (1740) is particularly striking.

38. Réau, *Saint-Pétersbourg,* cites at length contemporary voices which criticize the despotism with which the building measures were forced through. "The Tsar, the Tsar alone, has fallen in love with these marshy arms of the river, where he did not intend to build a city for the use of people but only as a residence for himself. . . . The climate, too hot or too cold, resembles, in its cruelty, the changing moods of the despot," wrote the Polish poet Michewicz. As late as 1839, Custine calls the site of St. Petersburg the most inhospitable in the world. However, voices could be heard on the other side, thus J. Müller, *Tableau de Saint-Pétersborg* (1810): "Even someone who has travelled through all of Europe

and America declares that St. Petersburg, thanks to its position on the most beautiful river in the world, represents by its size and the magnificence of its buildings something unique of its kind. It has taken less than a hundred years for repeated and ruthless efforts finally to tame this river, so that in the kaleidoscope of palaces and parks, the banks of its many arms unite into a picture of the dominion of the spirit over nature."

39. Hamilton, "St. Petersburg," excels all other descriptions to which I have had access.

Chapter Seven

1. I know of no special literature on Prague as a work of urban planning, but there are hints in many of the works about Prague. Further; Jaroslaus Schaller, *Beschreibung der königlichen Residenzstadt Prag,* 4 vols. (Prague, 1794–97); Karl Bosl, *Handbuch der Geschichte der böhmischen Länder,* 4 vols. (Stuttgart, 1966–67), useful also for gaining access to the whole literature. Further: Oskar Schürer, *Prag* (Vienna, 1935); Johanna von Herzogenberg, *Prag,* 2d ed. (Munich, 1966); see also K. Swoboda, ed., *Barock in Böhmen* (Munich, 1969); Ferdinand Seibt, ed. *Bohemia Sacra* (Düsseldorf, 1974).

2. Schürer, *Prag,* p. 27, citing G. Jacob, ed., *Arabische Berichte von Gesandten an germanischen Fürstenhöfen des 9. und 10. Jahrhunderts* (Berlin, 1927).

3. Summarized by Ennen, *Die europäische Stadt,* pp. 57ff (with bibliography).

4. See Gutkind, *City Development,* vol. 7, pp. 32, 49–50, 89.

5. H. Ludat, "Frühformen des Städtewesens in Osteuropa" in *Studien zu den Anfängen des Städtewesens,* 1955/56, pp. 541–53.

6. On the political iconography of the Charles Cathedral, see H. Sedlmayr, "Die gotische Kathedrale Frankreichs als europäische Königskirche," in *Epochen und Werke* (Vienna, 1959); Victor L. Kotrba, in *Bohemia Sacra,* pp. 511–48.

7. R. Hausherr, "Zu Auftrag, Programm und Büstenzyklus des Prager Domchores," *Zeitschrift fur Kunstgeschichte* 34 (1971): 21–46.

8. Götz Fehr, *Benedikt Ried: Ein deutscher Baumeister zwischen Gotik und Renaissance* (Munich, 1961) and "Benedikt Ried und seine Bauhütte," in *Gotik in Böhmen* (Munich, 1969).

9. Summarized by Erich Bachmann in *Barock in Böhmen.*

10. Once again we are faced with a literature that is highly differentiated and can only be comprehensively surveyed by an expert on Vienna. For an introduction, see H. Hassinger, "Kunsthistorischer Atlas Wiens," *Österreichische Kunsttopographie* 15 (1916); H. Tietze, *Wien* (Vienna and Leipzig, 1931); K. Öttinger, *Das Werden Wiens* (Vienna, 1951). The most succinct summary is H. Sedlmayr, "Das Werden des Wiener Stadtbildes," in *Epochen und Werke,* vol. 2, pp. 257–65.

11. H. Aurenhammer, "Ikonologie and Ikonographie des Wiener Belvederegartens," *Wiener Jahrbuch für Kunstgeschichte* 18 (1956): 86ff.; F. Novotny, *Prinz Eugen und sein Belvedere,* exhibition catalog (1963); H. and G. Aurenhammer, *Das Belvedere in Wien* (Vienna and Munich, 1971), with bibliography.

12. On the iconology of the Karlskirche, see H. Sedlmayr, "Die Schauseite der Karlskirche in Wien," in *Epochen und Werke,* vol. 2, pp. 174–87.

13. Öttinger, *Das Werden Wiens.*

14. H. Tietze, "Geschichte und Beschreibung des St. Stephandomes," *Österreichische Kunsttopographie* 23 (1931). On the political presuppositions for the individual phases of

building, Nikolaus Grass, *Der Wiener Dom: Die Herrschaft in Osterreich und das Land Tirol* (Innsbruck, 1968).

15. The best description of the history of the Hofburg is still M. Dreger, "Baugeschichte der K. K. Hofburg in Wier," *Österreichische Kunsttopographie* 14 (1914).

16. See Öttinger, *Das Werden Wiens*.

17. H. Sedlmayr, "Osterreichs bildende Kunst," in *Epochen und Werke*, vol. 2, p. 275.

18. G. Wienner, "Die Verbauung der Wiener Klostergärten in Josephinischer Zeit," *Jahrbuch des Vereins für die Geschichte der Stadt Wien* 12 (1959/60): 145ff.

19. R. Wagner-Rieger, ed., *Die Wiener Ringstraße—Bild einer Epoche*. The following had appeared at the time this work was written: vol. 1, R. Wagner-Rieger, *Das Kunstwerk im Bild* (Vienna, 1964); vol 4, A. Kieslinger, *Die Steine der Ringstraße* (Wiesbaden, 1972); vol. 6, E. Lichtenberg, *Wirtschaftsgeschichte und Sozialstruktur* (Wiesbaden, 1970); vol. 8(i), H. Chr. Hoffmann and others, *Das Wiener Opernhaus und seine Architekten, Eduard von der Nüll und August Sicard von Sicardsburg* (Wiesbaden, 1972); vol. 9(i), N. Wibiral and others, *Ringstraßendenkmäler* (Wiesbaden, 1973).

20. For maps and evidence, presented in a model manner, see Lichtenberg, *Wirtschaftsgeschichte* (vol. 6 of Wagner-Rieger, *Ringstraße*).

21. Edmund N. Bacon, *Townplanning, Past and Future* (New York, 1967), p. 179 and figure on p. 178, stresses these two areas; see also W. Köngeter, *Die Ostwestachse von Paris: Ihr Werden und ihre Schönheit*, diss. (Stuttgart, 1931).

22. A document of political ideology rather than of practical urban planning is the plan of Paris by M. Patté in *Monuments érigés en France à la gloire de Louis XV* (Paris, 1767). In this plan (which is frequently reproduced), nineteen squares were included that various architects wanted to make into a Place Louis XV. Even Notre Dame was to be sacrificed to one of these; the whole lot would have destroyed the city.

23. "Si j'étais Maître en France je voudrais faire de Paris non seulement la plus belle ville qui existât, la plus belle ville qui ait existé, mais encore la plus belle ville qui puisse exister." Cited from Louis Hautecoeur, *Paris,* 2 vols. (Paris, 1972), p. 430. In the course of my reading about Paris, Hautecoeur's splendid summation became my most important source of information.

24. Since the 18th century, no work about Paris, however comprehensive, has failed to mention the limitations of its choice of material. At the same time, I know of none that defends its principle of selection other than by pointing out that it is presenting a selection of what is most important. Even the introduction to Prefect Turgot's plan (fig. 171) of 1740, stresses that it is impossible to reproduce "l'immensité de cette Capitale et la magnificence de toutes les parties qui la composent." See primarily M. Poëte, *Formation et évolution de Paris* (Paris, 1911); *Une vie de cité: Paris de sa naissance à nos jours,* 4 vols. (Paris, 1924–31); *Paris; Son évolution créatrice* (Paris, 1938); P. Lavedan, *Histoire de Paris* (Paris, 1960); Chr. Beutler, *Paris und Versailles,* Reclams Kunstführer (Stuttgart, 1970). Delamare's statements about Paris as a task for urban planning, in *Traité de Paris* (Paris, 1722), vol. 1, pp. 83–129, and vol. 4, pp. 10ff., are unrivaled.

25. Hautecoeur, *Architecture classique*, vol. 1, p. 297.

26. The leading roles played by the Paris workshops has been stressed especially in W. Sauerländer, "Die kunstgeschichtliche Stellung des Westportals von Notre Dame in Paris," *Marburger Jahrbuch für Kunstwissenschaft* 17 (1959): 1ff.

27. Hautecoeur, *Paris,* pp. 70–71, 90.

28. There are different estimates of the population. J. C. Rüssel, *Late Ancient and Mediaeval Population* 1958), gives 53,000 laymen, 6,000 clerics, and 6,000 students in 1292 and estimates 90,000 in 1350. In my opinion he underestimates the density of settlement. According to him there were about 100,000 people living in Paris in the middle of the 16th century, whereas the Venetian ambassador speaks of 300,000 in 1500 and 500,000 in 1545. Hautecoeur, *Architecture classique,* vol. 1, p. 279, talks of 415,000 in the year 1637 and of the same number a century earlier. But he stresses the decline in population—because of the Fronde—to 200,000 in 1650. The number 750,000 for 1700, cited in "Curiosités de Paris," is too high. We are on firmer ground with 550,000 in 1801 after the losses caused by the Revolution, with 1,000,000 in 1851, and with 2,700,000 in 1900.

29. Hautecoeur, *Paris,* p. 496.

30. As far as I know, no one has written an interpretation of the Louvre as a document recording the change in the kings' perception of themselves.

31. Millard Meiss, *French Painting in the Time of Jean de Berry, the Limbourgs, and their Contemporaries* (New York, 1974).

32. T. W. Gaetgens, *Napoleons Arc de Triomphe,* Abhandlungen der Akademie der Wissenschaften in Göttingen, Phil.-Hist. Klasse III, No. 90, (Göttingen, 1974).

33. The massive plans are in Hautecoeur, *Paris,* p. 437.

34. On the doctrine of the state our of which the *Places* arose, cf. U. Keller, "Reiterdokumente Absolutistischer Fürsten," *Münchener Kunsthistorische Abhandlungen* 2 (1971): 54ff. The *embellissement* of Paris, as a program, was first demanded by Henry IV in 1601 at a meeting of the authorities. See Hautecoeur, *Architecture classique,* vol. 1, p. 295.

35. Sir John Summerson, *Georgian London* (Baltimore, 1962), p. 24, quotes, in this connection, an estimate for 1885 by Sir Benjamin Hall.

36. John Gwynn, *London and Westminster Improved, illustrated by plans. To which is prefixed a Discourse on Public Magnificence* (London, 1776). Cited in Gutkind, *City Development,* vol. 6, p. 264. Gwynn goes on to say, "The narrowness of the streets and the unaccountable projection of the buildings, which confined the putrid air, and joined with other circumstances, such as the want of water, and the concurring consequence of the increase of filth, rendered the city scarcely ever free from pestilential devastation."

37. Steen Eiler Rasmussen, *London, the Unique City,* 2d ed. (Oxford, 1937). The first edition was published in Danish in 1934. This work, which was influenced by Werner Hegemann, *Städtebau nach den Ergebnissen der allgemeinen Städtebau-Ausstellung,* vol. 2 (Berlin, 1913), pp. 272–306, is also the starting point for the present descriptions of London. Photographs of the buildings in the historical districts appear in *A Survey of London,* published by the London County Council, vols. 1–37, 1900–1972 (continuing).

38. Martin Biddle and Daphne M. Hudson, *The Future of London's Past* (Worcester, 1973), presents model pictures of the topography of the Roman city and its relation to all that came later.

39. Gutkind, *City Development,* vol. 6, p. 170, takes the numbers from R. A. Pelham, "Fourteenth-Century England" in H. C. Darby, ed., *A Historical Geography of England, before A.D. 1888* (London, 1936), pp. 231–35.

40. H. M. Calvin, ed., *The History of the King's Works,* vol. 1 (London, 1963).

41. "Erat . . . ingenio subtilis . . . audax et potens in armis . . . in extruendis aedificis

et machinis, aliusque ardius operibus ingeniosus artifex, et in toquendis hominibus inexorabilis carnifex." Cf. Calvin, *King's Works,* vol. 1, p. 45, and vol 2, p. 707, note 7.

42. Braunfels, *Monasteries of Western Europe* (London, 1972), pp. 173–74.

43. John Stow, *A Survey of London* (London, 1603; new ed. 1842). In contrast to contemporary and older Italian guides, London is here described house by house, and the author also describes whatever he can find out about the inhabitants of the houses. In the process, he stresses the beauty of the ancient buildings.

44. These ordinances are printed in Rasmussen, *London,* pp. 67–68, 72ff.

45. Ibid., p. 95.

46. The plans drawn up by Wren and his competitors are central to almost all research into urban planning. He developed his regular new order—which was to start at the "piazza" of St. Paul's, leaving the open space in front of the Royal Exchange free—according to Roman models and 16th century theories of urban planning. If this plan had been carried out, the city would have acquired, as early as the 17th century, the character of a 19th century urban expansion dominated by the monotony of every sort of uniformity (see above, Introduction). Gutkind, *City Development,* vol. 6, p. 255, has correctly pointed out: "Wren's plan is, therefore, a representative example of city planning ideas current in the 17th century. But it remained on paper, and looking back from our vantage point with the convenient wisdom of hindsight, we find it was an exercise in out-of-date patternbook planning which would have imposed on London a design totally alien to its character and its spontaneous and unregimented growth."

47. Gutkind, *City Development,* vol. 6, p. 257.

48. B. Beresford-Chancellor, *The History of the Squares of London* (London, 1907); the contrast between the squares and the *Places Royales* is stressed by Lavedan, *Histoire de l'Urbanisme,* 2d. ed., vol. 2 (1959), pp. 275–76. Rasmussen, *London,* p. 165; Gutkind, *City Development,* vol. 6, p. 26.

49. Rasmussen, *London,* p. 278.

Chapter Eight

1. On the development of the third city of Rome: Franco Borsi, *L'architettura dell'unità d'Italia* (Florence, 1966); Paolo Portoghesi, *L'eclettismo a Roma, 1870–1922* (Rome, 1968); Gianno Accasto, Vanna Fraticelli, and Renato Vicolini, *L'architettura di Roma Capitale, 1870–1970* (Rome 1971); Leonardo Benevolo, *Roma da ieri a domana* (Bari, 1971). This literature is summarized and reviewed by S. Kostof, "The Third Rome," *Journal of the Society of Architectural Historians* 32 (1973): 239–50.

2. Benevolo, *Roma.*

3. Thus A. J. Toynbee, *Cities on the Move* (London, 1970).

4. On the necessity for moving the capital, see ibid., p. 63.

5. The Via della Conciliazione was begun in 1936 by Mussolini and Pope Pius XI and completed in 1950 under Pope Pius XII. Its name recalls the concordat between church and state.

6. Aelius Aristides (A.D. 117–189) already condemns the number of stories in these buildings; *In Romam* § 8: "Rome bears on its shoulders a whole pile of other Romes of the same size, heaped on top of one another. . . . If the city were to be laid out flat so that

the different Romes which now rise up into the air were to lie next to one another on the ground, the rest of Italy, I believe, insofar as it is not yet covered by Rome, would be completely overlaid by it."

7. Russell, *Population,* pp. 64–65, arrives, on the basis of an absurd assumption, at a population of only 172,000 for the imperial period. He defines the 42,000 *insulae* as "apartments" with an average of 3.5 inhabitants in each; to this he adds the 1,790 *domi* as larger units. The *insulae* were blocks of dwellings, and there is no reason to doubt the reports of their horrible, inhumane overcrowding, which has been described by Lewis Mumford, *The City in History* (New York, 1961), pp. 228 ff., as well as by others. We have to reckon that there was a population of 1,500,000 at the zenith of the development. Gutkind, *City Development,* vol. 6, p. 422, considers Russell's computation (his computations have proved right in many other cases) to be correct here too.

8. The numbers are taken from the *Enciclopedia Italiana,* art. "Roma," vol. 39 (1949), p. 789.

9. As early as Diderot's *Encyclopédie,* in the article on Rome, it was stressed that Paris was six times and London seven times as large as the Eternal City. Amsterdam was twice as large.

10. On the movements which led to the establishment of a senate on the Capitol, see F. Gregorovius, *Geschichte der Stadt Rom im Mittelalter,* book 8, chap. 3.

11. On the development of the Vatican: F. Castagnoli, G. Cecelli, G. Giovannoni, and M. Zocca, "Topografia e urbanistica di Roma," in *Storia di Roma,* vol. 23 (Bologna, 1958); Gutkind, *City Development,* vol. 4 (1964), pp. 414–39; still good is G. Dehio, "Die Bauprojekte Nikolaus' V and L. B. Alberti," *Rep. für Kunstwissenschaft* 3, (1880): 241ff.

12. A. Munoz, *Domenico Fontana architetto.* Quaderni Italo-Svizzeri III (Rome and Bellinzona, 1944).

13. J. S. Ackermann, *The Cortile del Belevedere* (Vatican City, 1954); H. Brunner, *The Statue Court in the Vatican Belvedere* (Stockholm, 1974), pp. 19ff.

14. King Ferrante of Naples, in 1471, recommended to Sixtus IV that the streets be straightened and extended as a security measure. Braunfels, *Mittelalterliche Stadbaukunst,* p. 103; Lavedan (1959), p. 41.

15. Luigi Salerno, *Via Giulia, una utopia urbanistica* (Rome, 1974).

16. C. L. Frommel has mapped forty-two new places of which only three or four are outside the medieval settlement areas.

17. There is no better summary in a recent work than in L. v. Pastor, *Geschichte der Päpste,* vol. 10, pp. 422–99. Even S. Giedion's celebrated presentation in *Space, Time and Architecture* 5th ed., rev. and enl. (Cambridge, Mass., 1967), contains little that is not in Pastor. H. Keller, *Kunstlandschaften,* p. 172, contains one of the best summaries. Bacon, *Townplanning,* pp. 128–29, gives a good pictorial representation.

18. Pastor, *Geschichte der Päpste,* vol. 10, pp. 439ff.

19. Cf. Introduction, note 2, above.

20. Lavedan (1959), p. 171 stresses, as a principle of the baroque, "Donner sans espace véritable l'illusion de l'espace."

21. A masterly description in H. Kauffmann, *Giovanni Lorenzo Bernini: Die figürlichen Darstellungen* (Berlin, 1970); see also Norbert Huse, *Gianlorenzo Berninis Vierströmebrunnen,* diss. (Munich, 1967); the special relationship to the Pamphili pope is described in R. Prei-

mesberger, "Obeliscus Pamphilius," *Münchener Jahrbuch der bildenden Kunst* 3, no. 25 (1974): 77–162.

22. Ath. Kircheri, *Ad Alexandrum VII Pont. Max. Obelisci Aegyptiaci nuper Isaei Romani rudera effossi interpretatio hieroglyphica* (Rome, 1666).

23. For a summary of the Kircher texts, see Kauffmann, *Bernini,* p. 175, and R. Preimesberger, "Pamphilius," pp. 116ff.

24. A basic work is Herbert Siebenhüner, "Das Kapitol," in *Rom, Idee und Gestalt* (Munich 1954). Summaries in James S. Ackermann, *The Architecture of Michelangelo* (London, 1961), pp. 54–74, and Herbert von Einem, *Michelangelo* (Berlin, 1973), pp. 181–88. Outstanding, on account of their historical documentation and the wealth of illustrative material, are Renato Bonelli, "La Piazza capitolina," in *Michelangelo architetto* (Turin, 1964), pp. 425–98, and C. Pietrangeli, *Il Campodoglio di Michelangelo* (Milan, 1965).

25. Tilmann Buddensieg, "Zum Staatsprogramm im Kapitolsplan Pauls III," *Zeitschrift für Kunstgeschichte* 32 (1969): 192–93.

26. Charles de Tolnay, "Beiträge zu den späten architektonischen Projekten Michelangelos," *Jahrbuch der Preußischen Kunstsammlungen* 52 (1931): 176–81.

27. Thus Hans Sedlmayr, "Das Kapitol des della Porta," in *Epochen und Werke,* vol. 2 (Vienna and Munich, 1960), pp. 46–56.

Epilogue

1. References and concepts in Hans Kauffmann, "Die Kölner Domfassade," in *Der Kölner Dom: Festschrift des Zentral-Dombau-Vereins* (Cologne, 1948), pp. 78–137.

2. Adolf von Hildebrand, *Gesammelte Schriften,* ed. Hennig Bock (Cologne and Opladen, 1969), pp. 257–58. New ed., P. P. Rubens, *Palazzi moderni di Genova* (Genoa, 1956).

CREDITS

Reductions of plans, generally on a larger scale, to the essentials which are presented here were made by G. Klewitz: 173; J. Partenheimer: 84, 86, 87, 88, 89, 163; H. Pothorn: 1, 13, 28, 29, 38, 48 (a and b), 59, 65, 85, 101, 116, 123, 130, 133, 146, 165, 166, 168, 175, 178, 185; D. Schneider: 6, 57, 71; R. Schreiner: 14, 33, 36, 67, 72, 111, 127, 135, 142.

Figures 5, 8, 10, 18, 19, 34, 37, 41, 44, 45, 49, 50, 51, 52, 54, 55, 56, and 58 were taken from collections of engravings.

Photographs were furnished from the following institutions. German National Museum: 61, 62, 70, 74, 75, 82, 83, 90, 91, 93, 94, 96, 98, 99, 100, 104, 105, 106, 107, 108, 109, 110, 112, 114, 115, and 117; Staatliche Schlösserverwaltung Berlin: 112, 118, 126, 128, 134; Rheinfränkisches Museum, Würzburg: 136, 137, 138, 140, 144, 145, 149, 151, 153, 154; Historisches Landesmuseum, Vienna: 157, 158, 159, 160, 164, 167, 170, 171, 172, 174, 176, 177, 180, 182, 183, 184, 186; Graphisches Kabinett, Munich: 188 and 189.

Original photographs were provided by Alinari: 2, 3, 4, 25, 27, 30, 31, 181, 190; Anderson: 32, 43; Lala Aufsberg: 68; Max Baur: 141, 143; Foto Brugger: 64, 66, 95; Brogi: 23; Centro Internazionale per lo Studio della Cerchia Urbane: 26; Deutsche Fotothek, Dresden: 119; Giraudon: 97, 169; Gundermann: 60; W. Halm: 120; K. Kratsch: 156; Landesamt für Denkmalpflege, Salzburg: 125, 131, 132; Landesbildestelle Sachsen: 121; Foto Marburg: 63; Werner Neumeister: 155; Roger-Viollet: 15, 16, 20, 53, 139, 147, 148; H. Schreiter: 129; Schweizerisches Landesmuseum, Zürich: 35; H. Schmölz: 7; Städtisches Museum, Trier: 124.

The author owes especial thanks to Horst Schreiber, photographer at the Kunsthistorisches Institut of the University of Munich, who photographed most of the engravings and drawings reproduced in this work.

Index

(Italics indicate pages on which illustrations appear)

Aachen, 12, 112, 128, *140*, 141–44
Aalen, 112
Accasto, G., 389
Ackerman, J. S., 390, 391
Adam, Robert, xiii
Adolf II von Schauenburg, count of Holstein, 95
Aelius Aristides, 389
Aigues-Mortes, 151, *152*
Alberti, Leo Battista, 151, 164, 188, 347, 348, 371
Albert the Bear, 212
Albrecht, archduke, 173
Albrecht I of Hapsburg, duke, 298
Alessandro (Medici), duke, 67
Alexander the Great, 209
Alexander I, czar of Russia, 272, 274
Alexander VII (Chigi), pope, 358
Althan, 301
Altötting, 173
Ambras, castle, 298
Amiens, 314; cathedral, 5, 35
Ammanati, 61, 69
Amsterdam, 3, 7, 45, 79–82, 84, 102–5, *103*, *104*, 115, 126, 177, 199, 267, 293, 367, 369, 370
Ankara, 307
Anna Ivanovna, czarina, 269

Anna of Austria, 187, 254
Anno, bishop, 19, 22
Ansbach, 128, 175, 249
Antinori, 54
Antwerp, 45, 111, 115, 369
Aquileia, 15
Aretin, K. O. von, 382
Arezzo, 47, 59, 153
Aristotle, 47
Arlesheim, 231
Arno, bishop, 293
Arras, M. d', 284
Athens, 180
Augsburg, *14*, 15, 19, 27, 44, 49, 112, 114, *116*, 117, 123–25, *123*, *124*, 231, 233; cathedral, *14*; fountains, 124–25; Maximilianstraße, 4, 125, 371
Augustus the Strong, 185, 221–25
Augustus II, 223
Aurenhammer, H. and G., 386
Autun, 18
Auxerre, 18
Avignon, 345, 347

Babenbergs, the, 34, 296
Babylon, 276, 277
Bachmann, E., 386
Bacon, E. N., 8, 387, 390

Bähr, G., 222
Balzac, H. de, 316
Bamberg, 28, 33–35, *33, 34,* 231, 232, 236,
    246; residence buildings, 247
Bandinelli, Baccio, 68
Bandmann, G., 374
Barbari, Jacopo de', 83, 115
Barbarossa, emperor, 89, 141, 146, 243
Barberini, the, 358
Barcelona, 370
Bascarino, S., 383
Basel, III, 114, 115, 117, 231, 233
Bath, 336
Bayreuth, 128
Beaumont du Périgord, *156,* 156, 157
Beauvais, 8; cathedral choir, *36,* 37
Bedford, earl of (Francis Russell), 336
Behaim, Sebaldus, 116
Belgrade, 301
Bellinzona, 69
Benevolo, Leonardo, 389
Beresford, Maurice, 156, 381
Beresford-Chancellor, B., 389
Bergamo, 81, 82
Berlichingen, Götz von, 245
Berlin, 4, 7, 10, 114, 145, 175, 179, 185, 210,
    212–20, *213, 214, 216, 218, 219,* 249, 253,
    283, 303, 307, 370; Unter den Linden,
    214, 215, 217, 218, 333
Bern, 10, 41, 44, 45, 69, 70, 74–77, III,
    149, 156, 179
Bernini, 240, 292, 319, 347, 358, 359
Bernward von Hildesheim, 30
Berry, duc de, 187, 318
Berthold V, of Zähringen, 74
Beutler, C., 387
Biberach, 112
Biddle, M., 388
Binding, G., 385
Bloomfield, R., 383
Blume, G., 381
Böblinger, Mathias, 135, 138
Bock, Henning, 391
Boffrand, Germain, 227, 228
Bologna, 341

Bonacolsi, 191
Bonanno, 55
Bonelli, R., 391
Boni, A., 382
Boniface, St., 28, 243
Bonn, 231, *235,* 240
Bopfingen, 112
Bordeaux, 12, 41, *42, 43*
Borghese, the, 358
Borromini, 240, 347
Borsi, F., 389
Borst, O., 380
Bosl, K., 380, 386
Boullée, 317
Bourges, 18, 39; cathedral, 35, 38
Bramante, 192, 347–49, 357
Brandenburg, 234
Brasilia, 179
Braun and Hogenberg, 307, 321
Braunfels, W., 374, 375, 377, 378, 380, 389,
    390
Bremen, 45, 79, 101, 112, 114, 115, 117, 158
Bremerhaven, 168
Brescia, 82
Brinckmann, A. E., 8, 381, 385
Bristol, 329
Brix, M., 379
Brixen, 231
Bronx, the, 108
Brooklyn, 108
Bruchsal, 235
Bruges, 44, 45, 79, 84, 370
Brühl, count, 221
Brunelleschi, 54, 281
Brunner, Otto, 302
Bruno, archbishop, 22
Bruno, bishop, 244
Brussels, 39, 179, 283, 301
Buchau, 112
Buchhorn, 112
Buda, 289
Budapest, 180, 301
Buddensieg, T., 391
Bullinger, H., 384
Buontalenti, 67

Burckhardt, J., 183
Burghausen, 207
Burke, G. L., 379

Cachiagi, B., 377
Cairola, A., 378
Calais, *161, 162,* 163
Caligula, 357
Calvon, H. M., 382, 388, 389
Cambio, Arnolfo di, 49, 153
Canaletto, 117
Carbonesi, N., 383
Carotti, Francesco, 292
Carli, E., 378
Carlo Emanuele I of Savoy, 197
Carlo Emanuele II of Savoy, 197
Carlsburg, 168, 169, *171*
Carolingians, the, 12, 19, 27, 30
Carthage, 276, 277
Cassiodorus, 81, 378
Castagnoli, F., 390
Castellamonte, Amadeo and Carlo di, 197, 199
Castruccio Castracane, 60, 61
Catherine de Medici, 192, 318, 319
Catherine the Great, 273, 274
Cavalleri-Murat, A. S., 383
Ceccelli, C., 393
Cellini, Benvenuto, 68
Chandigarh, 179
Chanteheux, 228
Charlemagne, 15, 28, 144, 145, 311, 368
Charles Albert, elector of Bavaria, 208
Charles I of England, 338
Charles II of England, 333
Charles IV, emperor, 4, 128, 137, 144, 206, 282–87, 289
Charles V, emperor, 67, 115, 123, 164, 166
Charles V, France, 315, 318
Charles VI, emperor, 299
Charles VIII of France, 325
Charles XII of Sweden, 172, 268
Charlesville, 159
Chartres, 18, 36, 39, 314; cathedral, 15, 35, 38
Chiaveri, G., 222, 383

Chichester, *173*
Chiemsee, 234
Chigi, Agostino, 234
Chlodwig, 311
Chrodegang von Metz, 15
Chur, 69, 111, 114, 231, 232
Cividale, 82
Civitali, Matteo, 59
Claudius, emperor, 342
Clement II, pope, 34
Clement VII, pope, 352
Colbert, 257–59
Colloredos, the, 292
Colmar, *113*, 132
Cologne, 5, 7, 8, 15, 18–28, *20, 21, 24,* 39, 44, 112, 114, 115, 117, 128, 233, 234, 237, 303, 323, 327, 334, 343, 368; churches, 21–27, 118; city wall, 118
Colonnas, the, 358
Commercy, 227
Constance, 112, 231, 233, 235, 246
Constantine II, emperor, 344
Constantinople (Istanbul), 55, 276, 277, 314, 342, 344
Copenhagen, 101, 182, 283
Corvinus, Matthias, 289
Cosimo I (Medici), 47, 67, 181
Cosimo de' Medici (the Elder), 54, 61
Cotte, Robert de, 146, 316, 322
Coventry, 329
Cracow, *280,* 370
Craig, James, xiii, 369
Cromwell, Oliver, 329
Custine, 385
Cuvilliés the Elder, 208
Czernins, the, 291, 292

Dacca (Bangladesh), 179
Dachau, castle, 5, 209
Dahlberg, Erich, 167, 170, 171
Dante, 47, 49, 67
Danzig, 45, 79, 84, 101, 170, 370
Darby, H. C., 388
Dehio, G., 5, 390
Deintzenhofer, Leonhard, 34, 225

De la Croix, H., 382
Delft, 102
Descartes, 368
Diderot, 390
Dinkelsbühl, 112, 132, 135
Domitian, emperor, 358
Dortmund, 112
Dreger, M., 387
Dresden, 185, 220–26, *222, 225,* 230; Japanese Palace, 224, 228; Zwinger, 221, 224, *225–26,* 229, 230
Dubrovnik, 45, 79, 82
DuChamp, M., 316
Duisburg, 112
Dupérac, Etienne, 362, 364
Dürer, 126, 237
Durham, 157

Eberhard, Ludwig, duke of Württemberg, 181
Echter von Mespelbrunn, Julius, 245
Edinburgh, xiii, 87, 369
Edward I of England, 156, 157
Edward III of England, 161
Edward VII of England, 333
Edward the Confessor, 330
Egloffstein, Count A. von und zu, 384
Eichstätt, 231, 232
Elmer, G., 166, 381, 382
Einem, H. von, 391
Ekbert von Andechs-Meran, bishop, 34
Elizabeth, czarina of Russia, 270, 272
Elizabeth I of England, 334
Emmanuel Filibert of Savoy, 193, 195
Engelhardt, B., 138
Ennen, F., 375, 386
Ensinger, Matthias, 79
Eosander von Göthe, 218, *219*
Erhard, Michael, 138
Erlangen, 175, 249
Ernst, M., 380
Erthals, the, 235, 253
Escher, K., 378
Eßlingen, 112, *133, 134*
Eugene, prince, 248, 294, 302

Eutin, 231, 234
Ewig, Eugen, 375

Falmouth, U.K., 157
Fanelli, G., 377
Fehr, G., 386
Fehrbellin, 215
Félibien, 256, 259, 385
Ferdinand I of Hapsburg, 283, 296
Ferrante, king of Naples, 390
Ferstel, Heinrich von, 303
Feulner, A., 381
Fiedler, H., 376
Filarete, 151, 158, 164
Fischer von Erlach, the Elder, 301
Fischer von Erlach, the Younger, 218, 240, 241, 292, 294, 300
Fleischhauer, W., 383
Fleming, minister, 224
Flint, 157
Florence, 3, 5, 10, 13, 18, 26, 42, 44, 46, *48,* *49–54, 52, 53, 54,* 56, 59, 63, 87, 113, 117, 126, 202, 334, 343, 345, 368, 370; Baptistery, *48, 52;* bridges, *48,* 50, 69; campanile, *52,* 53; cathedral, 37, 47, *48, 52, 53,* 371; churches, *48,* 50–53; fortresses, *48,* 67; gates, *48,* 50; Laurentium, 68; Loggia dei Lanzi, *52,* 53, 210; Medici palace, 68; Mercato Nuovo, *52;* Mercato Vecchio, *48,* 49, *52;* Piazzas, 49, *52,* 53, 55, 68, 85, 361; Pitti palace, *48, 53,* 67, *68,* 69, 183; Strozzi palace, 4; Uffizi palace, *48, 53,* 69, 90; Vecchio palace, 47, *48, 52, 53, 54,* 68, 93, 153, 183, 371; Via Calzaiuoli, *52,* 53
Fontaine, Pierre François, 322
Fontana, Domenico, 347, 349, 354, 356–58
Forster, Ludwig, 303
Francis I of France, 193, 318, 322
Francis III of Lorraine, 227
Francis Joseph I, emperor, 294, 303
Frankfurt, 113–15, 140, 144–47, *145,* 303; churches, 144, 146
Franks, the, 12
Franz G., 380
Fraticelli, Vanna, 389

Frederick I, king of Prussia, 217, 219, 261, 263

Frederick II, emperor, 70, 137, 183, 221

Frederick III, emperor, 127, 187, 296

Frederick VI, burgrave of Nuremberg, 213

Frederick Augustus III, elector (King Augustus II of Poland), 220–21

Frederick the Great, 114, 215, 217, 260–62, 266

Frederick William I ("The Great Elector"), 161, 213–15, 261

Freeden, M. von, 384

Freiburg im Breisgau, 28, 74, 112, 156

Freiburg im Üchtland, 69, 74, 156

Freising, 231, 232, 236

Freudenstadt, 149, 150

Friedberg, 112

Friedel, H., 380

Frisoni, D. G., 181

Frommel, C. L., 390

Fugger, Jakob, 123

Fuhrmann, F., 384

Fulda, 28

Fürstenried, castle, 5, 209

Gabriel, J. A., 317, 321, 326

Gaetgens, T. W., 388

Gallas, Johann Wenzeslaus, count, 292

Gebauer, J. H., 376

Geibach, castle, 247

Geneva, 69

Gengenbach, 112

Genoa, xiii, 45, 55, 80, 87, 369

George III of England, 333

George IV of England (Prince Regent), 337

Gerhard, Hubert, 124

Gericke, Otto von, 160

Gerlach, B., 376

Gerstenberg, H. A., 376

Gertner, Madern, 146

Ghent, 44, 45

Giacondo, Fra, 325

Giedion, S., 390

Ginori-Lisci, L., 377

Giotto, 51

Giovannoni, G., 390

Giry, A., 381

Giustiniani, the, 358

Godeau, Siméon, 219

Godehard, saint, 31

Goerck, surveyor, 107

Goethe, Johann Wolfgang von, 114, 118, 145, 147

Goethert, K., 375

Göllersdorf, 225

Gondi, Jean François de, archbishop of Paris, 254

Gondi, the, 54

Gonzagas, the, 191, 192

Goslar, 27, 112, 140–44, *142, 143*

Goths, the, 12

Göttingen, 112

Gozo, 164

Grabar, J. E., 385

Grado, 15

Granada, 184

Graß, N., 387

Grasser, Erasmus, 207

Graz, 298, 303

Gregorovius, F., 390

Gregory XIII, pope, 353, 354

Gregory of Tours, 22

Greifenclau, bishop of Würzburg, 248

Greifenclaus, the, 234

Greising, Joseph, 249

Grieß, Hans-Günther, 381

Grodecki, L., 382

Groß, Konrad, 129

Gross, W., 380

Großsedlitz, 224

Grub, H. G., 381

Guardi, 117

Guarini, Guarino, 198, 199, 201

Gubbio, 47

Guidoni, E., 377

Guinigi, Paolo, 61

Gundolf, bishop of Rochester, 330

Gurk, 234

Gustavsburg, 158

Gustavus II Adolphus of Sweden, 146, 168, 246

Gutkind, E. A., 157, 336, 381, 382, 386, 388–90

Gwynn, J., 388

Haarlem, 102

Haase, C., 373, 379

Habsburgs, the, 159, 234, 240, 290, 296, 298

Hadrian, emperor, 347

Haeckel, J., 385

Hagemann, W., 383

Hague, The, 81, 177

Halberstadt, 28, *29, 30,* 112, 237

Hall, B., 389

Halle, 28

Hamburg, 45, 79, 101, 112–14, 145, 158

Hamilton, G. H., 385, 386

Hanover, 303

Hatsch, H., 384

Hansen, Theophil, 303, 306

Hardouin-Mansard, Jules, 256, 259

Harrachs, the, 301

Hassinger, H., 386

Hauberat, 146

Haussmann, 317, 326

Hausherr, R., 386

Hautecoeur, Louis, 228, 384, 387, 388

Havelberg, 234

Hegemann, W., 388

Heidelberg, 5, 188, *189*

Heilbronn, 112

Heimpel, W., 384

Heinrich Jasomirgott, margrave, 296

Heintz, David, 75

Heliopolis, 357

Hempel, E., 383

Henrietta Adelaide of Savoy, 208

Henry II, emperor, 28, 31, 33, 34, 141, 234

Henry II of France, 309, 315, 318

Henry III, emperor, 126, 142

Henry III, duke of Bavaria, 186

Henry III of England, 331

Henry III of France, 318, 322

Henry IV, emperor, 24

Henry IV of France, 307, 319, 322, 325

Henry V, emperor, 24, 144

Henry VIII of England, 332, 333

Henry the Lion, 98, 205

Henschel, W., 384

Hentzen, A., 382

Héré E., 227, 229, 383

Herlihy, D., 377

Herzog, E., 27, 28, 376, 380

Hetzilo, bishop, 32

Heuss, Theodor, 384

Hildebrand, A. von, 369, 391

Hildebrandt, Lukas von, 217, 225, 242, 252, 299, 300, 301

Hildesheim, 6, 28, 30, *31,* 32, 231; Convent of the Holy Cross, *51*

Hinz, S., 382

Hofer, P., 378

Hoffmann, H. Chr., 387

Hohenlohes, the, 235

Hohenstaufens, the, 110, 131, 134, 136, 144

Hohenzollerns, the, 127, 213

Holl, Elias, 125

Holstein-Gottorps, the, 234

Hopfer, Joseph Daniel, 302

Howard, Ebenezer, 151, 368

Hubala, E., 217, 225, 379

Hubert, J., 375

Hübler, H., 379

Hudson, D., 388

Hughes, Q., 382

Hugneney, J., 381

Hugot, L., 380

Huguenots, the, 174, 175

Huse, N., 390

Ingelheim, Franz von, 146

Ingolstadt, 207

Innocent X (Pamphili), pope, 358, 359

Isabella, wife of Archduke Albrecht, 173

Isny, 112

Istanbul. *See* Constantinople

Jackson, H., 379

Jacob, G., 386

Jacobs, J., 8, 374

Jäger, W., 380
Jenisch, P. J., 181
Jennesson, 228
Jerome, saint, 3, 356, 391
Jerusalem, 277
Jetropkin, 274
John, king of Luxembourg, 284
John I, duke of Brandenburg, 212
John III, elector of Saxony, 221
Jones, Inigo, 332
Joseph I, emperor, 299, 303
Joseph II, emperor, 147, 224, 299, 303
Julian the Apostate, emperor, 13
Julius II, pope, 349
Juvarra, Filippo, 198, 199, 202–4

Kahn, Louis L., 179
Kalmar, *168*, 169
Karl August of Weimar, 253
Karlshafen, 175
Karlsruhe, 176
Kassel, 5, 175, 249
Kaufbeuren, 112
Kauffmann, G., 378
Kauffmann, H., 390, 391
Kaufmann, E., 381
Keller, G., 72
Keller, H., 376, 378, 390
Keller, U., 388
Kempten, 112
Kempten, Jakob von, 171
Kent, William, 333
Keussen, H., 375
Keutschach, Leonhard von, archbishop, 237
Keyser, E., 380, 381
Kieslinger, A., 387
Kinskys, the, 291
Kircher, A., 391
Klebel, E., 374, 380
Klee, Paul, 8
Klosterneuburg, 296
Knobelsdorff, 219, 263
Knorre, E. von, 380
Kömstedt, R., 384
Köngeter, W., 387

Königshofen, 252
Konrad of Freising, bishop, 206
Konrad III, emperor, 144
Kotrba, V. L., 386
Kovernholmen, *168,* 169
Kretschmayr, H., 379
Kronburg, 268
Kubach, E., 375
Kuenberg, count, Max Gandolf, 240
Kunibert, bishop, 22
Kunze, H., 376

La Fontaine, Jean de, 153
Landshut, 7, 114, 186, *190,* 207; Castle
    Trausnitz, 189
Landskrona, 168, 169, *170*
Landwehr, G., 380
Lang, S., 381
Langobards, the, 12, 15, 59
Lang von Wellenburg, Matthäus, arch-
    bishop, 237
Laon, 39; cathedral, 5, 38
Laparelli, F., 382
Largiader, A., 378
La Rochelle, 80
La Scarperia, 153, *154*
Lausanne, 69, 75
La Vallière, Mme, 259
Lavedan, P., 8, 374, 381–83, 387, 389, 390
Le Blond, 268, 272
Le Corbusier, 151, 179, 368
Ledoux, 317
Leipzig, 145, 224
Le Mans, 18
Le Mercier, 152
Leningrad. *See* St. Petersburg
Le Nôtre, 219, 258, 268
Leo IX, pope, 352
Leonardo, 51, 192
Leopold, duke (consort of Maria
    Theresa), 227
Leopold von Anhalt-Dessau, 161
Leopold III, margrave, 296
Lersner, Achilles August, 144
Leutkirch, 112
Le Vau, Louis, 254, 257, 319

Levron, J., 385
Leyden, 102
Lichtenberg, E., 387
Lichtenstein, princes of, 234, 291, 301
Liechtenstein, prince, 248
Liège, 28, 231
Limburg brothers, 187
Limoges, 18
Lincoln, U.K., 329
Lindau, 112
Lisini, A., 377
Liverpool, 157
Lobdeburg, Hermann von, bishop, 243
Lobkowitz, Caramuel, bishop, 192
Lobkowitzes, the, 289, 291, 301
Lodron, Paris, count, archbishop, 239, 240, 246
Löffler, F., 384
Londinium, 328
London, 4, 6–8, 19, 44, 179, 185, 210, 215, 277, 281, 283, 302, 310, 322, 326–39, *328, 329, 331, 338,* 343, 345, 367, 368; Admiralty, 333, 339; bridges, 330, 334; Buckingham Palace, 333, 338, 339; Charing Cross, 338, *339;* City, 3, 327, 330–32, 339; Covent Garden, 336, *337;* Houses of Parliament, 333, 339; Mall, 333, 338; National Gallery, 338, *339;* parks, 334, 335, 337; St. James's Palace, 333, 335; St. James's Square, *336;* St. Paul's Cathedral, 38, 334, 335, 339; Tower, 187, 318, 330; Trafalgar Square, 338, 339; Westminster, 3, 285, 327, *329,* 330–33; Whitehall, 332, 333, 338
Longhena, Balthasare, 94
Lorenzetti, Ambrogio, 64
Lorenzo il Magnifico, 47, 61
Loretto, 173
Lother I, emperor, 18
Lotz, W., 379
Louis the Bavarian, emperor, 206, 207
Louis the Fat, of France, 314
Louis VII, 314, 324
Louis IX, 314, 315
Louis XIII, 254, 259, 315
Louis XIV, 187, 188, 253, 254, 256, 259, 261, 266, 267, 301, 313, 315, 316, 320, 326, 359

Louis XV, 221, 256, 257, 272, 316, 320
Louis XVI, 256
Louvain, 45
Lübeck, 5, 10, 41, 42, 79, 80, 84, 95–102, *96, 97, 101,* 105, 112, 114, *115,* 117, 128, 149, 158, 170, 231, 234, 369, 370; churches and convents, *96, 97, 98, 99;* Danzelhaus, 99, 100; town hall, *96,* 100
Lucca, 16, 46, 49, 55, *58,* 59, 153, 189, 202; cathedral, *58,* 59–61; San Michele, *58,* 59, *60*
Ludat, H., 375, 386
Ludovico il Moro, 192
Ludovisi, the, 358
Ludwigsburg, 181, *182,* 185
Ludwig the German, 144
Ludwig the Pious, 144
Lüneburg, 28
Lunéville, castle, 227, 228, 230
Lusini V, 377
Lutetia, 13, 311
Lyon, 18; cathedral, 35

Maderna, 347, 348
Madrid, 8, 184; Prado, 338
Magdeburg, 28, 112, 160–61, 237, 282
Maier, P. J., 377
Maintenon, Mme de, 259
Mainz, 231, 233, 237, 246, 252, 264; Favorite, 247; Martinsburg, 233
Malgrange, La, castle, 227, 228
Manhattan, 45, 78, 79, 100, 105–9, *106, 107.* *See also* New York
Mann, A., 375
Mannheim, 176, *178,* 188
Mansard, 254, 258, 259
Mansfield-Fondi, 301
Mantua, 7, 191–93, 209, 301
Marcel, Etienne, 316
Maretto, P., 379
Marghareta, duchess of Parma, 67
Maria Giovanna, 197, 199
Maria of Hungary, 159
Maria Theresa, 227, 299, 302
Marie, A., 385
Marienbourg, 159

Mark, saint, 85
Marseilles, 45, 80
Martin V (Colonna), pope, 345
Martini, Simone, 64
Maschke, E., 380
Mathilde, margravine, 59
Max III, Joseph, elector, 208
Max Emmanuel of Bavaria, 5, 208, 209, 227
Maximilian I, elector, 187, 206, 207
Mayer, T., 374
Mazarin, cardinal, 187, 254
Mazzarial, G., 379
Mazzini, E., 378
Medici, the, 54, 238
Medina, 164
Meersburg, castle, 235
Meiner, C., 76, 378
Meinwerk, bishop, 32
Meiss, M., 388
Meissner, J., 379
Mclk, 296
Mell, Johann, 171
Memmingen, 112
Merian, 32, 70, 115, 139, 145, 146, 180, 321
Merovingians, the, 12, 13, 15
Merseburg, 234
Mestre, 95
Metternichs, the, 234
Metz, 18, 117
Meyer, O., 384
Meyer-Barkhausen, W., 375
Michelangelo, 51, 90, 153, 347, 348, 357, 358, 360–64
Mielke, F., 262, 385
Milan, 3, 7, 18, 39, 179, 183, 301, 327, 341, 345; Castello Sforzesco, 183, 195; cathedral, 37
Minden, 234, 368
Miozzi, E., 379
Montefeltro, Federigo de, 190
Monteriggioni, 153
Montespan, Mme de, 258, 259
Montfort, Simon de, 331
Montreuil, Pierre de, 314
More, Thomas, 151

Moritzburg, 224
Morot, P., 383
Moscow, 274, 283, 315
Moy, Count Johannes, 384
Mrusek, J. J., 376, 382
Mühlhausen, 112
Müller, J., 385
Müller, W., 382
Multscher, Hans, 138
Mumford, L., 389
Münster, 187, 188, 233, 368
Münter, G., 381
Munich, 4, 28, 39, 179, 182, 184, 185, 187, 204–12, *205, 208, 210,* 245, 283, 293, 319; churches, 204–8; gardens, 206, 210; squares, 204, 210, 211
Munoz, A., 390
Muratori, S., 83, 379
Mussolini, 389

Naegeli, W., 378
Nancy, 5, 176, 182, 185, 220, 226–30, *228,* 262; Place Stanislas, 221, 226, *230;* Place de la Carrière, 228, *230*
Naples, 7, 8, 45, 80, 301, 345
Napoleon I, 28, 39, 122, 164, 166, 204, 274, 302, 303, 309, 316, 320, 326, 337, 339
Napoleon II, 320
Napoleon III, 318, 326
Nash, John, 333
Naumburg, 237
Necker, 260
Nelson, 339
Negri, T. O. de, 378
Nette, J. F., 181
Neumann, Balthasar, 34, 125, 181, 218, 248, 249, 252, 299
Neumann, Johann-Christoph, 223
New Amsterdam, 106, 370
Newcastle-upon-Tyne, 157
New Glasgow, 370
New Orleans, 370
New York, 7, 177. *See also* Manhattan
Nicholas V, pope, 347
Nicholas I, czar, 272
Nicola, *154,* 155

Nicolai, Friedrich, 119, 216, 383
Niebelschütz, E. von, 380
Niemeyer, Oskar, 179
Nijmegen, III
Nîmes, 343
Nolhac, P. de, 385
Norberg-Schulz, C., 374
Nordhausen, 112
Nördlingen, 5, 112, 132
Norwich, 329
Nüll, E. van der, 303, 304
Nuremberg, 7, 42, 44, 49, 112, 114–16,
   126–31, *126, 127, 129,* 140, 142, 186, 370;
   St. Lorenz, 126, 129, *130,* 131, 206; Ma-
   rienkapelle, 128, 131; St. Sebaldus, 126,
   128, 129, *130,* 131; Schöne Brunnen, 128,
   131
Nymphenburg, castle, 5, 144, 209, 227

Odo (goldsmith), 331
Öttinger, K., 386, 387
Offenburg, 112
Ogoccione della Faggiola, 60
Olmütz, 28, 234
Oranienburg, castle, 219
Osnabrück, 28, 231, 368
Ottobeuren, 132
Otto the Great, emperor, 22, 30
Otto III, emperor, 213
Ottokar II, king of Bohemia, 281, 298
Ottokar III, king of Bohemia, 285
Ottonians, the, 19, 27
Oxford, 329

Paderborn, 32, 112, 231, 368
Padua, 82
Paganuzzi, G. B., 379
Palermo, 7, 55, 345
Palladio, xiii, 89, 93, 94
Palmanova, *159*
Pamphili, the, 358
Paris, 3, 5, 7, 10, 15, 18, 19, 35, 39, 50, 117,
   177, 179, 185, 187, 204, 210, 215, 262, 277,
   283, 301, 303, 307–27, *320,* 330, 333, 334,
   337; Arc de Triomphe, 333, 339; Arc de
   Triomphe (du Caroussel), 320; Bastille,
187, 318, *325,* 330; bridges, 321–23, *323,*
325; Champ de Mars, 322; Champs-
Elysées, 309, 321, 333; Cité, 187, 307, 308,
309, 311, *312,* 313, 317; Collège des Quatre
Nations, 322, *323;* Dôme des Invalides,
222, 322; Eiffel Tower, 322; Faubourg
St. Germain, 324; gates, 308; Grand
Châlelet, 318, 322; Hôtel de Ville, 307,
314, 316, 317, 322; Ile Saint-Louis, 317, *325;*
Louvre, 3, *186,* 187, 254, 299, 306, 309,
310, 318, *319,* 322, 332, 338, 367; Marais,
324, 325; Notre Dame, 313, 314; Opéra,
326; Palais Bourbon, 322; Palais de
Chaillot, 322; Pavillon de la Reine, 326;
Pavillon du roi, 326; Petit Châtelet, 318,
322; Place de la Concorde, 309, 321, 322,
326; Place de l'Etoile (Place Charles de
Gaulle), 309, 318, 321, 326, 339; Place des
Vosges, 321, *325,* 326; Quartier Saint-
Denis, 316; Quartier Saint-Martin, 316;
Royal Axis, 6, 309, *310,* 321, 371; Samari-
taine, 322, *323;* squares, 325–26; Sainte
Chappelle, 314; Saint-Germain des Prés,
19, 311, 314; Saint-Martin des Champs,
311, 314; Trocadéro, 322; Tuileries, 193,
254, 309, 317, 319–22; walls, *308,* 308, 314,
316, 318
Parisi, the, 311
Parler, Heinrich, 284
Parler, Peter, 128, 284–87
Parma, 7, 15, *16*
Passau, 232, *236, 237*
Pastor, L. von, 374, 390
Patté, M., 387
Patterweil, B. von, 381
Paul, J., 376
Paul III, pope, 361
Paul V, pope, 354
Pavia, 15, 18, 26, 81
Pazzi, the, 54
Pée, H., 380
Pelham, R. A., 388
Percier, Charles, 322
Permoser, Balthasar, 224
Perrault, 319
Persepolis, 276

Perugia, 47
Peruzzi, 348
Peschgen, G., 383
Peter the Great, 172, 262, 267–69, 272, 274
Peter II, czar, 269
Petri, F., 374
Petrini, Antonio, 249
Pevsner, N., 384
Peyrot, A., 383
Pfeiffer, G., 379, 380
Pfister, C., 383
Pfister, R., 385
Pfullendorf, 112
Phelps-Stokes, I. N., 379
Philadelphia, 8
Philip II of Spain, 159, 184
Philip IV of Spain, 203
Philip Augustus, King of France, 50, 315, 318
Philippeville, 159, 160
Philip the Brave, 151
Philip the Fair, 151
Piccolominis, the, 292
Piedmont, 343
Pienza, 149, 150, 192
Pierotti, P., 155, 377, 381
Pietrangeli, C., 391
Pignatti, T., 379
Pillnitz, 224
Pinder, Wilhelm, 149
Pippin von Heristal, 22
Piranesi, 117
Pirenne H., 374
Pisa, 16, 17, 45, 47, 49, 54, 56, 59, 153
Pisano, Giovani, 61, 64, 67
Pistoia, 49, 56, 57
Pitti, the, 54
Pius II, pope, 149
Pius IV, pope, 238
Pius VI, pope, 345
Pius XI, pope, 389
Pius XII, pope, 389
Planitz, H., 376
Plato, 47, 151, 368
Plymouth, 329
Podebrad, Georg von, king of Bohemia, 287

Poëte, M., 387
Poleggi, E., 378
Poll, B., 380
Pommersfelden, castle, 247
Pompadour, Mme. de, 322
Pöppelmann, Matthäus David, 223–25, 229, 383
Portoghesi, P., 389
Posen, 234
Potsdam, 177, 185, 197, 216, 230, 260–66, 264–65, 293, 317, 326, 367; Sanssouci, 4, 260, 261, 266
Prague, 3, 4, 7, 10, 39, 128, 179, 206, 224, 230, 234, 252, 277, 278–94, 278, 296, 298, 301, 315, 322, 330, 333, 370; Belvedere, 289; cathedral, 4, 37, 206, 284, 285, 286, 287; Hradcany (city), 278, 279, 282, 289, 290–91; Hradcany (castle), 278, 284–88; lesser quarter, 278, 281, 283, 290–91; new town (Neustadt), 278, 283; old town, 278; Palais Czernin, 292; Vladislav hall, 288, 289; Vysherad, 278, 283
Preimesberger, R., 391
Premyslids, the, 284
Pruinai, G., 378
Pruntrut, 231

Quercia, Jacopo della, 67
Quedlinburg, 27, 112
Queens (N.Y.), 108

Ragusa (Dubrovnik), 45, 79, 82
Ramella, V., 383
Raphael, 346–48, 352
Rasmussen, Steen Eiler, 327, 388, 389
Rastrelli, 273
Rave, P. O., 383
Ravenna, 15, 18
Ravensburg, 112, 131
Réau, L., 385
Regensburg, 19, 39, 112, 114, 117–22, 120–21, 128, 231, 233, 234, 368; cathedral, 37, 119; town hall, 119, 122
Regunmar, bishop, 296
Reichle, Hans, 125
Reims, 18, 19, 314; cathedral, 35

Reincke, H., 379
Reitzenstein, Freiherr von, 249
Restif de la Bretonne, N. E., 316
Retti, Riccardo, 181
Reuther, H., 383, 384
Reutlingen, 112, 132, *135*, 136
Reval, 101, 370
Richelieu, cardinal, 152
Richelieu, town, 152–53
Ried, Benedikt, 287, 288
Riemenschneider, Tilman, 137, 285
Rietschel, S., 376
Riga, 79, 98, 101
Rinaldi, Antonio, 273
Rohault de Fleury, G., 377
Romano Giulio, 192
Rome, 5, 7, 10, 15, 18, 55, 177, 179, 183, 187,
    230, 253, 276, 340–65, *353, 355*, 367; Au-
    relian wall, 341, 343, 345, 353; Belevedere
    (court and garden), 348, 349; Borgo,
    347, 352; Caracalla baths, 344; Castello
    S. Angelo, 187, 318, 330, 347, 348, *351*,
    352; Capitol square and palace, 357,
    360–65, *361, 362, 364*; churches, 344–46,
    353–57, 359; Colosseum, 356; Forum,
    361; fountains, 354, 359; Lateran, 345,
    357, 358, 361; Marcus Aurelius column,
    357, 361; national monument, *364;*
    piazzas, 350, 357, 358; Piazza Navona,
    225, 357–59, *360;* Piazza del Popolo, 241,
    350, *351, 355*, 357, 358; Piazza di Spagna,
    357; Piazza S. Pietro, 4, 6, 309, 348, *349,*
    357, 358, 365; Piazza Venezia, 343, 357;
    Palazzo Farnese, 4; Ponte S. Angelo
    (pons Adriana), 347, 350, 352, 356; Porta
    del Popolo, 350, 352, 355; Porta Pia, 356;
    Quirinal, 345, 357; Sistine Chapel, 349;
    St. Peter's, 187, 335, 336, 344, 345, 347,
    349, 356; streets, 343, 350, 352, 355; Tiber
    city, 344, 345; Trajan's column, 356, 357;
    Trastavere, 352, 358; Vatican, 345, 347,
    352, 357, 358, 371; Villa Montalto, 353
Rörig, F., 373, 379
Rosenbergs, the, 289
Rosenfels, L., 382
Rossellini, 347, 348

Rossi, A., 17, 375, 379, 382
Rostock, 101
Rothenburg ob der Taube, 112, 113, 132,
    136–37, *136*
Rottweil, 112, 135, 136
Royale, Mme, 199
Rubens, P. P., 332, 369
Rucellai, the, 54
Rudolph II, emperor, 289, 290, 298, 299
Rüssel, J. C., 388

Saarbrücken, 112
Sage, Walter, 381
St. Andreä-Levant, 234
Saint-Cloud, 260
Saint-Denis, 311
St. Gall, 111
Saint-Germain-en-Laye, 260
St. Petersburg (Leningrad; Petrograd), 6,
    10, 177, 179, 185, 197, 210, 215, 220, 267–
    75, *268, 270, 271*, 293, 302, 307, 367; Acad-
    emy of Arts, 273; Admiralty, *268,* 269,
    270, 271, 274; House of the 12 Councils,
    269; Marble Palace, 273; Peter and Paul
    Fortress, 267, *268, 271;* Saint Isaac Ca-
    thedral, 271, 274; Smolny convent and
    cathedral, *273;* Stock Exchange, 269;
    Summer Palace, *271,* 274; Vasilyevsky Is-
    land, 269; Winter Palace, 269, 270, *271,*
    273, 274
Saint-Simon, duke, 253
Salisbury, cathedral, 38, *39*
Salt Lake City, 174
Salzburg, 10, 12, 37, 187, 231–33, *233*, 236–
    42, *238, 241,* 244, 246, 248, 319; castles,
    churches, and monuments, 237–41; ca-
    thedral, 239, 240; Franciscan church
    and convent, 237, *238;* Ursuline church,
    241, *242;* residence, *238,* 240; streets and
    squares, 238–40
Samonà, G., 379
San Francisco, 2
Sangallo, Antonio di, 67
San Gimignano, 47
San Giovanni Val d'Arno, 153, *154*
San Paolesi, Piero, 377

Sansovino, Jacopo, 90, 91, 92
Sauerländer, W., 387
Scamozzi, Vincenzo, 238
Schaller, J., 386
Schedel, Hartmann, chronicler, 245
Scherf, A., 384
Scherpenheuvel, 173, *174*
Scheuerbach, A., 384
Schickward, Heinrich, 149
Schleißheim, castle, 5, 209, 227
Schlesinger, W., 375–77
Schlüsselburg, 268
Schlüter, Andreas, 125, 217, 220, 272
Schmidt, Friedrich von, 303, 306
Schönborn, Friedrich Karl, 248
Schönborn, Johann Philipp, 246
Schönborn, Johann Philipp Franz, 248
Schönborn, Lothar Franz, 34, 247, 252
Schönborns, the, 240, 246
Schürer, O., 386
Schultheiß, W., 380
Schwäbisch-Gmünd, 112, 264
Schwäbisch-Hall, 112, 113
Schwartz, W. H., 377, 378
Schwarzenbergs, the, 289, 291, 301
Schweinfurt, 112, 113
Schwemmer, W., 380
Scudery, Mlle de, 385
Seberich, F., 384
Seckau, 234
Sedlmeier, R., 385
Sedlmayr, H., 37, 241, 294, 302, 374, 381, 384–87, 391
Seibt, F., 386
Seinsheim, prince-bishop, 253
Seld, Jörg, 115
Semper, G., 303
Seneca, 342
Sens, 18
Sersanders, Andries, 168
Sforcesca, 158
Sforzas, the, 192
Shaw, William, 333
Siebenhüner, H., 391
Siena, 5, 6, 8, 10, 42, 44–47, 56, 59, 61–67, *62, 64, 65,* 113, 153, 202, 345, 370; ca-
thedral, 61, 64, 65, *66,* 66; Palazzo Pubblico, 47, 61, 64, *65,* 66; Torre di Mangia, *65*
Sigismund, emperor, 213
Silvestre, Israel, 117
Simson, O. von, 37, 376
Sitte, C., 8, 374
Sitticus, M., 238, 241
Sixtus IV, pope, 349, 390
Sixtus V, pope, 238, 349, 352, 356, 357
Soissons, 18
Solari, Santin, 238
Solothurn, 111
Spalato (Split), 82
Spatio, Giovanni, 289
Speyer, 27, 112, 117, 231, 233, 235, 246
Spezza, Andrea, 290
Spoleto, 18
Stadions, the, 234
Stalpaert, Daniel, 105
Stanislas I, king of Poland (Prince Lescyynski), 185, 221, 229
Starhembergs, the, 301
Staten Island, 108
Stethaimer, Hans, 237
Stettner, M., 387
Stockholm, 101, 167, 172, 182, 283
Stoß, Veit, 114
Stow, John, 334, 388
Strahm, H. A., 376, 378
Straßbourg, 28, 114, 117, 231, 233
Straubing, 207
Stropp, H., 380
Strozzi, the, 54
Stuttgart, 179–81, 253, 319
Stuyvesant Town, 108
Sully, Maurice de, 35, 313
Summerson, Sir J., 388
Swoboda, K., 386
Syrlin, Jörg, 138

Tasniere, Giorgio, 203
Tessin, Nicodemus, the Elder, 169, 171, 172
Tessin, Nicodemus, the Younger, 172
Thangmar of Hildesheim, 31, 376
Theodoric, saint, 85, 87

Theseider, E. D., 375

Thuns, the, 234, 292

Thun, Count Guidobaldo, 240

Thun, Count Johann Ernst, 240

Tiepolo, Domenico, 248

Tietze, H., 386

Tintoretto, 89

Toalini, E., 377

Tolnay, C. de, 391

Torcello, 15, *16*

Tours, 18

Tout, T. F., 381

Toynbee, A., 389

Trento, 231, 232

Trezzini, 272

Trier, 13, 15, 18, 26–27, *26*, *232*, 233, 246, 343; basilica and residence, *232*, 233; cathedral precinct and main market, *26, 27*

Tschan, F. J., 376

Tulln, 296

Turgot, prefect, 321, 387

Turin, 10, 26, 87, 182, 184, 185, 193–204, *194, 195, 196*, 212, 215, 217, 223, 253, 293, 303, 317, 326, 343; Piazza Castello, 196, 197, *199, 200*, 200; Piazza di Città, *194*, 201; Piazza S. Carlo, 197, *198*, 200; residence (Palazzo Reale), 196, 197, *202*

Udine, 81, 82

Überlingen, 112

Ulm, 5, 7, 44, 112–14, 131, 132, 137–40, *139*, 142; minster, 137, *138, 139*

Ulrich, saint, of Augsburg, 14

Ulrich von Ensingen, 135

Ur, 276

Urban VII (Barberini), pope, 358

Urbino, 190, *191*

Urschlechter, A., 380

Utrecht, 32, 111

Valletta, Jean de la, 164

Valletta, 163–66, *165*

Vasari, Giorgio, 47, 68, 69

Vauban, marquis de, 158

Venaria Reale, 197, 203–4, *203;* La Mandria, 204

Venice, 3, 10, 18, 45, 79, 80–95, *83, 84, 92*, 98, 108, 115, 116, 159, 202, 224, 345, 367, 370; basin of St. Mark, *92, 93;* buildings and monuments, 89–94; doge's palace, 87, 90, 93, 94; library, 90, 91, 94; Piazza S. Marco, 4, 6, 84, 85, *87,* 87, *88,* 88, *91,* 361, 367, 371; Rialto, 84, 94; S. Gimignano, 90, 92; St. Giorgio Maggiore, 81, 93, 94; S. Marco, 81, 85, 87, 90, 92, 93, 94; S. Maria della Salute, 81, 93, 94, 222; Zecca, 90–92, 94

Verler, P., 385

Verona, 18, 26, 82, 89

Versailles (palace and town), 4, 5, 152, 176, 177, 185, 187, 191, 197, 230, 253–60, *255, 258*, 265, 269, 270, 327, 367, 369; Appartement des Bains, 257; Clagny, 259; Grande Ecurie, Petite Ecurie, 259; Grands Communs, *255, 258*; Trianon de Porcelaine, 225, 228, 258, 259

Vicenza, 82, 262

Vicolini, R., 389

Victor Amadeus II (Vittorio Amadeo), 198, 203, 204

Victor Emmanuel II, 341

Victoria, queen of England, 333

Vienna, 7, 28, 44, 145, 179, 185, 187, 210, 212, 224, 230, 252, 253, 277, 283, 285, 293, 294–307, *295*, 315, 333, 345, 367; Belvedere, 3, 226, 301, 302; Burgtheater, 305, 306; Hofburg (and Alte Hofburg), 298, *299, 299, 300*, 305, 306; opera house, 304, 306; Ringstraße, 4, 9, 303, *304*, 306, 321, 367; St. Stephen's cathedral, 4, 206, 294, *295*, 296, *297*, 298; Schönbrunn, 144, 294, 300; Votivkirche, 303, 304

Vienne, 18

Vigevano, 192, *193*

Vignola della Porta, 347, 364

Villani, G., 47, 50, 377

Ville, Jadot de, 299

Ville-Franche-sur-Meuse, 159

Visconti, the, 183, 192

Vittozzi, Ascanio, 197, 199, 201

Vladislav II, king, 287, 288

Vöge, W., 139, 380

Voltaire, 260, 385
Volterra (town), 47
Voss, H., 376
Vries, Adriaen de, 124

Wackerbarth, count, 223, 224
Wagner-Rieger, R., 387
Waldsteins, the, 291
Wallenstein, 192, 289
Wangen, 112
Wärnskjold, 169
Warsaw, 182, 224, 230
Washington, D.C., 177, 179, 342
Webb, Sir Aston, 333
Weinrebe, Brune zur, 146
Weisman, W., 379
Weißenburg, 112
Weil die Stadt, 112
Weingarten, convent, 132
Wenceslas, saint, 284
Wenceslas I, king, 279
Werner, J., 380
Werner, W., 381
Wetzlar, 112
Weyres, W., 375
Wibiral, N., 387
Wiener Neustadt, 187, 296, 298
Wienner, G., 387
William I of Prussia, 215
William III of England, 332, 333
William the Conqueror, 329, 330
Wimpfen, 112
Windsheim, 112
Winterthür, 111
Wisby, 98
Wittelsbachs, the, 234

Wittlsbach, Ferdinand von, 246
Woensam, Anton, 25, 115, 117
Wolf-Dietrich, bishop of Salzburg, 237, 238
Wolff, Jakob, 131
Wolsey, cardinal, 332
Wood, John (father and son), 336
Worms, 112, 117, 231, 233
Wortmann, R., 380
Wrangel, field marshal, 171
Wren, Sir Christopher, 125, 335
Wright, E., 378
Würzburg, 125, 181, 187, 231–33, 236, 242–53, *243, 244, 247, 250–51, 252,* 306; castle, *247, 249, 252;* cathedral, 244, *247,* 248, 249; Echter (Julius) hospital, 245, *247;* Haug convent, *247,* 249; Marienburg (fortress), 3, 243, 246, *247;* Marien-kirche, 3, 243, 245, *247;* Neustift, *247;* Schönborn chapel, 249, 252; St. Burck-hard, *247;* town hall, 245, *247;* university, 245, 252

York, 329
Ypres, 15, *16*

Zahn, E., 375
Zähringer, the, 70, 74, 75, 156
Ziani, Sebastiano, doge, 89
Zocca, M., 390
Zuccalli, Gasparo, 240
Zucker, Paul, 8
Zug, 111
Zurich, 4, 44, 69–74, *71, 72,* 179
Zwingli, Ulrich, 72